THE **MOUNTAINS SHALL DRIP SWEET WINE**

BIBLICAL THEOLOGY FOR LIFE

THE MOUNTAINS SHALL DRIP SWEET WINE

A Biblical Theology of Alcohol

JOHN ANTHONY DUNNE

general editor JONATHAN LUNDE

ZONDERVAN ACADEMIC

The Mountains Shall Drip Sweet Wine
Copyright © 2025 by John Anthony Dunne

Published by Zondervan, 3950 Sparks Drive SE, Suite 101, Grand Rapids, MI 49546, USA. Zondervan is a registered trademark of The Zondervan Corporation, L.L.C., a wholly owned subsidiary of HarperCollins Christian Publishing, Inc.

Requests for information should be addressed to customercare@harpercollins.com.

Zondervan titles may be purchased in bulk for educational, business, fundraising, or sales promotional use. For information, please email SpecialMarkets@Zondervan.com.

Library of Congress Cataloging-in-Publication Data

Names: Dunne, John Anthony, 1986- author | Lunde, Jonathan, 1960- editor
Title: The mountains shall drip sweet wine : a Biblical theology of alcohol / John Anthony Dunne ; general editor Jonathan Lunde.
Description: Grand Rapids, Michigan : Zondervan Academic, [2025] | Series: Biblical theology for life | Includes bibliographical references and index.
Identifiers: LCCN 2024035554 (print) | LCCN 2024035555 (ebook) | ISBN 9780310516095 paperback | ISBN 9780310516101 ebook
Subjects: LCSH: Wine--Biblical teaching | Alcohol--Biblical teaching | Drinking in the Bible | Bible--Criticism, interpretation, etc.
Classification: LCC BS680.W55 D86 2025 (print) | LCC BS680.W55 (ebook) | DDC 220.8/64121--dc23/eng/20250320
LC record available at https://lccn.loc.gov/2024035554
LC ebook record available at https://lccn.loc.gov/2024035555

Scripture quotations unless otherwise noted are taken from The Holy Bible, New International Version®, NIV®. Copyright © 1973, 1978, 1984, 2011 by Biblica, Inc.® Used by permission of Zondervan. All rights reserved worldwide. www.Zondervan.com. The "NIV" and "New International Version" are trademarks registered in the United States Patent and Trademark Office by Biblica, Inc.® • Scripture quotations marked ESV are taken from the ESV® Bible (The Holy Bible, English Standard Version®). Copyright © 2001 by Crossway, a publishing ministry of Good News Publishers. Used by permission. All rights reserved. • Scripture quotations marked KJV are taken from the King James Version. Public domain. • Scripture quotations marked NETS are taken from *A New English Translation of the Septuagint*, ©2007 by the International Organization for Septuagint and Cognate Studies, Inc. Used by permission of Oxford University Press. All rights reserved. • Scripture quotations marked NRSV are taken from the New Revised Standard Version Bible. Copyright © 1989 National Council of the Churches of Christ in the United States of America. Used by permission. All rights reserved. • Scripture quotations marked NRSVue are taken from the New Revised Standard Version Updated Edition. Copyright © 2021 National Council of Churches of Christ in the United States of America. Used by permission. All rights reserved worldwide.

Any internet addresses (websites, blogs, etc.) and telephone numbers in this book are offered as a resource. They are not intended in any way to be or imply an endorsement by Zondervan, nor does Zondervan vouch for the content of these sites and numbers for the life of this book.

All rights reserved. No part of this publication may be reproduced, stored in a retrieval system, or transmitted in any form or by any means—electronic, mechanical, photocopy, recording, or any other—except for brief quotations in printed reviews, without the prior permission of the publisher.

Without limiting the exclusive rights of any author, contributor or the publisher of this publication, any unauthorized use of this publication to train generative artificial intelligence (AI) technologies is expressly prohibited. HarperCollins also exercise their rights under Article 4(3) of the Digital Single Market Directive 2019/790 and expressly reserve this publication from the text and data mining exception.

HarperCollins Publishers, Macken House, 39/40 Mayor Street Upper, Dublin 1, D01 C9W8, Ireland (https://www.harpercollins.com)

Cover design: Rob Monacelli
Cover photo: © Atattoo69 / Shutterstock
Interior design: Kait Lamphere

Printed in the United States of America

John Anthony Dunne does an excellent job of describing alcoholic drinks in the biblical world, how alcohol is portrayed in biblical imagery, and even the relevance of things like "new wine" for Christian hopes about the future. At the same time, he provides an uncompromising exposition of biblical prohibitions against drunkenness and recognizes the gravity of abusing alcohol as well as the risks of alcoholism. Dunne provides a sane and sober analysis of what is for many a difficult topic of the Bible: alcohol and the Christian life.

> REV. DR. MICHAEL F. BIRD, Deputy Principal at Ridley College, Melbourne, Australia

This is more than a book to help Christians determine whether to drink or not to drink. It is more than an encyclopedia of every mention of alcoholic beverages in the Bible (although it is thorough in its scope). It is more than even a book about wine in the Bible. In this volume, Dunne explores how the biblical authors employ images—literal and figurative—of beer, wine, wine growing, and winemaking. He helps us see the wide-ranging use of such images to signal variable theological themes, including exile, judgment, restoration, blessing, and eschatological abundance. If you wonder if there is all that much to say about wine in the Bible, there is! And you'll find it here. I highly recommend this comprehensive and accessible book.

> JEANNINE K. BROWN, The David Price Professor of Biblical and Theological Foundations, Bethel Seminary, Saint Paul, Minnesota

What I love about this rich biblical theology of the symbolism, production, and use of alcohol is the theologically mindful posture that Dunne gifts to us—whether you imbibe or not—that is aware of how alcohol represents both the goodness of God as well as the responsibilities of his people. John Dunne doesn't merely tackle the modern debates about alcohol in Scripture but resurrects the ancient enchantment of alcohol, seeing it as a divine gift and miracle. He enables us to see the picture unfolding regarding our covenantal relationship with God and one another and how the production and use of alcohol orients us toward creation and new creation. This book is more than an academic study—it is a promise.

> AIMEE BYRD, author of *Saving Face*, *The Hope in Our Scars*, and *Recovering from Biblical Manhood and Womanhood*

If, as the psalmist observes, wine makes the human heart glad, then so also will reading John Anthony Dunne's discussion of its place in Christian Scripture. He is rigorous and informative without being dull and pedantic. In short, Dunne has produced a sober analysis of an intoxicating topic!

> COURTNEY FRIESEN, Professor of Religious Studies and Classics at the University of Arizona and author of *Reading Dionysus*

John Anthony Dunne has brewed up for us a rich and refreshing biblical theology of alcohol, a theme that is as vital as it is (until now) underexplored. His distillation of the technical, cultural, and theological aspects of fermented drinks is sure to gladden the hearts of many. Three cheers for the author!

> REV. DR. ANDREW JUDD, Deputy Principal and Lecturer in Old Testament, Ridley College, Melbourne, Australia, and author of *Modern Genre Theory: An Introduction for Biblical Studies*

With a range of insights into not only the material production of alcoholic beverages but also thoughtful understanding within material, literary, and social contexts, Dunne's book is clearly the new essential work for anyone interested in understanding drinking in the Bible. Whether wine, beer, or otherwise, Dunne's work sheds light not only on this consumptive act in the Bible but also on biblical society and life more broadly. Whether one is a Jew, a Christian, or just otherwise interested in biblical drinking, this is an indispensable and comprehensive look at this element of biblical life.

> Rabbi Drew Kaplan, host of the podcast, The Jewish Drinking Show

Lay person, seasoned theologian, and would-be archaeologist alike will benefit from John Dunne's up-to-date and very lucid exposition of the many biblical passages that revolve around a fermented beverage, preeminently grape wine. He unlocks the metaphorical complexity and richness of this ethereal beverage in God's covenant with Israel and the Last Supper's foreshadowing of the heavenly banquet promised by the prophets and in the book of Revelation.

> Patrick McGovern, Scientific Director of the Biomolecular Archaeology Project for Cuisine, Fermented Beverages, and Health, University of Pennsylvania Museum, author of *Ancient Wine: The Search for the Origins of Viniculture* and *Ancient Brews: Rediscovered and Re-Created*

In this book, Dunne provides a valuable resource for understanding the many ways that Scripture alludes to alcohol use, especially the many theological points that use this imagery. Dunne is both informative and poetic in his approach to the topic.

> Madison N. Pierce, Associate Professor of New Testament at Western Theological Seminary, Holland, Michigan

Dunne has produced a work that is rich and detailed as he explores the biblical traditions around alcohol. In a work that is both scholarly and pastoral, *The Mountains Shall Drip Sweet Wine* offers an insightful theology of alcohol that invites the reader to move beyond typical taboos around whether Christians should or should not drink. Dunne opens the ancient world and the biblical text to demonstrate that wine and alcohol provide a critical thread running through the Bible that relates to God's engagement and love for the world. This is a book that challenges unfounded negative assumptions about alcohol and celebrates the gift of wine as a critical theological sign and symbol of God's kingdom.

> Mark W. Scarlata, Senior Lecturer in Old Testament, St Mellitus College, author of *Wine, Soil, and Salvation in the Hebrew Bible and New Testament*

The Mountains Drip Sweet Wine is a brilliant addition to the growing collection of work that focuses on alcohol and drinking in the Bible. Dunne provides thorough detail on every aspect of viticulture and also does not ignore the important role of beer that was consumed widely in the ancient world. Insightful exegesis of a range of relevant biblical passages is illuminating for all readers, whether new to the study of alcohol in biblical texts or well acquainted. What comes across most strikingly is how central alcohol was to the ancient cultures that Dunne explores, saturating nearly all aspects of life from the social and religious to the economic and political. Despite the distance of many centuries, alcohol still plays a prominent role in our own lives, and it is therefore intellectually vital that we reflect on how biblical texts and their interpretation have shaped our contemporary attitudes and preferences surrounding alcohol consumption. In doing this, Dunne challenges our assumptions and misconceptions regarding wine and beer and provides us with a way to appreciate the many references to alcohol that are spilt across the pages of the Bible.

> Rebekah Welton, Lecturer in Hebrew Bible, University of Exeter, author of *"He Is a Glutton and a Drunkard": Deviant Consumption in the Hebrew Bible*

For

T. J. Bernstein
Robert Bolgeo
Greg Franklin
Travis Lodes
Jason Smyth
Calvin Sodestrom

May the wine of friendship never run dry.

CONTENTS

Detailed Table of Contents xi
Abbreviations xvii
Series Preface xxiii
Author's Preface xxv

QUEUEING THE QUESTIONS

  1. Introducing a Biblical Theology of Alcohol 3

ARRIVING AT ANSWERS

  2. The Types of Alcoholic Beverages in the Bible 13
  3. Mixed Drinks and Dilution 31
  4. The Production and Economics of Alcoholic Beverages 40
  5. Cultivating God's Vineyard 57
  6. Alcohol in the Temple System 76
  7. Restrictions and Prohibitions of Alcohol 87
  8. Abstinence and Fasts from Alcohol 97
  9. Consuming Alcohol Wisely 115
10. Drunkenness and Vulnerability 124
11. The Loss of God's Vineyard 141
12. The Cup of Wrath 159
13. Eschatological Abundance of Wine 176
14. The Eschatological Banquet 194
15. The Last Supper and the Blood of Christ 209
16. The Eucharist and Early Christian Meals 220

REFLECTING ON RELEVANCE

17. Alcohol for Today 237

Scripture and Other Ancient Literature Index 255
Subject Index 273
Author Index 283

DETAILED TABLE OF CONTENTS

Abbreviations xvii
Series Preface xxiii
Author's Preface xxv

QUEUEING THE QUESTIONS

1. Introducing a Biblical Theology of Alcohol 3
    The Complexity of the Issue 3
    The Nature of the Book 7
    The Shape of the Book 9

ARRIVING AT ANSWERS

2. The Types of Alcoholic Beverages in the Bible 13
    Categorizing Ancient Alcoholic Beverages 13
    The Two-Wine Theory 15
    Fully Fermented Wines 18
    New Wines 19
    Grape Must and Sweet Wines 21
    Sour Wine and Vinegar 23
    Beer 24
    Conclusion 28
    Relevant Questions 30

3. Mixed Drinks and Dilution 31
    Mixed Drinks 31
    Diluted Wines 33
    Conclusion 39
    Relevant Questions 39

4. The Production and Economics of Alcoholic Beverages 40
    The Production and Economics of Wine 40
        Planting and Cultivating Vineyards 41
        Harvesting and Treading the Grapes 43
        Wine Storage and Trade 45
        The Economics of Vineyards 47

  The Economics of Wine Consumption 49
  The Production and Economics of Beer 54
  Conclusion 56
  Relevant Questions 56

5. Cultivating God's Vineyard 57
  The Land Promise 57
    Blessings and Extensions of the Promise 58
    The Promised Land and Its Viticultural Potential 59
    The Blessing of Wine and Covenantal Stipulations 61
  Wine Consumption on Holy Days 65
    The Feast of Trumpets 66
    Purim 66
    The Feast of Tabernacles 68
    Passover 69
  The Song of Songs: Wine and Sexuality in the Land 70
  Conclusion 74
  Relevant Questions 75

6. Alcohol in the Temple System 76
  Tithes of Alcohol 76
  Libations of Alcohol 78
    The Content of Libations 79
    Libation in Judges 9 81
  The Temple as a Source of Great Food and Wine 83
  Conclusion 86
  Relevant Questions 86

7. Restrictions and Prohibitions of Alcohol 87
  Explicit Restrictions in the Old Testament 87
  Explicit Restrictions in the New Testament 93
  Conclusion 96
  Relevant Questions 96

8. Abstinence and Fasts from Alcohol 97
  Samson 98
  Hannah and Samuel 100
  Job 101
  Jeremiah 102
  The Rekabites 102

    Esther 103
    Daniel 104
    John the Baptist and Jesus 105
    "The Weak" and "The Strong" in Romans 14–15 109
    Timothy 110
    Conclusion 113
    Relevant Questions 114

9. Consuming Alcohol Wisely 115
    Proverbial Wisdom on Alcohol 115
    Ecclesiastes and Drinking "under the Sun" 119
    Conclusion 123
    Relevant Questions 123

10. Drunkenness and Vulnerability 124
    Vulnerability to Sexual Exploitation 125
    Vulnerability to Violence 131
    Vulnerability to Divine Judgment 136
    Conclusion 139
    Relevant Questions 140

11. The Loss of God's Vineyard 141
    Privation as Judgment 141
    Israel as God's Vineyard 146
        Israel as God's Vineyard in Psalm 80 147
        Israel as God's Vineyard in Hosea and Jeremiah 147
        Israel as God's Vineyard in Ezekiel 148
        Israel as God's Vineyard in Isaiah 150
        Israel as God's Vineyard in Jesus's Teachings 152
    Conclusion 157
    Relevant Questions 158

12. The Cup of Wrath 159
    Harvesting and Treading 160
    The Cup of Wrath 163
        The Contents of the Cup 164
        Passing the Cup 169
        The Cup of Gethsemane 172
    Conclusion 174
    Relevant Questions 175

13. Eschatological Abundance of Wine 176
    Viticulture and Restoring the People. 176
    Viticulture and Revitalizing the Temple 179
    Mountains Dripping Sweet Wine in Joel and Amos 181
    The Wedding at Cana. 187
    Conclusion 192
    Relevant Questions. 193

14. The Eschatological Banquet 194
    A Feast Celebrating the Death of Death 194
    The Teachings of Jesus 197
        The Question about Fasting. 197
        Feasting in Jesus's Lukan Parables 198
        The Last Supper. 202
    The Marriage Supper of the Lamb 205
    Conclusion 208
    Relevant Questions. 208

15. The Last Supper and the Blood of Christ 209
    Was the Last Supper a Passover Meal?. 209
    Covenantal Blood. 210
    The Third Cup of the Passover Meal?. 213
    The Upper Room Discourse 215
    "Drink My Blood" 217
    Conclusion 219
    Relevant Questions. 219

16. The Eucharist and Early Christian Meals 220
    Identity and Ethos at Early Christian Meals 220
    Participation and the Eucharist in 1 Corinthians 10–11 223
    Drunkenness and the Spirit-Filled Community in Ephesians 5:18 . . . 228
    Conclusion 232
    Relevant Questions. 233

REFLECTING ON RELEVANCE

17. Alcohol for Today 237
    The Giver of All Good Gifts. 239
    A Diversity of Consumptive Habits. 240
    The Ritual Use of Alcohol 245

Creation and Embodiment 247
Art and Creativity. 248
The Abuse of God's Gifts 250
God Is Eager to Restore 252

Scripture and Other Ancient Literature Index. 255
Subject Index 273
Author Index. 283

ABBREVIATIONS

Abbreviations of ancient sources in this book follow the conventions of the *SBL Handbook of Style* (2nd ed.); some additional abbreviations are also included.

AB	Anchor Bible
ABD	*The Anchor Bible Dictionary*. Edited by David Noel Freedman. 6 vols. New York: Doubleday, 1992
ABV	Alcohol by Volume
ACCS	Ancient Christian Commentary on Scripture
AGUSA	Assemblies of God USA
AHRW	*Alcohol Health and Research World*
AIL	Ancient Israel and Its Literature
AJBI	Annual of the Japanese Biblical Institute
ANE	Ancient Near East
ANET	*Ancient Near Eastern Texts Relating to the Old Testament*. Edited by James B. Pritchard. 3rd ed. Princeton: Princeton University Press, 1969
APG	Agora Picture Book
AT	Alpha Text
AYB	Anchor Yale Bible
AYBRL	Anchor Yale Bible Reference Library
BAC	Blood Alcohol Content
BAR	*Biblical Archaeology Review*
BARIS	British Archaeological Reports International Series
BBE	Beiträge zur biblischen Exegese
BCOTWP	Baker Commentary on the Old Testament Wisdom and Psalms
BDAG	Danker, Frederick W., Walter Bauer, William F. Arndt, and F. Wilbur Gingrich. *Greek-English Lexicon of the New Testament and Other Early Christian Literature*. 3rd ed. Chicago: University of Chicago Press, 2000
BDB	Brown, Francis, S. R. Driver, and Charles A. Briggs. *A Hebrew and English Lexicon of the Old Testament*
BECNT	Baker Exegetical Commentary on the New Testament
BGBE	Beiträge zur Geschichte der biblischen Exegese
BHGNT	Baylor Handbook on the Greek New Testament
BibInt	*Biblical Interpretation*
BibInt	Biblical Interpretation Series

BNTC	Black's New Testament Commentaries
BPT	*Biblica et Patristica Thoruniensia*
BRev	*Bible Review*
BS	The Biblical Seminar
BSac	*Bibliotheca Sacra*
BWANT	Beiträge zur Wissenschaft vom Alten und Neuen Testament
BZAW	Beihefte zur Zeitschrift für die alttestamentliche Wissenschaft
CBET	Contributions to Biblical Exegesis and Theology
CBQ	*Catholic Biblical Quarterly*
CBTS	Catholic Biblical Theology of the Sacraments
CIL	*Corpus Inscriptionum Latinarum*. Berlin, 1862–
COQG	Christian Origins and the Question of God
COS	*The Context of Scripture*. Edited by William W. Hallo. 3 vols. Leiden: Brill, 1997–2002
CT	*Christianity Today*
DPL²	*Dictionary of Paul and His Letters*. Edited by Scot McKnight, Lynn H. Cohick, and Nijay K. Gupta. 2nd ed. Downers Grove, IL: IVP Academic, 2023
DSD	Dead Sea Discoveries
DSSSE	*The Dead Sea Scrolls Study Edition*. Edited by Florentino García Martínez and Eibert J. C. Tigchelaar. 2 vols. Leiden: Brill; Grand Rapids: Eerdmans, 1997–1998
EDEJ	*The Eerdmans Dictionary of Early Judaism*. Edited by John J. Collins and Daniel C. Harlow. Grand Rapids: Eerdmans, 2010
EEC	Evangelical Exegetical Commentary
ESV	English Standard Version
ExpTim	*Expository Times*
HALOT	*The Hebrew and Aramaic Lexicon of the Old Testament*. Ludwig Koehler, Walter Baumgartner, and Johann J. Stamm. Translated and edited under the supervision of Mervyn E. J. Richardson. 4 vols. Leiden: Brill, 1994–1999
HCSB	Holman Christian Standard Bible
HSM	Harvard Semitic Monographs
ICC	International Critical Commentary
IPA	India Pale Ale
JBL	*Journal of Biblical Literature*
JETS	*Journal of the Evangelical Theological Society*
JIBS	*Journal for Interdisciplinary Biblical Studies*
JME	*Journal of Molecular Evolution*
JR	*Journal of Religion*

JSNT	*Journal for the Study of the New Testament*
JSNTSup	Journal for the Study of the New Testament Supplement Series
JSOT	*Journal for the Study of the Old Testament*
JSOTSup	Journal for the Study of the Old Testament Supplement Series
JWR	*Journal of Wine Research*
KEK	Kritisch-exegetischer Kommentar über das Neue Testament
KJV	King James Version
KTAH	Key Themes in Ancient History
KTU	*Die keilalphabetischen Texte aus Ugarit.* Edited by Manfried Dietrich, Oswald Loretz, and Joaquín Sanmartín. Münster: Ugarit-Verlag, 2013. 3rd enl. ed. of *KTU: The Cuneiform Alphabetic Texts from Ugarit, Ras Ibn Hani, and Other Places.* Edited by Manfried Dietrich, Oswald Loretz, and Joaquín Sanmartín. Münster: Ugarit-Verlag, 1995
L&N	Louw, Johannes P., and Eugene A. Nida, eds. *Greek-English Lexicon of the New Testament: Based on Semantic Domains.* 2nd ed. 2 vols. New York: United Bible Societies, 1989
LAB	Liber antiquitatum biblicarum (Pseudo-Philo)
LAI	Library of Ancient Israel
LCL	Loeb Classical Library
LHBOTS	Library of Hebrew Bible/Old Testament Studies
LNTS	Library of New Testament Studies
LSTS	Library of Second Temple Studies
LTQ	*Lexington Theological Quarterly*
LXX	Septuagint
MT	Masoretic Text
NAC	New American Commentary
NASB	New American Standard Bible
NEA	*Near Eastern Archaeology*
NET	New English Translation
NETS	*A New English Translation of the Septuagint.* Edited by Albert Pietersma and Benjamin G. Wright. New York: Oxford University Press, 2007
NDBT	*New Dictionary of Biblical Theology.* Edited by T. Desmond Alexander, Brian S. Rosner, D. A. Carson, and Graeme Goldsworthy. Downers Grove, IL: IVP Academic, 2000
NIAAA	National Institute on Alcohol Abuse and Alcoholism
NICNT	New International Commentary on the New Testament
NICOT	New International Commentary on the Old Testament
NIDOTTE	*New International Dictionary of Old Testament Theology and Exegesis.* Edited by Willem A. VanGemeren. 5 vols. Grand Rapids: Zondervan, 1997

NIGTC	New International Greek Testament Commentary
NIV	New International Version
NKJV	New King James Version
NLT	New Living Translation
NovT	*Novum Testamentum*
NovTSup	Supplements to Novum Testamentum
NPNF¹	*Nicene and Post-Nicene Fathers*, Series 1
NPR	National Public Radio
NRSVue	New Revised Standard Version Updated Edition
NSBT	New Studies in Biblical Theology
NTL	New Testament Library
NTS	*New Testament Studies*
OBT	Overtures to Biblical Theology
OTL	Old Testament Library
OTP	*Old Testament Pseudepigrapha*. Edited by James H. Charlesworth. 2 vols. New York: Doubleday, 1983, 1985
PACS	Philo of Alexandria Commentary Series
Pal. Hist.	Palaea Historica
PEQ	*Palestinian Exploration Quarterly*
PNAS	*Proceedings of the National Academy of Sciences of the United States of America*
PNTC	Pillar New Testament Commentary
PSL	Princeton Science Library
RB	*Revue biblique*
ResQ	*Restoration Quarterly*
RJ	*Reformed Journal*
RM	*Research in Microbiology*
RSV	Revised Standard Version
SAM	Studies in Ancient Medicine
SBC	Southern Baptist Convention
SBL	Society of Biblical Literature
SBLMS	Society of Biblical Literature Monograph Series
SHBC	Smyth & Helwys Bible Commentary
SNTSMS	Society for New Testament Studies Monograph Series
SR	*Scientific Reports*
STAC	Studien und Texte zu Antike und Christentum
SwJT	*Southwestern Journal of Theology*
TDNT	*Theological Dictionary of the New Testament*. Edited by Gerhard Kittel and Gerhard Friedrich. Translated by Geoffrey W. Bromiley. 10 vols. Grand Rapids: Eerdmans, 1964–1976

TDOT	*Theological Dictionary of the Old Testament.* Edited by G. Johannes Botterweck and Helmer Ringgren. Translated by John T. Willis et al. 17 vols. Grand Rapids: Eerdmans, 1974–2021
TOTC	Tyndale Old Testament Commentaries
UBS	United Bible Societies
UBSHS	United Bible Societies Handbook Series
VT	*Vetus Testamentum*
VTSup	Supplements to Vetus Testamentum
WBC	Word Biblical Commentary
WTJ	*Westminster Theological Journal*
WUNT	Wissenschaftliche Untersuchungen zum Neuen Testament
ZECNT	Zondervan Exegetical Commentary on the New Testament

SERIES PREFACE

The question "What does the Bible have to say about that?" is, in essence, what the Biblical Theology for Life series is all about. Not unlike other biblical explorations of various topics, the volumes in this series articulate various themes in biblical theology, but they always do so with the "So what?" question rumbling about and demanding to be answered. Too often, books on biblical theology have focused mainly on *description*—simply discerning the teachings of the biblical literature on a particular topic. But contributors to this series seek to straddle both the world of the text and the world in which we live.

This means that their descriptions of biblical theology will always be understood as the important *first* step in their task, which will not be completed until they draw out that theology's practical implications for the contemporary context. Contributors therefore engage both in the *description* of biblical theology and in its contemporary *contextualization*, accosting the reader's perspective and fostering application, transformation, and growth. It is our hope that these informed insights of evangelical biblical scholarship will increasingly become enfleshed in the sermons and discussions that transpire each week in places of worship, in living rooms where Bible studies gather, and in classrooms around the world. We hope that this series will lead to personal transformation and practical application in real life.

Every volume in this series has the same basic structure. In the first section, entitled "Queueing the Questions," authors introduce the main questions they seek to address in their books. Raising these questions enables you to see clearly from the outset what each book will be pursuing, inviting you to participate in the process of discovery along the way. In the second section, "Arriving at Answers," authors develop the biblical theology of the topic they address, focusing their attention on specific biblical texts and constructing answers to the questions introduced in section one. In the concluding "Reflecting on Relevance" section, authors contextualize their biblical-theological insights, discussing specific ways in which the theology presented in their books addresses contemporary situations and issues, giving you opportunities to consider how you might live out that theology in the world today.

Long before you make it to the "Reflecting on Relevance" section, however, we encourage you to wrestle with the implications of the biblical theology being described by considering the "Relevant Questions" that conclude each chapter. Frequent sidebars spice up your experience, supplementing the main discussion with significant quotations, illustrative historical or contemporary data, and fuller explanations of the content.

In sum, the goal of the Biblical Theology for Life series is communicated by its title. On the one hand, its books mine the Bible for theology that addresses a wide range of topics so you may know "the only true God, and Jesus Christ, whom [he] . . . sent" (John 17:3). On the other hand, contributing authors contextualize this theology in ways that allow the *life*-giving Word (John 1:4; 20:31) to speak into and transform contemporary *life*.

Series Editor
Jonathan Lunde

AUTHOR'S PREFACE

The present book was a long time coming. I first set out to synthesize the Bible's teachings on alcohol in August 2011 as my initial contributions to a brand-new blog that I helped launch, *The Two Cities*. It always felt like I had done too much legwork for just two blog posts, and so I had hopes of developing things further. Due to the helpful prodding of Katya Covrett at Zondervan Academic, the present book project became official in 2013, for which I am tremendously grateful. The whole team at Zondervan Academic (past and present) has been so enthusiastic over the years, not to mention remarkably patient, given my requests for extensions (*mea culpa*). I'll spare you all the wine puns about my thoughts needing to mature, but I do think the book benefited from more time. That meant that I could research ancient winemaking and brewing more extensively, and also that I could workshop my ideas in more contexts, including by giving papers at the annual, international, and regional meetings of the Society of Biblical Literature, the British New Testament Conference, the Evangelical Theological Society, the Society of Vineyard Scholars, the St Andrews Symposium for Biblical and Early Christian Studies, and the Twin Cities New Testament Symposium, and also by giving guest lectures at L'Abri International Fellowship (in Switzerland and Minnesota), Salem Covenant Church (New Brighton, MN), and Princeton Theological Seminary, as part of professor F. W. "Chip" Dobbs-Allsopp's class on "Wine and the Bible" in collaboration with Nathan Stucky's Farminary Project. To everyone who engaged my work in those venues, cheers and thank you.

As for specific acknowledgments, those consistent voices of encouragement over the years deserve first mention: my parents, my siblings and their families, Trevor and Rachel Cartwright, my fellow cohosts from *The Two Cities* podcast, and the indefatigable Gordon Franz. Many thanks to my students at Bethel Seminary who participated in my class "Wine and Meals in the Bible." They were all so engaged, giving me plenty of great feedback, and so I name them here: Chris Auer, John Beaugard, Orly Bisquera, Charity Blomberg, Andy Bramsen, Stuart Collins, Dan Cook, Lexi Folen, John Godin, Wendy Green, Lissa Hutcheson, Sullivan Keehr, Nick Klein, Dagny Lemunyon, John Patton, Paul Richard, Monica Ritchie, Jeffrey Smith, Amy Staley, Danny Steward, Sean Thomas, Dustin Thompson, Jill Utecht, Michael Wahlstrom, Christian Walk, Jessi Walk, and Seth Zielicke. Thanks are also due to my TA for that course, Rebekah Wold Defries, and to Austin Reichow-Chavez, who helped me find social-scientific studies and polling data. I also appreciate my DMin students Karen Beaumont and Brian Brunke, who conducted independent studies with me on alcohol in the American church.

I am especially grateful to everyone who read some or all of the first draft of my book and joined me for a merry night of debriefing, including: Jeannine Brown, Dan Cook, Aaron Downs, Andy Johnson, Laura Kozamchak, Rose Nelessen, J. D. O'Brien, Taylor Patz, Kavan Rogness, Amy Staley, and Casey Summers. Those who weren't able to attend but nevertheless provided feedback on parts of that first draft also include: Brad Blakeley, Nick Fox, Kaz Hayashi, Ryan Heinsch, Stephanie Kate Judd, Andrew Judd, Jennifer Pietz, Ben Rhodes, Mark Strauss, Sean Thomas, Dustin Thompson, Logan Williams, and Justin Winzenburg, as well as those who read the full draft and wrote extensive notes: Andrew Cowan and especially Deborah Fransway. The feedback and queries from Chris Beetham at Zondervan Academic were incredibly helpful at the copyedit stage as well.

Having colleagues who work broadly in this area and are willing to dialogue has been invaluable. I have known Gisela Kreglinger since my doctoral days at St Andrews, where I had the pleasure of participating in her reflective wine-tasting events and hearing her lecture on portions of what became her *Spirituality of Wine*. Gisela's expertise, passion, and sensibilities about wine have been inspiring to me. Patrick McGovern has been a warm dialogue partner, and I am honored that he engaged earlier drafts of this book. He is my academic hero in this field, given his expertise in archaeology and chemistry, and also his collaboration with my favorite brewery, Dogfish Head, in re-creating ancient styles of beer. Peter Hemstad, who is a grape breeder and the co-owner and COO of St. Croix Vineyards (Stillwater, MN), along with their head winemaker and production manager, Martin Polognioli, allowed me to help with harvesting and pruning on multiple occasions, and shared some of their insights with me while we worked. Rebekah Welton has become a good friend as a result of this project. I am grateful for her scholarship, her detailed feedback on my early drafts, and our delightful conversations—all of which have sharpened my thinking.

It must be said that this book is deeply indebted to Jonathan Lunde, the general editor of the Biblical Theology for Life series, who gave me invaluable feedback on earlier drafts of this book. Dr. Lunde (as I can't help but call him) was my former undergraduate professor, and in his "NT Use of the OT" class—the most formative class I would ever take—I chose to write my final paper on the use of Amos 9 in Acts 15, which was not on the shortlist of preapproved passages. His willingness to approve my topic in May 2008 (for a paper that wasn't due until the end of the following semester when the course was offered) meant that I could spend the whole summer researching in advance. Since that time, Amos's vision of sweet wine dripping down mountains has remained a constant fascination, and thus it is only fitting that this book is named after that passage as an acknowledgment of both where this research started and Dr. Lunde's role in giving it life.

Finally, I dedicate this book to my former housemates at "the Bora Residence," with whom I lived for two years during graduate school. When I first moved in, I only knew half of them, and those I did know I wasn't acquainted with outside of our mutual involvement in an on-campus ministry. As it happened, the circumstances necessitating my move were the most depressing and disorienting of my life. The generosity they showed me, someone outside of their immediate friend group, has always meant so much, considering that I was now trying to navigate my life with the realization that the vision that I had for myself would never materialize. Even more fitting for this book, though, that house was not simply the context in which I came to imagine a new trajectory for my life, but it was also where my own appreciation for fine beverages originated. Specifically, it was their knowledge of various styles of craft beer, and their interests in extending road trips to visit highly esteemed breweries, that made me passionate about excellence, nuance, and diversity in this space. My housemates were not only hospitable to me when I needed it most, but they gave me a gift—the gift of passion for the subject matter of this book. And so, to them I raise my glass. Since this book is part of a larger series called Biblical Theology for Life, I can think of no better toast than this—*L'chaim!*

John Anthony Dunne
Repeal Day (aka my birthday), 2023

PART 1

QUEUEING THE QUESTIONS

CHAPTER 1

INTRODUCING A BIBLICAL THEOLOGY OF ALCOHOL

Whether or not we personally drink alcohol, our Bibles are soaked with it. References to alcoholic beverages in Scripture are everywhere; sometimes they are literal and sometimes they are symbolic—from production to consumption to intoxication. The most common term for wine in the Old Testament, *yayin*, occurs 141 times, with an additional thirty-four occurrences of the Greek term *oinos* in the New Testament. However, these statistics—which in themselves convey the prominence of the theme—do not even come close to representing the fullness of alcohol's biblical representation. It would be overwhelming to itemize all of the additional terms in the Bible for wine and other intoxicating beverages and count off their occurrences. This would not even include the multiple terms related to the agricultural side of production, the equipment for winemaking, vessels for storage and drinking, the consumers of alcoholic beverages themselves, the effects of drunkenness, and more.

Alcohol is truly a major topic in biblical literature. If we ignore passages about alcohol, we will end up setting aside quite a bit of biblical material, and we will miss out on one of the richest topics presented to us in Scripture. We will also lose out on experiencing the richness that alcohol provides to other theological topics, such as creation, covenant, kingdom, temple, and more. Thus, references to alcohol are not just everywhere in Scripture; they are also quite robust, often possessing a great deal of symbolic structure and, if you like, theological tannins for readers to savor.

THE COMPLEXITY OF THE ISSUE

Despite the pervasiveness of alcoholic drinks in Scripture, it is too often the case that Christians reduce the topic to little more than proof texting. Typically, the debate concerning what the Bible has to say about alcohol is almost singularly conceived in terms of *permissibility*: *Does Scripture permit Christians to drink alcohol?* Many simply look for the definitive passages that seem to settle the debate once and for all. To be sure, this is a well-meaning question with practical implications, and it will be addressed in this book, but there are a few problems with this approach if it is the only framework we have.

To start, the question is far too generic. Although it seeks for wisdom, it will only receive generalizations and simplifications in return. Definitive answers work neither for the ancient text nor for our modern world. Christians today hail from widely divergent cultures, espousing dramatically distinct perspectives, so cookie-cutter answers are not serviceable. With this in mind, we should trade in the generic permissibility question for ones that are more sensitive to the complexity of the issue. *Does Scripture prohibit the consumption of alcohol for all people at all times? If permissible, should a Christian drink alcohol? If a Christian is going to drink, how should they do so? If a Christian chooses to abstain, do they need biblical justification for that decision?* These questions provide some added nuance to our original question, and yet they have only provided nuance *to one area of interest*—namely, individual permissibility. Certainly, when we ask permissibility questions, we ought to be sensitive to the fact that an issue like alcohol consumption is not straightforward. Yet additionally we need to recognize that there are other kinds of questions worth asking as well.

In addition to being more sensitive to the contexts of Christians, we need to be sensitive to the contexts of Scripture. We need more questions at our disposal than those pertaining to permissibility, because the themes related to alcohol in Scripture are actually quite complex. At a basic level, one of the things that becomes apparent about alcohol in the Bible is that some passages seem more positive, and others more negative. On the one hand, consider this example from Proverbs:

> Honor the LORD with your wealth,
>   with the firstfruits of all your crops;
> then your barns will be filled to overflowing,
>   and your vats will brim over with new wine. (Prov 3:9–10)

On the other hand, we have passages like this from the same biblical book:

> Wine is a mocker and beer a brawler;
>   whoever is led astray by them is not wise. (Prov 20:1)

When we simply ask permissibility questions alone, we might not know what to do with such a tension. Typically, Christians tend to opt for one of these types of texts as conclusive, prioritizing some texts over others. If we have a personal opinion on whether Christians are free to enjoy alcohol from a biblical perspective, our position is likely informed by the set of texts we see as most naturally aligning with our view. When we approach Scripture's teaching on alcohol only as a matter of permissibility, we will inevitably sideline a number of texts that do not appear to answer the question the way we want, or even at all. So, which do we prefer—the warning of Proverbs 20:1 or the blessing of Proverbs 3:9–10?

There are at least three problems with making an either-or choice here. One problem is that our undue selectivity will lead to a truncated account of Scripture's teaching. The *entire* biblical portrait should matter to us rather than just a piece of it here or there. In my estimation this is perhaps the most significant problem that needs to be corrected, though it is not the only one. A second problem pertains to the diversity of terms used for alcohol in the two passages from Proverbs: "new wine," "wine," and "beer" should not be conflated in our assessment of what Proverbs says about alcohol, let alone what the whole Bible says (see ch. 2 of the present work). A third and final problem to note is a failure to recognize the nuance of the biblical authors. In the examples above, do we recognize a difference between *abundance*, on the one hand, and *excessive consumption* on the other?

Equipped with different kinds of questions, we can arrive at a more informed, comprehensive, and theologically enriching account of alcohol in the Bible. For example, we need to ask *questions of content*. What types of alcohol are mentioned in Scripture? How were they produced? Were ancient wines commonly watered down? With these questions we are trying to ensure that we understand what the Bible is referring to when it mentions anything pertaining to alcohol. We can also ask *questions of function*. What kinds of images and symbols do the various biblical authors associate with alcohol production and consumption? How do the biblical authors connect the images and symbols of alcohol with broader biblical-theological topics that eclipse issues of permissibility? These types of questions highlight that we should expect distinct emphases in the biblical material. Finally, we can ask *questions of characterization and representation*. Who are the people who drink or abstain from alcohol, respectively, and what is their rationale for doing so? On what occasions and in what kind of spaces is alcohol consumed or avoided? With these questions we are looking for ways that alcohol consumption and abstinence are associated with certain people, times, and spaces.

As we ask these additional questions, we should not assume that all biblical writers will answer them *identically*. In fact, there is quite a biblical assortment when it comes to the connotations of alcohol. Thinking about this as a metaphor for a moment, we might compare the symbolic diversity to that of grapevine varietals within the world of wine. If you are familiar with many new-world wines in the Americas, Australia, New Zealand, and South Africa, they are often named after the dominant grapevine varietal that was used to create the wine (in the US, at least, the dominant varietal must be at least 75%). For example, a Merlot is a well-known red wine made primarily from Merlot grapes. The same is true of other wine styles that are named after a specific varietal, like Pinot Noir, Zinfandel, Sauvignon Blanc, etc. Old-world wines from Europe and the Mediterranean, by contrast, are usually named after the region where the wine was made, often referred to by the French term *terroir*, which places more emphasis on factors like climate and soil. Famous French examples include Côtes-du-Rhône, Beaujolais, Bordeaux, and Burgundy. Applying this dynamic of winemaking as a metaphor for the biblical material, we might say that Scripture's statements about alcohol can be clustered together in *symbolic varietals*. The metaphor helps us recognize the inherent diversity of the biblical material and also helps us to conceptualize the kinds of diversity that it contains. Rather than treat alcohol in the Bible like a cheap blend, we should cultivate an appreciation for its diversity, just like we would with a *full-bodied* Cabernet Sauvignon, or a *peppery* Shiraz, or a *buttery* Chardonnay. In a manner of speaking, although alcohol is pervasive in Scripture, it does not go down the same way each time. We should taste and see the nuance and become connoisseurs of its delicious complexity.

To illustrate the metaphor further, let me point out some obvious examples that usher us into the kinds of rich theological themes that will be explored in subsequent chapters. For instance, there are passages where alcohol-related imagery primarily conveys the notion of *God's wrath*. Take a look at one noteworthy example:

> God remembered Babylon the Great and gave her the cup filled with the wine of the fury of his wrath. (Rev 16:19b)

Without even unpacking anything in this passage, it is clear that the image is meant to terrify. "I'll have what she's having" is not a likely response that readers would have to this. And yet, at the same time, there are also a number of texts in the Bible that use similar language to refer to *God's restorative actions*. Accordingly, consider this text:

> On this mountain the Lord Almighty will prepare
> a feast of rich food for all peoples,
> a banquet of aged wine—
> the best of meats and the finest of wines. (Isa 25:6)

When we compare these two texts side by side, we can see the usefulness of categorizing them according to distinct symbolic varietals. Wine does not symbolize one thing in the Bible; it symbolizes many things, depending on the context. Playing with our metaphor of symbolic varietals, one of these examples is quite sweet and the other is bitter. How can the same symbol have such a different association? A tension exists in the biblical portrait, but what should we do with it? Is this a problem to be resolved, or a complexity to be savored? Alcohol is clearly not a basic symbol containing a single meaning or value but is rather capable of conveying very different things, depending on the context. The diversity of alcohol as a symbol is actually true of many metaphors in Scripture, such as leaven (yeast), salt, or even the world. Leaven, for example, can be used both as a positive image for the expansion of the kingdom of God (Matt 13:33; Luke 13:21), or as a negative image of the spread of false teaching and bad morals (Matt 16:6, 11–12; Mark 8:15; Luke 12:1; 1 Cor 5:6–8; Gal 5:9). As I will demonstrate in this book, alcohol presents us with an even greater theological diversity in Scripture than we have just seen.

THE NATURE OF THE BOOK

Even with the pervasiveness and complexity of alcoholic beverages in the Bible, there have not been many book-length studies that have explored it. A handful of books are an exception to this and are worth noting here briefly, since they will be dialogue partners throughout the book. Lothar Becker has produced the closest thing to an overview of the topic in the Bible.[1] His study provided a much-needed corrective to Robert P. Teachout and Samuele Bacchiocchi, who argued for a Two-Wine theory, which suggests that nearly half of the references to wine in the Bible are nonalcoholic (cf. ch. 2).[2] Carey Ellen Walsh offers a thorough archaeological overview of ancient Israelite viticulture (i.e., overseeing a vineyard), from production to the social dynamics of consumption.[3] Multiple studies on ancient Israelite viticulture could be noted that give more depth to a particular area of focus, but the strength of Walsh's work is her breadth and literary analysis.[4] Walsh's study also pairs nicely with the work of Patrick E. McGovern, whose comprehensive archaeological, chemical, and anthropological research on the origins and development of viticulture covers ancient Israelite practice alongside other ancient cultures.[5] Joel Butler and Randall Heskett deliver an accessible account of the wine industry's development historically, using the biblical material as a launching pad.[6] Their study supplements the work of Tim Unwin and Paul Lukacs respectively on the development of the wine industry up to the end of the twentieth century.[7] Gisela Kreglinger provides a theological and contemplative approach to wine in the light of Scripture and church history, drawing also from her personal experience of growing up on a vineyard in Franconia—firsthand experience that most authors in this space do not possess—and she invites readers to savor the goodness of God with every sip of wine as a spiritual practice.[8] Manuel Dubach addresses how the concerns related to drunkenness in the Old Testament are more related to societal impact than to drunkenness per se,[9] which is a perspective that Rebekah Welton also emphasizes in her own way, highlighting the social and religious concerns at the root of "deviant consumption" that go beyond excess.[10]

---

1. Lothar Becker, *Rebe, Rausch und Religion: Eine kulturgeschichtliche Studie zum Wein in der Bibel*, Theologie 23 (Münster: LIT, 1999).

2. Robert Paul Teachout, "The Use of 'Wine' in the Old Testament" (ThD diss., Dallas Theological Seminary, 1979); Samuele Bacchiocchi, *Wine in the Bible: A Biblical Study on the Use of Alcoholic Beverages* (Berrien Springs: Biblical Perspective, 1989).

3. Carey Ellen Walsh, *The Fruit of the Vine: Viticulture in Ancient Israel*, HSM 60 (Winona Lake, IN: Eisenbrauns, 2000).

4. For more in-depth archaeological studies, see, e.g., Rafael Frankel, *Wine and Oil Production in Antiquity in Israel and Other Mediterranean Countries* (Sheffield: Sheffield Academic, 1999).

5. Patrick E. McGovern, *Ancient Wine: The Search for the Origins of Viniculture*, rev. ed., PSL 66 (Princeton: Princeton University Press, 2019).

6. Joel Butler and Randall Heskett, *Divine Vintage: Following the Wine Trail from Genesis to the Modern Age* (New York: St. Martin's Press, 2012).

7. Tim Unwin, *Wine and the Vine: An Historical Geography of Viticulture and the Wine Trade* (London: Routledge, 1991); Paul Lukacs, *Inventing Wine: A New History of One of the World's Most Ancient Pleasures* (New York: W. W. Norton, 2012).

8. Gisela Kreglinger, *The Spirituality of Wine* (Grand Rapids: Eerdmans, 2016); idem, *The Soul of Wine: Savoring the Goodness of God* (Downers Grove, IL: IVP, 2019).

9. Manuel Dubach, *Trunkenheit im Alten Testament: Begrifflichkeit – Zeugnisse Wertung*, BWANT 4 (Stuttgart: Kohlhammer, 2009).

10. Rebekah Welton, *"He Is a Glutton and a Drunkard": Deviant Consumption in the Hebrew Bible*, BibInt 183 (Leiden: Brill, 2020).

Finally, Jordan D. Rosenblum has written a helpful introduction to rabbinic literature using fermented beverages as an entry point into the main themes and features of "the sea of Talmud," and so his study features many interesting analyses of rabbinic interpretation of biblical texts related to imbibing.[11]

Each of these studies is worthwhile in its own right, and they all have benefited me greatly. But what is clearly missing is a sustained biblical-theological approach to the full biblical witness on alcohol. For some reason this arena is missing from every major series on biblical theology, and it is not given any attention in such biblical dictionaries as the *New Dictionary of Biblical Theology* (*NDBT*) or the *Anchor Bible Dictionary* (*ABD*), to name just two. We can broaden this observation further to note that food generally is rarely engaged from this perspective.[12] As a biblical theology, the present book is concerned with synthesizing the biblical material, but it attempts to do so by allowing the rich diversity in the Bible to be seen. One way of conceiving biblical theology is that it involves a synthesis of biblical exegesis for the sake of the church—the community that regularly interprets biblical texts together.[13] As a Protestant, I focus directly on the sixty-six books that comprise our canon of Scripture, yet my hope is that this book will also be of value for Catholics and Orthodox alike, as well as Jewish readers and others interested in a Christian perspective on the topic. With respect to the larger canons of Catholics and the Orthodox, my stress on the diversity of symbols would only be enhanced by adding more textual material. Similar nuances appear in the Apocrypha, to be sure, but extracanonical texts and traditions will not be the focus of the present investigation, even though they will be referenced from time to time supplementally.

In the end I hope that this synthesis is indeed helpful *for life*, even as it includes but goes beyond questions of permissibility. One aim of this book is undoubtedly to provide an account of a biblical theology of alcohol in the sense that its discussions provide a basis for thinking through one's own personal approach to alcohol. But a biblical theology of alcohol is not eclipsed by one's personal consumption or nonconsumption of alcohol. A biblical theology of alcohol is for all Christians who love their Bible and try to live by it, whether they drink or not. The idea that alcohol in the Bible might be irrelevant to Christians who do not drink is like a Catholic priest saying that he does not need to know about the church's theology of marriage because he is not personally married. It is probably not unfair to say that most Catholic priests know much more about the theology of marriage than their married parishioners, despite their personal lack of participation in it. In other words, making sense of the references

---

11. Jordan D. Rosenblum, *Rabbinic Drinking: What Beverages Teach Us About Rabbinic Literature* (Oakland: University of California Press, 2020).

12. See Nathan MacDonald, *Not Bread Alone: The Uses of Food in the Old Testament* (Oxford: Oxford University Press, 2008), 7.

13. For a helpful taxonomy of approaches, see Edward W. Klink III and Darian R. Lockett, *Understanding Biblical Theology: A Comparison of Theory and Practice* (Grand Rapids: Zondervan, 2012).

to alcohol should be of interest to anyone who reads the Bible, even teetotalers (the term from the temperance movement for people who were *capital T, totally abstinent*).

THE SHAPE OF THE BOOK

The bulk of the book's contents is contained within the section called "Arriving at Answers," where we will be looking closely at the biblical material on alcoholic beverages. Chapters 2–3 address the main content questions for our study, including the "types" of alcoholic beverages in Scripture and whether there are many references to begin with (ch. 2), and also whether these beverages were often diluted with water to make their alcohol levels negligible (ch. 3).

Subsequent chapters address various function questions, stressing the diversity of images and symbols throughout Scripture (or "varietals," referring back to the viticultural metaphor). We begin with that in chapter 4 by looking at how alcoholic drinks literally functioned in ancient Israelite societies, including their production and use. From there we turn to look at positive biblical images of alcohol in the life of ancient Israel, where it is associated with blessings like sexuality and the covenantal promise of the land (ch. 5), and where it plays a key role within the temple system through libations to God and tithes for priestly consumption (ch. 6).

The next four chapters then explore potential problems and dangers related to alcohol. Chapter 7 contains a discussion on what types of prohibitions or restrictions Scripture explicitly makes regarding alcohol, and chapter 8 looks at the biblical characters who abstain from alcohol and why (to help us with questions of characterization). In chapter 9 we engage the wise, yet seemingly conflicting, counsel on the consumption of alcohol in Proverbs and Ecclesiastes. Chapter 10 then emphasizes the dangers that accompany drunkenness, including the vulnerability of sexual exploitation, violence, and divine judgment.

The next several chapters trace a thematic thread pertaining to alcohol within the development of exile, judgment, and restoration. The privation of alcohol is a motif for the curse of the covenant often associated with the exile (ch. 11), and God's judgment is presented as a cup of wrath, which is a parody of God's good gift of alcohol (ch. 12). Chapters 13 and 14 then look at the reinstatement of God's good gift of alcohol through the restoration and abundance that comes on the other side of disasters like the exile (ch. 13), and how a climactic feast will inaugurate the future era of abundance when God acts to restore all things (ch. 14). The next two chapters build on the imagery of the eschatological banquet and explore the use of wine in the Eucharist, both in the Last Supper that Jesus shared with his disciples (ch. 15) and with the ongoing celebration of that meal in the early church, as a foretaste of the feast to come (ch. 16).

In the final section of the book, "Reflecting on Relevance," I will turn to consider how the diverse theological portrait outlined in the "Arriving at Answers" section can be applied in various ways in the church today (ch. 17). In particular, the pluriform images will underscore the necessity of a diversity of approaches within the life of the church—approaches that should be greeted with respect and care for the good of our fellow siblings in Christ.

As this introductory chapter already makes plain, I refer to *alcohol* throughout this book rather than strictly to wine. Part of the rationale for this comes in the next chapter, where we will see that not all references to alcoholic beverages in Scripture are grape based, and hence this is not a biblical theology of *wine* solely. One advantage of referring to alcohol is this reminder of the diversity of beverages in Scripture. This outweighs the term's shortcomings, given that it is admittedly reductionistic, since there is certainly much more to wines and beers than the presence of alcohol, and also anachronistic, since biblical authors were unaware of chemicals like alcohol (and ethanol, to be more specific). However, I use the term alcohol heuristically for our benefit, because of its frequent usage in the US and other contexts as a shorthand for alcoholic beverages. Given that there are more kinds of alcoholic drinks on offer today, focusing on their common denominator aids us in questions of application. Additionally, my interest in what the Bible has to say about alcohol, rather than strictly wine, allows me to address biblical depictions of intoxication, which in many places never mention the content that led to the condition. I also use the terms *intoxicant* and *alcoholic beverage* interchangeably, and I define them, for the purposes of this study, as any substance that can alter one's emotions or behavior (i.e., intoxication) and that can modify them severely when consumed in excess (i.e., drunkenness).

As we finally turn to explore what the Bible has to say about alcohol, it is important to recognize that everyone approaches this topic having been shaped by their background and experiences. We all hold various tensions within us when we consider the role of Scripture *for life*, and this is certainly true for a topic like alcohol. Whereas I cannot assume, dear reader, what your disposition to alcohol is, I do think it is important that I show you my cards (since I was born and raised in Vegas after all). I am not an uninterested interpreter. In full disclosure, one of my favorite hobbies is exploring wineries, craft breweries, and cocktail bars across the US and around the world. I am also a homebrewer, and I love hosting craft-beer receptions, tastings, and cocktail parties. At the same time, I also have close family members who have had their lives upended by addiction to alcohol. Naturally, my perspective on this topic is shaped by my own background and experiences. So my goal is to try to respect the practical tensions that we might uniquely bring to this study, while at the same time offering my assessment of what Scripture has to say about alcohol holistically, in all of its diversity. I hope that, as we explore this rich biblical topic and all of its difficult practical issues, you will be challenged and encouraged along the way, whether you personally consume alcohol or not. There is a feast that awaits us all.

PART 2

ARRIVING AT ANSWERS

CHAPTER 2

THE TYPES OF ALCOHOLIC BEVERAGES IN THE BIBLE

Modern consumers of alcoholic beverages can choose from a variety of options within the three main categories of wines, beers, and spirits. In the ancient world, however, spirits of 40 percent (or higher) alcohol by volume (ABV) did not exist, since distillation developed in the medieval era. This means that beverages made with spirits were not around either, such as fortified wines. Which alcoholic beverages were available depended on various factors, such as cultural preferences, regional suitability, infrastructural supports, trade partnerships, and socioeconomic class. Broadly speaking, though, alcohol production in the ancient world included wines, beers, and meads (made from honey), which could at times be combined together to make a kind of "grog."[1]

When it comes to alcoholic beverages in the Bible, wine is recognized as the primary, if not the sole, beverage. Yet questions about the kinds of wines that biblical figures consumed, or what the various terms for wine mean, are rarely addressed outside of specialized books or dictionaries. Additionally, whether there are references to other drinks like beer or mead is not something that most Bible readers ponder, even though it is a matter of scholarly dispute. Answering these questions will help us better recognize how alcohol was enjoyed, and then also how it functioned both in daily life and in the biblical texts. The goal of this initial chapter in the "Arriving at Answers" section of this book is to provide clarity on the types of intoxicants mentioned in the Bible, as well as some of the common misunderstandings about them.

CATEGORIZING ANCIENT ALCOHOLIC BEVERAGES

The most common category of beverage in Scripture is grape based, but there are references to other fruit-based drinks and possibly even grain-based ones too. The Bible uses different terms to distinguish between types of wine, but the distinctions in Scripture are different from modern categorizations. Contemporary wines are categorized as red, white, rosé, sparkling, or dessert wine. If we have more familiarity with wine, we might further classify them by provenance or region (e.g., Napa Valley

---

1. See McGovern, *Ancient Wine*, 262–78, 279–98, cf. 186.

or Hunter Valley), or vine varietal (e.g., some reds include Malbec and Petite Sirah), unless they are a blend of varietals.

The Bible, however, does not really categorize wine by color, varietal, or provenance. An exception may be found in the term *soreq* (Isa 5:2; Jer 2:21; cf. Isa 16:8), often translated as "choice vine," which could refer to a species of vine that produces red grapes (cf. Gen 49:11).[2] Since there was a town called Sorek (Judg 16:4; same Hebrew spelling), it is likely that a vine called *soreq* designated either the vine's origin from that area before being replanted elsewhere, or its comparable quality to vines from Sorek.[3] Only twice does the Bible overtly mention the provenance of wine: Lebanon (Hos 14:7) and the city of Helbon in modern-day Syria (Ezek 27:18). We can assume that most wines in the region of ancient Israel, from the Late Bronze Age to the Hellenistic period, were reds (Prov 23:31).[4] References to a wine's color refer to it as dark (Gen 49:12; cf. Sib. Or. 14.292) or compare it to blood (Deut 32:42; Isa 34:5; 49:26; Ezek 39:17–20; Joel 3:13; Zech 9:14–15; Matt 26:28–29; Mark 14:24–25; Luke 22:17–18, 20; John 6:53–58; 1 Cor 10:16; 11:25; Rev 14:17–20; 17:6), even calling it the "blood of [the] grape[s]" (Gen 49:11–12; Deut 32:14; cf. 1 Macc 6:34; Sir 39:26; 50:15).

What gives red wines their color is when the *must*—expressed juice from grapes—ferments with the skins, known as *maceration*. Maceration would have been the most consistent way to ferment grape must in the ancient world because yeast residue collects on the skins, and yeast is needed to convert sugar into alcohol. Without maceration, though, the must would ferment from natural yeast strains in the air. White wines were possible, though they were trickier to make, and were often orange in color due to maceration. They gained prestige after the Hellenistic period (cf. Pliny the Elder, *Nat.* 14.11.80). In fact, a wall near a wine shop in the ruins of Herculaneum (destroyed by Mt. Vesuvius in 79 CE alongside Pompeii) colorfully advertises various options for wine, with a white wine listed as the most expensive (*Ad Cucumas* in insula VI.14).

Nowhere does the Bible refer to white wine, although there is some archaeobotanical evidence suggesting that white wine became more prominent in the Levant (the eastern coastal Mediterranean region inclusive of the land of Israel) during the Hellenistic period as wider trade increased.[5] Notably, Shevi Drori has been studying wild varietals in Israel-Palestine that have some claim to antiquity, including Dabouki, Marawi/Hamdani, Jandali, and Bittuni, among others (including some that are presently unnamed). Other than Bittuni, these varietals listed here would be used for white wines.[6] Although these varietals are indigenous to Israel-Palestine, debate about their antiquity persists.[7]

---

2. *HALOT* 3:1362.
3. So similarly Walsh, *Fruit*, 109–10.
4. So, e.g., Walsh, *Fruit*, 107–8; Dubach, *Trunkenheit*, 197.
5. Walsh, *Fruit*, 107; Michal Dayagi-Mendels, *Drink and Be Merry* (Jerusalem: The Israel Museum, 1999), 37.
6. Elyashiv Drori et al., "Collection and Characterization of Grapevine Genetic Resources (*Vitis vinifera*) in the Holy Land, towards the Renewal of Ancient Winemaking Practices," *SR* 7:44463 (2017): 1–12.

7. McGovern, *Ancient Wine*, 333, is not convinced about the antiquity of Marawi/Hamdani or Jandali.

> Most wineries in Israel-Palestine today use common European varietals, like Cabernet Sauvignon and Merlot, because winemaking was reintroduced in the nineteenth century by Baron Edmond Rothchild of Château Lafite in Bordeaux after it ended in the seventh century under Islamic control. Internationally, winemakers do not often use indigenous varietals because, although the main grapevine species for winemaking, *vitis vinifera*, produces thousands of grape cultivars, 99 percent of wines are made from just twenty-five varietals favored by market forces.[8] A few modern producers in Israel-Palestine, however, like Cremisan, Recanati, and Philokalia, have been making wines from local varietals.

If white wine is implied anywhere in the New Testament, the best candidate would be when Jesus turned water into wine.[9] One reason is because the text does not say that the miracle was *visibly discernible*, allowing for a resemblance between the wine and water. It was only *when the wine was tasted* that the miracle was recognized (John 2:9). Whether or not this suggestion is likely (see ch. 13), white wine is not assumed anywhere else in Scripture.

THE TWO-WINE THEORY

Some contemporary Bible readers, especially in the US, assume that the categories of wine represented in the Bible are actually "fermented" and "unfermented" respectively. This is known as the Two-Wine theory, notably defended by Robert Paul Teachout and Samuele Bacchiocchi.[10] This theory essentially affirms that positive references to wine refer to unfermented grape juice, whereas negative ones, especially involving drunkenness, point to alcohol.[11] Judging whether references to wine imply alcohol, however, based on whether its effects are clearly stated, is the equivalent of assuming today that references to coffee normally imply the decaffeinated variety, unless there are overt references to the effects of caffeine. It is little more than special pleading to suggest that beverages that are clearly intoxicants in many contexts simply are not alcoholic in the ones where it would conflict with a predetermined perspective on alcohol.[12]

Most importantly, however, this position fails to account for the way fermentation works. Everything needed for fermentation is found with the grape itself. Once the grapes are crushed, the yeast on the skins combines with the sugary must, and

---

8. McGovern, *Ancient Wine*, 364, 369; cf. 1.
9. So also, Butler and Heskett, *Divine Vintage*, 115.
10. Teachout, "Use of 'Wine'"; Bacchiocchi, *Wine*.
11. Cf. Bacchiocchi, *Wine*, 47–48.
12. Yet Teachout ("Use of 'Wine,'" 18) asserts that his study was not biased by preconceived beliefs.

fermentation begins. It is actually quite easy for grapes to ferment; they can even ferment on the vine, or while they are still in the collection receptacles after they are harvested, if the skin is broken. In fact, broken skin on grapes often leads to the presence of the best yeast for full fermentation, *Saccharomyces cerevisiae*.[13] Without this variety of yeast, wines will likely top out around 5 percent ABV just from the wild yeasts present on the skins and in the air. But with it, ancient wines could reach up to 14–15 percent.[14] This yeast is used intentionally by vintners and brewers today, but its use in winemaking can be detected as far back as 3150 BCE.[15] The likelihood of an ancient wine being fully fermented by *Saccharomyces cerevisiae* would be increased by the following factors: the use of grapes with broken skin, previous exposure to the yeast strain (since it is known to linger on equipment, infrastructure, and soil at breweries and vineyards),[16] and if fruit juices or honey were added as additional sources of sugar and yeast.[17]

Ancient wines probably varied greatly in ABV, but strong wines would be the only kind worth storing and aging because they would spoil otherwise. Thus, the very fact of ancient wine storage and trading, attested in the literary and archaeological record, suggests that sufficient fermentation was regularly achieved. In a telling moment, Teachout registers his amazement at descriptions of wine storage in the Bible, saying, "the liquid produce of the vineyard was stored (1 Chr 27:27) and used during the whole year," even though "no hint is given as to how grape juice was kept from fermenting."[18] The simple reason is that the juice was not kept from fermenting, and without sufficient fermentation it would have spoiled in those conditions.

Despite this fact, both Teachout and Bacchiocchi contend that there is ancient evidence for preserving grape juice from Greek and Latin sources.[19] The two primary methods were boiling the wine down (cf. Columella, *Rust.* 12.19), or submerging vessels of wine into cold bodies of water (producing *semper mustum* or *aiegleukos*; cf. Pliny the Elder, *Nat.* 14.11.83; Columella, *Rust.* 12.29; Cato, *Agr.* 120). Yet these and other methods do not receive mention in the biblical texts, nor is there evidence that they were practiced in ancient Israel. These methods also could not provide large-scale solutions to preserving must, given the quantities produced annually by each vineyard. Moreover, this discussion largely assumes that ancient people understood how fermentation worked, but in fact they did not, and instead they

---

13. Robert Mortimer and Mario Polsinelli, "On the Origins of Wine Yeast," *RM* 150 (1999): 199–204.

14. Patrick E. McGovern, *Uncorking the Past: The Quest for Wine, Beer, and Other Alcoholic Beverages* (Berkeley: University of California Press, 2009), 16; Walsh, *Fruit*, 187–88; Paul A. Henschke and Anthony Borneman, "Yeast," in *The Oxford Companion to Wine*, ed. Julia Harding and Jancis Robinson with Tara Q. Thomas, 5th ed. (Oxford: Oxford University Press, 2023), 848.

15. This was detected in Canaanite amphorae found in king Scorpion I's tomb in Abydos, Egypt. See Duccio Cavalieri et al., "Evidence for *S. cerevisiae* Fermentation in Ancient Wine," *JME* 57 (2003): 226–32. Cf. McGovern, *Ancient Wine*, 103–6.

16. Alessandro Martini, "Origin and Domestication of the Wine Yeast *Saccharomyces cerevisiae*," *JWR* 4.3 (1993): 165–76.

17. McGovern, *Uncorking*, 64, 137.

18. Teachout, "Use of 'Wine,'" 101.

19. Teachout, "Use of 'Wine,'" 396–403; Bacchiocchi, *Wine*, 107–19.

assumed that it was a magical or divine occurrence.[20] Boiling down the must, in particular, would not preserve the must *as juice* in most instances, since the cooking process was not designed to kill the yeast (which they did not know about) but to create a concentration, often in the form of a syrup, which was typically used as an additive to sweeten wine (cf. Columella, *Rust.* 12.21).[21] Similarly, submerging vessels of wine in bodies of water would only work if the water was deep and cold (which is not so simple throughout Israel), and it would only forestall fermentation as long as cold temperatures were maintained, since most yeasts prefer the warmth and would be reactivated unless retrieved during a particularly cold winter.

> Bacchiocchi claims, without support, that "the best wines were those whose alcoholic potency had been removed by boiling or filtration."[22] Despite the fact that no one from antiquity talked about "the best wines" like this, one prominent naturalist, Pliny the Elder (1st c. CE), said that "no other wine has a higher rank" than the Roman wine, Falernum, affirming that it is "the only wine that takes light when a flame is applied to it" (*Nat.* 14.8.63 [Rackham, LCL]). Taking light, of course, speaks to Falernum's high ABV. Conversely, Pliny mentioned another type of grape called "the good-for-nothing," since it was "the only vintage that does not cause intoxication" (*Nat.* 14.4.31–32 [Rackham, LCL]).

Indeed, the only way to stop the process of fermentation after the grapes have been crushed is through pasteurization, which was not fully understood until after the discovery of yeast by Antonie van Leeuwenhoek in the seventeenth century.[23] Developed by Louis Pasteur in 1865, pasteurization is the process of heating a liquid long enough and at the appropriate temperature to kill all microorganisms, including yeast cells. Pasteurization was first applied to winemaking in 1869 when a Methodist named Thomas Bramwell Welch (1825–1903) wanted to find a way to serve communion wine without alcohol.[24] This innovation led to the famous brand of Welch's grape juice. Now, for the first time, people could consume "unfermented wine" year-round, thanks as well to the invention of ice boxes in the nineteenth century and refrigerators in the early part of the twentieth century, without which Welch's grape juice would spoil, if not ferment.

Thus, despite the contention of the proponents of the Two-Wine theory, the

---

20. Lukacs, *Inventing Wine*, 1, 3.
21. McGovern, *Ancient Wine*, 309; Frankel, *Wine and Oil*, 43.
22. Bacchiocchi, *Wine*, 139.
23. Patrick E. McGovern, *Ancient Brews: Rediscovered and Re-Created* (New York: W. W. Norton, 2017), 17.
24. Michael M. Homan and Mark A. Gstohl, "Jesus the Teetotaler: How Dr. Welch Put the Lord on the Wagon," *BR* (2002): 29.

truth of the matter is actually that there are no references to "unfermented wine" in the Bible. The notion of a stable, unfermented grape juice is actually a modern invention.[25] This is also true regardless of which term for wine is used in the Bible, such as those often translated as "new wine," as we will see below. The reason is because grape must begins to ferment immediately and will be fully fermented in a matter of days. When we categorize ancient wines in terms of fermentation, we should speak of *fermenting* must and *fermented* wines. If an ancient person wanted to drink grape must, they could do so at the harvest in late summer (see also ch. 4).[26] Once everything was harvested, there would be no further opportunity until the following year.

Thus, the Bible does not distinguish between fermented and unfermented wines, nor does it make a distinction between wines the way modern wine-drinkers might expect, based on *terroir* or varietal. Nevertheless, the Bible does have its own categorization of wine as seen in the various terms from the original languages of Hebrew, Aramaic, and Greek. I contend further that biblical terminology is not limited to grape-based intoxicants, meaning that there are likely references to beer as well. In the following sections, we will explore those key terms.

FULLY FERMENTED WINES

In the three languages of the Bible, the primary words for fully fermented wines are *yayin* (Hebrew), *khamar* (Aramaic), and *oinos* (Greek). Residual sugar may remain, but each of these generally refer to wines that have completed fermentation and have aged to some degree since harvest. They also appear to be fairly interchangeable, since the Greek Septuagint (LXX) translates both *yayin* and *khamar* with *oinos*. Thus, they are broad terms, with some texts even referring to various kinds of *yayin* (Neh 5:18) and various types of *oinos* (Philo, *Drunkenness* 218).

Against Two-Wine theorists, many instances of *yayin* in the Old Testament, for example, are clearly presented as positive *and* inebriating through the use of Hebrew euphemisms. One of the blessings of *yayin*, for example, is how it brings *joy and gladness to the heart* of the consumer (Ps 104:15; cf. *oinos* in Sir 40:20), and makes life joyful (Eccl 10:19). *Yayin* also causes people to have "a good heart" (NIV: "high spirits"), which is another euphemism for intoxication, applied to Amnon (2 Sam 13:28), King Ahasuerus (Esth 1:10), and readers of Ecclesiastes (Eccl 9:7; NIV: "joyful heart"). In the story about Nabal, being "good in heart" from *yayin* meant that he was "very drunk" (1 Sam 25:36–37), which reveals that the euphemism implies the altering effects of intoxication, though not always to the point of drunkenness.

---

25. So also, e.g., Becker, *Rebe*, 145; Walsh, *Fruit*, 109.
26. Jack M. Sasson, "The Blood of Grapes: Viticulture and Intoxication in the Hebrew Bible," in *Drinking in Ancient Societies: History and Culture of Drinks in the Ancient Near East*, ed. Lucio Milano (Padua: Sargon, 1994), 401.

Two other rare Hebrew terms in the Old Testament seem to refer to a specialized wine. The first is *shemer*, which technically refers to wine sediment, called dregs or lees (cf. Ps 75:8 [75:9 MT]; Jer 48:11). In Isaiah 25:6, however, the term designates a superior kind of aged wine—a wine that aged unfiltered, but which would be filtered before consumption (cf. ch. 14). The second term is *khemer* (not to be confused with the Aramaic term *khamar*), which only occurs once in Deuteronomy 32:14 and is translated as "foaming"—"the foaming blood of the grape"—because the cognate verb means "to foam." Some scholars argue that the link to foaming means that *khemer* is wine that is still fermenting,[27] since foaming is a by-product of fermentation caused by the release of carbon dioxide when yeast converts sugar into alcohol. If carbon dioxide is unable to escape from a sealed vessel, though, the liquid will become carbonated. The foaming of *khemer*, then, might not suggest fermentation but rather carbonation. Similarly, Butler and Heskett suggest that *khemer* could designate a carbonated red wine, since the verb for foaming is also used in Psalm 75:8 (75:9 MT) with fully fermented wine, *yayin* ("foaming wine").[28]

Similar euphemisms for intoxication—often translated as being "cheerful," "gladdened," "merry," or "in good spirits"—are so commonplace that they occur in contexts that merely *assume* the presence of alcohol (Judg 19:6, 9, 22; 1 Kgs 21:7; 2 Chr 7:10; Eccl 7:2–3; Prov 15:15), including for Haman (Esth 5:9), the Philistines (Judg 16:25), and even Boaz (Ruth 3:7).

NEW WINES

The second most common term for wine in the Old Testament is *tirosh*, which is typically translated as "new wine." When the New Testament speaks of "new wine," it adds the adjective *neos* ("new") rather than using a term different from *oinos* (Matt 9:17; Mark 2:22; Luke 5:37–38; cf. Luke 5:39),[29] though *gleukos* is a rare exception (see discussion on sweet wines below). This further suggests that *oinos*, when it is not qualified by another adjective or phrase, refers broadly to fully fermented wine.

Much confusion persists about the nature of "new wine." Beyond Two-Wine theorists, many scholars contend that new wine designates unfermented wine.[30] In the New Testament, however, "new wine" designates *fermenting* and *newly fermented* wine, as seen in Jesus's parable of the wineskins (e.g., Mark 2:22), since new wine bursting old wineskins implies the pressure of carbon dioxide within a sealed wineskin during fermentation (cf. ch. 4).

The issue is not as straightforward in the Old Testament, however. Several scholars view *tirosh* as the raw material for wine (i.e., grapes).[31] Proponents of this regard Isaiah 65:8 as conclusive, since *tirosh* is in "the cluster of grapes," although

---

27. *HALOT* 1:330; Becker, *Rebe*, 218.
28. Butler and Heskett, *Divine Vintage*, 53.
29. Jesus's comment about drinking wine *new* in the coming kingdom does not apply (Matt 26:29; Mark 14:25). Cf. ch. 14.

30. BDB 440 glosses *tirosh* as "must, fresh or new wine"; L&N 1:77 (§6.197–98) regards *oinos neos* as "grape juice," or juice "in the initial stages of fermentation."
31. E.g., G. Fleischer, "תירוש," *TDOT* 15:655, 657.

this ignores how grapes can ferment on the vine. Others point to another passage in Isaiah that mentions consuming *tirosh* after it is *gathered*, suggesting that it refers to harvested grapes (Isa 62:8–9; cf. Deut 11:14). Although associations with the harvest seem accurate for *tirosh*, the proposal that *tirosh* refers to grapes does not. Rather, *tirosh* and grapes are likely connected by metonymy, meaning that grapes were linked to the telos of winemaking.[32] When texts mention *tirosh* alongside grain, the grape view finds some support, since grain is raw material. Yet when paired with grain in Joel 2:24, *tirosh* and oil overflow their respective vats, suggesting that both are *produced from* the raw materials of grapes and olives (cf. Hos 2:8, 22 [2:10, 24 MT]).[33] Moreover, Micah explicitly mentions drinking *tirosh* (Mic 6:15), making it more likely that *tirosh* is grape must than just grapes.

Yet other texts suggest that *tirosh* is not merely drinkable, but also intoxicating. *Tirosh* can "take away understanding" just like *yayin* (Hos 4:11) and euphemistically bring "cheer" (Judg 9:13). Further, its absence can cause "the merrymakers" to "groan" (Isa 24:7), just as they mourn the loss of *yayin* and *shekar* (Isa 24:9; on *shekar*, see below).[34] The intoxicating nature of *tirosh* is also corroborated by the way that the LXX translators do not make much of a distinction between *yayin* and *tirosh*, since they typically translate both with *oinos*.[35]

In this light, it is best to view *tirosh* as the desired result of the harvest—fresh wine. The evidence suggests that *tirosh* refers to the fresh batch of newly fermented wine that one can only enjoy once a year after harvest.[36] Passages, then, that seem like *tirosh* refers to grapes or grape must should be considered like those that mention *yayin* being expressed in winepresses (e.g., Isa 16:10; Jer 48:33). They anticipate what is to come from the whole viticultural process, eliding some steps in that process. But rather than view *yayin* and *tirosh* as essentially synonymous,[37] *tirosh* stresses that a wine is fresh and unaged (cf. virgins enjoying *tirosh* in Zech 9:17).[38] To be clear, *tirosh*'s freshness is not *pre-fermentation* freshness. Instead, *tirosh* designates fresh wine that is just as intoxicating as *yayin* and will become *yayin* with time.[39]

> The two exceptions to the LXX pattern of translating *tirosh* as *oinos* are revealing. Hosea 4:11 (LXX) renders *tirosh* with *methysma*, a generic term for an intoxicant that was needed because *oinos* was used for *yayin* in the same verse. Isaiah 65:8 (LXX) translates *tirosh* in the grape cluster with a word for grape (*rhōx*). Although this could support the raw-material view, it is notable that this decision only occurs here in a context about grape clusters. Everywhere else they render *tirosh* as an intoxicant (*oinos* or *methysma*).

---

32. The metonymical argument has been overstated in favor of *tirosh* being grapes; see S. Naeh and M. P. Weitzman, "TĪRŌŠ—Wine or Grape? A Case of Metonymy," *VT* 44.1 (1994): 115–20. Cf. Dubach, *Trunkenheit*, 48–50.

33. S. R. Driver, *The Books of Joel and Amos*, 2nd ed. (Cambridge: Cambridge University Press, 1915), 79–80.

34. J. J. M. Roberts, *First Isaiah: A Commentary*, Hermeneia (Minneapolis: Fortress, 2015), 314.

35. Bacchiocchi mistakenly insists that since *tirosh* was translated as *oinos*, then *oinos* can be unfermented (*Wine*, 61–62, 71).

36. Rightly Walsh, *Fruit*, 194–97.

37. So Oded Borowski, *Agriculture in Iron Age Israel* (Winona Lake, IN: Eisenbrauns, 1987), 113.

38. Dubach, *Trunkenheit*, 197.

39. Scholars who regard *tirosh* as a reference to grapes must also view its difference with *yayin* in terms of time, but do so incorrectly as before and after fermentation respectively. See Hinckley G. Mitchell, "Tirosh and Yayin," *JBL* 1 (1891): 70–72; Becker, *Rebe*, 99, 123, 218.

GRAPE MUST AND SWEET WINES

There are three Hebrew terms for grape must in the Old Testament, but they are rare. Two of them only occur once; one designates the juice (*dema*) expressed at harvest time that was dedicated to YHWH during the consecration of Israel's firstborns (Exod 22:29 [22:28 MT]),[40] and the other is included in a prohibition of grape juice (*mishrah*), along with all grape products, for the Nazirite vow (Num 6:3). The third term for grape must, *asis*, occurs the most, but only five times (Song 8:2; Isa 49:26; Joel 1:5; 3:18 [4:18 MT]; Amos 9:13).

The primary indication that *asis* refers to grape must is that the cognate verb *asas* means "to tread" (cf. Mal 4:3 [3:21 MT]), suggesting that *asis* comes from expressing juice by treading (cf. ch. 4).[41] The clearest examples are the passages in Joel and Amos that describe *asis* dripping down mountains, imagining a future when the grapes grown on the mountainsides are pressed to the point that the collection vats overflow right there on the hills (Joel 3:18 [4:18 MT]; Amos 9:13). It could also be that *asis* is technically a general term for any fruit juice, since *asis* and pomegranates are paired in Song of Songs 8:2.[42] Given how difficult it would be to produce a significant amount of pomegranate juice, however, it is more likely the *asis* there was accented with pomegranates, just as *yayin* in the same verse is flavored with spices.[43]

Asis is variously translated into English as "new wine," "sweet wine," or "nectar," to name a few, and such variety is also reflected in the Greek terms used in the LXX.[44] As we saw with *tirosh* above, *asis* is likewise a harvest term, being available for a short window of time each year after the initial treading of grapes. Since fermentation begins shortly after grape skins come into contact with the sugary must, it should be reiterated that *asis* is not "unfermented wine" or even "unfermented must."[45] Primary fermentation—when the bulk of the sugars are converted to alcohol—usually only takes about a week, and the initial presence of alcohol is detectable within a day.

The swiftness of the fermentation process helps to explain why even *asis can cause intoxication*.[46] For example, the prophet Joel calls for drunkards and consumers of wine (*yayin*) to mourn the absence of *asis* as a result of the locust plague (Joel 1:5). These imbibers were obviously not disappointed by a lack of grape juice but by the fact that there would not be any wine from that year's vintage. Moreover, the prophet Isaiah writes, in a context of judgment, that YHWH's enemies will become drunk on

---

40. The NIV clarifies this by translating it as "vats."
41. E.g., Becker, *Rebe*, 126 (cf. 99); Dubach, *Trunkenheit*, 198; Walsh, *Fruit*, 198.
42. E.g., Frankel, *Wine and Oil*, 198.
43. So also Walsh, *Fruit*, 197–99.
44. Cf. "new wine" (Isa 49:26 LXX), "sweetness" (Joel 4:18 LXX; Amos 9:13 LXX), and "juice" (Song 8:2 LXX) in NETS.
45. Contra *HALOT* 2:860; Eugene Carpenter, "עסיס," *NIDOTTE* 3:470.
46. Dubach, *Trunkenheit*, 198.

their own blood as with *asis* (Isa 49:26), implying again that *asis* can intoxicate.[47] If grape-based *asis* can cause drunkenness, that reinforces that *asis* should be regarded as "fermenting must" or even "sweet wine," with the sweetness stemming from the residual sugar that has yet to ferment. This seems to be why the Greek translators of Joel and Amos render *asis* as "sweetness" (*glykasmos*), emphasizing that the fermenting must is still sugary.

Elsewhere in the Bible there are references to sweet alcoholic drinks that do not specify how the sweetness was acquired, whether from incomplete fermentation (as with *asis*), sugary additives, or drying out the grapes into raisins first before extracting juice (cf. ch. 4). In the Old Testament, this includes references to "sweet drinks" (*mamtaqqim*) in Nehemiah 8:10 and Song of Songs 5:16. *Mamtaqqim* might also derive its sweetness from incomplete fermentation like *asis*, because it is also translated as *glykasmos* in the LXX just as *asis* is in Joel and Amos LXX.[48] In the New Testament, the Greek term *gleukos* in the story of Pentecost (Acts 2:13), implies a sugary wine. It is often translated as "new wine," but it should be clear that its "newness" implies that the fermentation of sugar has not fully completed.[49]

Gleukos in Acts 2:13 assumes fermentation to some degree because it was believed at Pentecost that those claiming to hear the disciples' message in their own language were drunk from it. This rare word occurs once in the New Testament, but in its other appearances it refers to fermenting must. For example, in Josephus's rendition of the Joseph story, the cupbearer squeezes out *gleukos* from grapes into Pharaoh's cup (*Ant.* 2.64), and in the Greek translation of Job, Elihu compares the urge in his stomach to respond to Job to being like bubbling *gleukos* about to make a wineskin burst (Job 32:18–19 LXX).[50] Yet the problem with this understanding of *gleukos* in Acts 2:13 is that Pentecost is a springtime festival and harvest occurs in late summer, so *gleukos* would not have been available. This has led to some creative solutions.[51] C. K. Barrett suggested that *gleukos* may pejoratively suggest that the people were getting drunk from "cheap stuff," based on Lucian's (2nd c. CE) contrast of *gleukos* with nicer wines (*Ep. Sat.* 22).[52] Yet it may just be that the comment was simply sarcastic, not least because *fermenting* wine would not have been available in the spring, but more importantly because no one was actually drunk at Pentecost anyway.[53]

---

47. Rebekah Welton argues that the verb for becoming drunk is a metaphor for becoming fermented. Thus, she suggests that YHWH will ferment his enemies' blood like *asis*. See "Yahweh the Wrathful Vintner: Blood and Wine-Making Metaphors in Isaiah 49:26a and 63:6," *JIBS* 4.3 (2002): 22–25.

48. *HALOT* 2:596 refers to *mamtaqqim* as "sweetness" and "sweet drinks" without comment on alcohol levels.

49. L&N 1:77 (§6.199) regard *gleukos* as "a new, sweet wine in the process of fermentation."

50. The Hebrew word in Job 32:19 is *yayin*, making this the only instance where *yayin* is translated as *gleukos*.

51. E.g., Joseph A. Fitzmyer insists, on the basis of evidence in the Temple Scroll (11QTª [11Q19] XVIII–XXI), that some Jews observed three Pentecosts (new grain, new wine, and new oil), and that Acts 2, set during the Pentecost of new grain, alludes to the previous Pentecost of new wine. See his *The Acts of the Apostles: A New Translation with Introduction and Commentary*, AYB (New Haven: Yale University Press, 1998), 234–35.

52. C. K. Barrett, *The Acts of the Apostles*, 2 vols., ICC (Edinburgh: T&T Clark, 1994), 1:125.

53. Eckhard Schnabel, *Acts*, ZECNT (Grand Rapids: Zondervan, 2012), 121.

> Bacchiocchi claims to find evidence of unfermented wine in Athenaeus's (3rd c. CE) discussion of *glykus* in *Deipnosophistae* 2.45e (not to be confused with *gleukos*). Athenaeus designated the Latin term *protropum* with the Greek word *glykus*—wine made from the "free run" of juice from grapes before being pressed (cf. ch. 4)—drawing attention to an expression of it from a Greek island called Lesbos. Bacchiocchi cites an English translation from 1854 that refers to this as "sweet Lesbian wine,"[54] which Bacchiocchi embarrassingly cites as "sweet lesbian *glykus*" and explains in this way: "the unfermented sweet grape juice is called 'lesbian—effoeminatum' because the potency of fermentable power of the wine has been removed."[55] Setting aside the gross misogyny and homophobia underpinning this claim, "Lesbian" was obviously the adjectival form of Lesbos, which Bacchiocchi clearly missed and distorted by adding his own Latin gloss ("effoeminatum") and by citing it with a lowercase "l".[56] Moreover, it is clear that *glykus* could cause inebriation because the point in context is that it affected rational capacities *less* than other wines.

SOUR WINE AND VINEGAR

Sour wine, or vinegar, appears a few times in Scripture (Heb. *khomets*; Gk. *oxos*). If alcoholic beverages are exposed to oxygen, whether intentionally or through improper storage, the alcohol converts to acetic acid and creates vinegar. Depending on when the sour wine is consumed, there would be varying degrees of alcohol left over, since the full conversion process can take a couple months in some cases. The resulting acetic acid is what makes one's teeth hurt (Prov 10:26), and vinegar is even aligned with poison in some contexts (Ps 69:21). Vinegar had many purposes, however, since it could be used as a preservative, a condiment for dipping bread (Ruth 2:14; cf. possibly Matt 26:23; Mark 14:20), a topical medicine for wounds (Prov 25:20), and a means of sanitizing water. In the Gospels' passion narratives, we see how sour wine was frequently used to quench thirst when it was offered to Jesus on the cross, even though the intent of the offer varies. In John's Gospel, Jesus receives sour wine from someone nearby (presumably a soldier) after declaring that he was thirsty (John 19:28–30) without any hint of malicious intent.[57] The jar was likely there for the

---

54. See *Deip.* II, 24 in Athenaeus, *The Deipnosophists, or The Learned Banqueters*, trans. C. D. Yonge, 3 vols. (London: Henry G. Bohn, 1854), 1:74.

55. Bacchiocchi, *Wine*, 60.

56. Moreover, the best manuscript evidence does not even refer to "Lesbian" *glykus* (see S. Douglas Olson, ed. and trans., *Athenaeus: The Learned Banqueters, Volume I: Books 1–3.106e*, LCL 204 [Cambridge: Harvard University Press, 2007], 257), which was likely added later on to explain what the Latin loan word meant to Greek audiences.

57. Cf. Patrick Faas, *Around the Roman Table: Food and Feasting in Ancient Rome* (Chicago: University of Chicago Press, 2005), 122; Jo-Ann Shelton, *As the Romans Did: A Sourcebook in Roman Social History*, 2nd ed. (Oxford: Oxford University Press, 1998), 80n10.

soldiers, since sour wine (a mixture of vinegar and water known as *posca* in Latin) was a favorite drink of Roman soldiers.[58] Luke records soldiers offering Jesus sour wine, presumably intended originally for their own consumption, but in Luke their offer is clearly intended to mock Jesus (Luke 23:36). In Matthew and Mark, bystanders offer Jesus sour wine in an attempt to aid him after they misunderstand his "cry of dereliction," assuming he was appealing for Elijah's help. This underscores its role as a thirst quencher, since it was offered to keep Jesus alive a little longer (Matt 27:48; Mark 15:36). These scenes resist easy harmonization, but they nevertheless underscore in their respective ways how sour wine (*oxos*) was a thirst quencher.

BEER

Whether or not the Bible refers to grain-based alcohol, or beer, is hotly debated. The disputed terms are the Hebrew words *sobe* and *shekar* in the Old Testament, and the Greek word *sikera* in the New Testament (a Semitic loanword). Both *sobe* and *sikera* are rare biblical terms, but *shekar* occurs twenty-three times, making it the third most used word in the Old Testament to refer to alcohol after *yayin* and *tirosh*.

Sobe occurs three times in the Old Testament (Isa 1:22; Hos 4:18; Nah 1:10). Most scholars contend that *sobe* is a generic term for an alcoholic beverage, and so it is often simply translated as "drinks" or the act of drinking (as a noun).[59] But since Isaiah 1:22 refers to *sobe* that has been diluted, many translations regard it as wine (so, e.g., NRSVue), and even a superior kind of wine (so, e.g., NIV; ESV). Yet, based on cognate evidence from Akkadian, some scholars contend that it is probably a reference to a wheat beer.[60] Without more evidence it is difficult to say what *sobe* is definitively other than an intoxicant, though it could refer to beer (so, e.g., NET).

Sikera is only found once in the New Testament (Luke 1:15), but it is the most commonly used Greek word in the LXX to translate *shekar* (cf. Lev 10:9; Num 6:3; 28:7; Deut 14:26; 29:6 [29:5 LXX]; Judg 13:4, 7, 14; Isa 5:11, 22; 24:9; 28:7; 29:9). Since *sikera* is a Semitic loan word, part of the case for determining what *sikera* is depends on what *shekar* is, to which we will turn next. But it is worth noting that the standard ancient Greek dictionaries gloss *sikera* as "beer."[61]

Scholars are largely unclear on what *shekar* is. Because *shekar* is cognate to the Hebrew verb for becoming drunk (*shakar*) and the noun for a drunkard (*shekor*), many English translations have rendered it as "strong drink" (notable in the KJV). This translation has led many Bible readers to misunderstand *shekar*. If wine is off

---

58. L. Th. Witkamp, "Jesus' Thirst in John 19:28–30: Literal or Figurative?," *JBL* 115.3 (1996): 494–95.

59. BDB 685 opts for "liquor." Cf. Walsh, *Fruit*, 203–4; Dubach, *Trunkenheit*, 33.

60. So, e.g., Roberts, *First Isaiah*, 28–30, 80; Joseph Blenkinsopp, *Isaiah 1–39: A New Translation with Introduction and Commentary*, AB 19 (New York: Doubleday, 2000), 186; *HALOT* 2:738; 4:1501.

61. BDAG 923; L&N 1:77 (§6.200).

the table for some conservative readers because it contains alcohol, surely "strong drink" is too! Norman Geisler, who argues that ancient wines were highly diluted with water (cf. ch. 3), maintains that modern wines should be forbidden because they are comparable to "strong drink," which he says is "forbidden in the Bible."[62] Even if the comparison between *shekar* and contemporary wine in terms of ABV is apt, *shekar* is plainly not forbidden in the Bible. *Shekar* was (1) poured out for libations on the altar in the tabernacle/temple (Num 28:7–10); (2) consumed as part of one's tithe to YHWH in a sacrificial meal (Deut 14:26); (3) recommended for the poor by King Lemuel's mother (Prov 31:6); and (4) lamented when taken away as a judgment of privation (Isa 24:9).[63]

So then, if *shekar* was not a forbidden drink, what was it exactly? Outside of "strong drink," the next most common translation for *shekar* is "fermented drink," because many scholars think it is a generic term for any intoxicant.[64] Scholars who do try to identify *shekar* as a specific type of alcoholic beverage have proposed grappa, date wine, or beer. Part of the difficulty in identifying one of these is that *shekar* is never overtly linked with its main source of fermentable sugars, whether grapes, dates, or grains. Yet what grappa and date wine have in common is that both of them could potentially be stronger in alcohol than standard grape-based wine, potentially explaining why *shekar* is cognate to terms for drunkenness.

Grappa in particular is a grape-based spirit, and those who identify it as the referent for *shekar* contend that its fermentable sugars likely come from grapes. One reason for this identification is because *shekar* is included in the Nazirite vow, prohibiting anything that comes from the vine (Num 6:3; Judg 13:14).[65] A grape spirit like grappa, however, is an improbable suggestion historically because its strong alcohol content is derived from distillation.[66]

Furthermore, the argument that *shekar* is made from grapes is by no means clear from the Nazirite passages. The inclusion of *shekar* could be intended to ensure that no kind of alcohol be consumed by Nazirites undertaking their vows, not just alcohol that is derived from the grapevine. Otherwise, if they are both

> Distilling alcohol requires a technical understanding about the different boiling temperatures for water (212°F / 100°C) and alcohol (173°F / 78°C), and appropriate equipment to collect the evaporated alcohol so that it can condense separately and produce a higher concentration of alcohol. Proper distillation was actually a medieval invention, although it had experimental precursors.

---

62. Norman L. Geisler, "A Christian Perspective on Wine-Drinking," *BSac* 139:553 (1982): 50, cf. 51.

63. See this fourfold breakdown in Michael M. Homan, "Beer, Barley, and שֵׁכָר in the Hebrew Bible," in *Le-David Maskil: A Birthday Tribute for David Noel Freedman*, ed. Richard Elliott Friedman and William H. C. Propp (Winona Lake, IN: Eisenbrauns, 2004), 25–26.

64. E.g., Frankel, *Wine and Oil*, 198; Sasson, "Blood," 399–400; Becker, *Rebe*, 128; Dubach, *Trunkenheit*, 201–5.

65. E.g., Lawrence E. Stager, J. David Schloen, Daniel M. Master, eds., *Ashkelon 1: Introduction and Overview (1985–2006)* (Winona Lake, IN: Eisenbrauns, 2008), 271, 309, 341; Philip J. King and Lawrence E. Stager, *Life in Biblical Israel*, LAI (Louisville: Westminster John Knox, 2001), 101–2; Robert Alter, *The Hebrew Bible: A Translation with Commentary*, 3 vols. (New York: W. W. Norton, 2019), 3:450.

66. The difference between grappa and brandy is that grappa is made specifically from pomace, the collection of skins and stems left over after pressing the grapes.

grape based, the pairing of *yayin* and *shekar* would seem to be redundant. Indeed, in Numbers 6:3 the vow includes abstinence from vinegar (*khomets*) made from *yayin* and also vinegar made from *shekar*. As mentioned in the previous section, vinegar can be produced from any type of alcohol, but if *shekar* is made from grapes, then stressing vinegars made from *yayin* and from *shekar* is redundant. It does not seem, then, that *shekar* is made from grapes (on the Nazirites, cf. ch. 7).

Date wine, on the other hand, was distinct from grape-based *yayin* and was a well-established alcoholic beverage in antiquity, being widely attested in ancient Egypt and Mesopotamia.[67] Patrick McGovern argues that *shekar* refers to date wine on the basis of Proverbs 20:1, which compares *yayin* to a mocker, and *shekar* to a brawler. Even though the proverb does not identify the ingredients used for *shekar*, the argument is that *yayin* is not as strong as *shekar*, and thus the sugar source for *shekar* must be greater than that of grapes.[68] Although dates do have a higher sugar content than grapes, that does not mean that the resulting alcoholic beverage would necessarily be stronger, because the yeast will peter out when the same level of ABV is produced (around 15%).[69] With reference to the proverb, though, if the second line that refers to *shekar* is meant to be a heightening of the first line (i.e., brawling is more excessive than mocking) rather than simply parallel to it, it by no means follows that the heightening would be due to the *actual* alcohol content. It could just as easily be heightened due to societal associations and perceptions of *shekar*.

> In many settings in the modern West, beer is often regarded as more of a party drink compared to the sophistication of wine. This reputation is persistent, even though on average wine has a much higher ABV than beer. The difference in perception is not the relative strength of wine and beer but the cultural associations with the habits and settings of consuming them. Part of the reason for this is that beer could be produced year-round (cf. ch. 4) and thus consumed in greater quantity. From what we know about beer in the ancient world, it held a similar reputation in certain cultures that predominantly made wine, like Greece and Rome.[70]

Although beer in the ancient world was not stronger than wine, often roughly 2–3 percent ABV without the addition of other sugary ingredients, Max Nelson notes that beer was commonly perceived by many to be the strongest intoxicant.[71]

---

67. For *shekar* as date wine, see Walsh, *Fruit*, 200–202.
68. McGovern, *Ancient Wine*, 235–36.
69. So also, Walsh, *Fruit*, 202, though she views *shekar* as date wine.
70. See esp. Max Nelson, *The Barbarian's Beverage: A History of Beer in Ancient Europe* (London: Routledge, 2008).
71. Nelson, *Barbarian's Beverage*, 72.

The point here is simply that Proverbs 20:1 is by no means conclusive in determining the nature of *shekar*, other than the fact that it is an intoxicant like *yayin*.

> Michael Homan contends that date wine is an anachronistic proposal for a handful of passages that predate the Babylonian exile in the sixth century BCE (e.g., Isa 5:11, 22; 24:9; 28:7; 29:9; Mic 2:11), since that is probably when Judahites were first introduced to it.[72] If one is inclined to date Old Testament texts more conservatively than Homan, that would strengthen this argument further.

This leads to the third and final suggestion that *shekar* refers to grain-based beer.[73] In favor of this proposal are a few different considerations. To start, *shekar* is derived from the Akkadian word for beer, *sikaru*.[74] Beer was also a common beverage among Israel's neighbors, especially in Egypt and Mesopotamia, and so it is hard to imagine that Israel would not consume it as well.[75] Furthermore, it is even harder to imagine that there would be no word for beer in Hebrew.[76] In the LXX, *shekar* is often translated as *sikera*, as noted earlier, which does not provide much help here because it is a Semitic loanword.[77] As J. J. M. Roberts points out, though, in one instance in the LXX the Greek translators of Isaiah 19:10 misread the Hebrew word for "wages" (*sekar*), which looks very similar to *shekar*, and rendered it as *zythos* in Greek, which is the word for Egyptian beer.[78] By the time of the Mishnah (3rd c. CE), it is clear that *shekar* was understood to be grain-based beer.[79] A tractate on the Passover describes how celebrants should get rid of *all grain-based foodstuffs* from their homes, and what it itemizes includes "Median beer [*shekar*], Edomite vinegar [*khomets*], Egyptian barley beer [*zitom*]" (m. Pesahim 3:1).[80] This is an intriguing reference because it clearly identifies *shekar* as a grain-based product. Incidentally, it also recognizes that certain vinegars can be grain-based as well (*khomets*), referring back to the previous discussion on why the two vinegars in Numbers 6:3 suggest that *shekar* is not made from grapes. If you have ever used malt vinegar on fried fish and chips at a British

---

72. Homan, "Beer, Barley, and שֵׁכָר," 31.
73. E.g., *HALOT* 4:1501; Michael M. Homan, "Beer and Its Drinkers: An Ancient Near Eastern Love Story," *NEA* 67.2 (2004): 92–93; idem, "Beer, Barley, and שֵׁכָר," 25–38; Jennie Ebeling, "Grains, Bread, and Beer," in *T&T Clark Handbook of Food in the Hebrew Bible and Ancient Israel*, ed. Janling Fu, Cynthia Shafer-Elliott, and Carol Meyers (London: T&T Clark, 2022), 109–10.
74. Roberts, *First Isaiah*, 79–80; Homan, "Beer, Barley, and שֵׁכָר," 29.
75. Homan, "Beer, Barley, and שֵׁכָר," 38.
76. Rightly Roberts, *First Isaiah*, 80. Contra King and Stager, *Life*, 103.
77. Elsewhere *shekar* is translated as a generic intoxicant (*methysma* in 1 Sam 1:15; Mic 2:11; *methē* in Prov 20:1; 31:6; cf. Isa 28:7) and once as *oinos* (Prov 31:4). Isaiah 56:12 is missing from the LXX.
78. Roberts, *First Isaiah*, 80.
79. As Magen Broshi admits, while arguing for date-based alcohol in ancient Palestine ("Date Beer and Date Wine in Antiquity," *PEQ* 139.1 [2007]: 55).
80. Jacob Neusner, *The Mishnah: A New Translation* (New Haven: Yale University Press, 1988), 233. The Hebrew was derived from sefaria.org.

pub, for example, you are well aware that vinegar can be made from beer. Although the Mishnah is a later source, the question that this evidence raises is whether *shekar* meant anything other than grain-based beer from its Akkadian derivation to the time of the Mishnah. I suggest that the evidence from the Mishnah shows that the identification of *shekar* as beer remained consistent.

Yet there are counterarguments to this proposal that deserve attention. The case against *shekar* being beer is at least threefold. First, the argument is that beer was not as strong as wine in the ancient world, which calls into question its association with cognate terms for drunkenness.[81] Second, beer required a significant amount of water to make (for the growth of grain and to produce the beer), but Israel did not receive as much rain as her neighbors in Egypt and Mesopotamia (and this is partly why those places were not ideal for producing wine; i.e., *viniculture*; cf. ch. 4).[82] Finally, *shekar* was used as a libationary offering in sacred space (cf. Num 28:7), and so it could not have been beer since it is not mentioned as a libationary offering anywhere else (cf. ch. 6).[83]

None of these counterarguments are insurmountable for the proposal that *shekar* refers to beer, however. In response to the first point, I have already addressed how *shekar* could be associated with drunkenness, even if it was not technically as strong as wine in the discussion on Proverbs 20:1 above. The second point, about the need for more water, misses the fact that anywhere people can make bread, they can make beer (cf. ch. 4). As for the third point, this fails to account for grain as a regular offering to YHWH (cf. ch. 6). It seems that a cultural bias against the use of beer in sacred space is what is contributing to this final argument. In fact, such a bias against beer can be seen in the scholarly interest in wine, which is more complicated to make than beer—beer being primarily a domestic beverage made by women who also baked bread.[84] When all of the evidence is considered and the arguments are weighed, I contend that the most likely understanding of *shekar* is that it refers to grain-based alcohol.

CONCLUSION

As we have seen, there is a clear diversity of terms for alcoholic beverages in Scripture. As a summary of only the main terms from what precedes, see figure 2.1 below.

---

81. Walsh, *Fruit*, 201.
82. Walsh, *Fruit*, 201.
83. E.g., Alter, *Hebrew Bible*, 1:581; Baruch Levine, *Numbers 1–20*, AB (New York: Doubleday, 1993), 219.
84. So rightly, e.g., Jennie R. Ebeling and Michael W. Homan, "Baking and Brewing Beer in the Israelite Household: A Study of Women's Cooking Technology," in *The World of Women in the Ancient and Classical Near East*, ed. Beth Alpert Nakhai (Newcastle: Cambridge Scholars, 2008), 46.

Figure 2.1: Glossary of the Main Types of Alcoholic Beverages in Scripture

Beverage	Hebrew	Aramaic	Greek
Fully Fermented Wine	*yayin*	*khamar*	*oinos*
Wine Aged on Lees	*shemer*		
Sparkling Red Wine	*khemer*		
New Wine	*tirosh*		*oinos neos*
Fermenting Must, or Sweet Wine	*asis, dema, mishrah, mamtaqqim*		*gleukos, glykasmos*
Sour Wine, or Vinegar	*khomets*		*oxos*
Beer	*shekar*		*sikera*
Wheat Beer (possibly)	*sobe*		

Having some clarity on what these terms mean will aid us in the rest of our study, since we can build on these distinctions and also set aside many of the common misunderstandings that have already been addressed.

We have also seen in this chapter that the common Two-Wine theory does not account well for the biblical evidence. In overviewing the most common terms above, it should be acknowledged that the theory would at least make some intuitive sense if the proponents of this view were claiming that the Bible clearly uses different terms—one set of terms to designate the good kind of wine, and one set of terms for the bad kind. In all of the instances where proponents of this theory have claimed to find unfermented juice, *the same terms* are used elsewhere in the Bible to cause intoxication and even drunkenness. If ancient Israelites and early Christians were so concerned about fermented beverages, why would they not create different terms to avoid confusion? The reason, simply, is because they did not share the modern concerns of teetotalers.

Yet, even though we now have clarity on the meaning of key terms and have highlighted serious issues with the Two-Wine theory, we also need to consider whether alcoholic beverages were watered down so much that their ABV was negligible, as many commonly assume. Water was certainly a known additive in the ancient world, among many other things, which means that the biblical terms for mixed drinks also need our consideration (which will supplement fig. 1). This is what we will explore next to complete our study of the biblical terms for intoxicating drinks.

RELEVANT QUESTIONS

1. If the way we categorize wines and other alcoholic beverages reveals something about us, what does the categorization of alcoholic beverages in the Bible suggest about the ancient cultures that consumed them?
2. Given that the Two-Wine theory cannot be supported biblically, does teetotalism need some other biblical justification in order for some Christians to remain teetotalers?

CHAPTER 3

MIXED DRINKS AND DILUTION

Our study of the various kinds of alcoholic beverages in the Bible will now be rounded out by looking at mixed drinks. Additives were incorporated into wines and other drinks for multiple reasons, such as preserving a beverage, covering up off-flavors, adding a new dimension to the taste, diluting the alcohol content to a desired amount, making a syrupy drink less viscous, or creating a medicine, among other possibilities. All kinds of ingredients were added to intoxicants in the ancient world, including tree resins, spices, herbs, honey, fruits, fresh water, sea water, salt, and more. This chapter will overview mixed drinks broadly in the Bible before turning specifically to address the commonly held notion that ancient wines were so diluted with water that their ABV was negligible.

MIXED DRINKS

We know from ancient sources that various ingredients were added to wines and beers, but in the biblical literature the evidence is surprisingly sparse. The Song of Songs provides the clearest examples of different ingredients added to wine, as can be seen in the reference to spiced *yayin* and *asis* accented by pomegranates (Song 8:2), although no verb of mixing is used. Drinking "my wine with my milk" (Song 5:1 NRSVue; cf. Apoc. Ab. 5.13) probably refers to drinking two separate beverages because of the curdling that would occur from combining them. Elsewhere when the Bible refers to mixed wine and mixed beer it is not clear what was mixed into them (cf. Pss 75:8; 102:9; Prov 9:2, 5; 23:30; Song 7:2; Isa 5:22; 19:14; 65:11), outside of one clear reference to the use of water in Isaiah 1:22 (more on that later). Although the Bible does not mention other ingredients overtly, this does not mean that they were not used.

For instance, tree resin, or pitch, is hardly mentioned as a wine additive in the biblical record, but resins were undoubtedly ubiquitous in the ancient world, as archaeological study on ancient storage vessels and amphorae reveals again and again. In fact, resin was probably the most common additive in ancient wine.[1] It was used (1) to provide a coating for the inside of storage vessels, and to help with sealing the lids to keep the wine from oxidizing (e.g., Pliny the Elder, *Nat.* 14.24.121; 14.25.127; 14.27.133–34); (2) to function as a preservative to help wine

---

1. McGovern, *Ancient Wine*, 70–71.

last longer (e.g., Columella, *Rust.* 12.20.3; 12.22–24; Pliny the Elder, *Nat.* 14.24.120; 14.25.124); and (3) to flavor wines, such as sparingly using myrrh (e.g., Columella, *Rust.* 12.20.5; Pliny the Elder, *Nat.* 14.15.92–93; 14.17.107). Pliny records that resin in Cyprus was the best, and that the resin from Judea was both too hard and too strong in aroma (*Nat.* 14.25.122). Perhaps then, the greater the use of resin, the more pungent the wine. Resin is still used for flavoring today in some modern wines, such as with Greek Retsinas. Yet the resinous notes in a modern Retsina are likely more subdued than ancient wines. As Paul Lukacs remarks, "Unless one drank [wine] right after the harvest, one would have tasted little fruit, as the wine's flavor would have resembled old tree sap more than grapes."[2] This is likely one of many reasons why ancient Israelites would want to distinguish fresh wine (*tirosh*) from aged wine (*yayin*).

> An analgesic interpretation of the wine offered to Jesus in Mark 15:23 is often based on a passage from the Babylonian Talmud (5th c. CE), which utilizes Proverbs 31:6 to address how wine should be given to a criminal about to be executed (b. Sanhedrin 43a). This fails to convince, however, because the proverb mentions wine without an additive, and the Talmud mentions frankincense, not myrrh.

The one overt example of the use of a tree resin in wine within the biblical record appears in Mark's passion narrative, when Roman soldiers offered Jesus wine mixed with myrrh as he was on his way to the cross (Mark 15:23). This is not to be confused with the offerings of sour wine (*oxos*) made to Jesus *while he was on the cross* (cf. ch. 2). The initial offering of mixed wine has often been interpreted as an attempt to aid Jesus during his suffering, interpreting the mixture as an analgesic.[3] Yet there is no reason to imagine that Roman soldiers charged with executing Jesus were taking pity on him.

If an excessive amount of myrrh was used, the wine would have been as undrinkable as gasoline, which would have meant that the soldiers were torturing Jesus with the drink.[4] This would certainly fit the parallel scene in Matthew, where Jesus is offered wine *mixed with gall*, an obvious reference to a poisoned wine (Matt 27:34). Yet, given that myrrh was regarded as the premiere Roman additive,[5] the soldiers could have been mocking Jesus with a special wine "fit for a king." This then aligns with other elements of inverted regal opulence in the narrative, like the purple robe and the crown of thorns (Mark 15:17).[6] Either a mocking or torture-inducing interpretation of the mixed wine fits the scene in Mark, over and against the analgesic interpretation. This is further corroborated by Matthew's replacement of myrrh with gall—a decision that was inspired in part to showcase that Jesus was experiencing the same mocking behavior as the psalmist, who received gall for food and sour wine for thirst from his enemies (cf. Ps 69:21).[7]

---

2. Lukacs, *Inventing Wine*, 7.
3. So, e.g., Heinrich Seesemann, "οἶνος," *TDNT*, 5:164; L&N 1:78 (§6.204); Paul Haupt, "Alcohol in the Bible," *JBL* 36.1–2 (1917): 80–81.
4. Erkki Koskenniemi, Kirsi Nisula, and Jorma Toppari, "Wine Mixed with Myrrh (Mark 15.23) and Crurifragium (John 19.31–32): Two Details of the Passion Narratives," *JSNT* 27.4 (2005): 384.
5. McGovern, *Ancient Wine*, 71, 131, 133, 309.
6. Craig A. Evans, *Mark 8:27–16:20*, WBC 34B (Nashville: Thomas Nelson, 2001), 501.
7. On the intertextuality of this episode and its reception in early Christian history, see John Anthony Dunne, "The Souring of the Ways: Anti-Jewish Readings of Psalm 69 and the Wine Offerings to Jesus," *JBL* 143.1 (2024): 105–24.

Another common additive to wines was actually other wines. Sometimes this was because a wine had become syrupy over time, such as Pliny's description of the famous "Consul Opimius" from 121 BCE. This wine was preserved up to the time of the first century CE because it was so revered, but since it had become a honey-like substance, it had to be added to other wines in order to be consumed (*Nat.* 14.6.55).[8] Rather than waiting years for a wine to age to a sweet aromatic substance, a much more common practice was to boil down must into a syrupy consistency to use as a sweetener for other wines (Columella, *Rust.* 12.19–21).[9]

Water was also used as an additive to reduce the viscosity of syrupy wines like the ones just mentioned,[10] or to reduce off-flavors or the strength of the alcohol content. Various kinds of water would be used as well. The Romans, for example, would sometimes dilute their wine with boiling water or even snow in the winter.[11] The Greeks would commonly use salt water in the form of a brine (Columella, *Rust.* 12.25.1) or directly from the ocean, provided it was not taken too close to the shore and was boiled first (*Rust.* 12.21.4–5). The reason is because the salt would help to preserve the wine and prevent off-tastes (*Rust.* 12.23.3). But just how much water was added, and did it significantly reduce the alcohol levels?

DILUTED WINES

Many are perhaps familiar with a notion that ancient wines were regularly diluted. Especially in some Christian circles, it is commonly assumed that, since wine was normally diluted with water, the final product hardly contained much alcohol.[12] For example, Geisler stated, "What the Bible frequently meant by wine was basically purified water."[13] A notion like this suggests not only that wine consumed in the time of the New Testament was very weak in alcohol but also that the primary reason for dilution was simply to find a safe way to drink water.[14] Without denying that this could influence some ancient consumers of wine, it wrongly conveys the sense that consuming wine was mostly a necessity rather than a craft that people cultivated and enjoyed, recognizing some as superior to others (as at Cana in John 2). Because of the confusion surrounding the topic of dilution, it is necessary to address it at greater length.

The addition of water to wine would normally occur at the time of consumption,

---

8. See Faas, *Roman Table*, 115.
9. Frankel, *Wine and Oil*, 43.
10. Lukacs, *Inventing Wine*, 8.
11. Faas, *Roman Table*, 90; Mary Beard, *SPQR: A History of Ancient Rome* (New York: Liveright, 2015), 455.
12. See, e.g., Everett Ferguson, "Wine as a Table-Drink in the Ancient World," *ResQ* 13.3 (1970): 141–53.
13. Geisler, "Wine-Drinking," 50.
14. Furthermore, the notion that alcoholic beverages were specifically cultivated because water was unclean to drink is a myth, as the plethora of fermented beverages in ancient China demonstrates, since boiling water for tea-drinking would have solved the problem of unclean water. See Edward Slingerland, *Drunk: How We Sipped, Danced, and Stumbled Our Way to Civilization* (New York: Little, Brown Spark, 2021), 31–35.

based on whatever ratio was desired. If the mixture occurred prior to trading or selling, it was considered fraudulent (cf. Pliny the Elder, *Nat.* 23.34). In the Hellenistic and Roman periods, we know that at Greek banquets, or symposia, wine and water were mixed for guests in a common receptacle, called a krater, and the ratio was determined by the symposiarch overseeing the festivities of the evening. At a Roman convivium, however, each guest would mix their own wine themselves within their own cups.[15] Either way, diluting wine was standard fare at Greco-Roman meals.

Various ratios for diluting wine are mentioned in antiquity, but a common ratio would be two or three parts water combined with one part wine. Athenaeus listed several different options for dilution ratios, including "unmixed" wine (known as the Scythian way), one part water to one part wine, as well as two-to-one, three-to-one, and even five-to-two. All of this highlights the lack of uniformity in the custom, even though it was customary for Greeks to dilute wine (Athenaeus, *Deipn.* 10.426b–427c). Homer (8th c. BCE) mentioned a ratio of twenty-to-one for the wine of Maronea (*Od.* 9.193–215), but the point of the passage is to incite amazement in the reader at how robust that legendary wine must have been, since it could be savored with even that much water. Pliny also recalled the legendary mixture for Maronean wine in Homer and noted that many in that city continue to use a ratio of eight-to-one for their wine (*Nat.* 14.6.54). Later rabbinic tradition in the Babylonian Talmud shows a preference for a three-to-one ratio (b. Pesahim 108b), though whether this reflects any first-century Jewish preferences is less than clear. In the Mishnah, one tractate records that a blessing should not be given over the wine until after it has been mixed with water (m. Berakhot 7:5).

Based on these types of references to dilution and more, Robert Stein argues that whenever wine appears in the New Testament and the surrounding culture, we should assume that it refers to diluted wine, unless the text explicitly says that it was "unmixed." Based on ancient dilution ratios, Stein further contends that it would take twenty-two glasses of ancient wine to consume the same amount of alcohol in two martinis today. As a result, Stein claims that although ancient wine in the time of the New Testament could make you drunk, it "would probably affect the bladder long before it affected the mind."[16]

The notion that mixing wine with water would make the ABV of wine in the New Testament negligible, however, is without evidence. This is because there is no way of knowing how much water would have been added, given that there is no descriptive evidence of this in the Bible, and because ratios varied by cultural context and individual preference. As the evidence for drunkenness found in literary and

---

15. Stuart J. Fleming, *Vinum: The Story of Roman Wine* (Glen Mills: Art Flair, 2001), 54.

16. Robert Stein, "Wine-Drinking in New Testament Times," *CT* 19 (June 1975): 11.

iconographical sources demonstrates, ancient people had no problem getting drunk if they wanted to do so, even from diluted wine.

Dilution was often a way to increase the volume of your wine to accommodate guests, as at Greco-Roman meals, and that did not necessarily equate to less alcohol being consumed. To illustrate this, imagine that you ordered a small Americano (with two shots) at a coffee shop to start your day. You would be consuming the same amount of caffeine as if you just ordered two shots of espresso, even though the Americano is made by diluting espresso with hot water. You might choose an Americano because you find the taste of straight espresso harsh, or it may not sit well in your stomach to drink espresso on its own. But choosing a small Americano over two shots of espresso in this scenario is not a choice to consume less caffeine (unless you expressly ordered decaf espresso). In the ancient world, when you diluted wine, you were often making it more like a session beer or a pub ale in ABV (i.e., 3–5%).

Yet should we really assume that wine is diluted when we find references to wine in the New Testament, or in the Bible more broadly, for that matter? The evidence in ancient Israel, when compared to New Testament times, is actually fairly thin. There are a handful of passages in the Bible that refer to mixed wine, without clarifying what the admixture was. Sometimes we find rare Hebrew nouns for "mixed wine," such as when Song of Songs refers to "blended wine" (*mezeg*) in the "navel" of the beloved (Song 7:2 [7:3 MT]); when Isaiah refers to filling bowls of "mixed wine" (*mimsak*) to the god, Destiny, in an oblique reference to idolatrous worship (Isa 65:11); when Proverbs describes the woes of those who "linger" over wine (*yayin*) and go after "mixed wine" (*mimsak*; Prov 23:30); and when the psalmist refers to a foaming cup of wine (*yayin khamar*) that is well mixed (*mesek*), which God will use to judge the wicked (Ps 75:8 [75:9 MT]; cf. ch. 12). In each of these cases it is more likely that mixing spices and other flavor-enhancing ingredients is in view than water. In the case of Proverbs 23:30, the context is describing the woes of intoxication, suggesting that the mixed wine is not significantly inferior to *yayin* in ABV, if at all. In Psalm 75:8, for example, it would not make sense in context to suggest that God's wrathful judgment has been diluted. Instead, we would expect the opposite point to be stressed (see discussion on Rev 14:10 and 18:6 below).

In a few other cases in the Old Testament, the Hebrew verb for mixing (*masak*) is used with reference to an alcoholic beverage, such as when Lady Wisdom (wisdom's personification) mixes wine (Prov 9:2, 5), and when Isaiah refers to people who are exceptional at drinking *yayin* and mixing *shekar* (*masak* in Isa 5:22) but who fail at

> For perspective, if you diluted a wine that is 14.6 percent ABV wine, which is the alcohol content of Meiomi Pinot Noir, at a three-to-one ratio—meaning that you poured the whole bottle (750 ml) into a large enough receptacle and then added three wine bottles' worth of water (2.25 liters)—the result would be three liters (or four wine bottles) of an alcoholic beverage of 3.65 percent ABV. This would be slightly stronger than some ales found at a British pub, including Greene King's IPA (3.6% ABV) and Belhaven Best (3.5% ABV), and you would have enough volume to fill five to six pint glasses, or twenty wine glasses (based on a five-ounce pour).

adjudicating justice in the courts (Isa 5:23). This verb is even used metaphorically to depict YHWH mixing together (*masak*) a spirit of confusion that makes those who drink it drunk in judgment (Isa 19:14). Once again, in none of these instances is the added ingredient mentioned. The only exception to this is Psalm 102:9 (102:10 MT), when the psalmist declares in his mourning that he eats ashes for bread and his drink is mixed (*masak*) with tears. The drink here is not necessarily alcoholic in nature, but the notion of mixing with tears could suggest, in an ironic way, that *masak* can refer to mixing with water. Yet this is by no means conclusive for the other examples that use *masak*. And even if it was, it would be noteworthy that the diluted wines only occur when they are specifically designated with their own (very rare) term.

There is, in fact, only one verse in the whole Bible that overtly refers to diluting an alcoholic beverage with water in a straightforward manner. Intriguingly, when it refers to the practice, it does not speak favorably of it. The prophet Isaiah aligns silver that has become dross with wine/beer (*sobe*; cf. ch. 2) that has been weakened or watered down (*mahal*).[17] Isaiah uses this image to refer to the faith of the people, which has gone from being pure to apostate (Isa 1:22).[18] Diluted alcoholic drinks, then, are a distortion of a *good* thing.

> Instead of recognizing how Isaiah 1:22 might address ancient Israelite perspectives on dilution, Robert Paul Teachout, a Two-Wine theorist, claims that Isaiah "must have been referring to a nutritional juice rather than a harmful intoxicant (which would be better diluted)."[19] Teachout's use of adjectives and his parenthetical comment betray that a priori assumptions guide his search for unfermented wine in the Bible.

Most scholars suggest that we do not have enough evidence to know for sure whether wine dilution was a common practice among ancient Israelites.[20] Others suggest that, on the basis of passages like Isaiah 1:22, ancient Israelites did not prefer to dilute their wine.[21] At the very least, Isaiah did not view the custom favorably (as he spoke prophetically on God's behalf). How widespread his view was is debatable, and the passages that refer to mixed wines noted above (Ps 75:8; Prov 9:2, 5; 23:30; Song 7:2; Isa 5:22; 19:14; 65:11) are not conclusive one way or another, since the incorporation of water is not specified (even with tears in Ps 102:9).

---

17. BDB 554, glosses the verb *mahal* as to "circumcise," or here, given the reference to an alcoholic beverage, as to "weaken."

18. Welton argues that the drink has become "olive juice," contending that "with water" is a later gloss (*"He Is a Glutton"*, 258n120).

19. Teachout, "Use of 'Wine,'" 178.

20. E.g., Leann Pace, "Feasting and Everyday Meals in the World of the Hebrew Bible: The Relationship Reexamined through Material Culture and Texts," in *Feasting in the Archaeology and Texts of the Bible and the Ancient Near East*, ed. Peter Altmann and Janling Fu (Winona Lake, IN: Eisenbrauns, 2014), 191.

21. E.g., McGovern, *Ancient Wine*, 235; Becker, *Rebe*, 125–26; Dubach, *Trunkenheit*, 197; Walsh, *Fruit*, 203.

The practice of dilution certainly developed over time in the regions of the Levant, however, and things do seem to have changed, as a clear passage in 2 Maccabees (2nd c. BCE) demonstrates: "it is harmful to drink wine alone or, again, to drink water alone, while wine already mixed with water is delicious and enhances one's enjoyment" (2 Macc 15:39 NRSVue). Clearly, by the time of the Hellenistic period, dilution of wine was more readily known and appreciated in the Levant thanks to Greek influence, which likely continued in some circles with later Roman influence.

In the New Testament there are only two passages that allude to the Roman practice of diluting wine, which appear in overt scenes of judgment in Revelation. The great harlot of Babylon, which is an allusion to the goddess Roma who represents first-century Rome, will be punished doubly for her deeds by receiving a "double portion" in her cup (Rev 18:6). As an image of judgment, the strength of the wine suggests that she will be made to be more incapacitated by the contents of her cup, which is a stronger ratio of wine to water than she is used to drinking. The fact that the wine is mixed directly in her cup reflects the Roman practice of wine dilution over against the Greek custom of mixing in a common krater. Elsewhere in Revelation, God's wrath is compared to unmixed (*akratos*) wine ("full strength" in Rev 14:10), suggesting that it is not diluted at all but will come in full force (cf. ch. 12). This is the only reference to unmixed wine in the New Testament, and given that the focus of Revelation is on first-century Rome, the common Roman practice of diluting wine makes apt the mention of undiluted wine here.

Even with this survey, there is certainly no need to question Stein's basic premise that dilution was common in the time of the New Testament. Even though it was common, however, that does not mean that it was common cross-culturally or that the same ratios of dilution were utilized. Stein acknowledges this, but in my view does not take this seriously enough. We should not make any generalizations about how ancient people mixed their wines. For example, Pliny the Elder notes that Greek wines should not be used for libations, specifically "because they contain water" (*Nat.* 14.23.119 [Rackham, LCL]). This both highlights that dilution was not viewed by Romans as appropriate for deities but also that Greeks diluted their wines more than Romans. Yet the Romans still diluted their wine, and they believed that anyone who did not was barbaric.[22] This of course meant that some people were known for not diluting wine as much or even at all, including Scythians and Germans,[23] and possibly even the ancient Israelites (as we have seen).

---

22. Katherine M. D. Dunbabin, *The Roman Banquet: Images of Conviviality* (Cambridge: Cambridge University Press, 2003), 20; Lesley Adkins and Roy A. Adkins, *Handbook to Life in Ancient Rome* (New York: Facts on File, 1994), 343.

23. Fleming, *Vinum*, 50.

Additionally, not everyone in antiquity equally appreciated all of the other common additives incorporated into intoxicants. The famous geographer Strabo (1st c. BCE–1st c. CE) thought the Libyans added too much seawater (*Geogr.* 17.1.14) and that the Gauls used too much resin (*Geogr.* 4.6.2). Pliny mentioned that the Romans could appreciate the common Greek practice of adding seawater if used sparingly, stating, "At the present time the most popular of all is the wine of Clazomenae [a Greek city], now that they have begun to flavour it more sparingly with sea-water" (*Nat.* 14.9.73 [Rackham, LCL]). Pliny even added his preference for using less pitch in wine, stating, "The most wholesome wine is that to which nothing has been added in the state of must, and it is better if not even the wine-vessels have been touched by pitch" (*Nat.* 13.24.46 [W. H. S. Jones, LCL]). He also stated that the best wines were consumed neat, or without anything added to it (*Nat.* 14.9.74; cf. Columella, *Rust.* 12.19.2). Of course, every wine was different, some needing more or less additives, and everyone's palette was different—this was just as true in the ancient world as it is today.

It does not seem appropriate, therefore, to interpret wine in the New Testament as always being diluted to a particular ratio, or even at all. In addition to the diversity of diluting and mixing just highlighted, there are at least two additional reasons. First, references to mixed wine are rare in Scripture, so the contention that mixed wine is the default, even if only referring to the New Testament, has little support. Second, when wine is mixed with some other substance in Scripture, that additive is either specified or unique terms are used to refer to the mixed wine.

> Philo of Alexandria (1st c. CE), a diaspora Jew, explains that the ancients would refer to wine *that had not been mixed with anything* by the simple Greek word *oinos* (*Planting* 154), which is also the word that we find throughout the New Testament (as well as the LXX). As part of an argument in which Philo maintains that wise people are permitted to become drunk, he makes this case by contending that the Greek verb for drinking wine (*oinoō*) is synonymous with the Greek verb for getting drunk (*methyō*).[24] Whether or not we, or Philo's contemporaries, would agree with this straightforward comparison, it highlights how *oinos* was perceived neither to be diluted inherently nor so diluted that its alcoholic value was rendered negligible.

---

24. See discussion in *Philo of Alexandria: On Planting: Introduction, Translation, and Commentary*, ed. Albert C. Geljon and David T. Runia, PACS (Leiden: Brill, 2019), 270, 273–74.

CONCLUSION

In this chapter we have seen that there are very few references to mixed drinks in the Bible and that they do not always specify what the additives were. See the relevant terms below in figure 3.1.

Figure 3.1: Short Glossary of Key Terms for Mixed Drinks

Mixed Wines (Hebrew)	*mesek, mezeg, mimsak*
Verb for Mixing (Hebrew)	*masak*
Unmixed (Greek)	*akratos*

Of course, in the ancient world many different kinds of additives were used, including water. Despite this fact, dilution was not common in ancient Israel and may have only become common in the region around the time of the New Testament. If we assumed that most mixed wines in the Bible referred to diluted wines, this would not mean that dilution was a common practice in ancient Israel. Moreover, even though dilution does become more common eventually, this does not mean that it should be assumed as the default mode of wine consumption nor indeed that a particular ratio was always utilized when it was.

Before we turn our focus to the symbolism, metaphors, and imagery that the biblical authors employ in relation to alcohol, we need to consider a couple of additional questions. The first pertains to how these kinds of alcoholic drinks were made, and the second has to do with how they functioned in society. We will address these topics in the following chapter.

RELEVANT QUESTIONS

1. If intoxicants were not merely consumed as a necessity in biblical times because of unsafe water, what other kind of values seem to be attributed to alcoholic beverages in the Bible?
2. Given that alcoholic beverages in the Bible were not diluted to a negligible ABV percentage, is another form of biblical justification needed to support Christian teetotalism?

CHAPTER 4

THE PRODUCTION AND ECONOMICS OF ALCOHOLIC BEVERAGES

Winemaking is a lucrative business in our contemporary setting, and it is often associated with "high culture." In many parts of the world people have access to a diversity of international wines, and plenty of them are reasonably priced. Yet many consumers still believe wine to be the proper domain of the elite. Only those with refined palates and deep wallets can truly appreciate wine, the common assumption goes. By contrast, wine was a much more common drink in ancient Israel. However, we will see that socioeconomic factors contributed to wine production, distribution, and consumption in some similar ways.

In chapter 2, we saw how the classification of wine and other alcohols does not neatly fit what we might expect when we compare it with various alcohol industries today. In this chapter we will see additional dissimilarities in terms of the production and economics of alcohol. We have already seen that wine receives far more attention than beer in the biblical record, and the same holds true for wine production over against beer production in the text as well. Since the Bible does not offer a comprehensive overview of wine and beer production—especially in the New Testament—this discussion will be supplemented with archaeological and additional literary evidence.

THE PRODUCTION AND ECONOMICS OF WINE

Wine is a celebration of place—what the French call *terroir*, which refers to the cumulative impact of the geology, soil, topography, microbes, and microclimate of the vineyard.[1] The topography and soil type of Israel varies greatly throughout the region, with the hills in the central part of Israel known for their semi-stony terra-rossa soil. Weather-wise, the hot and dry summers keep the vines from molding due to excess moisture.[2] At the same time, in order to receive an abundant and useful

---

1. On *terroir*, see Harm Jan de Blij, *Wine: A Geographic Appreciation* (Totowa: Rowman & Allanheld, 1983), 80–103. Cf. also Pliny, *Nat.* 14.8.70.

2. Walsh, *Fruit*, 27, 30, 33.

crop, sufficient rainfall is needed in the range of fifteen to thirty inches, coming mostly in the winter and spring.[3] Too little rain and there would be a smaller yield. Too much rain would lead to root rot and crop-destroying fungus. The Levant as a whole was uniquely conducive to growing grapes, in comparison with Mesopotamia and Egypt, which received more moisture (via rivers) and thus were better known for beer production.[4]

Grapes could be eaten raw after harvest, but their sheer volume necessitated that they be preserved somehow. Only nearby major cities would find it worthwhile to reserve larger portions of the yield for food (Columella, *Rust.* 3.2.1). Just as milk had to be consumed fresh or else was processed into yogurt, butter, or cheese, the same was true for grapes. Some methods were deployed to preserve grapes through winter (cf. Pliny, *Nat.* 14.3.15–19; Columella, *Rust.* 3.2.2), but in order to eat them long after harvest they typically needed to be dried into raisins (e.g., 2 Sam 6:19; 1 Chr 16:3). Yet grapes were primarily grown for the purpose of wine production.[5] This was the most desirable and strategic way to ensure that the grapes were not wasted, since alcohol is a preservative. Even today "grapevines are the world's most important fruit crop" in terms of production, and roughly 70 percent of grapes are used for winemaking.[6] Given the modern ability to preserve table grapes, raisins, syrup, and grape juice, that percentage was likely higher in the ancient world.

Planting and Cultivating Vineyards

Because ancient Israel was so good at producing wine, the biblical authors frequently make subsidiary references to viticultural practices, which starts with cultivating the land. Vintners, those who oversee vineyards, would remove any obvious stones (Ps 80:9; Isa 5:2) and curtail the growth of thorns and weeds (Prov 24:31; Isa 5:6; 27:4). Oftentimes vintners chose to terrace their vineyards on hillsides (e.g., 2 Chr 26:10; Ps 80:10; Isa 5:1; Jer 31:5; Joel 3:18; Amos 9:13), because the slope was ideal for distributing sunlight and preventing rainfall from accumulating.

After the vines were planted,[7] they were grown in three primary ways.[8] First, a vintner could allow the vines to grow along the ground.[9] Second, vines could be lifted up just slightly off the ground horizontally on short poles (cf. Varro, *Rust.* 1.8.6). Third, a vintner could use the trellising method by training vines to grow vertically up poles or even trees, which they naturally do in the wild and which made

---

3. Nathan MacDonald, *What Did the Ancient Israelites Eat? Diet in Biblical Times* (Grand Rapids: Eerdmans, 2008), 22.
4. Walsh, *Fruit*, 26.
5. Cf. Walsh, *Fruit*, 127–28, 209.
6. Richard E. Smart and Julia Harding, "Vine," in *The Oxford Companion to Wine*, ed. Julia Harding and Jancis Robinson, with Tara Q. Thomas, 5th ed. (Oxford: Oxford University Press, 2023), 803.
7. Planting seeds from grape pips was not as common as replanting vines from elsewhere. See Walsh, *Fruit*, 100.
8. See Walsh, *Fruit*, 113.
9. This likely includes the low-spreading vine mentioned in Ezek 17:6 (so Walsh, *Fruit*, 114). Although the very next verse (v. 7) mentions a vine that grows up toward the eagles overhead, which could suggest trellising (so MacDonald, *What Did*, 22).

harvesting easier.[10] Some ancient viticultural writers preferred the trellising method both for growth (Pliny, *Nat.* 14.4.3) and for the quality of wine (Columella, *Rust.* 4.19.3; 5.5.17). In ancient Israel, however, there was concern about this practice because Deuteronomy prohibits planting trees within vineyards (Deut 22:9). Despite that fact, some texts imply trellising with trees (cf. Ps 128:3; Song 6:11; 7:8; Luke 13:6), and others suggest it because people benefit from sitting under the shade of vines, which could involve trees (1 Kgs 4:25; Mic 4:4; Zech 3:10),[11] or not (cf. Judg 21:20–21; Ps 80:10; Ezek 19:11).[12] The most common practice, however, was growing vines along the ground, because the lack of residual moisture allowed for it.[13]

As the vines grow each year, vintners will prune them to promote growth (cf. John 15:2). If any branches continue to lack fruit, they are cut off and discarded (cf. John 15:6). The vintner does this with a knife or a pruning hook (cf. Isa 2:4; Mic 4:3; Joel 3:10). Pruning takes place at two main points each year. The first pruning is in the dormant season of winter, a few months after the harvest. The second occurs during summer, as the fruit is initially starting to appear, so as to encourage more growth. The clearest literary depiction in the Bible of the pruning process, outside of John 15, comes from Isaiah 18:

> For, before the harvest, when the blossom is gone
>   and the flower becomes a ripening grape,
> he will cut off the shoots with pruning knives,
>   and cut down and take away the spreading branches. (Isa 18:5)

In the context of this passage, the prophet Isaiah declares a word of judgment against Cush (Isa 18:6), which views pruning symbolically as a form of judgment that we see also in John 15:2, 6. But the reason that vintners prune vines is because, left alone, vines want to spread out in various directions. When vines are constrained, and when extra branches are cut off, vines exert their energy to produce grapes—and much more than they would without human intervention.[14]

Biblical law prohibited the use of any fruit grown in the first three years after planting, including vineyards (Lev 19:23). In the fourth year, the fruit was entirely dedicated to YHWH (19:24), presumably meaning that it should be offered as a libation or given as a tithe for priestly consumption. In the fifth and subsequent years, the fruit could be used for common consumption (19:25). In Deuteronomy 20, Moses told the men going to war not to depart if they had undedicated houses,

---

10. Borowski, *Agriculture*, 108–9. Elms were often regarded as the best tree for trellising (Columella, *Rust.* 5.6.5; *Arb.* 16; Pliny, *Nat.* 14.3.12; *Herm.* 51.1–4).

11. Peter A. Green, "Vineyards and Wine from Creation to New Creation: A Thematic-Theological Analysis of an Old Testament Motif" (PhD diss., Wheaton College, 2016), 248. Walsh (*Fruit*, 116–19) argues instead for "intercultivation."

12. Walsh, *Fruit*, 116.

13. Walsh, *Fruit*, 114–16.

14. Walsh, *Fruit*, 38.

unmarried women to whom they were betrothed, and unused vineyards. As for the vineyards, the Hebrew specifically refers to those yet to be *profaned* (*khalal* in Deut 20:6), meaning that they were not yet fit for common use after the fourth year (cf. 28:30).[15] Moses wanted these soldiers to return home lest they die in battle and fail to see the (literal) fruit of their labor. It was not just the fourth year's yields that were dedicated to YHWH but also the best of the firstfruits from each year (Exod 34:26; Num 18:12–13; Deut 26:1–2), as well as the first yield of each vat of wine (Exod 22:28–29; cf. *tirosh* in Deut 18:4). This is in addition to the annual tithe of 10 percent from the whole year's yield (*tirosh* in Deut 12:17–18; 14:22–23; Neh 10:37, 39 [10:38, 40 MT]; 2 Chr 31:5; *khamar* in Ezra 7:22).[16]

Vintners and laborers were also meant to cease working on the Sabbath, regardless of the time of the year, including harvest time (Exod 34:21). Nehemiah records an instance when he stopped people from working in vineyards on the Sabbath as they were treading grapes in the winepress and loading donkeys for the transportation of wine (*yayin*) and grapes (Neh 13:15). Sabbath observance on a weekly basis was also applied to the annual cycle of years so that a vineyard would need to lie fallow for the seventh year (Exod 23:8–13; Lev 25:1–4). Then once the cycle occurred seven times, there would be an additional Sabbath year known as the year of Jubilee (Lev 25:10–12). During all Sabbath years, as Exodus 23 and Leviticus 25 makes clear, vintners were neither meant to prune nor harvest grapes from "untrimmed" vines (*nazir*; cf. Num 6:5). Sabbath years were also supposed to be periods of generosity for the disenfranchised. If the poor requested anything during a Sabbath year, vintners were to provide from their threshing floor, flock, and even winepress (Deut 15:14).

Harvesting and Treading the Grapes

The grape harvest took place in late summer, and harvesters collected grapes as gleaners followed closely behind to take what was left behind for themselves (cf. Sir 33:16). Whatever had fallen was supposed to be left for the poor (Lev 19:9–10; 23:22; Deut 24:18–22), and travelers were also to be allowed to pass through vineyards to glean (Deut 23:24–25). Such a generous posture that Israel was meant to have for their own was not something they presumed from foreign kings during the wilderness period, since they promised not to travel through vineyards to avoid suspicion of stealing or gleaning (Num 20:17; 21:22).

Key infrastructure for vineyards often included a wall or fence around the perimeter to keep out animals, pests, and other humans (e.g., Num 22:24; Ps 80:12–13; Prov 24:31; Isa 5:2; Mark 12:1; cf. Song 2:15). Absent a wall (or an effective one), laws required compensation in kind to an owner of a field or vineyard who may have lost crops from someone else's flocks (Exod 22:4). Within the vineyard compound,

---

15. Alter, *Hebrew Bible*, 1:685.

16. Cf. ch. 6 for alcohol and sacred space.

vintners would also often set up a tower and a winepress (Isa 5:2; Mark 12:1). The tower would allow the vintner to see what was happening across the vineyard. It would also serve as a space for lodging during harvest and for the temporary storage of freshly made wine.[17] If a vintner did not have a tower, he and his family would erect tents and stay within the vineyard until the most opportune time to begin harvest (cf. Isa 1:8).[18] Winepresses were dug out of the bedrock for crushing grapes into must (i.e., the initial juice) and were often constructed within the premises of the vineyard itself.[19] There were thousands of winepresses in the time of ancient Israel, which highlights how productive their wine industry was.[20]

> Oddly, Gideon *threshed wheat* in a winepress (Judg 6:11), conveying the lengths that he went to in order to evade the Midianites.

Treading grapes by foot was the most common method for crushing grapes and extracting their juice in ancient Israel (e.g., Judg 9:27). The Bible refers to treading grapes as a joyous occasion full of shouting, no doubt because of the fun of trampling, the pleasure of completing another harvest, and the excitement at the prospect of new wine (Isa 16:10; Jer 48:33).

One common method for producing a stronger, sweeter wine was to first dry out the grapes before expressing juice. This would concentrate the sugar-to-water ratio, resulting in a sweeter, and often stronger, wine (cf. Columella, *Rust.* 12.27, 37, 39; Pliny, *Nat.* 14.11.80–85). The Phoenicians and Canaanites appear to have used similar methods, based on the inscriptional evidence from a jar found at Lachish for "raisin wines."[21] This suggests that ancient Israelite vintners would have known and possibly made raisin wines, even though there do not appear to be any distinctive terms used for this type of wine in the Bible. At any rate, the strongest wines in ancient Israel were likely made from methods that included drying out the grapes first.

The styles of winepresses varied in the land of Israel during the Iron Age (1200–586 BCE), but the dominant design included a designated floor for treading the grapes (Heb. *gat*) and a collecting vat carved out of the ground.[22] Sometimes all of the grape must was collected into a single vat. If the winepress was large enough to have multiple vats, vintners could have tried to create different styles at once, or to separate out the best quality juice. The must produced simply by the weight of the grapes in the press, known as *protropum* by Romans, was often prized for producing the best wine (Pliny, *Nat.* 14.9.85). By contrast, juice collected by pressing grapes that were already trodden (to extract every last drop) was regarded as inferior. Regardless of how the grape must was obtained, it would flow downhill or through a pipe into

---

17. Shimon Dar, *Landscape and Pattern: An Archaeological Survey of Samaria 800 B.C.E.–636 C.E.*, 2 vols., BARIS 308 (Oxford: BAR, 1986), 1:157–58.
18. Walsh, *Fruit*, 136–42; McGovern, *Ancient Wine*, 217.
19. Walsh, *Fruit*, 142–43.
20. Magen Broshi, *Bread, Wine, Walls and Scrolls*, LSTS 36 (London: Bloomsbury, 2002), 147.
21. McGovern, *Ancient Wine*, 234, 369.
22. Walsh, *Fruit*, 162–65. For more on winepresses, see Frankel, *Wine and Oil*.

a collecting vat where fermentation would take place.[23] Most of the vats were outside without a covering, and so the initial fermentation process would be out in the open for several days.[24] Afterward the newly fermented wine was transferred into vessels for storage and secondary fermentation.[25] For larger vineyards with greater yields at harvest time, they probably did not let the must ferment in the initial collecting vats, because that would make the vats occupied when there were still grapes left to tread. In those instances, the must would be collected to ferment within storage vessels.[26]

Wine Storage and Trade

As mentioned in chapter 2, grape skins provided the yeast for fermentation and impacted the color of wine. In addition to grape skins, other grape particles from the must would create sediment, known as dregs or lees. These were often stored with the wine (Ezek 23:33), but they could be filtered out (cf. Isa 25:6) through straining devices with perforated holes in them.[27]

Commercial wines today are filtered with fining agents, typically animal or fish proteins, to attain visual clarity. Unless they are organic or kosher wines, modern wines are often not a vegan product (despite how strange that sounds for a beverage made from fruit).

Although ancient vintners did not use raw sugar or nonnaturally occurring sulfites, as many modern vintners do, they did add various ingredients to flavor and preserve the wine, like resin, salt, etc. (cf. ch. 2).

If wine is stored properly, being left alone for long stretches of time without exposure to light, air, or shifts in temperature, then the wine will stay good and even mature. This is received wisdom today, and it was also known in the ancient world (cf. Columella, *Rust.* 3.21.10; Pliny, *Nat.* 14.4.22). The Samaria ostraca, which include incised inscriptions on pottery sherds dating to the eighth century BCE, suggest that older wines were preferred.[28] Even Jesus acknowledges this, stating that old wine is better than new wine (Luke 5:39; cf. Sir 9:10). In a prophetic oracle from Jeremiah, the prophet likens Moab's stability to wine that has been stored properly and left undisturbed: "like wine left on its dregs, not poured from one jar to another" (Jer 48:11). The Hebrew text simply says that Moab was "left on its dregs," and so a wine metaphor is implied, though the LXX translators missed the association (Moab "trusted in his glory" in Jer 31:11 LXX [NETS]). Within the metaphor, because Moab has not gone into exile, "she tastes as she did, and her aroma is unchanged" (Jer 48:11). The image here is less focused on the positive maturation of wine than on not developing

Kosher wines today represent a development in biblical winemaking practices from the rabbinic period (cf. m. Avodah Zarah 2:3–4; 4:8–12; 5:1–12). For a wine to be kosher, in addition to following biblical laws of viticulture, only observant Jews are allowed to be involved in the process from the point of crushing/pressing the grapes until the wine is bottled, to ensure that it was never dedicated to an idol. Additionally, for Passover wines, it is also required that none of the equipment has any contact with grain.

---

23. Dar, *Landscape*, 1:147–48.
24. Dar, *Landscape*, 1:156. Stirring the fermenting must helps reduce oxidization when exposed to the air (Walsh, *Fruit*, 189).
25. MacDonald, *What Did*, 22.
26. Walsh notes cellars in Gibeon were likely used for this purpose (*Fruit*, 158–59).
27. McGovern, *Ancient Wine*, 225–28.
28. Walsh, *Fruit*, 58; Dayagi-Mendels, *Drink*, 35.

off-flavors through improper storage. Yet this vision of Moab changes swiftly; her wine will be poured out, and her jars will be smashed (Jer 48:12).

Wine was aged in various types of vessels (cf. Jer 40:10), but the main one mentioned in the biblical record is wineskins. Wineskins were portable wine containers made of goat or sheep skin and were the primary means by which travelers could bring wine on their journeys (1 Sam 10:3; 16:20; 25:18; 2 Sam 16:1–2). In a fascinating scene that reveals how wineskins were often used, the Gibeonites, who were one of the original inhabitants of Canaan (and archaeological evidence of winepresses suggests that they were prolific winemakers), evaded destruction during the Israelite conquest of Canaan by pretending that they lived far away and were just passing through. Their deceptive "proof" was old clothes and sandals, along with moldy bread and cracked wineskins (Josh 9:4, 13). The cracked wineskins implied that they were freshly filled at the start of the journey and had dried out after the wine was consumed. What was also implied by their "proof" was that they would have had greater resources at their disposal if they were locals, since the land was regularly characterized as a uniquely fertile place (cf. ch. 5).

Wineskins could also serve as long-term storage receptacles. Jeremiah refers to storing wine in wineskins and comments on how the wineskins should be filled up completely (Jer 13:12), undoubtedly to prevent oxidation (cf. Herm. 48.3). Because vinegar results from exposing alcohol to oxygen, sour wines were especially common among those who could not store wine properly, such as soldiers, travelers, and the poor.[29] As noted in chapter 2, if a *fermenting* wine is sealed tightly in a wineskin, the resultant pressure from trapping carbon dioxide could burst the skin. So when Job's friend Elihu feels "pressure" to respond verbally to Job's predicament, he compares his internal state to that of fermentation: "for I am full of words, and the spirit within me compels me; inside I am like bottled-up wine [*yayin*], like new wineskins ready to burst" (Job 32:18–19).[30] This is why Jesus says that new wine should not be put into worn-out wineskins, lest the skins burst (Mark 2:22). If *new wineskins* would occasionally burst from the pressure of fermentation, then certainly old wineskins would not stand a chance with new wine still fermenting.

For long-term storage, wine was most often put into fired clay vessels like the Greco-Roman amphorae, which had as their prototypes vessels used by ancient Canaanites and Phoenicians.[31] These had a pair of curved loop handles on their shoulders, a narrow spout, and a pointed base that acted as an extra handle. Large amphorae would also be used for the distribution of wine through trade (Ezek 27:18–19). Shipwrecks in the Mediterranean contain many amphorae from Phoenicia,[32] and numerous such vessels have also been found in Egyptian tombs and palaces, including

---

29. Faas, *Roman Table*, 122.
30. Butler and Heskett (*Divine Vintage*, 88) relate this to drinking too much new wine.

31. Virginia R. Grace, *Amphoras and the Ancient Wine Trade* (Princeton: Princeton University Press, 1961), 6.
32. McGovern, *Ancient Wine*, 346–47.

those of prominent Pharaohs like Scorpion I (ca. 3200 BCE).[33] The material evidence suggests that the Phoenicians were involved in an elaborate trading industry.[34] Biblical evidence also suggests this (cf. Hos 14:7), especially since Tyre, the major Phoenician city, imported wines from Helbon for themselves (Ezek 27:18). When King Solomon began to build the temple, he requested wood from Tyre. As compensation, he gave them "twenty thousand cors [a large, though unknown, measurement] of ground wheat, twenty thousand cors of barley, twenty thousand baths of wine [*yayin*] and twenty thousand baths of olive oil" (2 Chr 2:10 [2:9 MT]). This example reveals the trade value of Israel's goods and highlights just how prosperous the wine trade was.

Part of what gives wine its flavor is the vessel in which it ages. Unlike wooden barrels, amphorae would not contribute a pleasant flavor unless they were not sealed with resin (which was rare; cf. ch. 2).[35] Wooden barrels began to be used in the first century CE, but it would not be until the seventeenth century that glass bottles with cork came into use.[36]

> The Malkata ostraca, which are a collection of amphora fragments from King Amenhotep III's palace in Thebes, Egypt (ca. 1350 BCE), reveal that sometimes vintners would write information on amphorae concerning the quality, year, estate, and purpose of the wine. This practice anticipates the classifications found on many modern wine labels by thousands of years,[37] and it demonstrates that from a very early period, winemaking was an artistry and not merely a necessity.

The Economics of Vineyards

Producing wine was a precarious endeavor. If inclement weather, disease, or warfare arose, vineyards would suffer, and with it the vintner's economic stability. Additionally, if wine was not stored properly and became vinegar, then a year of hard work would have been in vain. As we have seen already, planting a vineyard was quite the investment, since Israel's law required four seasons before grapes could be used for common consumption. The precarity of a vineyard is also accentuated when one factors in lower life expectancies for people in the ancient world.[38] As Columella wrote, a plot of land could be used for more lucrative and less precarious purposes than a vineyard (*Rust.* 3.3.1–15). This is partly why the "woman of valor" from Proverbs 31 is so significant, beyond the obvious fact that women did not own vineyards in ancient Israel.[39] She is lauded specifically for having foresight in

---

33. McGovern, *Ancient Wine*, 85–106.
34. McGovern, *Ancient Wine*, 107–47.
35. McGovern, *Ancient Wine*, 368. On the use of resin, cf. ch. 2.
36. Unwin, *Wine*, 55.
37. McGovern, *Ancient Wine*, 124–25.
38. Walsh, *Fruit*, 20.
39. Welton, *"He Is a Glutton"*, 122.

the acquisition of a field and planting a vineyard (Prov 31:16). This also implies her ability to anticipate how conducive the land was for viticulture.

Under normal circumstances, vineyards that were fully functioning were key economic assets. As one metric, the eighth-century BCE prophet Isaiah prices a thousand vines at a thousand silver shekels (Isa 7:23). Given their value, vineyards could be sold, traded, or handed down to the next generation as a family business. Indeed, most vintners in ancient Israel produced wine for their own families, making wine less lucrative for them and also less accessible to those who did not own a vineyard.[40] King Ahab had hopes of purchasing Naboth's family vineyard, because it was in close proximity to the royal palace and because the land always provided a great yield. Ahab offered either a sum of silver or an exchange for another vineyard, so that he could turn the vineyard into a vegetable garden (1 Kgs 21:1–2). But Naboth refused because he wanted to keep the vineyard within the family line (21:3–4). This led Ahab's wife, Queen Jezebel, to conspire to kill Naboth and seize the vineyard, demonstrating its perceived value. Vineyards could also be given in exchange for various types of service, as when King Saul assumed that the people at Gibeah were bribed with gifts of vineyards for helping David escape (1 Sam 22:7), or when Elisha chides his servant Gehazi that it would be inappropriate to receive any kind of payment for healing Naaman, including vineyards (2 Kgs 5:26).

Kings and various political leaders were often in charge of vineyards (cf. Zech 14:10), but since vineyards required so much work, they delegated the work to others. First Chronicles ends with a series of genealogies of priests, Levites, musicians, and royal staff, including those in charge of the king's storehouses of wine (*yayin*), fields, vineyards, and more (1 Chr 27:27). King Uzziah, in particular, was known as someone who "loved the soil," and who had "people working his fields and vineyards in the hills and in the fertile lands" (2 Chr 26:10). Vintners with larger vineyards would also bring in additional laborers as well (cf. Matt 20:1–16), which often involved exploitation. Job cursed the wicked for exploiting poor laborers who glean in the vineyards (Job 24:6, 18) but do not benefit from the labor they provide (24:11).

Babylon also exploited the labor of the poor during the exile. Because vineyards were so economically resourceful, enemy vineyards were often destroyed in ANE warfare. In some instances, vineyards would be maintained as an asset for the conquering people. One of the chief things that attracted Assyria and Babylon to conquer the northern kingdom of Israel and the southern kingdom of Judah was, in fact, their vineyards.[41] When Nebuchadnezzar took the southern kingdom of Judah into exile, he brought the nobles to Babylon (Jer 39:9), but he kept behind some of the poor to work the vineyards (2 Kgs 25:12; Jer 39:10; 52:16). Gedaliah, the Babylonian commander in charge of the poor working the vineyards (Jer 40:7),

---

40. Walsh, *Fruit*, 43–59.

41. MacDonald, *What Did*, 23.

told the people how they had been spared from exile, and so they should serve the Babylonians by "harvest[ing] the wine [*yayin*], summer fruit and olive oil, and put them in your storage jars, and live in the towns you have taken over" (40:10).[42] When other Judahites from neighboring lands in Ammon and Moab heard about this, some returned to Judah to help the poor: "they harvested an abundance of wine [*yayin*] and summer fruit" (40:12). What was presented as regal beneficence was undoubtedly designed to produce loyalty,[43] as well as an abundance of wine for the benefit of the empire.

After Judahites reentered their land during the Persian period, Nehemiah records how new economic disparities with viticulture emerged. To start, Judah was a vassal state within the Persian Empire, and so the land ultimately belonged to the Persians (Neh 9:35–37). Additionally, in the midst of a famine, some vintners were "mortgaging" their fields and vineyards in order to get grain (5:3). Others had to borrow funds to pay off regal taxes on their vineyards (5:4) and subjected their children to slavery to avoid their fields and vineyards being repossessed due to financial defaulting (5:5). Nehemiah's primary concern in all of this was the lack of societal help being given to everyone's fellow countrymen amid their return from exile. Thus, Nehemiah called for debts to be canceled, all interest accrued to be given back—including money, grain, new wine (*tirosh*), and oil—and for fields and vineyards to be returned to their original owners (5:11). Because of Nehemiah's efforts, those exploiting the vineyard owners agreed to return all that they had taken (5:13–14).

Vineyards were therefore vulnerable and contested spaces. They were vulnerable to the elements, the ill will of others, and the machinations of their owners. Vineyards were contested insofar as they were sites that elicited the envy of those with the power to evict their owners and to take the vineyards for themselves. The precarity of owning and maintaining a vineyard was thus relative to the amount of financial and social capital an ancient Israelite possessed. For the rich and powerful, vineyards were less precarious. But as you go down the economic spectrum, the precarity increased. As for the poor, they regularly lacked access to wine, even though they were often exploited for its production.

The Economics of Wine Consumption

The average Israelite from the ancient world had limited access to wine, especially if they did not own their own vineyard. As such, wine would be saved for special occasions, including the annual festivals in the liturgical calendar (cf. ch. 5) or ad hoc feasts.[44] One particular Hebrew term for feasting, *mishteh*, specifically highlights

---

42. Of course, fermented wine is not harvested, so the passage elides the grape harvest by focusing on its goal—wine. Rightly Alter, *Hebrew Bible*, 2:992. Contra Bacchiocchi (*Wine*, 66–69), who argues that this proves that *yayin* can be unfermented.

43. So Alter, *Hebrew Bible*, 2:990.

44. Welton, *"He Is a Glutton"*, 131–32.

alcohol consumption. The noun *mishteh* derives from a Hebrew verb for drinking (*shatah*), because drinking was the main feature of a *mishteh*,[45] and increased drinking is what distinguishes it from a meal.[46] Although the kind of alcoholic beverage consumed may not be explicitly indicated, the festive nature of the *mishteh* suggests more highly valued beverages—wine, if you had it. A *mishteh* could be enjoyed by royalty and non-royalty alike, but such were less frequent for the average person.

Although wine was consumed across the economic strata of ancient Israelite society, wine was often associated with regal opulence. "Most references to drunkenness," P. P. Jenson affirms, "are to kings and the wealthy, who could afford the quantities required."[47] They also had more leisure time with which to consume wine compared to the average person. One thinks immediately of the boisterous feasts and excessive drinking throughout Esther, consistent with its palatial setting. At the coronation of David (1 Chr 12:39–40 [12:40–41 MT]), there was a three-day festival characterized by "eating and drinking," including, of course, wine (*yayin*). The Queen of Sheba was impressed by the opulence of King Solomon, including his lavish dining set and the spread on the table, as well as his cupbearers and the fact that his goblets were gold (1 Kgs 10:5, 21; 2 Chr 9:4, 20; cf. Esth 1:7). When speaking of Hezekiah's wealth (2 Chr 32:27–29), the Chronicler depicts his building projects, possessions, livestock, and storehouses of new wine (*tirosh*),[48] grain, and oil (32:28). King Rehoboam fortified multiple towns during his reign, to build better defenses throughout Judah, and he supplied these places with "food, olive oil and wine [*yayin*]" (11:11). When non-regal figures put on elaborate feasts, like Nabal, they could be compared to a king's banquet without needing to specify what that entails (1 Sam 25:36).

The regal association of wine and feasting is important background for considering the significance of the admonition to King Lemuel at the end of Proverbs, since it seems to run counter to it:

> It is not for kings, Lemuel—
>> it is not for kings to drink wine [*yayin*],
>> not for rulers to crave beer [*shekar*],
> lest they drink and forget what has been decreed,
>> and deprive all the oppressed of their rights.
> Let beer [*shekar*] be for those who are perishing,
>> wine [*yayin*] for those who are in anguish!
> Let them drink and forget their poverty
>> and remember their misery no more. (Prov 31:4–7)

---

45. BDB 1059. Cf. Becker, *Rebe*, 142; Walsh, *Fruit*, 225–26.
46. Dubach, *Trunkenheit*, 27, cf. 27–30.
47. P. P. Jenson, "שכר," *NIDOTTE* 4:113.
48. Storehouses full of *tirosh* rather than *yayin* highlight the beginning of the wine maturation process.

The proverb provides two reasons why kings and rulers should not drink wine and beer (*shekar*). The first reason is because of their administrative responsibilities in leading and governing, and the second reason is because the poor and lowly are in better need of it. We have seen that wine regularly carries regal connotations, and a proverb like this seems to assume those connotations, even as it inverts the socioeconomic norm. The poor undoubtedly do not have the same access to alcohol as kings do, which suggests that royal provision is in view. Highlighting alcohol as something that leads to forgetfulness, the proverb speaks to how it is preferable that the downcast forget their sorrows than that kings forget their responsibility to care for them (cf. ch. 7). Ecclesiastes similarly upholds regal figures who do not feast every morning over those who do, most likely because of the same sorts of implications regarding the execution of regal responsibilities (Eccl 10:16–17; cf. ch. 9).

In Proverbs there is a warning about how wine consumption, among other things, can lead to poverty: "whoever loves pleasure will become poor; whoever loves wine [*yayin*] and olive oil will never be rich" (Prov 21:17). Part of what is implied here is not only the cost of these items but also that whoever loves them will presumably want a lot of them. Additionally, in another proverb it is more expressly stated that enjoyment of wine will decline one's productivity and thus hinder them from earning a living: "listen, my son, and be wise, and set your heart on the right path: Do not join those who drink too much wine [*yayin*] or gorge themselves on meat, for drunkards and gluttons become poor, and drowsiness clothes them in rags" (Prov 23:19–21). The concerns behind these proverbs highlight the socioeconomic precarity of wine consumption, especially among those who were not themselves already among the elite.[49]

Nothing highlights the disparity of wine consumption between kings and the average person like the role of cupbearers. Cupbearers were like ancient sommeliers who provided kings with wine, but with much higher stakes. One of their jobs was to taste the wine to prove that the wine was not drugged. In the Joseph story, Pharaoh's cupbearer was in prison, but we are not told why (Gen 40:1–3). He may have been suspected of foul play, or simply offered a distasteful wine to Pharaoh. Joseph anticipated the cupbearer's reinstatement, however, by interpreting his dream in which he squeezed grapes into Pharaoh's cup (40:9–13). This probably spoke to the royal preference for wine even in Egypt, where wine was far less accessible to the average person and beer was much more common. The cupbearer was reinstated when Pharaoh hosted a feast, or *mishteh* (40:20), which must have featured wine specifically over beer, since the baker who met his demise would also have been the brewer (more on bread and beer below).[50]

---

49. Welton argues that poverty is not in view here but rather idolatrous cultic activity like incubation and the ritual tearing of clothing, associating the critique of excess less with its *results* and more with its *associations* ("He Is a Glutton", 269–77).

50. Butler and Heskett, *Divine Vintage*, 38–39.

Nehemiah was a cupbearer in Susa, the capital of the Persian Empire, before he returned to the land and helped with the rebuilding efforts as governor (Neh 1:11; 2:1). It seems that in Nehemiah's case, being a royal cupbearer had put him in a better economic position than most.[51] This is demonstrated when Nehemiah rejected remuneration for his efforts: he never ate the people's food or took any land (5:16, 18b) and contrasted that with how governors normally receive forty shekels as compensation, in addition to food and wine (*yayin* in 5:15). Nehemiah's wealth is also suggested by his extravagant dinners, which included a lot of wine. As he describes it:

> A hundred and fifty Jews and officials ate at my table, as well as those who came to us from the surrounding nations. Each day one ox, six choice sheep and some poultry were prepared for me, and every ten days an abundant supply of wine [*yayin*] of all kinds. (Neh 5:17–18a)

Indeed, it makes sense that a former royal cupbearer would have both the means and the appetite for lavish fare, including all kinds of *yayin*.

Nehemiah's example is a great foil for those who come under the ire of the prophets. Unlike Nehemiah, who was generous with his wealth, the prophets were enraged by people who neglected the poor in order to satiate their own drunken appetites (Amos 5:11; Zeph 1:13; cf. Hag 1:6). As Joseph Blenkinsopp states, "The accusation of addiction to strong drink is a common topos in the prophetic tradition of protest directed against state bureaucrats and an *urban* elite."[52] Indeed, the prophet Joel describes the nations' treatment of God's people as being like selling a girl for wine (*yayin*) and drinking it (Joel 3:3 [4:3 MT]). Even though this is an analogy for precarious international relations, it also implies instances of the exploitation of human beings in the process of acquiring wine.

The writings of the prophet Amos are particularly noteworthy on this point. In Amos's opening oracles of judgment against the nations (Amos 1–2), he included as one of several indictments against the northern kingdom of Israel the fact that they drank wine that was "taken as fines" in the house of their "G/god" (Amos 2:8). Being "taken as a fine" suggests that the wine was either the fine itself or that the money received as a fine was used for wine.[53] The problem seems to be, given Amos's socioeconomic concerns, that these fines were not fair. It was "indulgence at public expense,"[54] and so their worship was not acceptable to YHWH. The wine being consumed in a house of worship in Amos 2 is consistent with how Amos critiques the rich for neglecting the poor as they participate in temple worship (cf. 5:21–24).

---

51. So Alter, *Hebrew Bible*, 3:842.
52. Blenkinsopp, *Isaiah 1–39*, 213–14 (emphasis original).
53. Shalom M. Paul prefers the latter (*Amos: A Commentary on the Book of Amos*, Hermeneia [Minneapolis: Fortress, 1991], 86).
54. Göran Eidevall, *Amos: A New Translation with Introduction and Commentary*, AYB (New Haven: Yale University Press, 2017), 116.

Later on, Amos targeted the rich who live comfortable and luxurious lives (Amos 6:4), as seen by their consumption of wine (*yayin*) from bowls and their use of extravagant lotions (6:6). It is possible that their consumption of wine was cultic or pertaining to temple observance, because the word for "bowls" typically refers to the basins used for grain offerings.[55] Additionally, they were participating in a *marzeakh* (6:7), which was a ritualized banquet known from Ugaritic literature (cf. also Jer 16:5), which seems to be a religious meal involving alcohol for the wealthy.[56] If so, this is another instance where ritual consumption of wine is critiqued because of a neglect for the poor. The problem that Amos explicitly has is that their leisure leads to them being devoid of concern for their fellow countrymen (6:6b) and for those without basic sustenance. Amos calls the women among this rich lot "cows of Bashan"—women who act harshly to the poor and needy, and then turn to request "drink" from their husbands (4:1). These "cows" may refer to idols of worship, but Alter argues it is likely a slur against the women of Samaria, who "indolently satisfy their appetite."[57] Amos's outrage regarding wine consumption is clearly motivated by socioeconomic concerns, and it highlights once again that accessibility to wine increased or decreased on a sliding scale relative to one's own capital (cf. Tob 4:15–16; Jas 5:5).

In contrast to this, the prophet Isaiah imagines a future era of restoration in which wine will be acquired without cost and without money (Isa 55:1–2; cf. ch. 13). In this passage we see an economic leveling, where all people have equal access to these good gifts from God when all things are restored. Moreover, within Isaiah's oracles themselves, this vision recalls the economic disparities highlighted in Isaiah 3 and 5, where the wealthy have "ruined" the vineyard and "crushed" the faces of the poor (3:14–15), and where they then drink excessively all day long in their grotesque life of leisure (5:11–12, 22). One day there will be equal access, and abundant access at that.

Such future abundance is prefigured in the wedding at Cana, when Jesus famously turned water into wine after they ran out of wine (John 2:1–11). Although much more will be said about this passage in chapter 13, it is worth mentioning here how this sign alludes back to a miracle by Elijah, in which he provided a needy widow and her son an unending supply of flour and oil when they lacked basic necessities (1 Kgs 17:14–16). In addition to the significant provisions that each supplied, the use of a similar idiom—"What is there between you and me?" (1 Kgs 17:18 LXX; John 2:4)—invites us to read these miracles together. As Leann Pace points out with respect to the Elijah narrative, wine is conspicuous by its absence because these people were so impoverished.[58] Yet what is lacking with Elijah, we find as a great

---

55. Welton, *"He Is a Glutton"*, 166. Cf. 134–37, 162–68.

56. See John L. McLaughlin, *The Marzēaḥ in the Prophetic Literature: References and Allusions in Light of the Extra-Biblical Evidence*, VTSup 86 (Leiden: Brill, 2001), 65–79 (on Amos 6, see 80–108).

57. Alter, *Hebrew Bible*, 2:1263.

58. See Pace, "Feasting," 195.

abundance with Jesus. Thus, the miracle at Cana further demonstrates that in the era of restoration there will be such an abundance that everyone will have plenty.

THE PRODUCTION AND ECONOMICS OF BEER

Beer production, by contrast to wine, was not as complex or as elaborate of a process. If you could make bread in the ancient world, you could make beer.[59] Beer is a grain-based alcohol, and there were a few ways to make it. The simplest way to make beer was to crumble pieces of bread, or *bappir* (a barley cake or a kind of sourdough), into water and let it sit.[60] This bread-water (or *wort*) would then ferment naturally through wild yeast strains in the air (or the culture from the sourdough), but sometimes grapes were also added, providing an additional source of sugar and yeast for fermentation.[61] Although the Bible does not describe this process, several ANE texts do, such as the Sumerian Hymn to Ninkasi (ca. 1800 BCE). It is possible, though, that Ecclesiastes alludes to the production of beer when it mentions casting bread on water (Eccl 11:1–2).[62] Another way to make beer, which was often combined with the process above, involved cooking a mixture of malted barley and water. Ambient yeasts, or those present in the vessels from previous use, would then convert those sugars into alcohol after the cooking process was completed.[63]

Beer was therefore more accessible than wine in many respects. Beer could be made any week of the year, whereas wine could only be made after the harvest in late summer.[64] Beer was also cheaper and easier to make. Obviously, no vineyard was required nor any major structures or equipment. Beer also did not need to be aged like wine. In fact, beer would not have aged well, because preservatives like hops had not been introduced to beer production yet, and ancient beer would not typically be high in alcohol (often 2–3% ABV).[65] This means that large storage vessels would not be needed either. For these reasons, beer was a horrible product for trade.[66]

Instead, beer was a simple, domestic beverage and was often made by women who typically did the baking. No additional equipment would be needed beyond what would be necessary for baking bread, and so the "archaeological correlates" for baking and domestic brewing are the same.[67] Thus, it is hard to discover *discrete* archaeological evidence for beermaking, since it is no different than evidence for breadmaking. Furthermore, beer residue (i.e., calcium oxalate, or beer stone) is less

---

59. See, e.g., Ebeling and Homan, "Baking," 45–62; Ebeling, "Grains," 108–9.
60. Ebeling and Homan, "Baking," 52–53; Ebeling, "Grains," 109.
61. McGovern, *Ancient Wine*, 84, 105, 186, 308.
62. Michael M. Homan, "Beer Production by Throwing Bread into Water: A New Interpretation of Qoh. XI 1–2," *VT* 52.2 (2002): 275–78.
63. Welton, *"He Is a Glutton"*, 100–102.
64. Ebeling, "Grains," 108.
65. Homan, "Beer and Its Drinkers," 85, 91.
66. Homan, "Beer and Its Drinkers," 86.
67. Ebeling and Homan, "Baking," 53–54.

detectable in amphorae and other vessels than wine residue (tartaric acid), in part because beer was not stored and aged the same way as wine.[68] There were actually only a few artifacts specific to beer, which reflect that ancient beer was often like fermented oatmeal. Two of them are worth mentioning briefly here.[69] First, there were drinking vessels with built-in perforated strainers to hold back bits of grain still in the beer. These vessels were found in Philistia and were originally labeled "beer jugs." But some archaeologists argued that they may have been used to filter out wine dregs instead.[70] Yet there is more recent support in recognizing that their purpose was for beer consumption,[71] and studies on ancient yeast cells found on pottery have helped to confirm that.[72] Second, there were straws, often made from reeds, which had iron or bone strainers placed on the ends, and those tips can be found in the archaeological record.[73] The straws allowed beer drinkers to push through the floating grain particles and filter out any additional bits (cf. Athenaeus, *Deipn.* 10.447b–c).[74]

In ancient Israel wine was the "most costly" form of alcohol, but beer may have been "more common"[75]—at least more common than the literary evidence suggests. Certainly, the biblical authors "foreground" wine, but the people who produced the Bible were not representative of the average Israelite. Along these lines, Welton critiques the prominence of wine as a "core element" of the ordinary Israelite diet, as conceived of in the so-called Mediterranean triad.[76] Wine's place as a staple is more secure when we are addressing the diets of the elite within ancient Israelite society (i.e., kings, priests, prophets), or the primary resources for trade. Welton argues further that the difficulties associated with producing and storing wine likely meant that wine was more associated with celebrations and feasts, and that beer was more likely the "staple" form of alcohol for the average person in ancient Israel.[77] Thus, wine received more attention in the literary record, at least in part because it was "more valuable, socially, ritually and economically, than beer."[78] In areas where wine was not produced as readily, such as Mesopotamia and Egypt, wine was even more of an elite beverage, with the common drink being beer.[79]

Herodotus, *Hist.* 2.77 (5th c. BCE), notes the dominance of grain-based alcohol in Egypt because of the lack of viticulture: "[The Egyptians] eat bread, making loaves which they call 'cyllestis' of coarse grain. For wine, they use a drink made of barley; for they have no vines in their country." (Godley, LCL)

---

68. Homan, "Beer and Its Drinkers," 86.
69. Cf. Homan, "Beer and Its Drinkers," 89–91, on cylindrical fermentation stoppers and jars with perforated bases.
70. Lawrence E. Stager, "The Fury of Babylon: Ashkelon and the Archaeology of Destruction," *BAR* 22.1 (1996): 64–65; King and Stager, *Life*, 102.
71. Ebeling and Homan, "Baking," 54–56.
72. Tzemach Aouizerat et al., "Isolation and Characterization of Live Yeast Cells from Ancient Vessels as a Tool in Bio-Archaeology," *mBio* 10.2 (2019): e00388–19.
73. Homan, "Beer and Its Drinkers," 86, cf. 88.
74. Ebeling and Homan, "Baking," 56–57.
75. Welton, *"He Is a Glutton"*, 121, cf. 99–121.
76. Welton, *"He Is a Glutton"*, 131–32. For the role of wine in the triad, see, e.g., Peter Garnsey, *Food and Society in Classical Antiquity*, KTAH (Cambridge: Cambridge University Press, 1999), 12.
77. Welton, *"He Is a Glutton"*, 121–32.
78. Welton, *"He Is a Glutton"*, 138.
79. Nelson, *Barbarian's Beverage*, 67; MacDonald, *What Did*, 13, 21; Walsh, *Fruit*, 21–27.

Beer was also consumed in ancient Europe, especially among the Gauls. Since there is no evidence of beer in ancient Italy, the Romans were not beer drinkers.[80] The available information seems to suggest that beer was probably consumed in places where wine was not easily produced. But if wine could be produced regionally, then wine seems to have been preferred.[81] To be sure, wine was more readily available in ancient Israel than in most neighboring countries. The average Israelite would have had greater access to wine than the average Egyptian, for example, and so the average Israelite probably much preferred wine over beer. But that does not mean that there was not a socioeconomic divide internal to Israel with respect to access to wine, as we have seen already.

CONCLUSION

In this chapter we have briefly explored how wine and beer were produced in ancient Israel, since that is primarily what the biblical record provides compared to the time of the New Testament (though the gap was somewhat filled through the works of first-century Roman agriculturalists and historians). We saw how much more elaborate the process and equipment were in the case of wine as compared to beer, and also that the biblical record also gives far more attention to wine over beer. Despite the literary discrepancy, at the very least beer would have been more common than the literature suggests.

Additionally, the ubiquity of wine in ancient Israel and the biblical record deserves a caveat—access to wine was socioeconomically determined. This issue adds a layer of complexity in the analysis of the biblical data and also highlights a key theme that runs throughout the text. As we will turn to explore in the following chapter, wine often symbolized the blessing and joy associated with God's provision of the land to his people. Even though not everyone had equal access to wine, the symbolism could still be appreciated, and the prophets and Jesus anticipated a day when everyone would be able to enjoy it equally.

RELEVANT QUESTIONS

1. What do biblical laws governing viticultural practices suggest about ancient Israelite perceptions of vineyards and winemaking?
2. How should socioeconomic factors impact how we assess biblical references to wine and beer, given the relative status of the biblical authors compared to the average person?

---

80. Nelson, *Barbarian's Beverage*, 67, 71.

81. Cf. Garnsey, *Food*, 118.

CHAPTER 5

CULTIVATING GOD'S VINEYARD

In ancient Israel, alcoholic beverages were commonly regarded as blessings from God. This was undoubtedly due in part to the fact that consuming alcohol often makes people feel happy and joyous. Although this would not have been known to ancient Israelites, alcohol triggers a release of dopamine in the brain, which tends to lead to positive feelings and emotions. Much more substantively, alcohol came to be understood as a divine gift as part of Israel's theology of the land and the covenant.

The land that God originally promised to Abraham and his offspring was known for its fertility and viticultural potential. As such, God's promise to bless the people through the land was understood in part as blessing them through wine. If the people remained obedient to God and upheld their covenantal relationship with him, they would continue to experience the land's delights. The people also celebrated God's covenant faithfulness in annual festivals, where wine consumption was customary. The use of wine as a celebration of the land is also seen in the erotic series of love poems of the Song of Songs, which brings together the gifts of alcohol and the land as part of its celebration of another divine gift—sexuality. In this chapter these themes will be explored in greater detail, beginning with the nature of the land promise itself.

THE LAND PROMISE

As part of the covenant that God made with the nomad Abram (i.e., Abraham), God promised him numerous offspring (Gen 12:1–2; 15:1–6; 17:1–7, 16; 22:17) who would bless the nations (12:2–3; 22:18) and eventually possess their own land (12:4–9; 15:17–21; 17:8). Yet they would not possess it immediately (15:12–16), foreshadowing Israel's experience in Egypt. Indeed, possession would also be delayed, if not compromised, because Abram and Sarai (i.e., Sarah) were unable to have children (cf. 11:30; 12:4; 16:1). After the events of the exodus (and wilderness wanderings) four hundred years later, Abram's miraculous offspring became numerous and took possession of the land through the conquest of Canaan. Yet prior to the post-exodus community entering the land, the promises made to Abram were reaffirmed and extended to each subsequent generation through the pronouncement of blessings.

Blessings and Extensions of the Promise

The extension of God's promises through pronouncing blessings begins with Abram's own experience. After God made promises to Abram (Gen 12:1–9), Abram received a blessing from an enigmatic figure named Melchizedek, who was "king of Salem" and "priest of God Most High" (14:18). Although the blessing's content did not concern matters of the land or viticulture, it reaffirmed that the God of promise was at work in ensuring their realization. Furthermore, Melchizedek's blessing was accompanied by a meal of bread and wine (*yayin* in 14:18), which symbolize and foreshadow the provisions that God will provide through the land.[1] This incident also highlights both the regal and priestly associations with wine that recur in the biblical tradition (cf. ch. 4).

Although Abram and Sarai initially assumed that the promise of numerous descendants would not be realized through their own union (hence the story of Hagar and Ishmael in Gen 16–25), Sarai gave birth to Isaac, who became the heir of the Abrahamic promises (Gen 17:19–21). Once Isaac was weaned, Abram (now Abraham), threw a "great feast" (*mishteh gadol* in 21:8) to celebrate God's miraculous commitment to his promises. This occasion must have included plenty of wine since a normal "feast" (*mishteh*) already showcases wine consumption.[2] Before Abraham died, he ensured that the promises that he received would continue to be extended to Isaac's offspring by having one of his servants promise to help Isaac find a wife (24:1–9).

Isaac would eventually father two sons—Esau and Jacob—but the Abrahamic promises were only extended to the latter. As it turns out, Jacob received his father's blessing through trickery. He initially duped his older brother Esau into giving up his birthright for a bowl of soup due to his (unexplained but extreme) hunger (Gen 25:29–34). Then Jacob impersonated Esau to his aging father in order to receive Esau's blessing. The context of this blessing was a meal with wine (*yayin* in 27:25), just as we saw with Melchizedek's blessing and with Abraham's celebration of Isaac's miraculous birth. The content of Isaac's blessing to Jacob included a reiteration of the expectation that Abraham's offspring would experience prominence relative to other nations (27:29). They would also enjoy agricultural fertility, including the "dew" from heaven, the "richness" of the earth, and an abundance of grain and new wine (*tirosh* in 27:28). These blessings, of course, point to their future realization in the land that was promised to Abraham.

Because Isaac had given this blessing to Jacob, even by chicanery, Esau would have to settle for a second-rate blessing (Gen 27:37). This blessing involves what amounts to an inversion of the blessings extended to Jacob (27:39–40). Most notably,

---

1. Butler and Heskett, *Divine Vintage*, 23; cf. 28.
2. In fact, Sarah's reaction at this *mishteh*—casting out Hagar and Ishmael—is partly explained by the effects of alcohol on her judgment. See Carey Ellen Walsh, "Under the Influence: Trust and Risk in Biblical Family Drinking," *JSOT* 90 (2000): 21–23.

there is a glaring omission of grain and new wine, and the benediction even states that Esau would live *away from* the "dew" of heaven and the "fatness" of the land. In other words, Isaac's "blessing" to Esau is something of a misnomer (27:41) and is really more of a curse.

Once Jacob (now Israel) was about to die, and his children reunited in Egypt at the climax of the Joseph story (Gen 37–50), Jacob pronounced blessings on each of his twelve sons, extending the Abrahamic promises to each of them (49:1–27). Each blessing reiterated elements of the main promises, but with regard to Judah in particular the theme of viticulture takes focus. Israel blesses Judah by proclaiming that he will defeat his enemies and then rule prosperously forever (49:8–10). The prosperity is depicted in terms of the foal being bound to the vine, and the donkey's colt being bound to the "choice vine" (49:11a NRSVue). In other words, there will always be viticultural work for these beasts of burden because so much will be produced. Judah's viticultural prosperity is also depicted in this blessing through the image of his garments being washed in wine (*yayin*) and the blood of grapes (49:11b). Given the militaristic victory at the start of the benediction, Judah's *blood*-stained garments work on two levels. In addition to signifying viticultural abundance, it also metaphorically connotes the continual defeat of Judah's enemies, which in turn will ensure unthwarted viticultural activity. Judah's eyes are further described as darker than wine (*yayin*), and his teeth as whiter than milk (49:12). The defeat of enemies (49:8–10) leads to a wise and peaceful rule of prosperity (49:11–12), which underscores how thriving agriculture is predicated on factors like political stability and militaristic security.

As this overview highlights, God's promises to Abraham were reiterated to subsequent generations through pronouncing blessings. The prospect of viticulture and wine production in those blessings suggests a trajectory that would culminate in Abraham's offspring finally inheriting the promised land and cultivating it to produce great wine.

The Promised Land and Its Viticultural Potential

The promised land was a source of immense agricultural productivity and was prized in part for its ability to grow vines. Scholars believe that the Levant is where humans first encountered the wild grapevine, before it was properly cultivated.[3] Viticulture was thus a crucial aspect of the land's fertility.

Famously, though, the promised land was characterized as "a land flowing with milk and honey" (e.g., Exod 13:5). This moniker highlights that the land was a fertile place, at the very least. Yet this saying seems to have an additional nuance, as Nathan MacDonald points out. This phrase is often repeated both in anticipation of receiving

---

3. McGovern, *Ancient Wine*, 332.

the land prior to the conquest and at the very end of the conquest, or in nostalgic hindsight of what was lost during the exile.[4] As such, it is a "teleological expression,"[5] and even an eschatological one. The statement idealizes the land's fertility in terms of milk and honey,[6] but the land's fertility was chiefly realized through agriculture of fruit trees and vineyards (cf. Deut 8:7–9; Let. Aris. 112).

Prior to entering the land, the biblical texts describe the land's fertility as unparalleled, and they do so with reference to viticulture. When the initial scouts from the exodus generation saw the promised land, they stressed how ripe and heavy the grapes were (Num 13:20), requiring multiple men to carry a single cluster (Num 13:23–24; cf. 32:9; Deut 1:24–25). In addition to suggesting unparalleled fertility, this scene also highlights that the infrastructure for vineyards had already been established by the inhabitants of the land (cf. Neh 9:25). Indeed, the infrastructure was not merely in place already; it produced superb results. As McGovern states, "The highest praise in the ancient world was heaped on the wines of the Phoenicians and their Bronze Age ancestors, the Canaanites."[7] Thus, when Israel took possession of the land of Canaan, it would lead to their enjoyment of the land's great viticulture immediately, rather than needing to wait several years to see those results (cf. Deut 6:11; Josh 24:13; LAB 23.11).

> "The Tale of Sinuhe" (12th c. BCE) is an Egyptian text that depicts ancient Canaan ("Yaa") as a richly fertile land, known for its wine:
>
> It was a splendid land, called Yaa.
> Figs were there, along with grapevines:
>   wine flowed more plentiful than water.
> A land of honey, endless with olives,
>   and fruits of every kind bent down its branches.
> And there was barley there, and emmer;
>   The land lay well, luxuriant with livestock.[8]

Furthermore, the lack of work needed to begin enjoying the land's viticultural produce amplifies how fruit symbolizes leisure. The reason for this is that fruit does not require cooking before consumption.[9] This notion is even present in the story

---

4. MacDonald, *Not Bread Alone*, 55, 108; idem, *What Did*, 3–9, 11.

5. MacDonald, *Not Bread Alone*, 108.

6. See Rebekah Welton, "Ethnography and Biblical Studies: 'A Land Flowing with Milk and Honey' as a Case Study for Re-Contextualizing a Familiar Phrase," *BibInt* 30 (2022): 1–20.

7. McGovern, *Ancient Wine*, 345.

8. John L. Foster, *Ancient Egyptian Literature: An Anthology* (Austin: University of Texas Press, 2001), 131.

9. MacDonald, *What Did*, 29.

of the garden of Eden, where Adam and Eve had access to readily available fruit that did not require work to enjoy, and after their transgression pain was increased in their work (Gen 3:17–19).[10] Thus, the large cluster of grapes that the spies bring back in Numbers 13 provides an image of rest to the weary generation preparing for war and longing for stability in the land. The New Testament author of Hebrews likewise compares entrance into the land with coming into a place of rest (Heb 3–4).

Yet prior to entering into the land, the initial post-exodus generation was kept away from enjoying the land and its viticulture because of their unbelief. Instead, they wandered in the wilderness for forty years (Num 14). During that time, among the grumblings of the people, Dathan and Abiram complained that Moses neither brought them to a land "flowing with milk and honey" nor to a land full of vineyards (Num 16:14). The wilderness was an "evil place" (20:5a), which was contrasted with the land's fertility in terms of grain, figs, pomegranates, water, and vines (20:5b). While the people were in the wilderness, YHWH miraculously provided manna from heaven and water from a traveling rock to sustain them, and YHWH kept them from eating bread, or drinking wine (*yayin*) and beer (*shekar*), so that they would know that YHWH was their God (Deut 29:6). The wilderness generation lacked comforts, as well as the means of producing their own food, highlighting their complete dependence on God. This is something that the generation that entered the land needed to remember as well; even though the land would enable them to produce bread, wine, and beer, the people needed to acknowledge their reliance on God in order to avoid being cast away from the land and its attendant blessings.

The Blessing of Wine and Covenantal Stipulations

Israel's need to rely on God as provider even after they had taken possession of the land is emphasized in the covenant after the exodus. When God gave Israel the law and established a covenant with Moses, explicit stipulations governed covenant life. Corporate obedience would lead to further blessings within the land, such that, among other things, the land would produce an abundance of wine and the people would remain unhindered in their production and enjoyment of it by foreign oppressors, famine, or pestilence. Disobedience, however, would threaten the enjoyment of God's gift.

To be clear, this is not some ancient version of the "prosperity gospel." For one, this dynamic pertains to a historical national covenant with a particular group of people. Additionally, these were promises made to a preindustrial, agrarian society in which most aspects of life were highly precarious. What the pattern of the covenantal stipulations shows, however, is that God's gift was *unconditioned*, given to them without any prior conditions, but it was not *unconditional* in the sense that the people

---

10. MacDonald, *What Did*, 29.

could neglect their covenantal commitments.[11] The land was indeed a gift, and it was a gift that needed to be stewarded according to the terms of the covenant. The covenantal stipulations are chiefly articulated in the Torah, but before outlining how they are expressed it is worth highlighting that wine is often regarded as a divine blessing in its own right.

Two psalms in particular highlight this fact in different ways. Psalm 104 praises God for all his great works throughout creation, including his provision for different wildlife. When the psalmist turns to God's provision for humankind, he chooses to highlight the gift of cultivating plants that cause the earth to bring forth "wine [*yayin*] that gladdens human hearts, oil to make their faces shine, and bread that sustains their hearts" (Ps 104:14–15). The image of God's provision here goes beyond basic needs to include the pleasures of life: oil for cosmetic purposes and wine to be enjoyed for its intoxicating effects ("gladdens hearts"). Even though it is people who cultivate the earth's plants for these purposes, they are cultivating resources that God gave them, and so all of it is ultimately attributed to God's care and provision. Wine is further associated with joy that comes from God in Psalm 4. A sad and weary psalmist cries out to God for his mourning to end, praying, "Fill my heart with joy when their grain and new wine [*tirosh*] abound" (4:7 [4:8 MT]). The psalmist here longs for the kind of joy that accompanies a good harvest (hence *tirosh*), and since God provides the harvest he provides the joy from new wine too. Even from these two examples in the Psalms, it is clear that God is the one who blesses his people through the provision of wine.

Although wine is the result of human ingenuity and hard work, God is the one who provides the natural resources to make wine production possible. All of this is predicated, however, on the ongoing obedience of the people. As Isaiah forecasts at the beginning of his prophetic oracles, the prospect of eating "the good things of the land" (Isa 1:19) is held out as a covenant blessing for those who are obedient to God. Proverbs similarly links agricultural blessing with devotion to God: "honor the Lord with your wealth, with the firstfruits of all your crops; then your barns will be filled to overflowing, and your vats will brim over with new wine [*tirosh*]" (Prov 3:9–10). The way that YHWH is honored in this proverb is through offering him the firstfruits, which refers to a tithe intended for priestly consumption or libationary offerings in sacred space.[12] We will explore temple tithes in more detail in the following chapter, but for now it is worth noting how obedience to God in this way leads to such great agricultural abundance that the storehouses of grain and new wine cannot contain the yields from the harvest. The proverb here reflects the idea that God blesses obedience and also that God is ultimately in control of the agriculture.

---

11. This language is drawn from John M. G. Barclay, *Paul and the Gift* (Grand Rapids: Eerdmans, 2015).

12. Michael V. Fox, *Proverbs 1–9: A New Translation with Introduction and Commentary*, AB 18A (New York: Doubleday, 2000), 152.

God's blessing of the people seems to reach its zenith with the kingdom of Solomon, when the people lived well: "they ate, they drank and they were happy" (1 Kgs 4:20). They also experienced stability and security in the land: "everyone [lived] under their own vine and under their own fig tree" (4:25). This image of flourishing, expressed through the enjoyment of meals and the ability to pursue viticulture, was a blessing that God bestowed to honor the wisdom of Solomon—a wisdom that God in fact gave to Solomon to help him rule well (4:29–34; cf. 3:5–9). Upon receiving that wisdom, Solomon's first move was to throw a feast (*mishteh*) in order to celebrate God's additional blessings (3:15). After Solomon used his wisdom to oversee the construction of the temple (1 Kgs 6–8), YHWH visited him a second time and warned him that the blessings that he and his kingdom were enjoying rested on his ongoing obedience and leadership (9:1–9). If Solomon failed, the people would be removed from the land and the temple would be abandoned (9:7–8). This dynamic illustrates the other side of the prospect of blessings for obedience, which are outlined in more detail in the covenantal stipulations in the Torah.

The covenantal arrangement is stated clearly to the wilderness generation in Deuteronomy 11:26–28:

> See, I am setting before you today a blessing and a curse—the blessing if you obey the commands of the Lord your God that I am giving you today; the curse if you disobey the commands of the Lord your God and turn from the way that I command you today by following other gods, which you have not known.

Throughout Deuteronomy it is repeated that keeping the laws and stipulations of the covenant will allow the Israelites to remain in the land and live a long life within it (e.g., Deut 4:25–26, 40; 6:2–3, 18; 8:1, 6–7, 11–20; 11:8, 16–17, 31–32; 12:1; 15:4–5; 16:20; 25:15; 27:3; 30:18; 32:46–47). When the people keep God's covenant, several positive blessings ensue (28:1–2, 9, 11, 13–14). Both the people and the land will be fruitful (7:12–13; 28:3–5, 9, 11; cf. Lev 26:9). Elsewhere in the Psalms, agricultural fertility is also used as a metaphor for the fertility of the people, where the man who fears YHWH is blessed with a wife like a vine and children like olive trees (Ps 128:3). Deuteronomy similarly affirms that Israel will not be infertile (Deut 7:14), and they will overtake their enemies (7:16; 28:7). These blessings also include weather conducive for agricultural fertility. They will not experience plagues (7:15), and God will provide rain (11:13–14; 28:12; cf. Lev 26:3–5). The resulting fertility of the land will include grain, "new wine" (*tirosh*), and oil (Deut 7:13; 11:14). Indeed, upholding God's laws will lead to a hyperabundance that disrupts the normal annual cycle of harvest and viticultural farming: "your threshing will continue until grape harvest and the grape harvest will continue until planting" (Lev 26:5; cf. 25:19–23).

> After the prophet Elijah calls down fire from heaven upon an altar (which the prophets of Baal were unable to do), Elijah tells King Ahab to go eat and drink (1 Kgs 18:41–42). Previously, Elijah had affirmed that the drought would not end unless he himself prayed for it to happen (17:1). Elijah's command was therefore a proleptic sign to King Ahab that the rain was about to come back. So instead of rationing amid a drought,[13] it was time to feast.

God is steadfast to his covenantal promises, but God will also punish the disobedient and those who do not keep their end of the covenantal stipulations (Deut 7:9–11; 28:15; cf. 28:45, 58–59). YHWH will respond to such unfaithfulness by withholding rain, leading to the inability of the land's soil to produce (11:17; 28:24; cf. Lev 26:20). This obviously stretches far beyond the realm of wine, but a lack of rain would massively impact viticulture. The curses include other aspects of agricultural devastation, such as pestilence and plagues (Deut 28:18, 20–21, 38–39, 42, 59–61; cf. Lev 26:25). The chief curse is the very loss of the land that was promised to them in their experience of exile away from it (Deut 28:47–50, 63–64; cf. 4:27; Lev 26:32–33). In fact, the loss of the land will be seen as a perpetual reminder of their disobedience and failure to keep the covenant (Deut 29:20–28). Leviticus says that the land itself will enjoy the Sabbaths it did not have when the people lived in it (Lev 26:34–35). As part of the curse, they will plant vineyards, and yet the enjoyment of those vineyards will be left for others (Deut 28:30, 33; Lev 26:16–17). Although vineyards will be planted and tended, neither the grapes nor the wine will be enjoyed because it will all be consumed by worms (Deut 28:39). The nation who takes over their land will consume all of their grain, all of their oil, and all of their "new wine [*tirosh*]" (28:51). The people of Israel will no longer enjoy the produce of the land, and neither will God; the sacred sites will be destroyed, and he will no longer smell the fragrant aromas of their offerings and sacrifices (Lev 26:30–31; cf. ch. 6).

However, the final covenantal word is not judgment but restoration. The text anticipates the people turning back to YHWH in obedience (Deut 30:9–10), even in the midst of their exilic experience (cf. 4:30–31), leading to a renewed realization of God's blessings. God will remember the land and the covenant with the original three covenant partners, Abraham, Isaac, and Jacob (Lev 26:42–44). Even though their disobedience resulted in curses, God promises that he will not ultimately reject them (26:44).

At the end of Deuteronomy, Moses pronounces a final blessing and warning to the generation about to enter into the land (Deut 33). The blessing portion of

---

13. Alter, *Hebrew Bible*, 1:510.

his speech resembles the blessings of Melchizedek, Isaac, and Jacob noted earlier, especially with reference to the land's capacity for grain, "new wine" (*tirosh*), and the dew from the heavens (33:28). In making this pronouncement, Moses extends the Abrahamic promises to the next generation—the generation that will finally begin to experience the land's bounty. The promises are genuine, but all of Deuteronomy serves to warn Israel about the dangers of thwarting them. Indeed, in a sad twist, all of the promises that are realized through covenantal obedience can themselves lead to covenantal infidelity. This is ironically the "burden of blessing."[14] After Israel begins to thrive in the land, Moses warns that their reliance on God may dissipate and so activate the covenant curses (cf. ch. 11). Thus, Moses emphasizes that it is necessary to remember their covenantal obligations to avoid this fate.[15]

In this way, the gift of a lush land harkens back to the original place that God gave humanity—the garden of Eden.[16] As many scholars have noted, Genesis 1–3 functions like a prologue to the story of the Old Testament, prefiguring both the reception of the land and exile from it. Indeed, because the land was recognized partly as a gift of viticulture, Israel was often depicted as God's "vineyard." Yet the contexts in which this metaphor is used often address Israel's exile from the land (cf. ch. 11). Nevertheless, at this point we can acknowledge that the metaphor of Israel as God's vineyard underscores how the land was productive viticulturally. Furthermore, exile from God's vineyard is not the end of the story. Restoration in the land is a centerpiece of Israel's eschatological hope, envisioning the consummation of the full blessings that the land has to offer, including viticulture (cf. chs. 13–14). The biblical storyline thus unfolds along a trajectory of reclaiming God's creation through vineyards all the way from the garden of Eden, to the promised land, and on through to the new creation (Isa 65:17–25).[17] Despite the fact that the covenant will be broken and the people will be exiled from the land, God's promise to bless through viticultural abundance is a thread that we will continue to see.

WINE CONSUMPTION ON HOLY DAYS

Ancient Israelites also demonstrated that they upheld wine as a joyous blessing by customarily consuming it during holy days, festivals, and other noteworthy celebrations. As we saw in chapter 4, the average Israelite would have a greater degree of access to wine during yearly festivals and other civic celebrations than they typically enjoyed throughout the year. This meant that wine often had a festive and even liturgical connotation. As such, they consumed wine as part of the religious observance of the occasion itself.

---

14. I owe this phrase to Peter Vogt.
15. MacDonald, *Not Bread Alone*, 83–85.
16. On the comparison of Eden and Canaan, see Green, "Vineyards," 97–111.

17. This theme is traced in Green, "Vineyards."

In the modern world it is common to assume that holiness and alcohol do not mix. In certain parts of the US, at least, we are accustomed to the idea that liquor shops might be closed on Sundays—"the Lord's Day." The assumption is that the sale and consumption of alcohol run counter to the religious significance of the day. Without contravening any county or state laws, it is at least worth acknowledging that this modern assumption would be foreign to ancient Israelites and the biblical authors. Some of the more noteworthy festivals, for which there is biblical evidence of alcohol consumption, include the Feast of Trumpets and Purim, as well as two of the three pilgrim festivals: the Feast of Tabernacles and Passover.

The Feast of Trumpets

During the start of the Feast of Trumpets in Nehemiah's day (cf. Lev 23:23–25), when Jerusalem's walls were finally rebuilt, a great celebration ensued. The people were originally moved to tears when Ezra read and explained the law to them (Neh 8:1–8), but Ezra, Nehemiah, and the other teachers called on them to stop mourning and instead to celebrate, because "the joy of the LORD is your strength" (8:9–10). They told the people to cultivate that joy in this context through the festive celebration of food and "sweet drinks [*mamtaqim*]" (8:10). Instead of mourning, they should enjoy these things because, as the text says twice, "this day is holy" (8:9–10; cf. Lev 23:24). The term that the NIV renders as "sweet drinks" refers simply to "sweetness" in Hebrew, but most scholars understand this to be a reference to alcoholic beverages, such as sweet wines.[18] Contextually, the description of people eating and drinking with great rejoicing during the festival suggests the presence of intoxicants (Neh 8:12). In a parallel account of this scene in 1 Esdras 9:50–55, the text contains an added euphemism of joyful consumption (9:54), highlighting how the "sweet drinks" in Nehemiah were viewed as alcoholic. Thus, rather than *avoiding* alcohol because of the sacredness of the occasion, reading God's law within the rebuilt walls of Jerusalem during the Feast of Trumpets *necessitated* a festive response to God's goodness.

Purim

Purim is the festival that is introduced in the story of Esther, celebrating Israel's great reversal of fortune. On the day that would have undermined the Abrahamic covenant when all the Jewish people were set to be annihilated (Esth 3:6, 13)—the day chosen when Haman cast lots (*pur* in 3:7)—the Jews instead overtook their enemies (9:1). As a festival tale celebrating this great turn of events, Esther is a story that is itself full of feasting. Depending on how one counts them, there are between

---

18. Cf., e.g., Becker, *Rebe*, 126.

eight and ten different banquets (*mishteh*) in the story of Esther. Interestingly, food is never mentioned, only wine (*yayin*; cf. 1:7, 10; 5:6; 7:2, 7–8).[19]

One of the notable features about the feasting in Esther is that they often come in pairs. The story opens with the king throwing a one-hundred-and-eighty-day feast (*mishteh*) for his provincial diplomats (1:3), only to follow that up immediately with a seven-day feast (*mishteh*) in the capital city of Susa for all who would like to attend (1:5). When Esther is made queen in the place of Vashti after gathering virgins from the provinces, the king hosts "a great banquet" (*mishteh*), celebrated as "Esther's banquet" (*mishteh*) (2:18). The king then assembles the virgins from the provinces for "a second time" (2:19). It is unclear why this would be necessary, but at the very least it continues the theme of doublets. When Esther requests a banquet (*mishteh*) with the king and Haman (5:4–6), she asks for another banquet (*mishteh*) on the next day with the two of them (5:8). Then, when the Jews defeat their enemies over two consecutive days in the provinces and the capital, the narrator explains that this is why Purim is celebrated as "a day of joy and feasting [*mishteh*]" (9:17, 19, 22) on two different days in urban and rural settings respectively (mirroring the banquet guests in Esth 1).

Excessive feasting is clearly seen by how it is usually followed up by even more feasting. The ancient historian Herodotus emphasizes the Persian appetite for wine and even how diplomats incorporated it into their decision-making process (*Hist.* 1.133), and Esther likewise highlights ancient Persian indulgence of wine throughout. At the second royal feast in the beginning of the story, there was an abundance of "royal wine" (*yayin*), which was served liberally in golden "goblets" and other extravagant vessels (Esth 1:7). The party had one rule, and one rule only: "drink with no restrictions" (1:8a). Whatever people wanted to drink, the king commanded that it be served to the guests (1:8b). It was during this second regal banquet that the incident with Vashti took place. When King Ahasuerus was "in high spirits from wine" (*yayin* in 1:10), he wanted to parade Vashti around in her crown in front of everyone in attendance (1:11). Perhaps it is implied that she would wear *only* the royal crown, as the Talmud states (b. Megillah 12b). When this command came to Vashti during her own banquet (*mishteh*) with the women (Esth 1:9), she refused (1:12), leading to the search for her replacement.

The feasting thus gives the regal sphere of the story a precariousness, especially at the outset. Yet it is not until Haman is spurned by Mordecai, after Esther is made queen, that there is direct antagonism against the Jewish people. Frustrated that Mordecai did not acknowledge his promotion by bowing (Esth 3:1–2), Haman convinces the king to send out an edict announcing that everyone who belongs to Mordecai's people should be killed.

---

19. MacDonald, *Not Bread Alone*, 207.

> Herodotus notes how customary it was to bow to men of higher rank and status in Persia (*Hist.* 1.134), which we see Queen Esther do herself when she falls prostrate before the king (Esth 8:3). The traditional explanation that Mordecai did not want to worship Haman is foreign to the story. Mordecai refuses to bow due to an ancestral feud, since he was a descendant of Saul and Haman was a descendent of King Agag (cf. 1 Sam 15).[20]

Once Haman and the king had sent off the edict, they "sat down to drink," while the turmoil in the capital ensued (Esth 3:15).[21] The posture is one of hubris and smug celebration—a feast that comes far too soon (cf. ch. 10 of the present book). It is also set in sharp contrast to Esther's decision to fast upon hearing this news (Esth 4:16; cf. ch. 8 of the present book).

Excessive feasting is also one of the ways that the story deploys hyperbole, which is seen elsewhere in Haman's plot to kill every Jew and the excessive height of the pole for impaling Mordecai, making the story *carnivalesque* in character.[22] Since Esther is an etiology for the origin of the festival of Purim, that festive spirit runs throughout the retelling of the story. This is especially demonstrated by one tradition that dictates that, during the public reading of Esther, celebrants ought to consume enough alcohol that they are unable to distinguish between shouts of "blessed be Mordecai" and "cursed be Haman" (b. Megillah 7b).[23] This later tradition, at the very least, is clearly rooted in the festive alcohol consumption already present in the story itself and serves to celebrate the survival of the Jewish people.

The Feast of Tabernacles

The Feast of Tabernacles was a harvest-time celebration commemorating God's provision for his people during the wilderness wanderings.[24] Celebrants would dwell in makeshift tents (*sukkot*) as a reminder that God continues to provide for his people through the harvest of grain and grapes (Deut 16:13). The seven-day festival (Lev 23:34), which would take place in the middle of the seventh month of the Hebrew calendar (Ethanim/Tishri), culminated in a final eighth day as a special convocation (cf. Lev 23:36; Num 29:35; Neh 8:18; John 7:37; cf., e.g., Jub. 32.27–29; Philo, *Spec. Laws* 1.189; 2.204; *Moses* 2.153; Josephus, *Ant.* 3.10.4; 11.5.5; 11.5.8; 12.7.7). No work was to be conducted on the first or eighth day, but otherwise people

---

20. For further discussion, see John Anthony Dunne, *Esther and Her Elusive God: How a Secular Story Functions as Scripture* (Eugene, OR: Wipf & Stock, 2014), 35–40.

21. Imbibing is clearer in the LXX (*kōthōnizomai*).

22. So Adele Berlin, *The JPS Bible Commentary: Esther* (Philadelphia: Jewish Publication Society, 2001), xvi–xxii.

23. For more discussion on rabbinic thought surrounding Purim, including the exhortation to restraint in the midst of great feasting during Purim, see Rosenblum, *Rabbinic Drinking*, 187–89.

24. For an extensive study, see Håkan Ulfgard, *The Story of Sukkot: The Setting, Shaping, and Sequel of the Biblical Feast of Tabernacles*, BGBE 34 (Tübingen: Mohr Siebeck, 1998).

were free to work. Dwelling in booths at harvest time was likely strategic for vintners in particular (cf. ch. 4) since it provided a way to identify the most opportune time to start harvesting. Biblical texts do not mention wine consumption overtly in any Feast of Tabernacles passage, though one text might allude to it euphemistically (2 Chr 7:8–10). Many passages, however, do prescribe libationary offerings of wine (cf. ch. 6), and, as I argue later in this book (cf. ch. 13), the festival informs Amos's epilogue about the eschatological abundance of wine that will accompany the rebuilding of David's tent (*sukkah* in Amos 9:11; see 9:11–15). Despite the lack of references to wine consumption, though, it is hardly controversial that a festival linked to the grape harvest would celebrate wine.

In fact, the Greek philosopher Plutarch, writing in the late first or early second century CE, compared both the Feast of Tabernacles and the Sabbath with the bacchanalia associated with the adherence to Dionysus, the Greek god of wine (*Mor.* 671D–E). It was probably the case that some Jews did syncretistically interpret their religious festivals and customs in Dionysian terms, but many others would have been revulsed by the association (cf. 2 Macc 6:7). For our purposes, it is simply worth noting that the Feast of Tabernacles and the Sabbath were known for wine consumption by the time of Plutarch, at least (on the Sabbath, cf. also b. Eruvin 61a).

As the tradition of the Feast of Tabernacles developed, the public reading for the festival eventually came to be Ecclesiastes. On the one hand, the melancholy of the text fits the meandering vibe of the wilderness generation. Yet Ecclesiastes consistently upholds the desire to enjoy the pleasures of life, including food and drink, for as long as one has life, which coheres with the ethos of harvest celebration as well (cf. ch. 9).

Passover

The traditional Passover seder, which celebrates God's deliverance of Israel out of Egypt, is well-known for including the consumption of four cups of wine, each of which has its own symbolic representation (cf. m. Pesahim 10).[25] Surprisingly, though, in the original instructions for the Passover meal in Exodus, there are no references to wine as part of the celebration outside of prescribed libationary offerings (cf. ch. 6). Wine is also not mentioned in the descriptions of Passover when Israel entered the land after the conquest (Josh 5:10–12), when King Josiah led reforms to celebrate Passover as it was originally intended (2 Kgs 23:21–22; cf. 2 Chr 35:1–19), and in Ezekiel's vision of the festival's role in the restored temple era (Ezek 45:21–25). Indeed, nowhere outside of the records of the Last Supper does the Bible ever suggest that wine was consumed during Passover (Matt 26:27–29; Mark 14:23–25; Luke 22:17–18, 20; 1 Cor 11:25). Technically these passages never mention wine; only

---

25. On the seder's development, see Baruch Bokser, *The Origins of the Seder* (Berkeley: University of California Press, 1984). For a succinct summary of rabbinic regulations related to the four-cups tradition, see Rosenblum, *Rabbinic Drinking*, 183–87.

"the cup" and "the fruit of the vine" are mentioned. But Jesus's comments about his blood suggest that he and his disciples were all consuming red wine together (and no one would be consuming grape juice in the spring; cf. ch. 2). The earliest extant reference to consuming wine in the Passover tradition is in Jubilees 49.6 ("and all of Israel remained eating the flesh of the Passover and drinking wine and praising and blessing and glorifying the Lord the God of their fathers"), which predates Jesus by a couple centuries (2nd c. BCE).[26] Clearly, the incorporation of wine into the celebration of Passover must predate the writing of Jubilees at least, but whether the four-cups tradition was known prior to the second century BCE is a separate question altogether (cf. ch. 15).

Subsequent Passover tradition assigned Song of Songs, a poetic celebration of sexual intimacy, for public reading during the festival. In making this move, Song of Songs was read as an allegory for God's love for Israel—a love so strong that he brought her out of Egypt. In later Christian tradition, a similar allegorical reading developed about Christ's love for the church. Yet as longstanding as these reading strategies are within Judaism and Christianity, they do not do justice to the subject matter of sexuality. Sexuality in the Song need not be read as an allegory of the love of God when it is recognized that sexuality itself is a gift from a loving God. As the poetic lyrics of the Song demonstrate, one good gift from God informs the meaning of the others.

THE SONG OF SONGS: WINE AND SEXUALITY IN THE LAND

In the Song—which oscillates between perspectives of a female lover, a male lover, and her friends—a young couple and their love is compared to nature, landscapes, agriculture, viticulture, plants, animals, and wine. As such, their relationship is conceptualized with reference to, and in the context of, the land.[27] This also includes the many euphemisms for sexual organs, sex acts, and sexual desire throughout the Song.

The relationship between sexuality and wine culture is important to recognize, but it is often obscured by those who read the Song allegorically. If the text is not read as celebrating the blessing of sex, then the way that it extols the blessing of wine will likely be lost on the reader as well. Indeed, the allegorical readings of the Song seem far more motivated by discomfort with sexually explicit literature in Scripture than with how metaphors typically work. At their most basic level, metaphors compare how one thing is like another thing. The thing described is called

---

26. O. S. Wintermute, "Jubilees," *OTP* 2:140.
27. See esp. Elaine T. James, *Landscapes of the Song of Songs: Poetry and Place* (Oxford: Oxford University Press, 2017).

the *tenor*, and the imagery deployed is called the *vehicle*. Thus, it would strain the use of metaphor to say that a metaphorical vehicle in the Song—such as a vineyard or wine—represents a specific sex act (the tenor), and then say that the tenor is an additional vehicle for some element of divine love (another tenor). No allegory is needed in a text that already uses metaphor and euphemism to describe its tenor or subject matter—sexuality. To be sure, marriage and sexuality are metaphors elsewhere for the divine-human relationship, as we see in Hosea and in the "bride of Christ" imagery. Yet in those instances, sexuality is the vehicle, whereas in the Song it is the tenor. And as the tenor in the Song, sexuality is often associated with the vehicle of viticulture, accentuating the nuances of joy and blessing associated with alcohol production and consumption.

The Song often compares love with wine and affirms that love is greater. When the Hebrew word for "love" (*dod*) appears in the plural (*dodim*) in the Song, which is often, it refers to acts of love, or *lovemaking*.[28] The young woman declares that the young man's lovemaking is "more delightful than wine [*yayin*]" (Song 1:2), which is echoed again in the "praise" of their friends (*yayin* in 1:4). Later on, the male lover exclaims to the woman, "How much more pleasing is your love than wine [*yayin*]" (4:10b).[29] These comparisons convey that both wine and sex are pleasurable embodied experiences in their own right and suggest that the romantic couple enjoyed them together. Yet the poetic lyrics affirm that lovemaking is superior to wine because of its greater ability to intoxicate and bring pleasure. The friends of the couple intimate as much when they call for them to "drink your fill of love" (5:1b). The NIV translation here does not do justice to what the friends are commending to the couple by obscuring the references to lovemaking (*dodim*) and to getting drunk (*shakar*). The friends are extending the imagery of sex as a superior form of wine consumption, and thus their summons to drunkenness is a metaphorical plea to experience the full inebriation of sex.[30]

Elsewhere the Song continues the theme of the superiority of lovemaking over wine. When the woman declares that she wants to be led "to the banquet hall" (Heb. "house of wine [*yayin*]"), where the male's "banner over her" or "gaze upon her" will be loving (Song 2:4), one may assume that this describes something like a flirtatious night out grabbing drinks. Yet it more likely extends lovemaking's superiority to wine by conveying that places where lovemaking occurs become a kind of wine bar. The latter option is supported by the embrace mentioned in verse 6, where one of the male's hands is placed under the woman's head and the other is around her body, suggesting that they are lying down. In other words, to be in that position of warm

---

28. Duane Garrett and Paul R. House, *Song of Songs and Lamentations*, WBC 23B (Nashville: Thomas Nelson, 2004), 200.

29. The NIV obscures the plural form of *dod* (i.e., "lovemaking") throughout the Song.

30. Roland E. Murphy, *The Song of Songs: A Commentary on the Book of Canticles of the Song of Songs*, Hermeneia (Minneapolis: Fortress, 1990), 157.

sexual embrace is like being transported to a wine bar. In another poem the woman wishes she could take the man to her mother's house and give him "spiced wine [*yayin*] to drink, the nectar [*asis*] of my pomegranates" (8:2). These do not refer to her mother's hospitality of offering the young man alcoholic beverages but rather refer to sexual actions shared between the two of them. That the woman is referring to a sexual act in the home that she grew up in is paralleled with the reference to arousing the male lover under the apple tree where he was both conceived and birthed (8:5).

Passionate kissing is also a sex act compared with wine consumption in the Song. As the woman longs for the "the kisses of his mouth" (1:2), she compares the young man's mouth with "sweetness itself [*mamtaqqim*]" (5:16a), using the same Hebrew term for a sweet alcoholic beverage as we saw in Nehemiah 8:10. Likewise, the man affirms that the best wine (*yayin*) is in the woman's mouth (Song 7:9 [7:10 MT]). In response to the male lover, the woman adds, "May the wine go straight to my beloved, flowing gently over lips and teeth" (7:9).[31] The comparison probably suggests that wine was being consumed while the couple was kissing; the lovers' mouths still taste like wine.

In addition to the mouth, other body parts are associated with wine. The woman compares her own body to a garden full of delights for the male lover to enjoy (Song 4:16). Thus, the consummation of their sexual union is described by the man as enjoyment of what the garden has to offer:

> I have come into my garden, my sister, my bride;
>> I have gathered my myrrh with my spice.
> I have eaten my honeycomb and my honey;
>> I have drunk my wine [*yayin*] and my milk. (Song 5:1)

Later on, the young man tells his lover that her "navel is a rounded goblet that never lacks blended wine [*mezeg*]" (7:2 [7:3 MT]). Although some scholars argue that this is a straightforward reference to the navel or belly button,[32] most likely the "navel" is a metonymy for the woman's genitalia.[33] This is likely because the man's description of the woman's body moves upward from her feet to her head, with the reference to the navel appearing after the thighs and before the belly (7:1–5). Furthermore, as we saw above, lovemaking has already been overtly compared with alcohol (1:2, 4; 4:10; 5:1).[34] In the same chapter, the male lover also likens the woman's breasts to "clusters of grapes on the vine" (7:8), drawing attention to their similarity in shape, though

---

31. Wine does not reappear in the Hebrew; the NIV clarifies what is in view.

32. So, e.g., Richard S. Hess, *Song of Songs*, BCOTWP (Grand Rapids: Baker, 2005), 214.

33. So, e.g., Tremper Longman III, *Song of Songs*, NICOT (Grand Rapids: Eerdmans, 2001), 194–95; Iain M. Duguid, *The Song of Songs: An Introduction and Commentary*, TOTC 19 (Downers Grove, IL: IVP Academic, 2015), 144.

34. Duguid, *Song*, 144.

elsewhere the woman's breasts are likened to twin gazelles (cf. 4:5; 7:3), suggesting that in the heat of the moment there is no need for consistent imagery.

Viticulture is also used to represent sexuality in the Song. We have already seen how the Song compares breasts to grape clusters (7:8), and bodies to gardens (4:16), but references to vineyards also abound. Sexual arousal in particular is compared to the viticultural cycle. Love should not be awakened before the right time (2:7; 3:5; 8:4), which is then described in terms of the growth of a vineyard during spring. This alludes to the fragrances of flowers in vineyards (1:14), as well as to the blossoming and budding of vines (2:13; 6:11). In one instance that demonstrates how a vineyard in springtime represents the awakening of sexual desire, the couple plans to get away to the "countryside" (7:11). The young woman says to her beloved that they should "go early to the vineyards to see if the vines have budded, if their blossoms have opened, and if the pomegranates are in bloom—there I will give you my love [*dodim*]" (7:12 [7:13 MT]). Here the springtime vineyard does not merely represent sexual arousal but also becomes a site of sexual encounter as well.

With vineyards representing sexuality in the Song, the warning about foxes in the vineyards should be interpreted as threats to the couple's intimacy: "catch for us the foxes, the little foxes that ruin the vineyards, our vineyards that are in bloom" (Song 2:15). The image of the vineyards being in bloom further demonstrates the point above about the springtime vineyard representing sexual arousal. The reference to foxes in the Song could then refer to any number of hindrances to the couple that they need to guard against, just as vintners need to protect their vineyards from pesky foxes.

> Varro, the first-century BCE Roman agriculturalist, writes that when vineyards grow vines along the ground, "the foxes often share the harvest with man" (*Rust.* 1.8.5–6 [Hooper and Ash, LCL]). The threat of foxes, and the use of trellises to keep foxes away from the fruit, is even the subject of one of Aesop's fables, "The Fox and the Grapes." Foxes also destroy vineyards, though in a highly unusual way, in the story of Samson (Judg 15:4–5).

The metaphorical references to vineyards in the Song also help to make sense of instances where literal vineyards are juxtaposed with metaphorical ones. Early in the Song, the woman declares, "My mother's sons were angry with me and made me take care of the vineyards; my own vineyard I had to neglect" (Song 1:6). The vineyards that the woman has to care for now are the literal vineyards owned by her brothers, but the reference to her own vineyard should be understood metaphorically as a reference to her beauty and sexuality. The NIV translation implies that the woman was forced to neglect her own literal vineyard in service of her brothers' literal vineyards, but this is misguided for a few reasons. First, women did not typically own their own vineyards (though see Prov 31:16), so this is an unlikely reading from the get-go.[35] Second, the Hebrew more accurately says that she did not keep her vineyard, which, if taken to mean that she was sexually active, could explain the

---

35. Welton, *"He Is a Glutton,"* 122.

anger of her brothers. Otherwise, that element is left unexplained.[36] Given the stress on not awakening love before its proper time throughout the Song, it is preferable to understand her own lack of attention to her vineyard as suggesting her inattention to ancient conventions of beauty.[37] As she mentions, she has been laboring in the vineyards in the open sun, and her skin has been overly exposed (1:5–6). Additionally, her devotion has been dedicated to the family vineyards, and so she has not tended to *her own*. Most likely this aspect of the woman's story is meant to highlight how her exploration of her own sexuality was suppressed by her brothers, which sets up the exploratory nature of the eroticism in what follows throughout the Song.

The metaphorical interpretation of her own vineyard in Song 1:6 also anticipates the metaphorical references to her body with elements of viticulture in the rest of the poetic material.[38] Additionally, the juxtaposition of literal vineyards with a metaphorical reference to the woman's sexuality seems to occur again later in the Song, when the woman compares her "vineyard" with the vineyards owned by Solomon: "Solomon had a vineyard in Baal Hamon; he let out his vineyard to tenants. Each was to bring for its fruit a thousand shekels of silver. *But my own vineyard is mine to give*; the thousand shekels are for you, Solomon, and two hundred are for those who tend its fruit" (8:11–12; emphasis added). By stressing that her own vineyard (her body) is for her to give, the woman is exercising her agency and selectivity with regard to her sexuality.

As we have seen, the lyrics of the Song simultaneously celebrate the land and its associated blessings (vineyards, wine, etc.), alongside the celebration of sexuality. Again, one of God's great gifts to humanity is used metaphorically to describe another one. An important caveat to this is provided by Elaine James, who stresses that the metaphors of the bodies and the sexuality of the lovers should not be overdetermined so as to miss the poetic emphasis on how the lovers are also delighting in the goodness of the natural world.[39] In other words, the vehicle is not merely chosen to convey something about the delightfulness of the tenor; the vehicle itself is a source of delight. So metaphors, once recognized and understood, are not to be dispensed with, because they remain constitutive of the meaning conveyed. The joy and pleasure often associated with both sexuality and alcohol consumption makes the comparison apt.

CONCLUSION

The joy of wine is clearly one of the main varietals of wine symbolism in the Bible, to draw upon my earlier metaphor (cf. ch. 1). As a divine gift, then, wine could be:

---

36. See also Alter, *Hebrew Bible*, 3:588–89.
37. Hess, *Song*, 57–59.
38. James, *Landscapes*, 35–36.
39. See James, *Landscapes*, 55–87.

(a) invoked when blessing others and was used to bless others; (b) crafted from the land that God gave to Israel; (c) consumed when celebrating the great acts of God in Israel's history during religious festivals; and (d) enjoyed as a pleasurable experience that affirms bodily existence. Yet the blessings of wine and a thriving viticulture were covenantally conditioned on the obedience of the people. God blesses an obedient people with pleasurable alcohol, and yet there is a dark flipside to that if the covenant is broken. The privation of God's good gifts as a curse of the covenant will be explored in chapter 11.

All gifts are designed to initiate and maintain relationships, and this is true with God's gift of the land with its capacity for viticulture. As a reciprocal gift exchange, then, the blessings of the land were given back to God in the form of offerings and libations in sacred space. It is to the other side of this covenantal gift exchange that we now turn.

RELEVANT QUESTIONS

1. How might we recognize a glass of wine today as a covenantal blessing from God now that, for many of us, wine is not tethered to our life in the land?
2. What habits can help us grow in our appreciation of life's pleasures (including but not limited to alcoholic beverages) that reorient us to the land and the places that produced them?

CHAPTER 6

ALCOHOL IN THE TEMPLE SYSTEM

If the land and its abundance constitute covenantal gifts from God, as we saw in the previous chapter, then in the temple system we see the other side of the gift exchange in which the covenant people gave gifts back to God. What farmers produced in the land is what God provided, and so returning some of the best produce in the form of offerings was only fitting. Sacred space, the temple and the tabernacle before it, was the primary site of that gift exchange. This was not merely because it was the place where offerings were made but also because a thriving sacrificial cult would further lead to more abundance in the land as a covenantal blessing.[1] As a result, the temple became known as the center of agricultural fertility and a source of great food and wine.

With reference to alcohol in particular, the gifts given back to God in this instance included tithes given to priests for their own consumption and also libations poured out to God in worship upon the altar. In this chapter we will look at the use of alcohol for tithes and offerings, and then turn to see how sacred space itself came to be viewed as a place where an abundance of food and alcohol could be found to delight God's people.

TITHES OF ALCOHOL

As we saw in chapter 4, viticultural laws required that vintners dedicate the fourth year of the vineyard's produce to YHWH (Lev 19:24), offer the firstfruits of every harvest (Exod 34:26; Num 18:12–13; Deut 26:1–2; cf. Prov 3:9–10) and the first yield from their vats (Exod 22:28–29; Deut 18:4), and then also tithe 10 percent of the annual yields of wine (*tirosh* in Deut 12:17–18; 14:22–23; Neh 10:37, 39 [10:38, 40 MT]; 2 Chr 31:5; *khamar* in Ezra 7:22). This means that in addition to mundane usage, every vineyard in Israel had a sacred purpose. As Leviticus says, every tithe is holy because it belongs to YHWH (Lev 27:30).

What ancient Israelites were meant to do with the offerings of firstfruits and other

---

1. The words "cult" and "cultic" in academic biblical studies designate rituals within any sacrificial system. These terms should not be confused with the sociological term "cult" for fringe religious groups, or indeed with the occult.

tithes differs in some respects between Numbers and Deuteronomy. In Numbers, part of the purpose of the tithe was to provide for the material needs of the priests and Levites, since the nature of their service restricted them from holding any land of their own (Num 18:1–32). What the people tithed was essentially designed to take care of the Levites and their families. This included the offering of firstfruits and "the finest new wine [*tirosh*]" with it (18:12; Heb. "the fat of the new wine"). Once the Levites had received all the tithes, they were then supposed to tithe a tenth from what they received and give that to the priests as a "tithe of the tithe" (18:25–32), including the yields from the winepress (18:27, 30). As we will see in chapter 7, priests were meant to abstain from consuming alcohol while serving in sacred space, but when they were not serving, they were free to consume (cf., e.g., Jdt 11:13; Tob 1:7 [see NRSVue]; Jub. 32.10–15; T. Levi 8.5; 11QT^a [11Q19] XXI, 3–4; Philo, *Virtues* 95; Josephus, *J.W.* 5.13.6).

In Deuteronomy, there is still a notion that the tithes were meant for Levites because of their unique role within the twelve tribes (Deut 18:1–5; cf. *tirosh* in 18:4), but the tithes were not meant exclusively for the Levites. Instead, they were supposed to be consumed by the person offering them along with their local Levites at "the place the LORD your God will choose" to dwell (12:17–19; 14:22–23). These versions of the tithe describe a cultic meal. The firstfruits were also meant to be taken to the house of YHWH and given to the priests (26:1–11), though it is unclear if they were all meant to consume them together. For those who lived too far away from "the place the LORD your God will choose," they did not need to bring their tithes with them to sacred space but could instead purchase what they would like to consume when they got there (14:24–26). Listed as options for people to enjoy along with their local Levites are both wine (*yayin*) and beer (*shekar*) in Deuteronomy 14:26. On every third year, the annual tithe was meant to be collected locally for the Levites as well as the less fortunate, including orphans, widows, and sojourners (14:28–29; 26:12–13).

It is notable that "new wine" (*tirosh*) is not mentioned for the meal with local Levites in Deuteronomy 14:26, since the annual tithe mentioned in verse 23 includes *tirosh*. The fact that *tirosh* is not mentioned highlights how it is often used with reference to the harvest of fresh wine (hence its inclusion in the annual tithe). Since verse 26 describes wine that was purchased, it is not referring to fresh wine from the recent vintage (hence *yayin*). For those who doubt whether *yayin* refers to a fermented beverage, the coupling with *shekar* here demonstrates that the consumption of alcohol was part of one's tithe to God, which was meant to be consumed with Levites, no less.

The reason for the disparity in the purpose and procedure of tithing between Numbers and Deuteronomy is difficult

> The apostle Paul appeals to priests in 1 Corinthians and how they receive food sacrifices and offerings in the temple (9:13) when arguing for his apostolic right to receive benefits from the congregation for his apostolic labor (9:4). He also appeals to other kinds of workers as well, like those who plant vineyards and are able to enjoy their fruit (9:7).

to determine, with chronological development and geographical variation being common suggestions, but it is possible that the difference is a matter of emphasis, since Levites were recipients of the tithe either way.[2] Without resolving the matter here, it is simply worth noting how alcohol was explicitly included in the holy tithes given to Levites and priests, reinforcing that all good things ultimately come from God (cf. ch. 5).

Some priests and Levites were specifically appointed to oversee the sacred vessels used for offerings, such as those that stored oil, wine (*yayin*), spices, and grain (1 Chr 9:29; cf. Neh 12:44). Nehemiah records that after the exile the tithes were collected in each town of Judah by the Levites (Neh 10:37), which adds another development to the procedures of tithing noted in Numbers and Deuteronomy. Nehemiah also reports how the oversight of the sacred vessels could be mismanaged, as in the case of a priest named Eliashib, who did not distribute the tithes properly from the storehouses to the Levites (13:4–9), including wine (*tirosh* in 13:5, 12), and so others had to be appointed to oversee the process (13:13).

LIBATIONS OF ALCOHOL

In addition to being a holy tithe, alcohol was also used as a libation, otherwise known as a drink offering. A libation was a ceremonial offering of liquid that was poured out upon the altar (Exod 29:40–41). In the tabernacle, and also the temple, there was a separate altar for burning incense where no drink offerings were allowed (Exod 30:9). Specialized jars and bowls were used for libations (Exod 25:29; 37:16; Num 4:7; Jer 52:19; cf. Zech 9:15), which were set on the table where the bread of presence was placed (Num 4:7).[3] Typically, a drink offering would accompany a grain offering or a burnt offering at the end of the sacrificial process (cf. 2 Chr 29:35a).

Libations were also incorporated into Israel's major festivals throughout the calendar. This includes Passover (Num 28:16–25; cf. 28:24), the Feast of Firstfruits during the Festival of Weeks (Num 28:26–31), the Feast of Trumpets (Num 29:6), the Day of Atonement (Num 29:11), and the Feast of Tabernacles (Lev 23:37; Num 29:16, 18–19, 21–22, 24–25, 27–28, 30–31, 33–34, 37–39). Likewise, in Ezekiel's vision of the restored temple (Ezek 40–48), he anticipates the renewed use of libations for festivals, new moons, and Sabbaths (Ezek 45:17). Yet in none of these passages is the precise contents of

> Paul utilizes imagery of libations, and specifically with reference to how they accompany the end of a sacrifice. He tells the Philippians that his ministry accompanied their faithful service by saying that he was "being poured out like a drink offering on the sacrifice and service coming from your faith" (Phil 2:17). At the end of 2 Timothy, he reflects on the end of his life as if he was "already being poured out like a drink offering" (2 Tim 4:6a; cf. Isa 53:12), referring to his imminent death (2 Tim 4:6b–7).

---

2. For a harmonized reading, see J. Gordon McConville, *Law and Theology in Deuteronomy*, JSOTSup 33 (Sheffield: JSOT, 1984), 68–87.

3. E.g., very shallow bowls called *phiale* were used for Greco-Roman libations. See Milette Gaifman, *The Art of Libation in Classical Athens* (New Haven: Yale University Press, 2018).

the drink offering specified (cf. also Ezra 7:17; 1 Chr 29:21; Joel 1:9; 2:14; Heb 9:10). However, it is most likely implied to be wine because, as we will see, wine is the most frequently mentioned libationary liquid. Indeed, if the text does not expressly state that the content was different than wine, we should assume it was wine.

The Content of Libations

The Bible is quite clear about the use of wine (*yayin*) for libations and drink offerings (Exod 29:40; Lev 23:13; Num 15:4–5, 7, 9–10; 28:14; Hos 9:4; cf. also Sir 50:15; Jub. 6.3; Josephus, *Ant.* 3.9.4; Philo, *Dreams* 2.183; *Spec. Laws* 1.134, 179). The Torah prescribes the precise amount to accompany each kind of sacrifice (Num 15:24; 29:24, 27, 30, 33, 37), which seems to correspond in proportion to the size of the animal. In other words, the more blood, the more wine. The libations were measured in hins, which are about four quarts or three and a half liters. For example, a quarter of a hin for a lamb (Num 15:5), a third of a hin for a ram (Num 15:7), and a half of a hin for a bull (Num 15:9–10). In Ezra, Darius the king decreed that the priests should be supported in their duties and that the people should send the priests whatever they might need on a daily basis, including wheat, wine (*khamar*), oil, and salt, so that they could make the prescribed offerings (Ezra 6:9–10; cf. 1 Esd 6:30–31). When Hannah finally gave birth to Samuel after praying for a son, she returned to the temple to offer up a young bull, flour, and wine (*yayin*) as gifts of gratitude to God (1 Sam 1:24), highlighting that wine held cultic significance for her even though she personally abstained (cf. ch. 7).

> Lamenting the destruction of the temple, 2 Baruch (1st or 2nd c. CE) imaginatively questions why wine would even be necessary to produce any more: "And you, vine, why do you still give your wine? For an offering will not be given again from you in Zion, and the first fruits will not again be offered" (2 Bar. 10.10).[4]

Beer seems to be another prescribed libationary liquid in the Torah. In Numbers 28:1–8, *shekar* is expressly required for libations accompanying daily food offerings at the sanctuary.[5] The *shekar* libations were to be "a quarter of a hin" for each lamb that was sacrificed (28:7). It is possible that the weekly Sabbath drink offerings mentioned next in Numbers 28 were also *shekar* even though the contents are not stated, since no new liquid is mentioned and the Sabbath drink offerings also accompanied the sacrifice of lambs (28:9–10). Further, it is not until verse 14 that

---

4. A. F. J. Klijn, "2 (Syriac Apocalypse of) Baruch," *OTP* 1:624.
5. For *shekar* as beer in this passage, see, e.g., Homan, "Beer, Barley, and שֵׁכָר," 25; idem, "Beer and Its Drinkers," 84; Welton, *"He Is a Glutton"*, 113.

wine (*yayin*) is mentioned for the drink offerings at the start of each new month (28:14–15).⁶ It would make sense that weekly libations of alcohol would be *shekar*, as the daily ones explicitly are, since beer could be produced more readily and also because grape-based and date-based alcohols were dependent on the harvest and good storage.⁷ As noted in chapter 2, most scholars view *shekar* as either a generic term for fermented beverages or one specifically made from dates or grapes, and it is believed further that *shekar* cannot be beer since elsewhere we do not get a sense that biblical libations were made from grain. Yet, given the prominence of grain offerings within Israel's cult and the fact that elsewhere in the ANE grain-based alcohols were used regularly for libations (cf., e.g., The Shamash Hymn [*COS* 1:117]; The Birth of Shulgi in the Temple of Nippur [*COS* 1:172]), it is highly likely that Israel would also use grain-based alcohol for libations.⁸ The only fruit-based liquids allowed at the altar according to the Mishnah, however, were those derived from olives and grapes (e.g., m. Terumot 11:3). If this tradition had ancient pedigree, which I doubt, this would rule out a date-based understanding of *shekar* and would only leave the possibility of a grape-based alcohol. Yet the grape-based explanation fails to explain why the term *shekar* exists and what distinct purpose mentioning *shekar* serves here. Even though *shekar* is not mentioned as often as *yayin* for biblical libations, the daily and weekly use of *shekar* in the cult speaks to its prominence, and I would argue that it helps to identify what it is too (i.e., beer). When it comes to the debate about *shekar*, this passage is perhaps the most controversial, given its use in the cult. Even the NIV, which often translates *shekar* as "beer" (cf. 1 Sam 1:15; Prov 20:1; 31:4, 6; Isa 24:9; 28:7; 29:9; 56:12), opts for "fermented drink" in this instance.⁹ I suspect that what is ultimately driving scholarly concerns here is modern sensibilities about beer more than anything else.

> *Shekar* is arguably listed as a distinct libationary liquid in the Temple Scroll (1st c. BCE–1st c. CE) from Qumran (11QTᵃ [11Q19] XXI, 9b–10): "They shall rejoice on this d[ay] at the appointed ti[me when they shall begin] to pour out a libation of drink [*shekar*], a new wine [*yayin khadash*], over the altar to YHWH, year by year."¹⁰ This translation seems to equate *shekar* and new wine appositionally, but I would argue that they are paralleled as two types of libationary liquids.

---

6. So too Welton, *"He Is a Glutton"*, 113.

7. Ezra 6:9 (noted above) is not likely an exception to this; King Darius decreed that the priests should be supplied daily with things like wine, not that they make daily offerings of wine.

8. The prohibition against grain offerings that are leavened (Lev 2:11) does not rule out the use of beer because alcoholic beverages are never regarded as "leavened" in the OT, and beer could be made without using baked bread (cf. ch. 4).

9. The NIV translates *shekar* generically as "fermented drink" elsewhere (Lev 10:9; Num 6:3; 28:7; Deut 14:26; 29:6; Judg 13:4, 7, 14), and as "drinks" on two occasions (Isa 5:11, 22).

10. Cf. *DSSSE*, 2:1243.

There are also multiple references to libations poured out to foreign gods as well (2 Kgs 16:13, 15; Isa 57:6; Jer 7:18; 19:13; 32:29; 44:17–19, 25; Ezek 20:28), though without specifying their contents. In one instance, however, it is a wine libation (*yayin* in Deut 32:37–38). In another, "mixed wine" (*mimsak*) is filled for the god Destiny, presumably for the purposes of libation (Isa 65:11).

There are only three explicit examples of nonalcoholic libations in the Bible. The first example is another non-Yahwistic libation like those just noted, where the psalmist refers to his refusal to make a libation of blood to other gods (Ps 16:4; cf. Jewish libations of blood in Philo, *Spec. Laws* 1.205; cf. Sib. Or. 8.493–94). The second is when David offered water to YHWH from the well of Bethlehem after refusing to drink it (1 Chr 11:18). The third and final example is the use of water libations during the Feast of Tabernacles. As we saw in chapter 5, this feast centered on the harvest, celebrating the rains that made it possible, and included a tradition of pouring out water on the altar each day (cf. m. Sukkah 4:9–10; 5:1–2).[11] These three examples reinforce the fact that alcohol was the default libationary liquid in the Bible—both *yayin* and *shekar*.

Of course, not everything could be libated, and traditions developed to specify what was off-limits. The Mishnah, Tosefta (2nd–3rd c. CE), and the Babylonian Talmud prohibit improperly stored wine that turned into sour wine and vinegar (m. Sheqalim 4:9; m. Terumot 3:1; 11:2–3; m. Mo'ed Qatan 2:2; t. Menahot 9:9; b. Bava Batra 97b). The Talmud also prohibits both weak wines made from pomace and white wine (b. Bava Batra 97b).[12] Philo mentioned that drinks mixed with honey were not permitted (*Spec. Laws* 1.291). Outside of Judaism, proclivities about libations existed as well. Pliny the Elder, for example, notes that wines made by people who trampled grapes with "sore feet" were not permitted. Greek wines were also not allowed because they "contain water," meaning that only undiluted wine was permitted for their deities (*Nat.* 14.23.119 [Rackham, LCL]). The divine preference for undiluted offerings was also shared by YHWH (cf. Isa 1:22). Indeed, according to Judges 9, wine (*tirosh*) even *cheers* God (9:13), which is intriguing enough to warrant extended discussion.

Libation in Judges 9

The statement that wine (*tirosh*) cheers God is part of a tale told by Jotham, a son of Gideon and brother of Abimelech. Abimelech had just conspired with his uncles to kill all of his brothers and so make him king among the Shechemites (Judg 9:1–5). As a veiled critique of what just transpired, Jotham, the lone surviving brother, tells the Shechemites a tale about a forest, full of trees, trying to determine which one of

---

11. Jesus's offer of rivers of living water during the Feast of Tabernacles alludes to this background of water libation (John 7:37–39).

12. See Frankel, *Wine and Oil*, 200.

them should rule over all the others (9:7–15). As they deliberated, the trees looked to four main candidates: the olive tree, the fig tree, the vine, and then finally the thornbush. The first three each declined to rule because they were busy doing more germane things. The vine, for instance, asks, "Shall I leave my wine [*tirosh*] that cheers God and men and go hold sway over the trees?" (9:13 ESV). Then the thornbush finally says that if the other trees want to be subservient to it, they can take shelter in its shade. Otherwise, a fire will come and destroy them all (9:15).

Jotham's tale contains a provocative window into the cultic practice of libations.[13] The euphemism "cheers" points to the intoxicating effects of *tirosh* (cf. Ps 104:15), and the notion that *tirosh* could have such an effect *on God* implies that libations are in view (intriguingly, this is the only biblical passage that refers to *tirosh* for libation). Yet because the Hebrew word for God here is the plural *elohim*, some translators prefer to see this as a reference to the gods (so, e.g., NIV; RSV; NRSVue). But despite the formal plurality, *elohim* often refers to the one God of Israel, and so several translations render *elohim* here as "God" (see, e.g., ESV; KJV; NKJV; NASB; CSB). Whenever plural gods are intended in Judges, there are key contextual clues, which are lacking here in Judges 9:13.

> The contextual clues in Judges that make a plural referent for *elohim* clear is the addition of (a) adjectives (i.e., "new gods" [5:8], "other gods" [2:12, 17, 19; 10:13–14], "foreign gods" [10:16]); (b) pronouns (i.e., "their god(s)" [2:3; 3:6; 8:33]), with the exception of YHWH being explicitly named (i.e., "the Lord their God" [3:7; 8:34]); and (c) overt reference to nations (2:12; 6:10; 10:6) or idols (17:5; 18:24, 31). In a few instances, *elohim* also refers to a *singular non-Yahwistic deity* (i.e., Baal [6:31; 8:33], Chemosh [11:24], Dagon [16:23–24], and "their god" [9:27]). The one contextual argument that could favor a plural reference to gods is that *elohim* is paired with the plural noun "men,"[14] but given how Judges qualifies every other reference to non-Yahwistic deities, it seems more likely that the unqualified *elohim* refers to Israel's God.

In fact, the earliest interpreters of Judges 9, the translators of both Greek traditions, clearly opt for the singular form of *theos*, and thus have Israel's God in view (Judg 9:13 LXX [A, B]). Further, since Jotham is telling the story, he is more likely referring to the God of Israel than to non-Yahwistic deities, even though the Shechemites had their own god (9:27). Moreover, at the outset of the riddle, Jotham

---

13. E.g., George F. Moore, *Judges: A Critical and Exegetical Commentary*, ICC (Edinburgh: T&T Clark, 1910), 247–48.

14. So Barry G. Webb, *The Book of Judges*, NICOT (Grand Rapids: Eerdmans, 2012), 276.

implores the Shechemites to listen to his words so that "God [*elohim*] may listen to you" (9:7). In the light of this discussion, there seems to be no real justification for translating *elohim* as "gods" in Judges 9:13. The motivation behind the plural translation appears to be one of embarrassment: *surely God is not inebriated by alcohol!* This is probably why one of the Greek versions of Judges says that wine cheers humanity with a merriment that comes from God (Judg 9:13 LXX [A]), and also why Pseudo-Philo's rewritten version of Judges 9 makes no mention of God being cheered (LAB 37.2).

Undoubtedly this is a personification since God did not literally consume drink offerings. But this is no different than the anthropomorphic notion that sacrifices and offerings constitute a "meal" for God, where the altar is his table and the aroma ascending to heaven "pleases" him (cf., e.g., Gen 8:21).[15] Some biblical texts, such as Psalm 50:12–14, critique the idea that God actually consumed the food or drink offered to him. It should be clear, however, that even in rejecting the idea that God *literally* consumed what was offered to him, the passage implies that enough people understood sacrifices and offerings this way. Both notions of a savory aroma "pleasing" God and fresh wine "cheering" God are personifications that highlight that God accepts the offerings given to him.

As the narrative of Judges 9 progresses after Jotham's tale, we see that his parable has a prophetic quality to it. Sometime later a division emerged between Abimelech and the people of Shechem, and a battle ensued. The Shechemites recruited a warrior called Gaal, son of Ebed, by throwing a big festival for him and treading the winepress (9:27). As Jotham's tale anticipates, the town of Shechem was decimated by fire (9:49), but Abimelech was ultimately defeated before he could set fire again (9:52–55). The narrative also mirrors Jotham's story with the reference to winemaking since it was during "a festival in the temple of their god" (9:27) that Gaal and his people decided to help Shechem. This showcases the broad application of what the vine says in Jotham's tale about the way wine cheers the divine and human realm (9:13).

THE TEMPLE AS A SOURCE OF GREAT FOOD AND WINE

As part of the covenantal system of blessings for obedience and curses for disobedience (cf. ch. 5), the temple became the locus of agricultural fertility. A thriving cult meant thriving produce. If the agricultural yield was plentiful, then the resources sent to the temple would be exceptional, but if the output was down for any reason, that would impact what could be brought to the temple. Whether there would be an increase or

---

15. See Gary A. Anderson, "Sacrifice and Sacrificial Offerings (OT)," *ABD* 5:872, 877–78.

decrease in yield was also seen as a barometer of Israel's fidelity to the covenant with YHWH. This dynamic is explicated in Solomon's original festival celebrating the construction of the first temple. At that inaugural ceremony, Solomon commanded the people to come to the temple to pray if there was a lack of rain or if they were under the threat of plagues (1 Kgs 8:35–38; 2 Chr 6:26–30; cf. 2 Chr 20:9). If the people turned to request forgiveness from God, God would heal the land of drought, plagues, and pestilence because of his presence in the temple (2 Chr 7:12–14). Thus, there was a circularity to the gift giving within the temple system.

Because of this dynamic, the temple came to be viewed not merely as a catalyst for producing great resources but also as the site where they could be found. Since Israel's tithes and offerings were sent to the site of sacred space, that meant that the best food and wine in the land were given to the Levites, the priests, and to YHWH. The psalmist delights in being able to "dwell in the house of the LORD forever" (Ps 23:6), immediately after speaking of the great table and the overflowing cup that YHWH provides him (23:5; cf. ch. 10). As the psalmist declares elsewhere, "We are filled with the good things of your house, of your holy temple" (Ps 65:4b; cf. 63:1–5). Indeed, the psalmist believed that the temple was the source of these things in a more ultimate sense, since the temple was only able to store these great things if God first provided weather conducive to the harvests (65:9–13). God's house was also a place of provision because it was the site where regular feasting occurred (cf. Jdt 16:20). When the second temple was destroyed by Rome in 70 CE, the arch of Titus was built near the Roman Forum to commemorate the event. Among the temple's plunder displayed in the arch's engraving is a prominent menorah, along with a wine goblet.[16]

The temple as a source of, and catalyst for, great resources is portrayed symbolically through the representation of rivers issuing from it in multiple texts. This image is quite common and may have originally developed out of the fact that a spring lay underneath the temple—the Shiloah (Isa 8:6). There was also a reservoir nearby (Let. Arist. 89–90). In biblical depictions, sometimes the temple's river is composed of water, as in the "living water" of Zechariah 14:8 and the fountain in Joel 3:18. Unlike typical water, Ezekiel's vision of the temple's river emphasizes its regenerative properties for the land (Ezek 47:1–12). But even more atypical of water, two of the biblical depictions of the rivers that flow from God's house describe it as *intoxicating*.

The first example of this comes in Psalm 36. The psalmist proclaims the goodness of YHWH, with particular attention given to his love, justice, and faithfulness (Ps 36:5–6). When the psalmist turns to speak of God's provision, he affirms that those who "take refuge in the shadow of your wings" (36:7) will be able to "feast on

---

16. Cf. Othmar Keel, *Symbolism of the Biblical World: Ancient Near Eastern Iconography and the Book of Psalms*, trans. Timothy J. Hallett (Winona Lake, IN: Eisenbrauns, 1997), 343.

the abundance of your house" and to "drink from your river of delights" (36:8 [36:9 MT]). The "feasting" here is about being satiated (Heb. *ravah*) and clearly develops the idea that the cultic center is the site of all of the best food and wine in Israel. The LXX makes the scene unmistakably one of joyful intoxication in God's presence: "they will be intoxicated [*methyskō*] with the fatness of your house, and you will give them drink from the wadi of your delights" (35:9 NETS). The delightful wadi/river is symbolic of the intoxicating beverages that would be consumed at this feast.

The second reference to an intoxicating river issuing from God's house comes from Psalm 46. The psalmist declares, "There is a river whose streams make glad the city of God," a river that comes from "the holy place where the Most High dwells" (Ps 46:4 [46:5 MT]). As David Toshio Tsumura has convincingly argued, the language of "making glad" (Heb. *samakh*) is elsewhere used as part of a euphemism for intoxication (Ps 104:15; Eccl 10:19; cf. Ps 4:7 [4:8 MT]; Isa 24:7), and is associated with the effects of wine rather than river water.[17] Additionally, in context, Psalm 46:3 refers to how the waters of the river "roar and foam," which are terms that could convey fermentation (cf. Deut 32:14; Ps 75:8; and see ch. 2 for carbonation-based foaming).[18] The river's contents therefore gladden God's people just like wine does.

The intoxicating nature of the river in Psalm 46 was recognized by some early interpreters. For example, Philo interpreted it as symbolic of the "divine word" (*Dreams* 2.246–47), which "intoxicates" through its ability to bring true insight into God's wisdom. This, of course, turns the notion of intoxication on its head. Nevertheless, the point is that Philo recognized the connotations of intoxication, even if he explained the meaning differently. Notably, he says that this divine word is received "unmixed" in the "holy goblet of true joy" that comes from "the cup-bearer of God, the master of the feast" (*Dreams* 2.248–49). This interpretation of intoxication is similar to how the Odes of Solomon (2nd c. CE) speak of a great river associated with the temple (6.8) that gives life (6.10–18), and which is later called intoxicating (11.6–7). However, this intoxication is qualified immediately as one that does not lead to ignorance or foolishness (11.8–10).

Together Psalms 36 and 46 utilize the image of an intoxicating river flowing from sacred space as an imaginative extension of the temple's abundance and fertility. This type of imagery continued to develop and expand. The prophet Micah, for example, spoke of a river made of olive oil (Mic 6:7), but additionally rivers of wine can be found in a number of later texts alongside rivers of other contents, like milk, honey, and olive oil (cf. Apoc. Paul 23–27; 2 En. 8.5–6 [Slavonic; J]; Sib. Or. 2.318; 8.209–12). All of these images, which develop out of passages like Psalms 36 and 46, reinforce the notion of the temple as the locus of agricultural blessing and the

---

17. David Toshio Tsumura, "The Literary Structure of Psalm 46, 2–8," *AJBI* 6 (1980): 39.

18. Tsumura, "Literary Structure," 38–39.

source of the very best that God provides. With respect to these psalms, if the temple is thriving, then *everyone* will taste that great, intoxicating river.

CONCLUSION

In this chapter we have seen how prominent alcohol was in relation to Israel's temple system. Wine is mentioned the most with respect to the literary record as a tithe and drink offering, but beer was prevalent also since it was part of the daily libations and the weekly Sabbath libations (Num 28:7–10). Additionally, alongside wine, beer was consumed as part of an annual tithe (Deut 14:26).

In the wider context of Israel's covenant with YHWH, we see that God gave his people gifts in the form of viticultural abundance (a major symbolic varietal in Scripture; cf. ch. 1), and the people were meant to give gifts back to God in the form of tithes and offerings. The temple was the key site for the unfolding of this covenantal pattern, since it was the place where tithes and libations were directed, and it was the place from which blessings flowed back through the land. We will see how the inverse of the covenantal pattern leads to disaster in chapter 11, and also how the restored eschatological temple relates to thriving agriculture in chapter 13. Both of those discussions further develop the role of the temple in the covenantal scheme, and in the productivity of their viticulture.

In the next two chapters we switch gears, moving on from the role of alcohol and viticulture within the covenantal scheme to the question of abstinence. Why would certain people abstain from alcohol (ch. 8), and were there any restrictions to doing so (ch. 7)? Indeed, in the light of our discussion in this chapter we can ask, if God wants people to abstain from alcohol unilaterally, *why doesn't he himself abstain?*

RELEVANT QUESTIONS

1. How can we foster appreciation for God's covenantal gifts, including wine and beer, while simultaneously recognizing that the best belongs to God, even without a temple system today?
2. How should the association of wine and beer with sacred space contribute to our appreciation and respect for both?

CHAPTER 7

RESTRICTIONS AND PROHIBITIONS OF ALCOHOL

Many readers of Scripture, especially in certain contexts, might assume that whatever the Bible has to say about alcohol, it primarily restricts and prohibits its consumption. In this chapter, we will look at the explicit commands and laws that we find in Scripture related to the consumption of alcohol, especially for the Nazirites, priests, and church leaders. Laws pertaining to the cultivation of vineyards, the tithing of wine, and the use of libations in sacred space have already been explored in chapter 6. In this chapter we turn to how the Old Testament and New Testament restrict alcohol consumption in their respective ways. As we will see, there are actually very few restrictive passages altogether, and despite common assumptions the Bible nowhere prohibits the consumption of alcohol for all people at all times.

EXPLICIT RESTRICTIONS IN THE OLD TESTAMENT

In some Christian circles one could be forgiven for assuming that "thou shalt not drink alcohol" is one of the Ten Commandments. As we saw in chapters 5–6, God instead blessed Israel with alcohol through the covenant and prescribed its ritual use in the tabernacle and the temple. It was far from prohibited categorically. If God never wanted ancient Israel to drink wine (*yayin*), beer (*shekar*), "or anything you wish," for example, then God would surely not have prescribed their ritual consumption "in the presence of the Lord your God" (e.g., Deut 14:26). Moreover, if God required abstinence from his people, it would be quite strange, considering that God himself did not abstain from receiving alcohol through ritual libations (e.g., Num 28:7, 14). There are plenty of Old Testament laws concerned with prohibiting certain foods (cf. kosher laws, or *kashruth*, in, e.g., Lev 11; Deut 14), but alcoholic beverages are not among them. The food laws, of course, are clear on the consumption of pork for Israel—it should never be consumed (e.g., Lev 11:7; Deut 14:8), and so it should also never be used ritually in sacred space (cf. 1 Macc 1:47). If it was unclean for the people, it was also unclean for YHWH. The only exception to this principle was the sacrificial blood of animals offered to YHWH, which the people were not permitted to consume (Lev 17:13–14). Alcohol, however, was appropriate for both ritual and mundane use within covenant life. Later developments in rabbinic thinking, which provided the foundation for a kosher diet, would go on to prescribe certain laws around alcohol. However, these prescriptions included prohibiting gentile involvement in wine production, specifically when the grapes were crushed and while the wine was fermenting,[1] but they did not prohibit Jewish consumption of wine itself.

Despite the absence of alcohol from the Ten Commandments and the food laws, the Torah prescribes limits to alcohol consumption for two groups of people. The first are priests. Priests were to refrain from wine (*yayin*) and beer (*shekar*) while serving in sacred space (Lev 10:9), ensuring that they were able to perform their sacred obligations with accuracy and care (Lev 10:10). In Ezekiel's vision of the restored temple, this prohibition continues: "no priest is to drink wine [*yayin*] when he enters the inner court" (Ezek 44:21). Additionally, other ancient Jewish texts emphasize this pattern of priestly behavior. Yet this prohibition only applied to priests *while they were serving in sacred space*, and not at any other times. This is clear from multiple passages that affirm that priests regularly enjoyed wine, in particular as part of the tithes from the people (cf. ch. 6).

> The historian Josephus (1st c. CE) writes about temple sacrifices and describes how priests were characterized by being sober (*Ag. Ap.* 2.23). This association fits the prescriptions from the Old Testament regarding priestly sobriety while performing temple duties (cf. Ps.-Hec. 199; Philo, *Spec. Laws* 1.98, 100, 247–50; *Drunkenness* 126–27, 129, 137–38; Josephus, *J.W.* 5.5.7; *Ant.* 3.12.2). Priestly abstinence was also not limited to Israelite cultic practice (Plutarch, *Mor.* V 353b).

Nazirites are the second group that receive restrictions on alcohol. Specifically, Nazirites are supposed to abstain from alcohol during the time in which they undertake a voluntary vow. This vow, which anyone in Israel could make (Num 6:1–2), includes a pledge of abstinence from wine (*yayin*) and beer (*shekar*), grapes themselves, as well as vinegar made from either *yayin* or *shekar* (Num 6:3–4). As noted in chapter 2, acetic acid can develop from any type of alcohol, regardless of the source of the fermentable sugars (i.e., grapes, grain, etc.). The reason for abstaining from these things seems to be to avoid accidentally consuming something fermented. Grapes themselves can ferment on their own, especially if the skin is slightly punctured, which allows the yeast on the skins to convert the sugars inside.[2] Vinegar also can contain alcohol, especially earlier in the oxidization process. Yet why does the list of prohibited items for Nazirites undertaking their vow not include grain as well, especially if *shekar* refers to beer (cf. ch. 2)? There are two probable reasons: (a) grain was too central to ancient Israelite diet; and (b) grains are not susceptible to fermentation in the same way that grapes are.

In addition to abstaining from fermented beverages, alcohol-derived products, and fermented fruit, Numbers 6 also prescribes that Nazirites avoid cutting their hair (6:5) and avoid contacting a dead body (6:6–8). The vow could extend beyond these matters to include anything from which one wanted to abstain (6:21). The vow

---

1. Odelia E. Alroy, "Kosher Wine," *Judaism* 39.4 (1990): 452.   2. Sasson, "Blood," 404.

was not a permanent commitment of abstinence, however, but was a temporary obligation (6:4, 8, 12; cf. also 1 Macc 3:49; Philo, *Spec. Laws* 1.247–51). Once the duration of the vow ended, Nazirites underwent a special set of rituals to signify its conclusion (Num 6:13). They would start by bringing various offerings and sacrifices to the tabernacle, including libations (6:15, 17). Then they would shave their heads at the front of the tabernacle and toss the hair into the fire as one of several offerings (6:18). After the rituals were completed, Nazirites were then permitted to drink wine (*yayin*) once more (6:20).[3] It was only during the time of the vow that abstinence was binding. The vow was so serious, in fact, that encouraging Nazirites to drink wine (*yayin*) while they were on their vow, or indeed forcing them to do so, came under the prophetic ire of Amos (Amos 2:12).[4]

Aside from these laws for priests and Nazirites, there are no other restrictions in the Torah regarding alcohol consumption itself. It is noteworthy that these two sets of laws were both temporary, and they both pertained to certain people with particular offices, responsibilities, and commitments. They did not concern the average Israelite. The key distinction between the two sets of laws was that priestly abstinence was more iterative than Nazirite abstinence, but neither were expected to completely abstain from alcohol forever.

There is one final passage worth mentioning from the Torah, which is the only law that appears to relate to excess alcohol. To be sure, the Torah does narrate scenes of drunkenness that lead to sexual exploitation (cf. ch. 10). For our purposes in this chapter, however, those scenes do not constitute examples of explicit restrictions of alcohol. The final explicit command within the Torah appears in the brief account of the rebellious son in Deuteronomy 21:18–21. Moses declared that rebellious sons should be handled by the community in the following way: the parents should present their son to the townspeople and declare that their son has been "a glutton and drunkard" (Deut 21:20). Then the people should stone him in order to remove the evil from their midst (21:21). There is not a lot of detail here, which makes interpreting the legal matter rather difficult. If the text is restricting alcohol consumption in some way, it would appear to restrict excess. Yet there is probably more going on with this legislation than a restriction of excessive consumption. The son is specifically called "rebellious," which could suggest that excessive consumption has resulted in a pattern of behavior that is neither beneficial to his family nor to the community—hence the corporate judgment.

Furthermore, this passage should be read in light of Deuteronomy as a whole, which develops the theme of how covenant blessings—including the land and its

---

3. Numbers 6:20 does not overtly permit *shekar* once the vow is complete, but neither does it permit grapes or vinegar. Wine (*yayin*) is most likely a synecdoche for all food items that were temporarily prohibited.

4. M. Daniel Carroll R. notes that the *hiphil* stem suggests they were obliging the Nazirites to drink rather than merely offering wine to them (*The Book of Amos*, NICOT [Grand Rapids: Eerdmans, 2020], 195n244).

abundance—can cause people to forget God and assume they are self-reliant.[5] Nathan MacDonald suggests, therefore, that the rebellious son is likely a cipher for the collective people of Israel, who have become rebellious because of their abundance.[6] Moreover, as Rebekah Welton contends, the death penalty would be an extreme form of punishment for excessive eating alone, especially since abundance is often a sign of blessing (cf. ch. 5, and see the blessing of restoration in chs. 13–14).[7] In addition, as she points out, "there are no biblical laws against excessive consumption."[8] Why would the community need to expunge evil by executing someone who eats and drinks too much? Welton intriguingly argues that what is actually condemned here in Deuteronomy 21 is the *kind* of consumption, not the mere quantity of it.[9] Specifically, she maintains that idolatrous practices are in view, as a comparison of terminology in the passage with Isaiah 65:11–12 highlights, implying that the rebellion here is particularly a cultic rebellion against YHWH.[10] Capital punishment is more fitting for how the Old Testament addresses "idolatry, apostasy, and conjuration" elsewhere, making idolatry the most likely context for the rebellious consumption.[11] Thus, it seems preferable to read Deuteronomy 21 as not simply legislating against excess but rather as either condemning what excessive consumption could lead to (i.e., rebellion) or as reproving the context in which the rebellious consumption occurs (i.e., idolatrous worship).

Outside of the Torah, Proverbs contains a couple of passages that are sometimes viewed as outright prohibitions of alcohol. These are the prohibition against even looking at wine (Prov 23), and the maternal advice to King Lemuel that wine is not fit for kings (Prov 31). While these are examples of proverbial wisdom, and not direct laws, they nevertheless constitute biblical restrictions on alcohol worth considering here. We will look at each in turn, beginning with Proverbs 23:29–35, which deserves to be cited in full:

> Who has woe? Who has sorrow?
> > Who has strife? Who has complaints?
> > Who has needless bruises? Who has bloodshot eyes?
> Those who linger over wine [*yayin*],
> > who go to sample bowls of mixed wine [*mimsak*].
> Do not gaze at wine [*yayin*] when it is red,
> > when it sparkles in the cup,
> > when it goes down smoothly!
> In the end it bites like a snake

---

5. MacDonald, *Not Bread Alone*, 70–99.
6. MacDonald, *Not Bread Alone*, 97n76.
7. Welton, *"He Is a Glutton"*, 143–80.
8. Welton, *"He Is a Glutton"*, 270.
9. Welton, *"He Is a Glutton"*, 224–82.
10. Welton, *"He Is a Glutton"*, 235–37, cf. 250, 263–64, 280.
11. Welton, *"He Is a Glutton"*, 292.

and poisons like a viper.
Your eyes will see strange sights,
and your mind will imagine confusing things.
You will be like one sleeping on the high seas,
lying on top of the rigging.
"They hit me," you will say, "but I'm not hurt!
They beat me, but I don't feel it!
When will I wake up
so I can find another drink?" (Prov 23:29–35)

This proverb clearly conveys the effects of excess alcohol. It stings, poisons, causes disorientated vision, impacts mental capacities, impairs motor skills, and even leads to a disorientating hangover that feels like one had just been in a fight (and given the "needless bruising," they may have actually been in one).[12] Given all of this potential for where alcohol could lead, the proverb warns against even looking at wine. In other words, it offers the warning to avoid the catalyst that could result in such a sorry condition—the initial gaze. Michael Fox notes that the language of the wine "sparkling" (so the NIV) refers to the appearance of the eye of the consumer in the cup (the Hebrew reads woodenly: "when it gives in the cup his eye"). The point is that the eye would be reflected in the cup because of the dark color of the wine, which prefigures how the drunkard's own eyes will become bloodshot from excessive consumption in verse 29.[13]

This is clearly not a literal prohibition against looking at wine, however. The Greek translation of the verse makes this clear by prohibiting drunkenness (*methyskō*) from wine (Prov 23:31 LXX). In other words, the Greek rendering of the proverb unpacks the original Hebrew prohibition with reference to its ultimate concern or telos, namely, drunkenness. The Greek version of this proverb is what informs Ephesians 5:18, which contains the exact same wording about avoiding drunkenness from wine (more below in the NT section). Although this portion of the Hebrew proverb does not mention drunkenness (though see the context of 23:19–21), it certainly does describe drunkenness with its many depictions of the effects of excessive consumption. As a proverb then, this passage is providing wisdom and warnings for people to consider and should be interpreted in the light of how Proverbs addresses other forms of excess that are associated with folly and wickedness. These include such behaviors and signs of excess as sloth (6:6–11; 10:5, 26; 13:4; 15:19; 19:15, 24; 20:4, 13a; 21:25; 22:13; 23:21; 24:33–34; 26:13–16), sexuality (2:16–22; 5:1–23; 6:24–35; 7:5–27; 22:14; 23:27–28; 29:3; 30:19–20), wealth (28:8, 22), gluttony (23:2–3,

---

12. Michael V. Fox, *Proverbs 10–31*, AYB (New Haven: Yale University Press, 2009), 740–42.

13. Fox, *Proverbs 10–31*, 741.

20–21; 28:7), and choice food (15:17; 17:1; 23:3, 6). If the critique of drunkenness in Proverbs 23 is taken to be an outright prohibition of alcohol consumption, such would constitute a selective approach to Proverbs's critique of excess—unless one was also willing to say that Proverbs prohibits sleep, sex, money, and food. What is needed, then, is moderation and appropriate use of these good things.

Proverbs 31 also contains advice that King Lemuel received from his mother, including that drinking wine (*yayin*) and beer (*shekar*) is not fitting for kings (Prov 31:4). The logic of this regal restriction, which is similar to the priestly prohibition noted earlier, is that wine can compromise the capacities of kings to rule and adjudicate wisely, particularly with respect to caring for the poor (31:5). It appears that the proverb is straightforwardly calling for King Lemuel to commit to total abstinence of alcohol. This is unlikely, however, not least because Proverbs 31 goes on to commend a "woman of valor" who, among other things, purchases and oversees a vineyard (31:16), which would be used for wine production.

Yet more importantly, when we look closely at the maternal guidance in the opening of the proverb, King Lemuel's mother appears to be speaking hyperbolically about the potential dangers of alcohol for kings—namely, the dereliction of duty. As Bruce Waltke points out, the hyperbolic statements about alcohol in verse 4 are clear from the hyperbolic statements about women in verse 3.[14] King Lemuel's mother warns him to avoid giving his "strength" and his "way" to women, who can "ruin kings" (31:3). Simply put, verse 4 is not a call to abstinence any more than verse 3 is a call to celibacy. The point of the passage as a whole, as Richard J. Clifford states, is to provide "an admonition against the imprudent use of sex and alcohol . . . lest the luxury-loving king *forget* the *poor*."[15] As King Lemuel's mother continues her sage instruction, she says that wine (*yayin*) and beer (*shekar*) should be given to the poor because *they do have things that they need to forget* (31:6–7). In other words, "kings should not drink so that they do not forget the poor, while the poor should drink so that they may forget."[16] Waltke, among others, takes this as a "sarcastic" and "cynical" comment,[17] but more likely the point of the passage is that kings, who have abundant access to such resources, should provide consolation for the poor.[18]

> Sirach 31:27–29 (NRSVue) speaks clearly to the value of consuming wine (*oinos*) in moderation:
>
> Wine is very life to humans
>   if taken in moderation.
> What is life to one who is without wine?
>   It has been created to make people happy.
> Wine drunk at the proper time and in moderation
>   is rejoicing of heart and gladness of soul.
> Wine drunk to excess leads to bitterness of spirit,
>   to quarrels and stumbling.

---

14. Bruce K. Waltke, *The Book of Proverbs: Chapters 15–31*, NICOT (Grand Rapids: Eerdmans, 2005), 507.

15. Richard J. Clifford, *Proverbs: A Commentary*, OTL (Louisville: Westminster John Knox, 1999), 270 (emphases original).

16. Rebekah Welton, "Too Much Food and Drink: Gluttony and Intoxication," in *T&T Clark Handbook of Food in the Hebrew Bible and Ancient Israel*, ed. Janling Fu, Cynthia Shafer-Elliott, and Carol Meyers (London: T&T Clark, 2022), 359.

17. Waltke, *Proverbs: Chapters 15–31*, 508–9.

18. E.g., Dubach, *Trunkenheit*, 148–50; Welton, "Too Much Food," 359.

If the poor need alcohol in order to forget their misery, how much more do they need those in power to be mindful of them to help reduce their misery?

These are the only texts in the Old Testament that contain overt restrictions of alcohol. The portrayal of drunkenness, and even the mockery of it, will be addressed later on (cf. chs. 10 and 12). Insofar as the Old Testament does contain explicit restrictions, the context and the responsibilities of the consumer are crucial for interpreting them. Even Proverbs 23:31, with its advice against gazing at wine, needs to be understood in relation to how Proverbs uniquely provides wisdom and warnings. There are no laws in the Old Testament that dictate that all people at all times should abstain from alcohol. But does that change when we get to the New Testament?

EXPLICIT RESTRICTIONS IN THE NEW TESTAMENT

In the New Testament, there is actually less material that restricts alcohol consumption than in the Old Testament. Intriguingly, alcohol restriction is missing from the sort of places we might expect to find it, especially if early Christians did abstain from alcohol, such as the record of the Jerusalem Council in Acts 15. Four prohibitions were given to gentiles joining the Jewish Jesus-followers out of deference to Jewish scruples. Although three out of the four pertained to Jewish food laws, none involved alcohol (Acts 15:20; cf. 15:29; 21:25). In fact, the broader context of Amos 9:11–12, which the apostle James cited at the Jerusalem Council (Acts 15:15–17), speaks of mountains flowing with sweet wine (Amos 9:13, Heb. *asis*). This is elided from James's quotation, but it is interesting to consider since the Council concluded that four prohibitions were sufficient for gentile believers in Christ, and nothing was made of intoxicating beverages.

As we saw in the Old Testament, the New Testament does contain restrictions of alcohol consumption for those with particular leadership responsibilities. For instance, in the Pastoral Epistles, overseers should not be drunkards (1 Tim 3:3; Titus 1:7), and deacons must not be "indulging in much wine [*oinos*]" (1 Tim 3:8). The older men ought to be "temperate," or perhaps "sober" (Titus 2:2), and the older women should not be "addicted to much wine [*oinos*]" (Titus 2:3). The word translated here as "addicted" is a Greek verb for enslavement: "do not be enslaved to wine." These restrictions were not calls for total abstinence, however. In fact, it was the false teachers who were promoting such ascetic practices (1 Tim 4:3a), which undermine God's good creation and the fact that everything should be received with thanksgiving (1 Tim 4:3b–5). Abstinence also conflicted with the perceived medicinal value of wine (*oinos* in 1 Tim 5:23), which Paul needed to help Timothy recognize (cf. ch. 8).

The only other overt restriction in the New Testament comes in Ephesians 5:18, in which Paul writes, "Do not get drunk on wine [*oinos*], which leads to debauchery." As noted above, Paul is here drawing on the Greek translation of Proverbs 23:31 (or a similar proverbial tradition which derived from it).[19] In context, the matter of excessive wine consumption is part of what it means to be wise rather than foolish (Eph 5:15, 17), to utilize one's time well "because the days are evil" (5:16), and to do the Lord's will (5:17). The rationale for the prohibition of excess wine consumption in verse 18 is provided in terms of the result of drunkenness—the vice of debauchery (*asōtia*), or sexual indulgence, which extends the ultimate concern of the Greek translation of Proverbs further.

It is important to stress here that Paul is not saying that debauchery is *in wine itself*. One ancient Jewish text does say that debauchery is inherently contained within wine (*oinos* in T. Jud. 14.1; 1st c. BCE–1st c. CE). Like Paul, that text draws on the language of Proverbs 23:31 LXX, and it states that the "evil spirit" of debauchery (*asōtia*) is found within wine (*oinos*) itself (T. Jud. 16.1). Although both texts speak of debauchery in relation to wine, the Testament of Judah sees debauchery as one of four "evil spirits" *contained within wine* (along with "desire," "heated passion," and "sordid greed"),[20] whereas Paul affirms that *drunkenness through wine* leads to debauchery.[21] Accordingly, the Testament of Judah says something much more drastic about wine than Paul does in Ephesians. Furthermore, even though the Testament of Judah speaks strongly against wine generally, in the very next verse it points to the possibility of drinking wine in moderation: "If you drink wine [*oinos*] in merriment, showing due respect for the fear of God, you shall live. But if you drink without restraint and the fear of God departs, the result is drunkenness and shamelessness sneaks in" (16.2).[22]

> "'Wine maketh glad the heart of man' (Ps civ. 15), says the Psalmist. How then does wine [*oinos*] produce drunkenness? For it cannot be that one and the same thing should work opposite effects. Drunkenness then surely does not arise from wine [*oinos*], but from intemperance."
>
> St. Chrysostom (4th–5th c. CE), *Homilies on Ephesians*, "Homily 19" (*NPNF*[1] 13:138)

The Pauline prohibition in Ephesians 5:18 applies to all Christians, not just leaders; instead of being filled with wine, believers should be filled with the Spirit. Both the prohibition and the command are second-person plural (i.e., "y'all"), as are the pronouns "you" and "your" in the passage. Furthermore, after the prohibition and command in verse 18, the passage develops with references to public acts of worship (Eph 5:19–20). The corporate context for the passage highlights that the concern here is not strictly with personal consumption of alcohol but rather with communal disruption. It is related in some respects to Paul's frustrations with the eucharistic drunkenness of some of the Corinthians (1 Cor 11:17–22), as we will see in the lengthier treatments on both

---

19. See Thorsten Moritz, *A Profound Mystery: The Use of the Old Testament in Ephesians*, NovTSup 85 (Leiden, Brill: 1997), 94.
20. H. C. Kee, "Testaments of the Twelve Patriarchs," *OTP* 1:799.
21. William J. Larkin, *Ephesians: A Handbook on the Greek Text*, BHGNT (Waco, TX: Baylor University Press, 2009), 124.
22. Kee, "Testaments," 799.

of these passages in chapter 16. For now, it is sufficient to note that Ephesians 5:18 contains a clear restriction of excess consumption.

Because Paul believed that drunkenness could lead someone to act foolishly, he regarded drunkenness as a vice. It can be found in two separate vice lists designed to highlight the types of habits that will characterize people who will not inherit the kingdom of God (1 Cor 6:10; Gal 5:21). Drunkenness belongs to the realm of the flesh (Gal 5:21) and outsiders (1 Cor 5:11), and when it becomes a habitual lifestyle, one is vulnerable to all of the other vices that are uncharacteristic of God's kingdom. Some ancient philosophers, like Plato, considered drunkenness to be a vice, but believed that without drunkenness one could not develop certain virtues like self-control (cf. Plato, *Laws* II 270e–272d).[23] For Paul, however, drunkenness was not a vice that could give way to virtue but was a vice that could hinder one from entering the kingdom of God. Drunkenness is not a fruit of the Spirit in Galatians—what we might consider to be a virtue list—even though the ninefold nature of the *singular* fruit of the Spirit resembles a grape cluster with nine grapes (Gal 5:22–23). Instead, drunkenness is one of the vicious works of the flesh (5:19–21). Thus, a life characterized by drunkenness is not the means to self-control, but rather the energizing work of the Spirit produces it (cf. 5:23). The contrast between drunkenness and the work of the Spirit in Galatians parallels Ephesians 5:18, where the contrast to being drunk with wine is to be filled with the Spirit (cf. ch. 16).

> Drunkenness is surprisingly not listed as a vice in most New Testament vice lists (cf. Rom 1:29–31; 2:8–9; 2 Cor 12:20–21; Eph 5:5; Col 3:5, 8–9; 1 Tim 1:9–11; 2 Tim 3:1–5), though it does appear in 1 Peter 4:7. Outside of the New Testament, drunkenness is listed more regularly in early Christian literature (e.g., 1 Clem. 30.1; Herm. 65.5–6; Acts Andr. 57[6]; Acts John 35; Acts Thom. 36, 58, 124; cf. also 3 Bar. 8.5; 13.4).

> Third Baruch 4.17 [Greek] (1st–3rd c. CE) speaks to the dangers of excess wine consumption as leading to vice: "For (no) good derives from it [i.e., wine]. For those who drink excessively do these things: Brother does not have mercy on brother, nor father on son, nor children on parents, but by means of the Fall through wine [*oinos*] come forth all (these): murder, adultery, fornication, perjury, theft, and similar things. And nothing good is accomplished through it" (cf. 3 Bar. 4.17 [Slavonic]).[24]

In addition to these warnings about how drunkenness will hinder entrance into the kingdom of God, there are additional eschatological warnings that call for sobriety in the face of the eschaton and divine judgment. These will be addressed in

---

23. Mark Forsyth, *A Short History of Drunkenness: How, Why, Where, and When Humankind Has Gotten Merry from the Stone Age to the Present* (New York: Three Rivers, 2017), 54.

24. H. E. Gaylord, "3 (Greek Apocalypse of) Baruch," *OTP* 1:669.

chapter 10, however, because they do not provide explicit prohibitions or restrictions on alcohol itself, and because they fit a broader theme of vulnerability that will be more fully explicated there. Other than these, there are no additional restrictions against alcohol consumption in the New Testament.

CONCLUSION

In this chapter we have seen that there are not many explicit restrictions related to alcohol in the Bible. People with particular responsibilities and commitments, including priests, Nazirites, kings, and church leaders, receive direct restrictions on excess and also commands regarding the need for periods of abstinence. Apart from the restriction of excess (Eph 5:18), no other restriction applies to all people at all times. Additionally, Paul makes clear that drunkenness is a vice that will keep one from entering the kingdom of God (1 Cor 5:11; Gal 5:21). Even in doing so, however, he does not overtly provide a restriction on alcohol consumption outside of warning about excessive consumption. Nevertheless, despite the lack of overt prohibitions and restrictions in the Bible, some biblical figures chose to abstain from alcoholic beverages. Understanding why is the focus of the following chapter.

RELEVANT QUESTIONS

1. Why do so many people, both inside and outside Christian circles, often assume that the Bible prohibits alcohol for everyone?
2. Why might it be good, in some cultural contexts, to adopt a more restrictive posture toward alcohol?

CHAPTER 8

ABSTINENCE AND FASTS FROM ALCOHOL

Despite what is commonly assumed about the relationship between religious observance and alcohol consumption, abstinence from alcohol was very rare among ancient Israelites and early Christians outside of prescribed days of fasting (e.g., Esth 9:31; Zech 8:19). This is discernible not least through the relatively few examples of people who chose to abstain in Scripture, but also from the prevalence of viticultural metaphors in the Bible. Notably, there is no evidence of a major sect within Second Temple Judaism (6th c. BCE–1st c. CE) abstaining from alcohol collectively and completely, outside of what Philo records about the Therapeutae (cf. *Contempl. Life* 73–74).[1] This includes the Pharisees, Sadducees, Zealots, and early Jesus-followers. This also applies to the Essenes, even though Josephus refers to them as sober and quiet, sharing a "perpetual sobriety" (*J.W.* 2.8.5)[2] and abstaining from wine at times (2.15.1). Whereas it seems that the Essenes were abstemious, that is not the same as abstinent. Most likely Josephus means that the Essenes did not drink to the point of drunkenness.[3] With regard to the occupants at Qumran (which may or may not have been Essenes), there is even evidence of utensils used for pouring wine,[4] and the texts found in the nearby caves—including the most sectarian ones like The Community Rule (1QS)—refer to the consumption of wine (cf., e.g., *tirosh* in 1QS VI, 4–6 and "the drink of the congregation" in VI, 20–VII, 25). They were a strict community with a robust concern for ritual purity, but these scruples did not entail total abstinence from alcohol.

Some early Christian heretical groups that developed in the second century CE, such as the Marcionites and the Encratites, developed ascetic practices that rejected the consumption of wine, among other things. This even included the removal of wine from the celebration of the Eucharist in exchange for water or another beverage (cf. Acts Pet. 2; Acts Paul 25).[5] Broadly speaking, however, early Christianity was not a movement characterized by abstinence.

---

1. Veronika E. Grimm, *From Feasting to Fasting: The Evolution of a Sin: Attitudes to Food in Late Antiquity* (London: Routledge, 1996), 28–32.
2. Flavius Josephus, *Josephus: The Complete Works*, trans. William Whiston (1737; repr., Nashville: Thomas Nelson, 1998), 726.
3. See Broshi, *Bread*, 161.
4. See Jodi Magness, *The Archaeology of Qumran and the Dead Sea Scrolls* (Grand Rapids: Eerdmans, 2002), 116.
5. On early Christian Eucharists without wine, see esp. Andrew McGowan, *Ascetic Eucharists: Food and Drink in Early Christian Ritual Meals* (Oxford: Oxford University Press, 1999).

Nevertheless, there are biblical examples of individuals and small groups that abstained. What motivated these people was neither that they believed intoxicants were inherently bad and always prohibited, nor a conviction that good religious people simply ought to abstain. Rather, there were specific contextual reasons for their voluntary abstinence. We will turn to look at a handful of named people and groups who chose to abstain for a short fast, a period of their lives, or permanently, which include Samson, Hannah, Samuel, Job, Jeremiah, the Rekabites, Esther, Daniel, John the Baptist, Jesus, the "weak" and the "strong" (Rom 14–15), and Timothy.

SAMSON

Samson is the first canonical example of a named character who abstains from alcohol, or rather, who was *supposed to abstain*. Samson, who was one of the judges of Israel, was meant to keep a strict Nazirite code for the entirety of his life, even from gestation. This prescription comes when an angel appears to Samson's mother and declares that although she is barren (Judg 13:2–3), she will have a son who will be a Nazirite *from the womb to the tomb* (13:5, 7). Thus, in essence she must undertake the pledge during pregnancy and refrain from drinking wine (*yayin*) or beer (*shekar*) (13:4, 14), and eating any unclean food (13:4–5, 7) or "anything that comes from the grapevine" (13:14).[6] Furthermore, the angel declares that after Samson is born his hair must never be cut (13:5). Although this scenario might suggest that Samson was destined for great things, he was far from exemplary.

In fact, the Nazirite vow itself creates a number of tensions within Samson's story. This includes his contact with animal corpses, because he eats honey from a lion's carcass after killing it near a vineyard (Judg 14:5, 8) and then offers it to his parents without telling them (14:9). He also uses a donkey's jawbone as a lethal weapon (15:15–17), despite the prohibitions of touching dead animals in Numbers 6 (not to mention the ethics of killing). It also includes his sexual conduct, such as marrying a Philistine woman from Timnah (14:10), visiting a sex worker (16:1), and, most notably, revealing to Delilah that the secret of his strength lies in his uncut hair (16:17).

But for our purposes the main issue is his consumption of alcohol. When Samson marries the Philistine woman, he participates in a great seven-day feast (*mishteh* in Judg 14:10, 12, 17; *potos* in LXX). During the feast, Samson tells a number of riddles to his new wife's countrymen, which is a common drinking trope.[7] It turns out that the whole wedding was a ruse, and Samson goes on to kill several men in Ashkelon (which, once more, should be most problematic to us), after he begins to

---

6. Trent C. Butler, *Judges*, WBC 8 (Nashville: Thomas Nelson, 2009), 324.

7. So, e.g., MacDonald, *Not Bread Alone*, 125–27; cf. Butler, *Judges*, 336; Dubach, *Trunkenheit*, 88–89.

burn with anger, perhaps due in part to the effects of inebriation (14:19). Moreover, when Samson returns and finds that his wife has been given to another person, he lights the tails of three hundred foxes who bring devastation to grain, olive trees, and vineyards (15:5), further highlighting his brash character and impulsivity. When we look at this list, it hardly seems that he had any commitments at all, let alone a permanent Nazirite vow.

With regard to Samson's apparent consumption of alcohol, the problem is not that he was consuming alcohol in and of itself, but that he was under a lifelong vow to abstain. It is the *violation of the vow* that was problematic. If Samson had been a typical Nazirite, such a feast would not have raised any flags, provided he was not under the vow at that given time.

Based on the description of the Nazirite vow from Numbers 6, Samson's commitment was noticeably stricter, being lifelong rather than temporary. This could reflect the development of a local variation on the Nazirite vow.[8] Yet despite the strictness of the vow in Judges 13 relative to Numbers 6, Samson hardly kept any of it outside of growing out his hair. The rabbis would later distinguish between three types of Nazirites: temporary ones, permanent ones, and permanent ones like Samson who do not need to make offerings when they become impure from contacting dead animals (m. Nazir 1:2). Yet it is not just Samson's contact with corpses that undermines the legitimacy of his Nazirite vow. It is also his consumption of alcohol, even though it is implicit (this is not overtly addressed in the Mishnah; cf. m. Nazir 2:4; 4:3, 5; 5:3; 6:1–2, 4, 9; 8:2; 9:1).

> The problem with violating vows is highlighted when the "man of God" from Judah in 1 Kings 13 did not keep his commitment to fasting from bread and water (13:8–9), lied about it, and then was mauled by a lion (13:20–25).

Perhaps the only portion of the Nazirite vow that applied to him was the proscription regarding cutting his hair (Judg 13:5), since that is the only element *overtly prescribed for him*. In fact, abstinence was only explicitly commanded for his mother. But if it did not apply to him, in what sense was Samson a Nazirite *from the womb*? The fact that his mother abstains from these things suggests that Samson was also meant to abstain from them. His mother's abstinence also serves to provide a comic contrast with his lifestyle.[9] Samson is thus a character who fails to live up to the standards expected of him, which is par for the course in the story of Judges.

Despite this fact, Samson is a great place to start our character study on abstinence, because he provides a foil for the first character who does abstain from alcohol—Hannah. She is under no compulsion to abstain, unlike Samson, but she chooses to do so. She also seems to choose this for her son, Samuel.

---

8. So, MacDonald, *Not Bread Alone*, 124n69.

9. See, e.g., Butler, *Judges*, 323–26; Webb, *Judges*, 351–52.

HANNAH AND SAMUEL

Hannah was a barren woman who prayed for a son at the temple in Shiloh. If YHWH granted her request, she promised that she would consecrate him to YHWH's service and that no razor would ever touch his head (1 Sam 1:11). The story is reminiscent of the Samson narrative, both through the theme of barrenness and through the Nazirite-like promise to refrain from cutting her son's hair. The allusion to Samson, and indeed the contrast, is clearer in the Hebrew order of the biblical books because Judges leads right on into 1 Samuel (Ruth breaks up the flow of these texts in the Greek order). What makes Hannah's prayer intriguing is that while she is there in sacred space, the priest Eli sees her from a distance, notices her lips moving, but does not hear any words. He supposes that Hannah must be drunk, and essentially tells her to lay off the wine (*yayin* in 1:13–14). She had actually just come to the temple from a sacrificial meal with her husband and their broader family. It was after "eating and drinking" (1:9) that Hannah left to pray at Shiloh, which suggests that Eli's supposition might not have been entirely unfounded.[10]

> Alcohol consumption is often implied in mundane or non-festive settings, where the text merely says that the characters were "eating and drinking." The clearest examples of this are when "drinking" is mentioned without any reference to an alcoholic beverage directly, and yet one of the characters becomes inebriated, as happens with Uriah (2 Sam 11:11, 13) and King Ben-Hadad (1 Kgs 20:12, 16). When "eating and drinking" does not imply the presence of alcohol, an alternative beverage is usually stated (e.g., water in 1 Kgs 19:6–8).

Eli's concern could be rooted in the fact that drunkenness in sacred space was prohibited, at least for priests (cf. Lev 10:8–11). Yet Hannah tells him that she had not consumed either wine (*yayin*) or beer (*shekar*), but instead was *pouring out her soul* in prayer (1 Sam 1:15). This may be intended as an allusion to libations, further underscoring that she had not done anything with alcohol that day. Then Eli blessed her, and YHWH granted her a son named Samuel (1:20).

After Samuel was weaned, Hannah brought her baby into the presence of YHWH to be dedicated (1 Sam 1:22). Pertaining to this, an ancient manuscript from the Dead Sea Scrolls contains a line here that Samuel will be "a Nazirite unto eternity" (4QSam[a] [4Q51] V, 22 [my trans.]; cf. m. Nazir 9:5). Even if this line is not original, it at least makes plain what is implied by Hannah's commitment that Samuel's hair would never be cut (1 Sam 1:11). At this scene of dedication, Hannah brought along sacrifices and offerings, including a bull, flour, and wine (*yayin* in 1:24). The wine, of course, would be poured out as a libation, which suggests that although Hannah did not personally consume alcohol, at least not in this brief story, she still recognized its appropriate cultic function within the worship of YHWH.

---

10. The LXX omits "eating and drinking," curtailing any possibility that Eli was correct.

It is not clear if Samuel himself was meant to abstain from alcohol. As noted already, there is an allusion to the Nazirite vow in 1 Samuel 1:11, and the text of 1 Samuel 1:24 from the Dead Sea Scrolls clearly makes him a Nazirite. The text as we have it in the Hebrew tradition never mentions that he abstained from alcohol or that he was required to do so because of his vow, but it may be implied. In the Greek tradition of 1 Samuel 1:11 (LXX), however, Hannah also commits Samuel to the avoidance of wine (*oinos*) and "strong drink" (*methysma*). There is a lacuna (or hole) in the Hebrew manuscript of 1 Samuel (4QSam^a [4Q51]) from the Dead Sea Scrolls at this precise spot, which would be enough room to fit this line, providing some possible evidence for the originality of this reading.[11] Yet even if that part about avoiding alcohol was unoriginal, it is probably safe to assume that abstinence is implied by the reference to Samuel's hair being uncut, since that restriction could be a synecdoche—a part of the Nazirite vow that stands for the whole of it.

JOB

Job is a story about a righteous man who is wealthy and successful, and who continues to be faithful to God even when all of his family, health, and possessions are taken from him. The narrative begins by noting that Job's children would regularly hold a feast together (*mishteh*) at the homes of his sons, one after another (Job 1:4). On one such occasion, as they were eating and drinking wine (*yayin*) together (1:13, 18), a strong wind caused the house to collapse and kill them all (1:19). Instead of feasting with his family on these occasions, Job would instead pray for them and make sacrifices on their behalf in case they sinned and "cursed God" while feasting (1:5).[12] Yet why would Job abstain from these feasts, and why was he so concerned to pray and make offerings for them?

Job's absence from these feasts could suggest that Job abstained from alcohol and perhaps also that he did not approve of their consumption of it (though the sheepshearing in 31:20 might imply otherwise; see discussion on sheepshearing festivities in ch. 10). For whatever reason, he continually chose not to feast with his children. But it is not the case that he thought they were sinful *because they were feasting*; rather, Job was concerned that they might sin *while feasting*, referring to a possibility that could arise in their vulnerable state of inebriation. David J. A. Clines argues that the language of "cursing God" specifically is listed as an extreme example of the worst sort of thing that one could do as a "secret sin" that would not

---

11. E.g., P. Kyle McCarter Jr., *I Samuel*, AB 8 (Garden City, NY: Doubleday, 1980), 53–54, 60–61; Ralph W. Klein, *1 Samuel*, 2nd ed., WBC 10 (Nashville: Thomas Nelson, 2000), 3.

12. The Hebrew reads "bless God" rather than "curse God" (cf. 2:9). Either "bless" is a euphemism for cursing, or "bless" is a scribal addition to remove the blasphemous phrase "curse God." See Norman C. Habel, *The Book of Job: A Commentary*, OTL (Philadelphia: Westminster, 1985), 88.

be remembered the next day. Clines argues further that this is a foreshadowing of Job nearly cursing God later on.[13]

There is no suggestion in the story that Job's children ever did sin. Yet if they did, Job was sacrificing on their behalf, which preemptively undercuts the suggestion from Job's friend Bildad that his children were killed as a punishment (Job 8:4). At the end of the day, it is not clear why Job was not feasting with his family, since he is never called a Nazirite or a priest. His abstinence may serve to highlight how righteous he was, but his abstinence pales in comparison to his proactive concern for his children.

JEREMIAH

Jeremiah is known as the weeping prophet due to the Babylonian exile. As such, he did not sit "in the company of revelers" and "[make] merry with them" (Jer 15:17), referring to the enjoyment of intoxicating beverages. There is a sense that Jeremiah feels ostracized by this. But he does not join them because these merrymakers believe that things will get better, whereas Jeremiah knows that they will not.[14] It is instead YHWH's word that brings him joy and that delights his heart (15:16), suggesting a pun on inebriation. Jeremiah's abstinence from alcohol, at least during the time of his prophetic oracles, reinforces how alcohol is associated with joy and blessing so often. Since he was in a perpetual state of mourning, he refused to imbibe.[15]

THE REKABITES

Jeremiah also mentions the Rekabites, who were a group known for their strict commitments, including abstinence. In a strange vision, Jeremiah is commanded to bring these Rekabites to the temple and have them drink wine (*yayin* in Jer 35:2). The prophet "set bowls full of wine [*yayin*] and some cups before the Rekabites and said to them, 'Drink some wine [*yayin*]'" (35:5). But they refused, and they explained that they had taken a vow to abstain because their father Jehonadab commanded them and their offspring not to drink wine (*yayin* in 35:6, 8, 14). Additionally, they were also prohibited from building houses, sowing seeds, and planting vineyards (35:7, 9). Instead of doing these things, they were commanded to live in tents (35:10), suggesting that the rationale behind the prohibitions was a familial intention to maintain a nomadic lifestyle.[16]

---

13. David J. A. Clines, *Job 1–20*, WBC 17 (Waco, TX: Word, 1989; repr., Grand Rapids: Zondervan Academic, 2017), 16.

14. William L. Holladay, *Jeremiah 1: A Commentary on the Book of the Prophet Jeremiah, Chapters 1–25*, Hermeneia (Philadelphia: Fortress, 1986), 459.

15. Jeremiah also employs an alcohol analogy, comparing his sadness and rage at his people's demise to that of a "drunken man" and "a strong man overcome by wine [*yayin*]" (23:9).

16. Becker, *Rebe*, 157; Walsh, *Fruit*, 6.

When this odd scene is finally explained (Jer 35:11–17), the Rekabites are held up as a remnant faithful to their vows (35:14), over against those who were repeatedly disobedient to God's laws. Their consistency and faithfulness are in view, not the content of their specific commitments. The Rekabites are praised for honoring their father (35:18–19), not for abstaining from alcohol, let alone refraining from building houses or planting seeds (cf. Jer 29:5), or even maintaining a vineyard.

ESTHER

Esther's three-day fast is an intriguing example of temporary abstinence, because her story is suffused with feasting (cf. ch. 5). In response to Haman's plot, and standing in contrast to the festive alcohol consumption, Esther fasts for three days in anticipation of her decision to go before the king unsummoned.

The fast itself calls into question the degree to which Esther enjoyed the royal fare, including that which might be expressly prohibited. This is not a question that is directly answered in the Hebrew version of the story, the one with which Protestants will be most familiar. But it is addressed in the later expanded versions of the story, like the Septuagint version that is part of the canon for Catholics and the Orthodox (cf. also the Alpha Text of Esther). For example, Esther explicitly asserts that she had never "eaten at Haman's table," nor had she "honored the king's banquet nor drunk the wine [*oinos*] of libations" (Esth 4:17 LXX [Addition C:28], NETS). In other words, in the Septuagint she was more regularly scrupulous about banqueting than just in this one instance of fasting.

Traditionally, Esther's fast is read as a religious act to petition God. But prayer is conspicuously absent from this scene in the Hebrew version, whereas the Greek versions supplement this part of the narrative with lengthy prayers (Additions to Esther C and D). In fact, God is not mentioned anywhere in the Hebrew story, nor are there any references to typical religious language or even specifically Jewish concepts or institutions. Moreover, fasting is actually not an inherently religious practice on its own. In fact, Esther's non-Jewish handmaids fast along with her, suggesting syncretism if it was religious (Esth 4:16). Elsewhere in the Old Testament there are a few examples where fasting is clearly not performed to petition God (cf. 1 Sam 31:13; 2 Sam 1:12; 1 Kgs 21:9, 12; 1 Chr 10:12; Dan 6:18). Furthermore, the absence of God in Esther does not need to be compensated. Rather, it should serve as an indication that Esther and Mordecai have not merely hid their Jewish identity to survive in Susa but have largely forgotten the significance of their identity as a result of assimilation in exile. This is perhaps nowhere more clearly seen than in the *timing* of Esther's fast.

Haman's edict went out on the thirteenth day of the first month (Esth 3:12), which is the month of Nisan. This is the day before the start of the Passover, and here we see an even greater threat to the Jewish people than was experienced at the exodus—namely, their entire extermination (3:6, 13). Thus, Esther's fast overlaps with the first three days of Passover. When Esther finally reveals the plight of her people to the king at the second feast, ultimately bringing about the demise of Haman, this also takes place during Passover. Yet nowhere does Esther acknowledge this. In fact, her words to the king directly *subvert* the whole Passover tradition. Esther requests that the king spare her life, and the life of her people, because they had been sold over to be exterminated. But she states that if her people had merely been "sold as male and female slaves," she would have kept silent, "because no such distress would justify disturbing the king" (7:4). This is a startling admission because Passover is the famous celebration of Israel's national redemption from slavery in Egypt.

> What further demonstrates Esther's neglect of the Passover in Esther 7:4 MT is how the Greek traditions in the Septuagint and the Alpha Text both change the reference to enslavement so that it is part of the *present* plight that Esther makes known to the king (Esth 7:4 LXX; Esth 7:4 Alpha Text). This is just one of many ways in which subsequent retellings of the Esther story have attempted to make it fit better with biblical tradition.

The irony here is just as strong as the words of the Jewish people in the Gospel of John when they tell Jesus that they "have never been slaves of anyone" (John 8:33). Esther's words to the king quite clearly demonstrate that there is no sense that Esther expected the God of the exodus to deliver his people once more. And yet the people are delivered, even though God's providence is not acknowledged at any point.

Thus, Esther's fast should not be read as religiously motivated but rather as a mourning ritual for her potential demise, because it is deadly to go to the king unsummoned (cf. Esth 4:11).[17] The excesses of alcohol consumption in the story of Esther certainly draw attention to her fast. And when we attend to the circumstances of it, we see that God is subtly at work behind the scenes, just as the Passover tradition lies subtly below the surface—even though the characters, including Esther, never recognize this. And because the Jewish people were delivered in the end, Esther's temporary fast gives way to feasting. Her abstinence from alcohol consumption in the story is temporary, and her partaking resumes after the pivotal moment of crisis.

DANIEL

Daniel is another character who chooses to abstain from alcohol, as well as other foods, at various points in his story, although he does not completely abstain. The most well-known example of Daniel's abstinence is when he refused to defile himself by eating the Babylonian king's food or drinking the wine (*yayin*) from his feasts (*mishteh*), when he was initially taken into captivity (Dan 1:5, 8). In doing this, Daniel did not appeal to dietary laws or restrictions, making his rationale unclear.

---

17. See discussion in Dunne, *Esther*, 47–56.

As Carol Newsom suggests, his reasoning may have stemmed from the uncertainty of what it looks like to be a Jew in this situation.[18] Rabbinic tradition does provide some rationale for abstaining from gentile wine, due to the concern of idolatry (cf. m. Avodah Zarah 2:3; 4:8–12; 5:1–12).[19] Even though the full articulation of that tradition is much later than Daniel, a similar logic may be implied. However, his motivation could simply amount to rejecting his captor's "beneficence" (cf. Ps 141:4) and mourning his people's captivity.

The reason that King Nebuchadnezzar provided his royal fare was because he wanted to select the best from among the young men to fulfill certain tasks (Dan 1:3–4). Instead of receiving the apportioned "food and drink [*mishteh*]" (1:10), Daniel requested vegetables and water. When the young men were all evaluated after ten days, Daniel and his friends were much better off than the others who "ate the royal food" (1:15). As a result, everyone was given vegetables and water instead of the king's food and the wine (*yayin*) from his feasts (*mishteh* in 1:16). Despite how it might appear at first, this scene is commenting neither on which diet is preferable nor on whether it is healthier to abstain from wine. Rather than promoting a diet worth implementing,[20] the scene is meant to be interpreted as a miracle.[21] God acted to improve the physical condition of Daniel and his friends *in spite of* their meagre diet—not because of it.

Years later, Daniel mentions another time of abstinence from "choice food," meat, wine (*yayin*), and lotions (Dan 10:3), while he was in a three-week state of mourning after receiving a confusing message from YHWH (10:1–3). His temporary abstinence from these things suggests that they were part of his regular lifestyle.[22] Thus, even Daniel himself did not maintain "the Daniel diet" from his earlier days in captivity. With Daniel's example, we see someone who abstained from alcohol at different points in his life during experiences of grief and trauma, but he was not someone who remained entirely abstinent.

JOHN THE BAPTIST AND JESUS

John the Baptist famously had a diet of "locusts and wild honey" (Matt 3:4; Mark 1:6),[23] whereas Jesus was known for more elaborate feasting. Yes, Jesus fasted for forty days (Matt 4:2; Mark 1:12–13; Luke 4:2), but that was prior to the launching of his public ministry, which was not characterized by fasting. The diets of Jesus and

---

18. Carol A. Newsom, *Daniel: A Commentary*, OTL (Louisville: Westminster John Knox, 2014), 48.

19. Wine was highly regulated out of concerns that gentiles may have used it as a libation to idols and other gods. See Rosenblum, *Rabbinic Drinking*, 66–95, 130–60, 237–42.

20. Contra Rick Warren and The Daniel Plan Team, *The Daniel Plan: 40 Days to a Healthier Life* (Grand Rapids: Zondervan, 2013).

21. Newsom, *Daniel*, 50; MacDonald, *What Did*, 25–26, 101.

22. Rightly, e.g., John J. Collins, *Daniel*, Hermeneia (Minneapolis: Augsburg Fortress, 1993), 143.

23. For more on John the Baptist's diet, see James A. Kelhoffer, *The Diet of John the Baptist: Locusts and Wild Honey in Synoptic and Patristic Interpretation*, WUNT 176 (Tübingen: Mohr Siebeck, 2005).

John the Baptist, including their respective approaches to alcohol, are contrasted in a couple of places in the Gospels. Although John the Baptist was the one who abstained from alcohol rather than Jesus, these two figures are worth discussing together, both because their diets are foils for one another and also because at the Last Supper Jesus did proclaim that he would abstain for the rest of his life.

In Luke, we are provided with an origin story that explains John the Baptist's dietary habits. The angel Gabriel appeared to John's father Zechariah, while he was serving as a priest in the temple. His message was that, despite his wife's barrenness (Luke 1:7), he would have a son who would never consume wine (*oinos*) or beer (*sikera*), and would be "filled with the Holy Spirit even before he is born" (1:15). This birth narrative is reminiscent of those of Samson and Samuel in many respects, including barrenness and prohibitions against alcohol. This could suggest that John is presented as a permanent Nazirite, just like them.[24] However, other restrictions pertinent to the Nazirite vow are not mentioned, such as not cutting his hair (cf. Num 6:5), which some suggest make the Nazirite vow unlikely.[25] If the Nazirite vow does not inform the restrictions on alcohol, it may be that the priestly regulations of alcohol are in view (cf. Lev 10:9) due to his father's occupation and the temple imagery of being "filled with the Spirit."[26] In this case, priestly temple service would be expanded to include John's entire life, which we never see for priests in the Old Testament. Consequently, neither the Nazirite nor the priestly explanation works perfectly, and it may be that a combination of regulations have been merged together in a unique and unprecedented way. If so, this would be fitting for John's unprecedented role as a herald of the Messiah.

With regard to their contrasting diets, Jesus is asked early on in his ministry why he and his disciples do not fast, since John the Baptist and his disciples fast along with the Pharisees (Mark 2:18–22; cf. Matt 9:14–17; Luke 5:33–39). Scripture did not prescribe consistent fasting, but fasting was likely intended to beseech God to bring about the kingdom. The nuances of Jesus's response to this question will be reserved for a fuller discussion later on (cf. ch. 14), since his answer pertains to themes of eschatological abundance and restoration. For our purposes in this chapter, we need to consider briefly what John was fasting from and what Jesus was enjoying. Since part of Jesus's response includes analogies involving a wedding (Mark 2:19–20) and the preservation of wine in wineskins (2:22), fasting from alcohol is most likely in view. Within the wedding analogy in particular, Jesus's claim is that his disciples should feast with him rather than fast, just as one feasts with a bridegroom (2:19).

---

24. Joseph A. Fitzmyer, *The Gospel According to Luke I–IX: Introduction, Translation, and Notes*, AB 28 (Garden City, NY: Doubleday, 1982), 326.

25. John Nolland, *Luke 1–9:20*, WBC 35A (Dallas: Word, 1989), 30.

26. François Bovon, *Luke 1: A Commentary on the Gospel of Luke 1:1–9:50*, 3 vols., Hermeneia (Minneapolis: Fortress, 2002), 1:36.

But, as he says, fasting will come when the bridegroom is taken away (2:20). Within the framework of the parable, Jesus has predicted his own death, but has he also predicted that his followers would remain abstinent from alcohol in his absence?

It is sometimes thought that an implication of the wedding analogy is that fasting from alcohol ought to characterize Jesus's disciples until the bridegroom returns to bring about the fullness of the kingdom (i.e., the second coming), but this interpretation reads too much into the passage. Jesus does not address the bridegroom's resurrection or return, but only that he will be taken away, suggesting that the disciples will fast as they mourn the bridegroom's death. When we account for the victory of the resurrection and the inaugurated presence of the kingdom through the advent of the Spirit and the enthronement of Christ, an interpretation that necessitates ongoing abstinence from alcohol does not do justice to the parable.[27] It also selectively restricts alcohol instead of all food, and it fails to recognize that fasting is a periodic practice rather than a permanent one. Thus, the inaugurated nature of the kingdom speaks to both Christian feasting and fasting, both of which can be done in anticipation of the fullness of the kingdom. Indeed, Craig Blomberg notes that although fasting was an early Christian practice (Acts 13:2–3; 14:23), it was never central or characteristic, and Paul even spoke out against the abuse of ascetic practices (Col 2:23).[28]

In another instance, Jesus addresses the reputations that arose from their respective dieting practices as part of his critique of "the present generation." He describes the generation as flighty and unsatisfied children making music in the marketplace and demanding different reactions to the different songs that they play (Matt 11:16–17; Luke 7:31–32). Within this context, this is a metaphor for how the present generation was critical of both of their diets. Jesus, the one who "came eating and drinking" (Matt 11:19; Luke 7:34), does not mourn when the children sing a dirge. However, John, who "came neither eating nor drinking" (Matt 11:18; cf. *oinos* in Luke 7:33), does not dance when they play their flutes. Furthermore, the present generation believed that John's fasting meant that he was possessed by a demon (Matt 11:18; Luke 7:33) and that Jesus's feasting meant he was "a glutton and a drunkard [*oinopotēs*], a friend of tax collectors and sinners" (Matt 11:19; Luke 7:34).[29] Jesus's conclusion encapsulates his response to the duplicitous reactions of the crowds: "wisdom is proved right by her deeds" (Matt 11:19), or, as Luke has it, "by all her children" (Luke 7:35).

Wisdom traditions are a strong influence in this passage more broadly. Jesus's

---

27. So similarly, e.g., I. Howard Marshall, *The Gospel of Luke: A Commentary on the Greek Text*, NIGTC (Grand Rapids: Eerdmans, 1978), 226; Darrell L. Bock, *Luke 1:1–9:50*, BECNT (Grand Rapids: Baker, 1994), 518.

28. Craig L. Blomberg, "The Most Often Abused Verses in the Sermon on the Mount and How to Treat Them Right," *SWJT* 46.3 (2004): 12.

29. Welton suggests that excess might not be implied, since eating with tax collectors and sinners makes the consumption "deviant" (*He Is a Glutton*, 291).

declaration about how his burden and yoke are light and easy (Matt 11:28–30), for example, resembles that of Wisdom in Sirach 6:28–30. In other words, then, whether you eat or drink is ultimately irrelevant. The wisdom of these respective diets is determined, not by the contents of the diets themselves but by the actions that result from them (i.e., Wisdom's deeds or children). This means, in part, that the crowds' respective assessments of Jesus and John the Baptist were wrong, but also that they failed to allow for a dietary spectrum wide enough to legitimize both of them. John the Baptist did not have a demon, but he was probably a bit wild relative to the status quo because of his anticipation of the *coming* kingdom of God. Jesus, however, was neither a glutton nor a drunkard, but such a reputation is only meaningful if he regularly ate with others and did not circumscribe his diet in a noteworthy way because of his belief in the *presence* of the kingdom of God.

Yet, at the Last Supper, just before his death, Jesus seems to finally announce a fast. He declares to his disciples that he will no longer drink the "fruit of the vine" until he drinks it again in the full arrival of the kingdom (Matt 26:29; Mark 14:25; Luke 22:18; cf. ch. 14 for the eschatological implications). With this statement, some scholars have argued that Jesus was informing his disciples that he was taking on a vow of abstinence from alcohol.[30] Whether or not John the Baptist was a Nazirite, clearly Jesus was not, based on his consumption of alcohol and awareness of viticulture, even though he was called "a Nazarene" (Matt 2:23). Rather than implying his Nazirite identity, Matthew is probably making a pun on Jesus's hometown, Nazareth, and the Hebrew word for Branch (*Nezer*), which is found in a few messianic texts like Isaiah 11:1 and Zechariah 6:12 (cf. Jer 23:5; 33:15). But it could be argued that Jesus finally made a Nazirite vow here at the end of his life.

However, abstinence should not be equated with the Nazirite vow, especially when other elements of the Nazirite vow are lacking (such as not trimming his hair).[31] Further, this interpretation would mean that Jesus was making this statement, in part, to explain to his disciples why he was not drinking from the cup with them. It seems best, however, to read his statement as indicating that the wine of their meal would be the last that he tastes.[32] In fact, this might be most clear in Matthew's version, since Jesus refers to "*this* fruit of the vine," referring to the wine of their meal.[33] In other words, he knew he was about to die, and he was predicting both his death and vindication.[34]

---

30. Notably Joachim Jeremias, *The Eucharistic Words of Jesus* (Oxford: Basil Blackwell, 1955; repr., London: SCM, 2011), 207–18.

31. Robert H. Gundry, *Mark: A Commentary on His Apology for the Cross* (Grand Rapids: Eerdmans, 2000), 843.

32. Joel Marcus, *Mark 8–16: A New Translation with Introduction and Commentary*, AYB (New Haven: Yale University Press, 2009), 959.

33. John Nolland, *The Gospel of Matthew*, NIGTC (Grand Rapids: Eerdmans, 2005), 1084.

34. E.g., Maurice Casey, *Aramaic Sources of Mark's Gospel*, SNTSMS 102 (Cambridge: Cambridge University Press, 1999), 243; W. D. Davies and Dale C. Allison, *A Critical and Exegetical Commentary on the Gospel According to Saint Matthew*, 3 vols., ICC (Edinburgh: T&T Clark, 1997), 3:475.

"THE WEAK" AND "THE STRONG" IN ROMANS 14–15

In Romans 14–15, Paul directly addresses issues that could divide the churches. Among these are questions pertaining to divergent scruples on food and alcohol. In particular, Paul singles out eating meat and drinking wine (*oinos*) as the dietary matters of controversy (14:3, 17, 21). Where the rubber meets the road, of course, is in shared meals. So, this passage is not strictly concerned about private food customs but about the conflicts created when people with various food scruples are represented at a common meal.[35] Paul handles the matter deftly in order to keep everyone eating together, even if they cannot countenance what others might be consuming. Elsewhere, Paul can be critical of those fixated on assuaging their bodily appetites (Phil 3:18–19), yet he can also be critical of those who criticize what another eats. Paul tells the Colossians, by virtue of participation in Christ's victory through baptism (Col 2:12–15), "do not let anyone judge you by what you eat or drink" (Col 2:16; cf. 2:20–23). Yet here in Romans 14–15 his tact is more circumspect, presumably because the scruples addressed are internal to the group in a large concentration.

Paul identifies two primary groups and addresses their respective scruples—that of the "weak" and the "strong." He affirms that it is the "strong" who choose to enjoy meat and wine, whereas the "weak" choose to abstain. Debates have been waged about the precise identity of these two groups. Without recounting all the options suggested in that discussion, most scholars have found it preferable to align the "weak" and the "strong" with the Jewish and gentile communities in the Roman churches, respectively.

> Francis Watson summarizes some of the reasons why the "weak" were primarily Jewish Christians: (a) the use of the word *koinos* ("unclean") in Romans 14:14 likely reflects Jewish categorization; (b) there is likely an allusion to the Sabbath in Romans 14:5–6a; (c) the eating versus faith dichotomy parallels the works of the law versus faith contrast earlier in the letter; and (d) Romans 15:7–13 is about how Jews and gentiles should be hospitable to each other.[36]

The fact that Paul does not call these groups "Jews" and "gentiles," respectively, suggests that we should not restrict each group hermetically to ethnicity. Ideological

---

35. Francis Watson, *Paul, Judaism, and the Gentiles: Beyond the New Perspective*, rev. ed. (Grand Rapids: Eerdmans, 2007), 176; John M. G. Barclay, "'Do We Undermine the Law?' A Study of Romans 14.1–15.6," in *Pauline Churches and Diaspora Jews* (Grand Rapids: Eerdmans, 2016), 41.

36. Watson, *Paul*, 176–77.

alignment, rather than ethnic identity, is forefront. At the same time, the scruples in view were most likely Jewish, even if they were not exclusively held by the Jews in the churches (i.e., they could have been held by gentile proselytes to Judaism).[37]

The dynamics in the passage, then, help us to understand how even though abstinence from wine and meat go beyond what is prohibited in Old Testament food laws, they still likely stem from Jewish scruples. The abstinence likely reflects a Jewish strategy in a gentile context.[38] This is similar to what we have seen with Daniel and the Greek versions of Esther (cf. also Jdt 12:1–4).[39] Thus, the abstinence in Romans 14–15 could be a tactic to avoid being polluted by idolatry—even though idolatry is not explicitly mentioned (unlike 1 Cor 8–10). Nevertheless, the avoidance of meat and wine in Romans 14–15 by the "weak" likely stems from some similar concerns.

Paul's advice in this situation is not that the "weak" change their diet but rather that the "strong" learn how to adapt and welcome those who do not share their views or habits pertaining to meat and alcohol (Rom 15:1–2). Paul's chief concern is that the "strong" do not give the "weak" a reason to stumble (14:13, 15, 19–21), and that the "weak" are not compromised by a sense that *they* need to adapt (14:14). As Paul says, whatever does not proceed from faith is a sin (14:22–23). This means that drinking alcohol can indeed be a sin for those who lack the faith to do so, even if it is not a sin for others. Although Paul does not provide a restriction to hinder the "weak" from consuming meat or alcohol, they should not go beyond what their own faith permits for as long as it continues to prohibit them.

TIMOTHY

The apostle Paul's colleague Timothy appears to be someone who abstains from alcohol, based on the offhand commands that he "stop drinking only water" and instead "use a little wine" for his stomach ailments (1 Tim 5:23). Within the context of 1 Timothy 5:17–25, which is focused mainly on the roles and responsibilities of elders with respect to handling sin in the community, verse 23 appears rather abruptly. Many translators and commentators view verse 23 as an aside and often place it in parentheses to signify this to readers. If verse 23 is not an aside, however, then it probably provides nuance to Paul's command that Timothy keep himself pure at the end of the previous verse (5:22).[40] In this rendering, the connection is that remaining pure does not entail the total rejection of alcohol. As such, it provides clarity for Timothy and also an implicit critique of the asceticism of the false teachers

---

37. Watson, *Paul*, 175.
38. Watson, *Paul*, 176; Barclay, "'Do We Undermine,'" 41; David G. Horrell, *Solidarity and Difference: A Contemporary Reading of Paul's Ethics*, 2nd ed. (London: Bloomsbury T&T Clark, 2016), 202.
39. Watson, *Paul*, 175.
40. William D. Mounce, *Pastoral Epistles*, WBC 46 (Nashville: Thomas Nelson, 2000), 318; Philip W. Towner, *The Letters to Timothy and Titus*, NICNT (Grand Rapids: Eerdmans, 2006), 376.

that Paul addressed elsewhere (4:1–5).⁴¹ This false teaching may have influenced Timothy about his own consumption of alcohol.

The assumption that most interpreters make at this point is that Paul must be recommending that Timothy consume wine in moderation.⁴² Accordingly, many scholars connect this command to the restrictions in the Pastorals that church leaders should not be excessive consumers of wine (see ch. 7). The wording of the restriction for deacons might seem to favor this interpretation, because deacons should not consume "much wine [*oinō pollō*]" (1 Tim 3:8), whereas Timothy should use "a little wine [*oinō oligō*]" (5:23).⁴³

Yet the problem with this interpretation is that it assumes that the Greek word in 1 Timothy 5:23 for "using" (*kraomai*) is synonymous with the standard verb for "drinking" (i.e., *pinō*), which does not appear in the verse.⁴⁴ When beverages in particular are *used* (*kraomai*), they serve a utilitarian purpose. The medicinal use of wine is clearly in view, given the reference to Timothy's stomach ailments.⁴⁵ This means that consuming wine for pleasure or for its *residual* health benefits (as commonly affirmed today) is not in view. Paul is not telling Timothy, in effect, "Be sure to have a glass of wine with dinner each night because it's good for you," but rather, "Don't forget to take your medicine!"

> Wine was used medicinally in part because of its ability to dissolve herbs and resins more thoroughly than water.⁴⁶ It could be used externally to treat wounds, as in the parable of the Good Samaritan (Luke 10:34), or internally as a sedative (3 Macc. 5.2, 10, 45, where it is used to drug elephants), or as a medicine in its own right (cf. T. Sol. 18.31, where it is used to treat the demon that causes diarrhea and hemorrhoids).

Paul's prohibition, "stop drinking only water" (*hydropoteō*), is also better translated as "stop being a water drinker." The word "only" does not appear in the Greek, though it may be implied.⁴⁷ Being a "water drinker" was not necessarily the same thing as being a teetotaler in today's parlance, though at times the term functions similarly. Many people would not exclusively drink water if they had access to other options.

---

41. See esp. Luke Timothy Johnson, *The First and Second Letters to Timothy*, AB 35A (New York: Doubleday, 2001), 281–82.

42. So, e.g., Kreglinger, *Spirituality of Wine*, 32, 168.

43. So most, see, e.g., Mounce, *Pastoral Epistles*, 318–19; Johnson, *First and Second*, 281–82; Towner, *Letters*, 375–76.

44. Cf., e.g., BDAG 1087–88; L&N §42.23.

45. This is how many early church fathers understood the passage, including Jerome, Chrysostom, Ambrose, and Augustine. See Peter Gorday, *Colossians, 1–2 Thessalonians, 1–2 Timothy, Titus, Philemon*, ACCS 9 (Downers Grove, IL: InterVarsity Press, 2000), 206–8.

46. McGovern, *Ancient Brews*, 100.

47. See, e.g., BDAG 832; Mounce, *Pastoral Epistles*, 319.

> To be sure, there are plenty of places where wine drinkers are contrasted with water drinkers (cf. *hydropoteō* in Hippocrates, *Nat. hom.* §9 lines 24–25). Circumstances may require water drinking, even if that is not one's preference, as Herodotus says about the Persians, who did not have good soil until they conquered the Lydians (*Hist.* 1.71). Likewise, Xenophon presents something similar in a speech attributed to Cyrus the Great about the need for soldiers to wean off wine and become water drinkers while on a militaristic expedition, due to lack of resources where they were traveling (*Cyr.* 6.2.26–29). But in the case of Daniel (LXX), who chose to be a water drinker instead of consuming the king's wine (Dan 1:12 LXX), he was not committing himself to a life of abstinence (cf. also Plato, *Resp.* 8, 561c, where fasting is more likely).

In this light, the medicinal advice to *use a little wine*, alongside the prohibition to stop being a water drinker, suggests that mere wine consumption is probably not in view. Instead, Paul is most likely giving ancient medical advice to Timothy about *how to drink his water*.[48] Using a little wine is Paul's way of saying, if you like, "no longer drink your water *neat*, but add a bit of wine to it." The reason for the advice is because consuming water was either the cause of, or an aggravating contributor to, Timothy's health problems.

> The ancient medical writer Hippocrates (5th–4th c. BCE), or one of his students, wrote a lengthy analysis of the different kinds of water and their respective benefits and side effects (*Airs, Waters, Places* §7–11; cf. Pliny, *Nat.* 31; Athenaeus, *Deipn.* 2.40f–46f).[49] One Hippocratic author (*Morb.* 3.6) even wrote about treating someone who had a dry tongue from an "ardent fever" by requiring the consumption of water (*hydropoteō*), because "water usually provokes vomiting" with such a condition. Then the patient would follow that up by using (*kraō*) some sweet wine (Potter, LCL).

Given the uncertainties associated with securing good drinking water, and the commonly held view that wine had medicinal value for the stomach (cf. Columella,

---

48. So also Daniel C. Arichea and Howard A. Hatton, *A Handbook on Paul's Letters to Timothy and to Titus*, UBSHS (New York: United Bible Societies, 1995), 133; Becker, *Rebe*, 202, cf. 223.

49. See discussion in Jacques Jouanna, *Greek Medicine from Hippocrates to Galen: Selected Papers*, trans. Neil Allies, SAM 40 (Leiden: Brill, 2012), 165–69.

Rust. 3.12.33, 38; Pliny, *Nat.* 23.35–36, 38–39, 41, 44, 51), wine was often added to water to purify it.[50]

> Bacchiocchi rightly argues that this passage is about the sanitation of water, but wrongly contends that Paul wanted Timothy to use *unfermented* grape juice to do so.[51] The passage requires alcohol for it to make any medical sense.

Athenaeus mentions that Hippocrates valued drinking water "from high elevations and deep-soiled hills," since it can bear only "a little wine" (*ton oinon oligon*). This suggests both that the best waters were the ones that did not need much wine added to it, and also that drinking water often did require adding some wine (Athenaeus, *Deipn.* 2.46d [Gulick, LCL]). Further, Jacques Jouanna notes that the medical writer Galen (2nd–3rd c. CE) regarded "watery wine" as the best kind of wine, medicinally speaking, because it would not cause the problematic effects that water and wine could cause on their own with respect to the head and the stomach.[52] Thus, in 1 Timothy 5:23, Paul is best understood as recommending that Timothy no longer drink "unmixed" water.

It may be accurate to regard Timothy as a person who abstained from alcohol. He may have continued to remain abstinent (with the caveat that he *used it* to purify his water), since, as I have argued, this verse is not suggesting that Timothy should begin drinking wine moderately. There is no reason to suppose, however, that the motive for his abstinence was that he had undertaken the Nazirite vow, or anything along those lines.[53] Instead, if Timothy was abstinent, he was most likely influenced by the same ascetic ideas that Paul was critiquing in the epistle (cf. 1 Tim 4:1–5). At the very least, outright rejection of alcohol was injurious to Timothy's health, and Paul wanted Timothy to realize that using a little wine in his water was appropriate, given his health concerns.

> Second Maccabees writes about the harm in drinking wine, as well as water, "alone" (2 Macc 15:39 NRSVue): "it is harmful to drink wine alone or, again, *to drink water alone*, while wine already mixed with water is delicious and enhances one's enjoyment" (emphasis added).

CONCLUSION

The biblically named characters and groups who abstained from alcohol did so in various ways and for different reasons. For most of them, such as Jeremiah, Esther,

---

50. See Robert J. Forbes, *Studies in Ancient Technology, Volume 1: Bitumen and Petroleum in Antiquity, The Origin of Alchemy, Water Supply*, 9 vols. (1964; repr., Leiden: Brill, 1993), 1:178; Lukacs, *Inventing Wine*, 9.

51. Bacchiocchi, *Wine*, 242–46.

52. Jouanna, *Greek Medicine*, 188.

53. As briefly suggested by George W. Knight III, *The Pastoral Epistles*, NIGTC (Grand Rapids: Eerdmans, 1992), 240.

Daniel, and Jesus, their abstinence was temporary and varied in length. Hannah and Job abstained in the crucial moments when they had opportunity to drink, which may suggest that they were always abstinent. But that is never stated. Based on what is overt in Scripture, only the Rekabites and John the Baptist abstained completely from alcohol. However, the text might imply that Samuel and the "weak" in Romans 14–15 did as well. Samson was meant to abstain, but failed to do so, and the nature of Timothy's abstinence is not entirely clear.

The rationale behind the abstinence of biblical characters is associated with a variety of things: (a) vows to God and family, as we see with Samson (antithetically), Samuel (possibly), the Rekabites, and John the Baptist; (b) death and mourning, as we see with Jeremiah, Esther, Daniel (in Dan 10 esp.), and Jesus; (c) prayer and cultic activity, as we see with Hannah and Job; (d) a strategy to avoid idolatry and other forms of impurity in gentile contexts, as seems likely with Daniel (in Dan 1) and the "weak"; and (e) an accommodation of the "strong," as they welcome the "weak" in community. None of these examples of abstinence is rooted in a sense that alcohol consumption is always restricted for everyone. The only possible exception to this might be Timothy, though that is unclear. If that was his rationale, it reflects the influence of false teaching in the region that Paul rejects and that he calls Timothy to reject as well.

Abstinence is therefore not predicated on overt prohibitions for all, as this chapter, along with the previous chapter, makes clear. Anyone can choose to abstain from alcohol for a period of time or permanently, and for whatever reason. Alcohol is not for everyone, but neither is abstinence. As we saw with Jesus and John the Baptist, both of their diverse approaches to alcohol have merit because neither abstinence nor consumption is good in and of itself. The wisdom of each approach is determined by the deeds that result (Matt 11:19) or the children that they bear (Luke 7:35). Indeed, knowing whether and when drinking is worthwhile requires wisdom, which is the subject of the next chapter.

RELEVANT QUESTIONS

1. How might we promote the wisdom of, as well as wisdom in, both abstinence and the consumption of alcohol? What would it take to foster communities that value the best in both approaches?
2. If you personally enjoy alcoholic beverages, what do seasons of abstinence and fasting look like for you?

CHAPTER 9

CONSUMING ALCOHOL WISELY

Wisdom is something that one acquires—that is, *if* one acquires it—with time. The reason is because time provides us with opportunities to appreciate the complexities of life. Wisdom defies simple explanations and easy answers, and it recognizes that some situations are too complex to approach rigidly. Wisdom also brings with it a unique vantage point on life, since the time it took to acquire it is oftentimes greater than the time that is left. When faced with an awareness of one's remaining time, wisdom brings a prioritization of what truly matters that puts everything else into perspective.

This dynamic is on display in the tension between Proverbs and Ecclesiastes, both of which provide wise instruction for their readers on many topics—including alcohol. Together, Proverbs and Ecclesiastes are perhaps the closest that readers will get to finding an evaluation of the pros and cons of alcohol consumption in the Bible. One of the fascinating things for our purposes is that they do this in different ways.[1]

PROVERBIAL WISDOM ON ALCOHOL

Proverbs calls readers to pursue a life of wisdom over against foolishness. Therefore, with regard to alcohol, this collection of proverbial advice often highlights the foolishness of drunkenness and warns about where consuming alcohol could lead. Furthermore, foolish people do foolish things with alcohol. Yet this is by no means the only perspective that Proverbs has to offer, and the reason is because wisdom is not so rigid as to provide a one-size-fits-all perspective.

As we have seen previously, on the one hand (cf. ch. 7), Proverbs can command someone not even to look at wine (*yayin* in Prov 23:31) and assert that wine (*yayin*) and beer (*shekar*) are more fitting for the poor than for kings (31:4). Yet on the other hand

> Sirach 39:26–27 (NRSVue) paints a picture of wine as integral to everyday life, but prone to abuse like anything else that is good and even necessary in life:
>
> > The basic necessities of human life
> >   are water and fire and iron and salt
> > and wheat flour and milk and honey,
> >   the blood of the grape and oil and clothing.
> > All these are good for the godly,
> >   but for sinners they turn into evils.

---

1. I do not assume that Proverbs and Ecclesiastes belong to a corpus of "wisdom literature," but rather I aim to juxtapose them because the concept of wisdom and its relationship to alcohol consumption are subjects that each of them shares, despite their formal and thematic differences. On the origins and problems with the label, see Will Kynes, *An Obituary for "Wisdom Literature": The Birth, Death, and Intertextual Reintegration of a Biblical Corpus* (Oxford: Oxford University Press, 2019).

(cf. ch. 5), Proverbs affirms that God provides an abundance of new wine (*tirosh*) to those who honor him through the way they steward their agricultural produce (3:9–10). Whereas examples like these might seem jarring to modern readers, this contrast fits the nature of proverbial wisdom. The point is that wisdom is needed, and simple conclusions are not helpful. Consider the intentionally juxtaposed proverbs where the reader is advised not to answer a fool in his folly, and then is immediately counseled to answer a fool in his folly (26:4–5). The rationale for answering and not answering a fool in each verse is different and not easily harmonized. The point is not to wed them together but rather to cultivate the wisdom necessary to know when each proverb is applicable. That aspect is no different with how Proverbs handles the topic of alcohol.

Within Proverbs, drunkenness is a form of excess that is portrayed as characteristic behavior of someone who is foolish and lacks wisdom. As one proverb states, "Like a thornbush in a drunkard's hand is a proverb in the mouth of a fool" (26:9). In other words, a proverb "wounds and lacerates"[2] if it comes from a fool, just as a thornbush would harm a drunkard that stumbled into it.

> "Eat, drink, and discourse in moderation. Of all things, moderation is best, but excess is grievous."
>
> Sibylline Oracles 2.141–42 (1st c. BCE–3rd c. CE)[3]

In a handful of apocryphal texts, wine is regarded as one of the strongest forces in the world, alongside women, kings, and truth (1 Esd 3–4; Josephus, *Ant.* 11.3.2–6; cf. Sir 19:2 on wine and women). In the account of 1 Esdras, the case made for wine's supremacy is that it leads the mind astray and does so equitably across socioeconomic status; it diverts the mind from its sorry financial state toward feasting; it changes how people talk about themselves and how they engage friends and family, even compelling people to do things like draw out their swords; and it causes people to forget the night before (1 Esd 3:17b–24).

The foolishness of drunkenness within Proverbs is fundamentally rooted in where drunkenness can lead a person. We already noted in chapter 4 how Proverbs regards "loving wine [*yayin*]" and drunkenness as economically foolish—stemming from a waste of money (Prov 21:17; 23:19–21). But Proverbs also critiques excessive alcohol consumption for causing drunk people to be unhindered from doing and saying things that they would be much less inclined to do while sober.

Proverbs 20:1 is a great example of this. It states, "Wine [*yayin*] is a mocker and beer [*shekar*] a brawler; whoever is led astray by them is not wise." Calling wine and beer a mocker and brawler respectively is strong language, and perhaps the strongest language in the Old Testament about alcoholic beverages. Yet, the language here is *telic*, focused

---

2. Waltke, *Proverbs: Chapters 15–31*, 353.

3. J. J. Collins, "Sibylline Oracles," *OTP* 1:348.

on the end result of imbibing. In other words, these beverages *can lead people* to become mockers and brawlers. Mocking and brawling are caricatures of behaviors that excessive alcohol consumption could foster—saying stupid things and acting violently. Since the focus is on being "led astray" by wine and beer in the second half of the proverb, it is not referring to the general consumption of alcohol. As Waltke affirms, "The proverb protects itself against contradicting this favorable side of wine and beer by restricting it to the inebriated."[4] This passage highlights how the chief concern that Proverbs has with alcohol is not its mere consumption but its excess, and most importantly for our purposes, where that excess *can lead* someone. For this reason, Proverbs 31:4 says wine and beer are not fit for kings, since kings could *be led to* forget the poor (31:5). Likewise, Proverbs 23:31 advises readers not to gaze at wine, since that could *lead to* sorrow and bruising (23:29), strange visions and saying something unwise (23:33), and waking up with a horrible hangover (23:35). This dynamic in Proverbs is even demonstrated by how Paul makes use of the Greek translation of Proverbs 23:31 in Ephesians 5:18, which is expressly about how drunkenness can lead to debauchery (cf. ch. 7). The negative focus on alcohol in Proverbs consistently pertains to an unwanted potential result from excessive consumption. Indeed, as Dubach affirms, the concerns about drunkenness in wisdom texts are more pragmatic than moral.[5]

Proverbs further develops the theme of how drunkenness can lead to foolish actions through metaphors of feasting with wicked people and even with Folly personified (e.g., Prov 7:1–27; 9:13–18). In one instance, Proverbs says that the wicked are people who

Sirach 31:25–26, 30 (NRSVue) provides a description of wine (*oinos*) as something that increases vices from bad to worse:

> Do not try to prove your strength by wine-drinking,
>   for wine has destroyed many.
> As the furnace tests the work of the smith,
>   so wine tests hearts when the insolent quarrel. . . .
> Drunkenness increases the anger of fools to their own hurt,
>   reducing their strength and adding wounds.

"eat the bread of wickedness" and who "drink the wine [*yayin*] of violence" (4:17). The Greek translation adds that the wicked get drunk (*methyskō*) off of the wine of violence, extending the image even further (Prov 4:17 LXX). The idea communicated through these metaphors regarding wicked people is that "their regular diet craves brutality."[6]

With the personification of Folly, the feasting metaphors have a sexual connotation. Folly greets a foolish man with kisses and mentions the sacrifices that she performed that day (Prov 7:13–14). This signals to the man that she now has a lot of meat for them to eat together.[7] Additionally, she summons the man to a drunken

---

4. Waltke, *Proverbs: Chapters 15–31*, 127.
5. Dubach, *Trunkenheit*, 286.
6. Bruce K. Waltke, *The Book of Proverbs: Chapters 1–15*, NICOT (Grand Rapids: Eerdmans, 2004), 291.
7. Rightly Alter, *Hebrew Bible*, 3:375.

sexual encounter with euphemisms: "Come, let's drink deeply of love till morning; let's enjoy ourselves with love!" (7:18). The blending of drunkenness and illicit sexuality here clearly highlights the foolishness of both.[8]

It is significant, however, that Wisdom is also personified as the host of her own feast (Prov 9:1–6), inclusive of freshly slaughtered meat and mixed wine (*yayin* in 9:2). Wisdom sends young women out into the streets to invite fools to her feast (9:3–4), beckoning, "Come, eat my food and drink the wine [*yayin*] I have mixed. Leave your simple ways and you will live; walk in the way of insight" (9:5–6). The metaphor of the feast is then unpacked in the rest of Proverbs as Wisdom continues to give instruction. Proverbs 15:15, for example, affirms, "All the days of the oppressed are wretched, but the cheerful heart [*tov leb*] has a continual feast [*mishteh*]." Having a "cheerful heart" at a *mishteh*, or drinking party, is only natural, and so we have a play on words here. That is to say, someone who is oppressed can possess a cheerful heart that allows them to feel like they were at a *mishteh*. The implication is that such a cheerful disposition will help the oppressed "to endure and to overcome their circumstances."[9] Wisdom offers a form of intoxication that increases wisdom, as opposed to physical intoxication, which so often curtails it (cf. Sir 1:16; Philo, *Good Person* 13; *Alleg. Interp.* 3.82; *Creation* 71; *Flight* 32, 166, 176; *Drunkenness* 147–48).

> Philo similarly associates the vine, as well as the insatiable consumption of wine (*oinos*), with folly and madness (*Planting* 148; *Dreams* 2.162, 169), and even calls unmixed wine (*akratos*) a poison (*Planting* 147).

Wisdom's feast is connected to her home, which she built herself with seven pillars (Prov 9:1), possibly implying that Wisdom resides in the temple (cf. Sir 24).[10] But Schipper contends that Wisdom's house here is not likely a cultic site, because the term used for slaughtering animals for food is not associated with cultic activity elsewhere, and the temple was not the only place where animals could be slaughtered (cf. Deut 12:13–19).[11] Instead, Schipper argues that the proper background is the Greek symposium, since at these events philosophical matters would be discussed, as guests drank wine that was mixed with water by the hosting symposiarch.[12] In fact, the Greek translation of Proverbs 9:2 seems to imagine a Greco-Roman banquet because it adds that Wisdom's wine was mixed into a krater, which was the common bowl used for mixing wine with water.

Whether or not the Greek symposium provides an explanatory background to this scene (dependent in part on the date of the final form of Proverbs), what was mixed into the wine here in Proverbs 9:2, 5 is not stated. It is more likely the case that the passage is referring to the incorporation of flavor additives like honey, herbs,

---

8. On the relationship between wine and sexual temptation in rabbinic literature, see Rosenblum, *Rabbinic Drinking*, 41–56, 105–6. On how sexual temptation can quickly lead to idolatry, see also Rosenblum, *Rabbinic Drinking*, 71–75, 116–19.

9. Waltke, *Proverbs: Chapters 1–15*, 625.

10. For a cultic interpretation, see William McKane, *Proverbs*, OTL (Philadelphia: Westminster, 1970), 362–65.

11. Bernd U. Schipper, *Proverbs 1–15*, trans. Thomas Krüger, Hermeneia (Minneapolis: Fortress, 2019), 326–27.

12. Schipper, *Proverbs 1–15*, 324–25.

or spices rather than water, since the evidence seems to suggest that ancient Israel was not fond of dilution (cf. ch. 3).[13] Dilution would also be even less likely if the consumption of wine here is associated with cultic meals at the temple (cf. ch. 6).

By contrast, the meal that Folly offers pales in comparison to Wisdom's banquet. Instead of mixed wine and fresh meat, Folly provides "stolen water" and "food [Heb. "bread"] eaten in secret" (Prov 9:17). The NIV renders *lekhem* in verse 17 as "food," since bread can be a metonymy for all kinds of food (cf. Gen 3:19), as it clearly is with Wisdom in verse 5. Yet the lack of reference to meat and wine in Folly's alternative feast could be indicative of the meager nature of the banquet that she offers. Even as a metaphor for associating oneself with wisdom and foolishness, respectively, the role of alcohol in their respective feasts suggests that the foolishness of alcohol consumption that we see so often in Proverbs is not germane to the act itself. If one is a frequent guest at the table of Folly, alcohol will likely be a catalyst for all sorts of foolishness. Yet if one receives insight from imbibing the wine of Wisdom, alcohol can truly be enjoyed wisely.

> Athenaeus (*Deipn.* 10.427f) cites a famous proverb in a context about why some people thought it was unwise to get drunk: "bronze reflects your appearance, but wine [*oinos*] reflects the mind" (Olson, LCL).

ECCLESIASTES AND DRINKING "UNDER THE SUN"

Ecclesiastes eschews much of the proverbial concerns about alcohol consumption and excess in the light of the limited amount of time that humans have to live "under the sun" (cf. 1:3, 9, 14; 2:11, 17–20, 22; 3:16; 4:1, 3, 7, 15; 5:13, 18; 6:1, 12; 8:9, 15, 17; 9:3, 6, 9, 11, 13; 10:5). As such, Ecclesiastes provides a foil to Proverbs. Both texts are concerned with wisdom and foolishness, but Ecclesiastes offers its wise perspective on life from the vantage point of life's eventual end.

In some instances, Qoheleth (the Teacher) has a viewpoint that is broadly compatible with Proverbs, since it does speak directly to the foolish use of alcohol and the problems to which it can lead. For example, Ecclesiastes shares a similar perspective to Proverbs 31 on regal feasting. Ecclesiastes commends regal figures who wisely feast "at a proper time," as opposed to doing so regularly or even daily, noting that they are a blessing to the land because they eat "for strength and not for drunkenness" (Eccl 10:17). This is contrasted with princes who "feast in the morning" (10:16), which is a practice that would obviously not be beneficial to proper governance, just as King Lemuel's mother warned (Prov 31:4–5). The Hebrew word translated as "feast" is just a standard term for "eating," but that is probably a euphemism for lavish consumption, given the reference to drunkenness in verse 17.[14]

In another example that shows some affinity with Proverbs, the Teacher also

---

13. As Schipper (*Proverbs 1–15*, 327) even admits. So also, e.g., Waltke, *Proverbs: Chapters 1–15*, 434; Fox, *Proverbs 1–9*, 299.

14. So Tremper Longman III, *The Book of Ecclesiastes*, NICOT (Grand Rapids: Eerdmans, 1997), 249.

declares that the day someone dies is better than the day of their birth (Eccl 7:1). For this reason, "it is better to go to a house of mourning than to go to a house of feasting [*mishteh*]" (7:2). Indeed, Qoheleth states that it is wise to live like this: "the heart of the wise is in the house of mourning, but the heart of fools is in the house of pleasure [*simkhah*]" (7:4). In a wordplay on intoxication, the Teacher affirms, "Frustration is better than laughter, because a sad face is *good for the heart*" (7:3; emphasis added). The reason for this counsel is the inevitability of death (7:2b)—if this is how life works, it is preferable to live that way. Yet despite offering this perspective, Qoheleth does not begrudge anyone who would prefer to feast instead, as the main thrust of his advice throughout Ecclesiastes makes clear.

For Qoheleth, everything "under the sun" is vanity. Ecclesiastes is one long reflection on how life is so unsatisfying because nothing lasts forever. Even the most extreme hedonistic pursuits, which ostensibly offer excitement, come and go without any lingering contentment. Because of this, everything is vanity. Noble pursuits and less noble ones are all ultimately conducted in vain. As Qoheleth states, "I applied myself to the understanding of wisdom, and also of madness and folly, but I learned that this, too, is a chasing after the wind" (Eccl 1:17). Does this mean that Qoheleth is setting out to mitigate all of the concerns that we saw in Proverbs?

The Teacher explains that his opinion on this began with a decision to experience folly for himself. The tale that he tells begins with a "test" that he received: "Come now, I will test you with pleasure to find out what is good" (Eccl 2:1). He initially rejects "laughter" and "pleasure" as undesirable (2:2), but he answers the call to be tested by pleasure, recalling how he "tried cheering myself with wine [*yayin*], and embracing folly" (2:3a). Yet he adds the caveat that his mind was "still guiding" him "with wisdom" as he did this (2:3a). Again, as the Teacher explains, what was motivating him above all was a desire "to see what was good for people to do under the heavens during the few days of their lives" (2:3b).

When Qoheleth turns to consider wisdom, madness, and folly, he regards wisdom as the greatest (Eccl 2:13), but he also expresses the futility of wisdom because "the same fate overtakes" the wise and the unwise, and both are forgotten (2:14b–16). Given the futility of it all, the Teacher states: "A person can do nothing better than to eat and drink and find satisfaction in their own toil. This too, I see, is from the hand of God, for without him, who can eat or find enjoyment?" (2:24–25). One might as well enjoy the good things of life, even though, as the chapter begins, it cannot bring ultimate satisfaction—*at least it is enjoyable while it lasts*. Similarly, Qoheleth stresses the meaninglessness that comes from the fact that sometimes the wicked prosper and the righteous suffer. This leads him to resound the refrain that it is simply best to enjoy life: "So I commend the enjoyment of life, because there is nothing better for a person under the sun than to eat and drink and be glad. Then joy will accompany them in their toil all the days of the life God has given them under the sun" (8:15).

The Teacher provides a similar sentiment of feasting in the face of life's futility in a handful of places. Intriguingly, he does so when he makes the well-known comment that God has placed eternity in the hearts of humanity (Eccl 3:11). Perhaps surprisingly, far from being a positive note, this fact is "frustrating" to Qoheleth.[15] Having eternity placed in our hearts is one of the "burdens" that God has placed on humanity (3:10), because everything returns to dust (3:18–21), and no one will be able "to see what will happen after them" (3:22b). In other words, the notion of eternity is burdensome because the Teacher's gaze is restricted by the closed horizon of death "under the sun." In the light of the weight of eternity, then, the teacher asserts, "I know that there is nothing better for people than to be happy and to do good while they live. That each of them may eat and drink, and find satisfaction in all their toil—this is the gift of God" (3:12–13). Indeed, since the living know they will die and the dead do not know anything (9:5), it is best to enjoy life: "Go, eat your food with gladness, and drink your wine [*yayin*] with a joyful heart, for God has already approved what you do" (9:7).

Another futile aspect of death is the fact that you cannot take any of the things you amass in this life with you when you die (Eccl 5:13–15). Thus, pursuing wealth is unsatisfying because you will always want more (5:10), and because it cannot go with you after death. When the Teacher reflects on the great things that he has done, like building houses and vineyards (2:4) and accumulating great wealth, possessions, and resources, he states: "I denied myself nothing my eyes desired; I refused my heart no pleasure" (2:10a). But this, he deemed, was all meaningless (2:11), because death ultimately steals everything.

Trying to amass wealth is also precarious to Qoheleth because everything is ultimately dependent on forces outside of one's control, even for those with all the power in the land: "The increase from the land is taken by all; the king himself profits from the fields" (Eccl 5:9). The implication here is that even the king is in a risky position because something could go wrong. In the light of this instability, the Teacher declares, "This is what I have observed to be good: that it is appropriate for a person to eat, to drink and to find satisfaction in their toilsome labor under the sun during the few days of life God has given them—for this is their lot" (5:18).

> Epic of Gilgamesh (ca. 2000 BCE), tablet X, column iii (Old Babylonian): due to the inevitability of death, the tavern-keeper, Siduri, tells Gilgamesh to enjoy all that life has to offer:
>
> Gilgamesh, whither rovest thou?
> The life thou pursuest thou shalt not find.
> When the gods created mankind,
> Death for mankind they set aside,
> Life in their own hands retaining.
> Thou, Gilgamesh, let full be thy belly,
> Make thou merry by day and by night.
> Of each day make thou a feast of rejoicing,
> Day and night dance thou and play!
> Let thy garments be sparkling fresh,
> Thy head be washed; bathe thou in water.
> Pay heed to the little one that holds on to thy hand,
> Let thy spouse delight in thy bosom!
> For this is the task of [mankind]! (*ANET*, 90)

---

15. Rightly Longman, *Ecclesiastes*, 118–21.

It is "God's gift" to be able to receive wealth from God and to be able to enjoy it (5:19). As Qoheleth says elsewhere, "A feast [Heb. 'bread'] is made for laughter, wine [*yayin*] makes life merry [*samakh*], and money is the answer for everything" (10:19).[16]

Qoheleth even obliquely commends readers to make beer in the face of the uncertainty of life (Eccl 11:1–2). He exhorts his audience to "cast your bread upon the waters," which has confused commentators for a long time. The NIV renders the verse as if Qoheleth is telling readers to ship grain across the sea as part of a trade of goods: "ship your grain across the sea; after many days you may receive a return" (11:1). As noted in chapter 4, "casting bread upon water" is most likely a shorthand reference to beer production, since a common way of making beer in the ancient world was to crumble up pieces of bread into water and allow it to ferment.[17] The second half of verse 1 also seems to allude to the process of waiting for the wort to ferment (i.e., the sugary bread water), when it speaks to finding it again after many days (i.e., after it has fermented). Verse 2 then highlights why Qoheleth is recommending the production of beer: "you do not know what disaster may come upon the land" (11:2). As Michael Homan states, "Qoheleth is recommending both beer production and consumption in perilous times."[18] This interpretation not only makes the most sense of a cryptic passage, but it also fits how Qoheleth consistently points readers to the enjoyment of alcohol in the face of life's precarity.

The perspective of Ecclesiastes is thus often deemed to be quite negative and depressing, but the end of the book provides an editorial frame to help interpret the whole (Eccl 12:9–14). The wisdom of Qoheleth is primarily an exhortation to enjoy what life has to offer, including wine, while you still have life to live. The ending of Ecclesiastes does not overturn this perspective, but it does add new connotations to what precedes.

The final section of the book was clearly written by someone other than Qoheleth, which is seen not least in the new perspective that it offers but also in how it mentions Qoheleth in the third person. The closing portion stresses that the "conclusion of the matter," regarding all of what was written previously, is that the reader should "fear God and keep his commandments, for this is the duty of all mankind" (Eccl 12:13). The reason is because God is ultimately the judge (12:14), which Qoheleth himself reminds the reader throughout the text (e.g., 3:17; 11:9). This final injunction does not undermine Qoheleth's perspective on eating and drinking in the face of death, since there is no final command to refrain from doing so. But the editorial frame at the end of Ecclesiastes does situate those injunctions more firmly in relation to the justice of God. In other words, we should enjoy what life has to offer with full awareness of his oversight of all things "under the sun."

---

16. As for money being the answer for everything, Longman explains that this conveys the idea that "money is necessary to buy the food and the wine and other enjoyments of this world" (*Ecclesiastes*, 252).

17. See especially Homan, "Beer Production," 275–78.

18. Homan, "Beer Production," 275.

Such a perspective provided by the canonical conclusion to Ecclesiastes is deepened if we broaden our canonical reflection to include the New Testament, which shows us that the logic of Qoheleth needs to be chastened by the fact that death will not have the final say. The logic behind the sentiment that Ecclesiastes offers, which is akin to "eat, drink, and be merry, for tomorrow we die," is challenged by Jesus in a parable about a man who hordes his harvest all to himself instead of considering others and being mindful of the judgment of God (Luke 12:19–21), and is also contested by Paul in the light of the resurrection (1 Cor 15:32). Thus, the editorial frame of Ecclesiastes already prompts us to lift up our gaze beyond the sun, and the New Testament merely asks us to keep looking further still.

CONCLUSION

Taken together, Proverbs and Ecclesiastes provide a great deal of variation on the matter of alcohol consumption. Both texts offer differing perspectives from each other, but they also contain internally nuanced outlooks as well. Neither addresses the topic of alcohol consumption in a one-sided manner. Proverbs has a positive place for alcohol consumption, but it also warns about the foolishness of excess consumption by stressing the dangers to which it can lead: neglecting obligations (Prov 31:4–5), poverty (21:17; 23:19–21), violence (20:1; 23:29, 35), and sexual indulgence (7:18). Ecclesiastes is not oblivious to the dangers of foolishness (cf. Eccl 2:1–3; 7:1–4; 10:16–17), nor does it commend foolishness to anyone (2:13). Qoheleth's approval of enjoying alcohol in response to the vanity of life is not a recommendation to consume alcohol to dangerous excess. Ecclesiastes is decidedly not in favor of destructive habits of drinking, since its primary aim is to commend a vision for enjoying life while you still have it.

Ecclesiastes therefore envisions a form of alcohol enjoyment that is life-giving and life-affirming in the face of death, whereas Proverbs is concerned to remind us that certain habits related to alcohol enjoyment are not so positive. The foolishness of drunkenness is thus primarily related to the foolish things that people do when they are drunk, but another aspect that makes drunkenness precarious is the way it makes someone vulnerable to what others might do to them while drunk. This is the subject of the following chapter.

RELEVANT QUESTIONS

1. What precisely constitutes excessive consumption of alcohol, and what exactly is problematic about it?
2. What practical steps are needed to enjoy alcohol without causing the negative effects of excessive consumption to come to fruition?

CHAPTER 10

DRUNKENNESS AND VULNERABILITY

Drunkenness is hard to define, both for the ancients and for us today. Complicating factors include the fact that some people have a higher tolerance for alcohol than others, which is partly based on biology and partly based on one's prior experience with alcohol. Additionally, cultural dimensions of how we conceive of drunkenness add confusion to the matter. For instance, some equate "being buzzed" with drunkenness, while others view the former as a precursor to the latter. Further complications stem from nuanced legal definitions in some countries, such as the US, where drunkenness is determined by having a blood alcohol content (BAC) above 0.08 percent. At the very least, it is clear that drunkenness arises from consuming excess alcohol and entails a loss of inhibitions, a decrease in motor skills, a lack of mental clarity, and the possible occurrence of various symptoms of sickness. All of this occurs on a sliding scale, however, leading to distinctions between light and severe intoxication (cf. Philo, *Drunkenness* 27).

In the biblical texts there are many metaphors and images used to depict drunkenness, but even so we do not get a clear definition. In various portions of the Bible there are references to how drunkenness can disrupt your mind, sight, emotions, stomach, and motor abilities. Drunkenness itself can also be a metaphor, as in Psalm 107, when it describes seafarers, tossed around in their ships by the ocean's waves, as fumbling about like drunkards (Ps 107:27).

Regardless of how we define it, the problems with drunkenness that the biblical material stresses are the negative things that can come from it, as with the disobedient son in Deuteronomy 21 (cf. ch. 7). It is even discernable when Job sacrifices for his family in case they inadvertently "cursed God" while feasting (Job 1:5; cf. ch. 8). But even further, drunkenness is linked with a propensity to violence in Proverbs 20:1. When Paul expands Proverbs 23:31 LXX to highlight how drunkenness leads to "debauchery," he is pointing out that people who are drunk are vulnerable to committing the vice of sexual indulgence (Eph 5:18). Thus, the negative side effects of drunkenness are frequently perceived to include regrettable behavior or the neglect of doing what is right. But what about the *vulnerability* of someone who is drunk to become a victim of exploitation, precisely because of their compromised state?

The critique of drunkenness in the Bible is not straightforwardly a matter of excess per se, but rather it is a matter of some failure or tragedy that could ensue from it, not only actively but also passively.[1] The danger, as Walsh explains, is that banqueting creates intimacy, and so should occur in particularly safe settings: "one drinks, in short, with those one trusts or wants to trust."[2] In safe and celebratory contexts, drinking beyond a state of mild intoxication is not inherently dangerous or problematic. An interesting example of this is when Joseph and his brothers become quite intoxicated (Heb. *shakar*) while feasting in the safe confines of Egypt's palaces (Gen 43:34).[3] In the aftermath of the meal, Joseph enacted a plan to frame Benjamin for thievery as a ploy to permanently reunite Joseph's whole family in Egypt (44:1–2, 5, 12, 16–17). Not surprisingly the deception works, in part because royal courtiers would believe that a higher degree of intoxication made Joseph vulnerable to thievery and also because the brothers were too intoxicated to notice.[4] Their level of intoxication is not presented as morally questionable, given Joseph's delight in seeing his family again during a horrible famine, though we do see how easily this could lead to chicanery.

Sometimes things can go much further awry, and trust can break down further in festive settings. This is why Louis Grivetti calls wine "the food with two faces."[5] In this chapter on the dangers of drunkenness, we will see how the Bible displays an overarching theme of how drunkenness can lead to various forms of vulnerability. These include vulnerability to sexual exploitation, violence, and divine judgment, which will receive their own treatment in turn.

VULNERABILITY TO SEXUAL EXPLOITATION

In several Old Testament passages where an egregious form of sexual deviance occurs, drunkenness contributes to the manipulation. In several other cases, the prospect of exploitation is part of the story, even if it does not occur. This theme starts with the very first occurrence of wine in the Bible—in the story of Noah, where this section begins.

In the flood story, Noah is presented as the first vintner, the inventor of wine. Like other creative geniuses depicted in "inventor sagas," Noah does not realize the power of his creation.[6] The very first biblical reference to alcohol appears when Noah plants a vineyard after the flood, drinks too much of his wine (*yayin*), and

---

1. On this understanding of drunkenness in the OT, see Dubach, *Trunkenheit*; Welton, *"He is a Glutton"*.
2. Walsh, "Under the Influence," 19.
3. See Dubach, *Trunkenheit*, 90–91.
4. Joseph's motivations for feasting with his brothers are worth considering as well in the light of Slingerland's notion of alcohol as a "truth-telling technology" that has been used to gauge trust from the ancient world to the present (Slingerland, *Drunk*, 124–33, 177–79).
5. Louis E. Grivetti, "Wine: The Food with Two Faces," in *The Origins and Ancient History of Wine*, ed. Patrick E. McGovern, Stuart J. Fleming, and Solomon H. Katz (Amsterdam: Gordon and Breach, 1997), 9–22.
6. Gerhard von Rad, *Genesis: A Commentary*, trans. John H. Marks, rev. ed., OTL (Philadelphia: Westminster, 1972), 136.

passes out naked in his tent (Gen 9:20–21). In the rewritten version of this story in Jubilees 7.1–6, the text adds that Noah made wine from his vineyard *in the fourth year after the flood*, likely highlighting that vineyards need cultivating before wine is produced, but also that Noah's actions were aligned with viticultural tradition prescribed in passages like Leviticus 19:23–25.

> The consensus of archaeological evidence has suggested that the grapevine was first intentionally cultivated by humans during the Neolithic period (ca. 6000 BCE) in the broader Transcaucasian area, which includes portions of modern Türkiye, Armenia, Georgia, Azerbaijan, Iran, etc. Intriguingly, in this regard, Mount Ararat from the Noah story (Gen 8:4) is found in eastern Türkiye today (i.e., Mt. Ağrı).[7] Recent studies challenge this consensus, however, contending that genetic evidence for grapevine cultivation indicates an earlier origin (by about 3,000 years), and that in addition to the Transcaucasian region, there was a simultaneous cultivation of the grapevine occurring in the Levant.[8]

Genesis presents Noah as a new Adam within a "new creation," with multiple allusions back to the opening creation stories. To start, after the flood the whole land was covered in water (Gen 7:19; cf. 1:2), and then the dry land became visible (8:1–5; cf. 1:9). Once the flood subsided, Noah and his family were instructed to be fruitful and multiply (9:1, 7; cf. 1:26–28), and then Noah became "a man of the soil [*ish hadamah*]" (9:20), harkening back to Adam, whose name (*adam*) resonates with his identity as "a man [*adam*] from the dust of the ground [*adamah*]" (2:7). Noah also lives up to his namesake (Heb. "rest"), bringing *comfort* from the curse on the land (5:29) that resulted from Adam's sin (3:17–19), by producing a relaxing beverage.[9] In Noah's case, however, it was a little *too* relaxing, leaving him naked in a vineyard-garden due ultimately to the effects of fruit, just as Adam was naked in a garden, having been led astray by fruit. Later tradition even identifies the tree of the knowledge of good and evil as a grapevine (cf. 1 En. 32.1–6; Apoc. Ab. 23.6; 3 Bar. 4.7, 15; Pal. Hist. 5.1). As Butler and Heskett suggest, the scene might itself imply that the forbidden fruit was fermented.[10] Finally, although initially Adam and Eve were not ashamed of their nakedness (Gen 2:25), Noah's situation was quite shameful, just as nakedness became shameful for Adam and Eve after they ate of the tree (3:7, 10–11, 21).

---

7. See, e.g., McGovern, *Ancient Wine*, 328, 331.

8. See Robin G. Allaby, "Two Domestications for Grapes," *Science* 379.6635 (2023): 880–81; Yang Dong et al., "Dual Domestications and Origin of Traits in Grapevine Evolution," *Science* 379.6635 (2023): 892–901.

9. Hanneke M. Wilson, "Bible," in *The Oxford Companion to Wine*, ed. Jancis Robinson, 4th ed. (Oxford: Oxford University Press, 2015), 80.

10. Butler and Heskett, *Divine Vintage*, 11.

The shame of Noah's drunkenness, though, is that it exposed him to manipulation by his son, Ham. It is not entirely clear, however, what Ham actually did while Noah was drunk. The traditional view is that Ham wanted to "look upon" Noah's naked body. Some scholars, however, have not been satisfied with this interpretation and have wondered if "nakedness" is a euphemism. If so, it would elide either Ham's sexual activity with his father Noah (paternal incest),[11] or with Noah's wife, Ham's mother (maternal incest).[12]

In favor of these two euphemistic interpretations is how they would frame the flood narrative with deviant sexuality, since it opens when the "sons of God" (i.e., angels) sire offspring with the daughters of men—the Nephilim (Gen 6:1–4).[13] The maternal-incest view is the more compelling option because Noah awakes to pronounce a curse against Ham's son, Canaan—not Ham himself (9:24–27). Since Canaan had not been born yet, he could be the cursed offspring of Ham's sexual impropriety with his mother. In this reading, the sexual deviance bookending the Noah story is amplified since the Nephilim and Canaan both emerge from unnatural sexual unions.

Nevertheless, both euphemistic interpretations are unlikely because in other scenes of sexual misconduct in Genesis the text is not so cryptic. In Genesis 9, there are no references to Noah's wife or even pregnancy. More importantly, these interpretations undermine how Noah's "nakedness" reinforces his connection with Adam. The reaction of Ham's brothers to cover Noah's nakedness suggests that exposure is the crime,[14] and the earliest interpretation of the story provides that reading (Jub. 7.7–13). What remains unclear within the traditional view is why Ham's son was cursed instead of Ham himself. One possible reason is found in a commentary from Qumran, which explains that Canaan was cursed because Noah had already blessed his sons—including Ham—and so a curse could not also be pronounced on Ham (4Q252 II, 7).

> In The Story of Aqhat (ca. 1550–1200 BCE), a man prays for a son, who, among other things, would be able to take "his hand when he is drunk, supporting him [when] sated with wine" (*KTU* 1.17 i 30).[15] This vision of a son's care for his father's drunkenness contrasts sharply with Ham's treatment of Noah.

---

11. Devora Steinmetz, "Vineyard, Farm, and Garden: The Drunkenness of Noah in the Context of Primeval History," *JBL* 113.2 (1994): 193–207.

12. E.g., John S. Bergsma and Scott W. Hahn, "Noah's Nakedness and the Curse on Canaan (Genesis 9:20–27)," *JBL* 124.1 (2005): 25–40.

13. Angels are called "sons of God" in the OT (Deut 32:8; Job 1:6; 2:1; 38:7; Dan 3:25), and 1 Enoch provides an early angelic interpretation of Genesis 6 (cf. allusions in 1 Cor 11:10; 1 Pet 3:18–22; 2 Pet 2:4–5; Jude 6).

14. Gordon J. Wenham, *Genesis 1–15*, WBC 1 (Waco, TX: Word, 1987), 200.

15. Nicolas Wyatt, *Religious Texts from Ugarit*, 2nd ed., BS 53 (London: Sheffield Academic, 2002), 258.

The scene depicts Noah in a shameful state as a result of his drunkenness, but his actions are not the ones that receive condemnation. Instead, the judgment concerns what Ham does to his drunken father.[16] This is similar to the pronouncement of judgment in Habakkuk against those who force their neighbors to get drunk so that they can look at their nakedness (Hab 2:15; cf. Lam 4:21). Noah's excess was precarious because it made him vulnerable to sexual exploitation, however we understand the exposure of his nakedness. Thus, there is an implicit warning against drunkenness—but specifically because there are those like Ham who are quick to take advantage of people in a compromised state.

Elsewhere, the examples that combine drunken vulnerability with sexuality are more overt, but the focus is still on *the machinations of those who are not drunk*, similar to what we saw with Ham. In the story of Lot, his daughters assumed that every other human was dead except the three of them after the judgment of Sodom and Gomorrah. So they devised a way to continue their family line (Gen 19:31) by getting their father drunk with wine (*yayin*) on successive nights and having sex with him while he was drunk (19:32–35). This is the etiology provided for the origin of the Moabites and the Ammonites (19:36–38), linking them with Canaan by way of their common origins in circumstances of drunkenness and sexual exploitation. Indeed, the broader scene is reminiscent of Noah, who similarly got drunk after a cataclysmic judgment. In my view, however, whereas the sexual deviance and subsequent pregnancies are clear in the Lot story, those things are at most implicit with Noah (and I would add that the Lot story shows that Genesis is not coy about sexual misconduct). Although the text provides no moral commentary on this story, we can see the precarious position in which drunkenness places people, because Lot did not know when his daughters came and went each night (19:33, 35).

There are a few other examples in Genesis that combine alcohol and the machinations of sexual trickery. Laban tricked Jacob into marrying his daughter Leah, despite Jacob's clear intentions with Rachel. The trickery occurred when Laban swapped his daughters at night, right after the feast (*mishteh*) celebrating Jacob's supposed marriage to Rachel (Gen 29:22). Presumably the cover of night had something to do with the confusion, but given the celebratory context and the presence of alcohol implied by the *mishteh*, inebriation probably contributed.[17] Similarly, Tamar duped Judah by intentionally pretending to be a sex worker at a sheepshearing festival. She did so as part of a plot to become pregnant because her previous two husbands had died, and she had no children (Gen 38:12–13). A sheepshearing was a celebratory occasion full of drinking to commemorate the end of a season of hard work (cf. 1 Sam 25:8; 2 Sam 13:23), making it a conducive context for her ploy. Tamar succeeded in becoming

---

16. So also, Welton, *"He Is a Glutton"*, 202.
17. Walsh, "Under the Influence," 27; Dubach, *Trunkenheit*, 87–88.

pregnant from her father-in-law, Judah, who did not recognize her because of the veil she wore over her face (Gen 38:14–15). But it is also probable that drunkenness, given the nature of the sheepshearing festival, had a role to play too.[18]

The way that festive events can devolve into something sinister is seen in another story from Judges (Judg 21:15–24). While celebrating an unnamed festival in Shiloh, women were snatched away by Benjamites hiding in the vineyards, who wanted to make these women their wives (Judg 21:19–21). The proximity of the festival to vineyards, and the context of feasting, suggests that the celebrants were inebriated. This would explain both how these Benjamite men were able to steal them away and presumably how the other men at the festival did not realize what was happening.

Sexual trickery with alcohol is also implied in the story of Ruth and Boaz, even though sexual activity does not seem to occur. Naomi, the mother-in-law of the newly widowed Ruth, devises a plot for Boaz to marry Ruth. The plan is that Ruth would go to the threshing floor after Boaz "ate and drank" at the end of a day of threshing grain (Ruth 3:2–3). Anticipating that Boaz would fall asleep in the granary from exhaustion and inebriation, she tells Ruth to "uncover his feet" and lay beside him until he wakes up (3:4). "Feet" can refer euphemistically to genitals in the Old Testament (cf., e.g., Exod. 4:25; Judg 3:24), suggesting that she exposed Boaz,[19] so that he would think they had had sex when he awoke.[20] As the event unfolds, Boaz was "in good spirits" at the end of the night and passed out in the granary (Ruth 3:7).[21] When Boaz awoke, he responded as Naomi had assumed by deciding to marry Ruth. The use of alcohol for sexual trickery here is strengthened by the way it ties in with the plot of Lot's daughters, since Ruth is a Moabite, and also with the plot of Tamar, since Boaz is from the line of Judah.[22]

King David also plotted to leverage alcohol for sexual deception in the story of Uriah, specifically in order to cover up his own sexual deviance with Uriah's wife, Bathsheba. After David had sex with Bathsheba, he devised a plan to send Uriah home to "eat and drink" with her and then sleep with her. If successful, Uriah would be unsuspicious of how Bathsheba became pregnant. After Uriah refused, because of his military responsibilities as a commander (2 Sam 11:11), David plotted to get Uriah drunk so that he would then go home and proceed as expected. But Uriah stayed put after they got him drunk (11:13). This is ultimately why David sent Uriah

---

18. Gordon J. Wenham, *Genesis 16–50*, WBC 2 (Waco, TX: Word, 1994), 368.

19. Kirsten Nielsen contends that Ruth uncovered herself at "the place of his feet." See *Ruth: A Commentary*, trans. Edward Broadbridge, OTL (Louisville: Westminster John Knox, 1997), 68–70. Nielsen adds that this explains Ruth's request that Boaz cover her with his wings (Ruth 3:9), since in this reading she is naked (*Ruth*, 73–74).

20. Some scholars do not hold this view; e.g., Daniel I. Block, *Judges, Ruth*, NAC (Nashville: Broadman & Holman, 1999), 683–88.

21. This is a euphemism for intoxication. Cf. Dubach, *Trunkenheit*, 89–90.

22. Nielsen, *Ruth*, 70–71.

out to the front lines to be killed (11:15–17). David's initial plots did not work, but his intentions fit this broader theme.

In none of the examples just surveyed is excessive drinking explicitly condemned. Instead, the scenes themselves depict the precarity of drunkenness, which opens one up to manipulation. Notably, these texts do not fault the inebriated person for what happened to them. Rather, the text focuses on the plots and machinations of others. Sometimes people cause harm or intend to shame the one who is drunk (e.g., Ham, Laban, David). In other situations, it is seen as a last resort and a means of survival, even while remaining deceptive and less than ideal. This is especially so with the women examples (e.g., Lot's daughters, Tamar, Ruth). Of the intoxicated men in these stories (Noah, Lot, Jacob, Judah, Boaz, and Uriah), only Judah receives any explicit critique, since his hypocrisy is revealed when he condemns Tamar for being pregnant (Gen 38:24–26). But Judah's error is not in feasting at the sheepshearing.

The instances of inebriation and sexual vulnerability so far have focused on the consumer's vulnerability to sexual schemes, but at times alcohol inhibits the consumer from preventing other people from being exploited. In the stories of Lot and the infamous Levite in Judges 19, respectively, townspeople come to a home that is entertaining guests with alcohol and demand to have sex with those guests (Gen 19:5; Judg 19:22), as strange as that sounds. In Genesis 19 the scene is a *mishteh* (Gen 19:2–3), and in Judges 19 those partaking were all "glad in their heart" (Judg 19:21–22 NETS).[23] Understandably, the people inside the home consuming alcohol were shown to be vulnerable to the sexual scheming of the townspeople. But clouded judgment is also implied by how the hosts in each case offer up the women staying there (Gen 19:8a; Judg 19:24), since—as the skewed logic goes—these hosts do not want to be inhospitable (Gen 19:8b; Judg 19:23). Although nothing happened to Lot's daughters, the most heinous example of sexual violence is perpetrated against the Levite's unnamed secondary wife (Judg 19:25–30). Judges itself stresses that this was incomparably evil, stating that nothing this awful had happened in Israel since the days of Egypt (19:30; cf. 20:6, 10, 13). The horrific death of the Levite's secondary wife is another example of how being drunk makes one susceptible to the machinations of others, but it also displays the precarity of trusting the impaired judgment of those who should provide protection.[24] It is that additional biblical emphasis on how drunkenness creates a vulnerability to violence, and even death, to which we now turn.

---

23. The Levite had been imbibing for several days previously at the home of his secondary wife's father (Judg 19:3–9), being told to stay and "enjoy yourself" (Judg 19:6; Heb. "be pleased to the heart"). The tragic event occurred subsequently after arriving in Gibeah and receiving hospitality from an old man, even though they did not need it because they had enough "bread and wine" (*yayin*) for their journey (Judg 19:19).

24. For more on thinking hermeneutically about scenes of sexual violence like these, see Phyllis Trible, *Texts of Terror: Literary-Feminist Readings of Biblical Narratives*, OBT (Philadelphia: Fortress, 1984); Rhiannon Graybill, *Texts after Terror: Rape, Sexual Violence, and the Hebrew Bible* (Oxford: Oxford University Press, 2021).

VULNERABILITY TO VIOLENCE

Many of the texts that portray drunken vulnerability are violent in nature. Most of these examples occur in militaristic contexts, though not exclusively, as seen in the deaths of Job's children when their home collapsed on them while feasting (Job 1:18–19; cf. ch. 8). Similarly, Proverbs 23 speaks of the needless bruises of drunkards and how hangovers feel like getting in a fight the night before (Prov 23:29, 35). Common elements where this theme of drunken vulnerability to violence occurs include the pride of those feasting and the premature nature of the feast.[25]

One of the best examples of this trope involves the haughty celebration of Belshazzar, the Babylonian king, who is overtaken by the Medes at "a great banquet" (*lekhem*) with lots of wine (*khamar*; Dan 5:1). "While Belshazzar was drinking his wine" (Dan 5:2), he gives orders to disgrace the vessels from the Jerusalem temple, utilizing them for his banquet. The Aramaic more straightforwardly says his order came "in the taste of wine," highlighting the presence of wine in his mouth when he gives the decree. The guests at the party proceed to drink wine from these vessels, profaning them, and praising other gods (5:4; cf. 5:23). On that night in which the sacred vessels were profaned, a disembodied hand appears and writes on the wall, "*mene, mene, tekel, parsin*" (5:25)—which Daniel interprets as meaning that their kingdom is coming to an end, being weighed and found wanting. On that night of haughty feasting, the Babylonian kingdom was overthrown by Darius and the Medes.

The downfall of Haman at Esther's feast is another great example of a pretentious figure overthrown at a banquet. Haman's presumption is on display throughout the story, both in his premature celebratory drinking in anticipation of the destruction of the Jews (Esth 3:15), and in his arrogant assumptions that he was being favored by the queen. Instead, Esther was playing the long con, using banqueting to her advantage. As an attempt to thwart Haman, Esther requested a feast (*mishteh*) with Haman and the king in response to the king's offer of half the kingdom (5:4–5).[26] As they were drinking wine (*yayin*) at the *mishteh* (5:6), Esther requested another feast the following day (5:8). Haman's presence at the banquet, the prospect of yet another one, and (no doubt) the lingering buzz from the feast (he was "happy and in high spirits"), had the effect of stroking his ego and lulling him into a false sense of security (5:9). Yet, after an unexpected turn of events, the king orders Haman to parade his arch nemesis, Mordecai, around town with royal fanfare. Immediately following this, Haman is rushed off to Esther's banquet (*mishteh* in 6:14), where they

---

25. These themes are so prominent that when some biblical stories are retold, the trope recurs, as when Jael overtakes Sisera (LAB 31:5–7), and when Delilah dupes Samson (LAB 43:6–7). As well, there are several other stories outside of canonical literature that use a version of this trope (see, e.g., 1 Macc 16:16; Jud. 13:2; Philo, *Spec. Laws* 3.126; Josephus, *Ant.* 10.9.4; 18.9.7; 19.1.4).

26. King Herod says something similar to Herodias's daughter at his birthday feast in the account of John the Baptist's death, linking John's demise with the precarity of feasting even though he was not a participant (Mark 6:14–29).

drank together (*shatah* in 7:1). As they were drinking wine (*yayin*) at this *mishteh* (7:2), Esther finally revealed Haman's plot to the king, resulting in the king leaving "the banquet [*mishteh*] of wine [*yayin*]" in fury (7:7). Returning to "the banquet hall" (*mishteh hayayin* in 7:8), the king mistakenly assumed that Haman was attacking his wife and sentences him to death. After Haman was executed, the Jews were victorious over their oppressors, leading to "feasting [*mishteh*] and celebrating" (8:17). As this final instance of feasting shows, banqueting is not strictly associated with the presumption of Haman, or indeed the king's buffoonery (cf. ch. 8), but also the celebration of life and the defeat of enemies.

The hubris of both Belshazzar and Haman was obviously foolish, as we also see in the story of Nabal (*nabal* means "fool" in Hebrew). At a festive sheepshearing (1 Sam 25:8), Nabal's foolishness is displayed when he spurned David's army and refused to give them resources after they refrained from roughing up his shepherds, making himself vulnerable to attack (25:5–11). Nabal's wife, Abigail, intervened and provided the angry troops with rations, including "two skins of wine [*yayin*]" (25:18), which calmed them down. Once Abigail returned home, she found Nabal in "high spirits" and "very drunk," because he had been throwing a "banquet [*mishteh*] like that of a king" (25:36). Nabal was therefore in the worst possible condition if an attack on his home had occurred. Even though nothing happened, Abigail told Nabal about what nearly transpired after he "was sober" the next morning—more straightforwardly, "after the wine [*yayin*] had left him" (25:37). This is a play on words because Nabal's name sounds similar to the Hebrew word for wineskin (*nebel*); wine left Nabal like wine leaves a *nebel*.[27] The news caused Nabal to endure a heart attack (or stroke),[28] and he died ten days later (25:38).

Clearly feasting makes you vulnerable to attack and is dangerous if you have active enemies pursuing you. In one of Isaiah's prophetic oracles, he instills a sense of urgency to a group at a feast that quickly needs to prepare for battle. "They set the tables, they spread the rugs, they eat, they drink!"—Isaiah prophesies, establishing a scene of feasting (Isa 21:5a). Then he shifts abruptly to the command: "get up, you officers, oil the shields!" (Isa 21:5b). The context of feasting and the sharp transition to lifting up one's protective guard highlights just how dangerous it is when we let our guard down.

In Homer's *Odyssey*, Odysseus lulls a flesh-eating Cyclops named Polyphemus to sleep by offering him multiple rounds of wine (*oinos*), causing him to fall over drunk, before Odysseus attacked Polyphemus by stabbing him in the eye (9.371–74).

Many other examples occur throughout the Old Testament, often involving the demise of a regal figure, or an aspiring one, during a state of inebriation. Abner, one of Saul's sons vying for

---

27. See David Toshio Tsumura, *The First Book of Samuel*, NICOT (Grand Rapids: Eerdmans, 2007), 592–93.

28. Alter, *Hebrew Bible*, 2:285.

his father's throne, was killed by his brother Joab at a feast (*mishteh* in 2 Sam 3:20, 27). Elah was king of the northern kingdom for two years, but his reign ended when his commander Zimri murdered him while he was "getting drunk" (1 Kgs 16:9). Adonijah, one of David's sons, prematurely declared himself to be king (1 Kgs 1:5) and hosted a big party full of "eating and drinking" to celebrate (1:9–10, 19, 25). But while Adonijah was feasting (1:41), David commanded Zadok the priest to anoint his son Solomon as king instead (1:32–35), leading to Adonijah's subsequent execution (2:13–25). The king of Aram, Ben-Hadad, was in the midst of battling king Ahab, when Ahab's men overcame the Aramean camp while Ben-Hadad was "drinking" (20:12) and "getting drunk" (20:16), causing them to flee (20:20).[29]

> Euripides, *Bacchae* (5th c. BCE), records the grotesque demise of King Pentheus from the power of wine when he is violently torn apart by the adherents of the god of wine, Dionysus (or Bacchus), who are in such a frenzied state from the influence of the deity that they do not realize what they are doing, including Pentheus's own mother (1118–24).

There are also a few instances when drunkenness creates a context for violent revenge. Samson, for example, was bound and captured at a feast, having lost his strength after Delilah cut his hair. But he prayed for one final show of force, bringing down the temple pillars he was chained to and killing three thousand people who were previously "in high spirits" (Judg 16:25). Likewise, David attacked Ziklag and the Amalekites who had just "raided the Negev" (1 Sam 30:1), destroying them all and reclaiming their spoils when the Amalekites were "eating, drinking, and reveling" (1 Sam 30:16).[30] Additionally, Absalom sought revenge against his brother, Amnon, for what he did to their sister, Tamar (2 Sam 13:1–22), leveraging the festive context of sheepshearing (13:23), and attacking when Amnon was "in high spirits from drinking wine [*yayin*]" (13:28).

Given this emphasis on susceptibility to violent enemies while feasting, Psalm 23 may contain an interesting nuance. The crucial portion to consider is how, after extolling YHWH for being a good shepherd (Ps 23:1–4), the psalmist says that YHWH is a good host too (23:5–6). Yet, in the light of the present discussion, it is striking to consider that YHWH prepares a table for the psalmist in the presence of his enemies and gives him an overflowing cup in that setting (23:5). The contents are not specified, but wine is implied,[31] and there is such an abundance (*ravayah*) that the cup keeps spilling. The LXX clearly presents this overflowing cup as containing an alcoholic beverage: "and your cup was supremely intoxicating" (Ps 23:5 [22:5 LXX] NETS).

The psalm emphasizes YHWH's protection, to be sure, as divine provision of a cup does elsewhere for the psalmist (Ps 16:5), but the presence of enemies could suggest that an overflowing cup of wine is dangerous. Scholars typically understand

---

29. Ben-Hadad fled again when the Arameans mistakenly thought that four men with leprosy were a large army, allowing the four men to eat and drink what they had left behind (2 Kgs 7:8).

30. This story is graphically intensified, and this trope is accentuated, in Josephus's description (cf. *Ant.* 6.14.6).

31. Contra the NLT, which has "overflows with blessings."

the enemies to be subdued, perhaps as captive prisoners looking on to David's victory feast,[32] or as props from a recent victory (i.e., their corpses).[33] Yet the text does not say explicitly that the enemies have been pacified. Just as the psalmist declares that he will not fear any evil while he is in the valley of the shadow of death because of YHWH's presence (23:4), there may very well be a precarity implied by the presence of enemies. The enemies and the dreadful valley are both dangerous, but the psalmist shows his trust in YHWH's protection and provision. The psalmist's anointing with oil in verse 5 suggests a regal setting for the banquet, but there is no political change of hand here unlike with other instances of this trope. The psalmist will not fear his enemies, even as he consumes enough alcohol for them to overtake him easily, because he knows that YHWH is in charge of the party.

As we have seen, most of the instances of this theme of drunken vulnerability concern leaders, particularly regal figures and commanders. The prophet Isaiah also makes use of some of the elements of this broader theme to chastise leaders. Accordingly, he depicts a vulnerability to violence that drunken leaders cause *for the people they are meant to lead*. In one image, Isaiah imagines the oppressive nations as "beasts of the field" coming to attack helpless sheep (Isa 56:9). Israel's leaders are like drunk shepherds who continue to ask for more wine (*yayin*) and beer (*shekar*), instead of protecting those sheep (56:12). This image—that of oppressive nations wreaking havoc on Israel because of "drunken" leadership—is a replication of an earlier oracle in Isaiah 28, which deserves attention.

In a pronouncement of woe against the leaders of Ephraim and Judah, Isaiah depicts both governing leaders and their constituents as drunkards. In the northern kingdom, the king is called the "pride of Ephraim's drunkards" (Isa 28:1, 3), and the valley in that area belongs to those "laid low by wine [*yayin*]" (28:1)—which is a militaristic metaphor describing the effects of alcohol. In the southern kingdom, the people "stagger from wine [*yayin*] and reel from beer [*shekar*]" (28:7a). The priests and prophets also "stagger from beer [*shekar*]," are "befuddled with wine [*yayin*]," and "reel from beer [*shekar*]," even while they see visions and make decisions (28:7b). As we saw in chapter 7, priests are not supposed to be drunk so that they can serve appropriately in sacred space. Here, however, the priests and prophets are so drunk that their tables are covered with vomit and feces (28:8). As a result, Isaiah addresses their inability to teach and speak for YHWH. Their drunken speech is so jumbled and meaningless (28:10; cf. 28:13) that only a newborn infant could possibly benefit from it (28:9). Translators tend to try to render their nonsensical speech with something intelligible, as the NIV does:

---

32. Derek Kidner, *Psalms 1–72*, TOTC 15 (1973; repr., Downers Grove, IL: InterVarsity Press, 2008), 129.

33. This could be rooted in ANE iconography on reliefs of royal banquet scenes. For an overview of this visual imagery, see Janling Fu, "Iconography of Food and Drink," in *T&T Clark Handbook of Food in the Hebrew Bible and Ancient Israel*, ed. Janling Fu, Cynthia Shafer-Elliott, and Carol Meyers (London: T&T Clark, 2022), 445–84.

For it is:
> Do this, do that,
> a rule for this, a rule for that;
> a little here, a little there. (Isa 28:10)

This traditional rendering conveys a sense that the drunken leaders are hypocrites who do not follow their own rules.[34] But the Hebrew is actually more garbled than this translation suggests, and in light of the comparison to the speech of infants in verse 9, the incoherence of verse 10 ought to be preserved.[35] Alter's translation conveys the nonsensical speech well, understanding the Hebrew as shortened forms of the words for vomit and excrement:

> For it is filth-pilth, filth-pilth,
> Vomit-momit, vomit-momit,
> A little here, a little there.[36]

The scatological tone here may be intended by the drunken priests and prophets *as their attempts to ridicule Isaiah's message*, like the taunts of a child, for being overly concerned with purity and similar matters.[37] But more likely, as Dubach suggests, Isaiah is criticizing the messages of the priests and prophets by associating their teachings with their refuse.[38] In other words, nothing good comes *from* them.

Regardless of the best way to translate the nonsense of the drunken leaders, Isaiah declares that a like-for-like judgment is coming, by way of the unintelligible speech of foreigners "with foreign lips and strange tongues," referring obliquely to the Assyrians (Isa 28:11).

> Paul cites this passage from Isaiah about the unintelligibility of the Assyrian language in 1 Corinthians 14:21 when stressing the need for corporate translation of "tongues" in the multilingual port city of Corinth.[39]

The result of hearing the drunken speech of the priests and prophets is that "as they go they will fall backward; they will be injured and snared and captured"

---

34. John N. Oswalt, *The Book of Isaiah: Chapters 1–39*, NICOT (Grand Rapids: Eerdmans, 1986), 512.

35. Gary V. Smith, *Isaiah 1–39*, NAC (Nashville: Broadman & Holman, 2007), 481–82.

36. Alter, *Hebrew Bible*, 2:709. As Alter explains, there is a "phonetic kinship" in Hebrew between the words for "precept" and "filth," as well as "line" and "vomit."

37. Brevard S. Childs, *Isaiah*, OTL (Louisville: Westminster John Knox, 2001), 207; Roberts, *First Isaiah*, 351.

38. Dubach, *Trunkenheit*, 145. Cf. also Welton, *"He Is a Glutton"*, 188–90.

39. See Ekaputra Tupamahu, *Contesting Languages: Heteroglossia and the Politics of Language in the Early Church* (Oxford: Oxford University Press, 2022).

(Isa 28:13). They were so incapacitated that they were too clumsy and too inattentive to avoid a trap. Though they think they will avoid devastation, haughtily claiming that they made "a covenant with death" (28:15), that pact will be "annulled," and destruction will ensue (28:18–19). This prefigures the Assyrian exile, here depicted as an imminent judgment coming upon unprepared drunkards, who will not be able to defend themselves. Since this is an expression of YHWH's judgment against them, we also see a clear example of how drunkenness can lead to a vulnerability to divine judgment as well—an aspect of the biblical portrayal to be addressed next.

VULNERABILITY TO DIVINE JUDGMENT

Although we are always vulnerable to divine judgment in one sense as finite humans, Scripture highlights how excessive alcohol consumption can exacerbate this. In the New Testament, drunken vulnerability is often cast in an eschatological light. A clear example of this is how Paul's prohibition against excessive wine consumption in Ephesians 5:18 follows from a reminder that believers should make wise use of their time "because the days are evil" (Eph 5:16). The underlying logic of this connection, which is more fully expressed elsewhere in the New Testament, develops the way that drunken feasting in the Old Testament precariously gives way to violent attacks and presents that precarity in relation to the overwhelming nature of divine judgment. In the Old Testament, there is already a trope of God's overwhelming judgment in the cup-of-wrath theme, which compares judgment to the experience of drunkenness. In many ways, the cup-of-wrath theme overlaps with and even extends aspects of the present chapter. Yet that theme will be treated separately in chapter 12 because of its unique role and features.

In the New Testament, believers are called to be ready for the imminent return of Christ, which encompasses the duality of judgment and salvation. Preparation for this event is often conveyed in terms of sobriety. Believers should be sober and alert, ready to receive Christ when he comes. They should also be equipped to avoid the ensuing judgment. As another iteration of the theme of drunken vulnerability, these passages share an apocalyptic orientation, making sobriety one of a handful of symbols for an alertness to the onset of potential judgment.

The use of sobriety to convey readiness for the end appears in Jesus's Olivet Discourse (Matt 24; Mark 13; Luke 21). This discourse, which Jesus delivers in the final week of his life, predicts the destruction of the temple when the Son of Man comes. Throughout the discourse, Jesus emphasizes that people need to prepare for that event. Contextually, then, drunkenness is depicted as an obvious distraction, causing that day to come "suddenly like a trap" (Luke 21:34). Just as "eating and drinking" led to people being overwhelmed by the flood in the days of Noah (Matt 24:38; cf. Luke 17:26–27), the same will happen when the Son of Man comes.

Jesus compares this deadly surprise to what a master would do upon returning unexpectedly from some time away to find his servant acting violently and "eating and drinking" with drunkards, instead of accomplishing the tasks he was given (Matt 24:49–51; cf. Luke 12:45–48).

In addition to being sober, Jesus uses several other apocalyptic images to depict what being alert for the judgment day looks like. He warns everyone to keep "watch" and "stay awake" to avoid being caught off guard (Matt 24:42; Mark 13:32–37; Luke 21:36; cf. Luke 12:37), as a sleeping person would be by a thief in the middle of the night (Matt 24:43). Elsewhere, Jesus also calls people to be dressed (Luke 12:35), to keep lamps burning through the night (Luke 12:35), and to keep waiting (Luke 12:36). Similarly, Jesus says in Revelation 16:15: "Look, I come like a thief! Blessed is the one who stays awake and remains clothed so as not to go naked and be shamefully exposed." All of these exhortations underscore that one must remain vigilant because the end could come when it is least expected. Within these apocalyptic exhortations, "eating and drinking" can be a distraction. But so too can getting married (Matt 24:38; Luke 17:27), along with "buying and selling, planting and building," as was the case with the destruction of Sodom in the days of Lot (Luke 17:28).

Outside of the Olivet Discourse, Peter and Paul both use many of these same tropes of eschatological sobriety and staying awake in the face of the end. Because "the end of all things is near," Peter writes that his audience should be "alert and of sober mind" (1 Pet 4:7) instead of being drunkards (*oinophlygia*) and carousers (*potos*), as they were formerly (4:3). Similarly, in light of the imminent return of Christ, Paul calls the church to be ready by doing the things that characterize daytime: being awake and being sober (1 Thess 5:6, 8; cf. Rom 13:11–13a). Otherwise, that day will come like a thief in the night for those unprepared (1 Thess 5:4–5), because they are doing the things that happen at night: sleeping and getting drunk (1 Thess 5:7; cf. Acts 2:15; Rom 13:12b–13).

In other texts, Paul develops a militaristic nuance to this imagery. For example, Paul exhorts believers to put on spiritual armor as part of their readiness for the oncoming judgment—armor that includes the "breastplate" of faith and love, the "helmet" of the hope of salvation (1 Thess 5:8), and the "armor" of light (Rom 13:12). The move from sobriety to clothing for warfare may seem like a mixture of metaphors. But given the theme of drunkenness leading to militaristic vulnerability that we have seen in this chapter, the connection flows quite naturally. If a soldier is not dressed appropriately for war but is instead drunk or asleep, the soldier will be overcome effortlessly. Within the logic of the imagery, then, eschatological sobriety and readiness for "war" looks like the manifestation of the virtues of faith, hope, and love.

First Peter also combines readiness for war with the theme of eschatological alertness. At the outset of the letter, the churches are called to have "minds that are alert and fully sober" in the light of the future revealing of Christ (1 Pet 1:13). The language of "minds that are alert," as the NIV renders it, smooths out the metaphor in the Greek, which is better translated as "girding up the loins of your mind." Girding loins often refers to being ready for war, and here it applies to one's mental clarity. The militaristic connection to sobriety is further seen when Peter calls for people to be "alert" and have a "sober mind" because "your enemy the devil prowls around like a roaring lion looking for someone to devour" (5:8). Given that the enemy is prowling, they should resist him and stand firm (5:9), extending the militaristic imagery further. This example in 1 Peter also adds the nuance that eschatological sobriety is not just necessary for anticipating divine judgment but is also for fending off the attacks of the devil with moral fortitude.

On the positive side of things, Paul also situates sobriety in relation to the reality of the future resurrection in 1 Corinthians 15. Paul says that if the dead are not raised, then we should eat, drink, and be merry because tomorrow we die (1 Cor 15:32). This saying comes from Isaiah 22:13 and expresses a defiant rejection of YHWH's plea for the people to mourn their sin with rituals of mourning (Isa 22:12). Instead of sadness and sorrow, the people were rejoicing, slaughtering animals for meat at a festival and drinking wine, channeling the slogan "for tomorrow we die" (22:13). This reflects how distant their hearts were from the spiritual contrition that God desired. As Paul utilizes the slogan in 1 Corinthians, the sentiment reflects a final celebration of life before it is taken away forever. Yet because Paul believes that death is not the last word, he calls for "sobriety" and for them to desist from sin (1 Cor 15:34). The NIV offers "come back to your senses" at 1 Corinthians 15:34, but something like "sober up" would be a preferable translation. If there is nothing beyond death to live for, then by all means enjoy yourself. But if there is more to come, then life should be characterized by an eschatological sobriety and moral alertness that is prepared for death's approach.

The imagery of sobriety that we have seen in these examples does not mean that all Christians need to become teetotalers any more than they need to become insomniacs or celibates or the like. The fact that the imagery should not be pressed too hard is seen through the inconsistent use of apocalyptic images. For example, consider what eschatological preparation looks like in the parable of the ten virgins (Matt 25:1–13), which appears right after Matthew's account of the Olivet Discourse. Five of the ten young women were ready for the bridegroom when he came for the wedding banquet, and the other five were not. While the women were asleep (25:5), a "cry rang out" at "midnight" for them to come to the wedding banquet and meet the bridegroom (25:6). What separates the women in the story is not those who slept and those who stayed awake, which we might expect, given the emphasis on alertness in the Olivet Discourse. Rather, the distinction is between those who had enough oil ready in their lamps and those who did not (25:3–4). Nevertheless, the culminating point of the parable is the same as the Olivet Discourse: "therefore keep watch" (25:13), even though no one in the parable stayed awake or kept watch literally. This observation similarly applies to the tropes of drinking and sobriety as well, since the young women were invited to a wedding banquet. We know from the parable of the new wineskins that Jesus believed that weddings ought to be times of feasting (Matt 9:15; cf. ch. 14). This is the case even though weddings are listed as a distraction from one's preparation for the coming judgment in the Olivet Discourse (Matt 24:38). These apocalyptic images are not consistent because they are not prescribing an absolute guideline for sleeping, marrying, or drinking.

What eschatological sobriety does point to, however, is the cultivation of virtues and a godly lifestyle that is expectant of the coming judgment against evil. With the divine-vulnerability motif, drunkenness is a metaphor; but literal drunkenness is not thereby approved. Whatever might keep someone from being eschatologically alert and morally prepared for divine judgment—including literal alcohol consumption—makes that person eschatologically "drunk," and thus ill prepared for the judgment once it comes.

CONCLUSION

As we have seen, this chapter primarily explores how drunkenness can cause vulnerability, whether it is a vulnerability to sexual exploitation, violence, or divine judgment (another distinctive symbolic varietal in Scripture). Drunkenness can be problematic in certain settings because it can lead to disaster. Most of the disasters that the biblical texts depict are not the moral failures of the drunken person but the plots of people who desire to abuse and harm the one who is drunk. In the New Testament, the potential vices that come with drunkenness are developed further. Literal drunkenness is condemned as something that should not characterize the people of God, because it will lead them away from the kingdom and inhibit preparation for the impending judgment. The calls for sobriety in the New Testament, however, are not calls to abstain from alcohol, because sobriety functions as an apocalyptic image for alertness, alongside other such images like being awake and being ready for war. Within the apocalyptic imagination that informs these texts, we must stay awake, stay dressed, and stay sober. Otherwise we will be vulnerable to an eschatological demise.

As noted earlier, there are additional examples of drunkenness leading to vulnerability, presented in the cup-of-wrath theme. Since that theme uniquely portrays God's own judgment as a kind of intoxicating beverage that causes drunkenness, it deserves its own sustained attention (cf. ch. 12). Yet since it also develops themes related to exile, it will need to be addressed after exploring exilic imagery in the Bible related to producing and consuming alcoholic beverages in the next chapter.

RELEVANT QUESTIONS

1. What practices should we implement so that we can promote contexts of trust and safety for the sake of others and ourselves when consuming alcohol?
2. If you consume alcohol, would it be accurate to describe your habits as conducive to eschatological sobriety?

CHAPTER 11

THE LOSS OF GOD'S VINEYARD

The curses of the covenant remained an ongoing threat to the kingdoms of Israel and Judah as a consequence of disobedience to the Mosaic covenant's stipulations. As we saw in chapters 5–6 of this book, there is a dark corollary to the divine blessings of viticultural abundance and flourishing viniculture, which is that those good gifts could be taken away. The present chapter therefore explores how alcohol was a blessing by highlighting specifically how the privation of it was a judgment from God. As a result, this study will also bring us back to the promise of the land and the vision of that land as one of viticultural potential, chiefly noting how Israel is often described as God's own vineyard. This is a theme that has not been explored at length yet in this book because it is primarily deployed with reference to Israel's idolatry and apostasy, which provoke the threat of exile, as we will see.

PRIVATION AS JUDGMENT

If Israel proves to be unfaithful to the covenant's stipulations, the enactment of the covenantal curses is inevitable. This is set out particularly in Deuteronomy 27–32 (cf. ch. 5). The prophets also repeat the same basic ideas, warning about impending calamities, which are climactically expressed in the Assyrian exile of the northern kingdom of Israel (722 BCE) and the Babylonian exile of the southern kingdom of Judah (586 BCE). Even after the exile, devastations were interpreted as God's judgment for violating the covenant. Among the many things impacted by God's judgment were those that were promised as blessings within the covenant, such as the fertility of the land and its viticultural output, revealing how judgment is often a privation of blessing. The concrete nature of the judgment of privation could take the form of militaristic destruction of vineyards, adverse weather conditions that hinder viticultural output, or various plagues that devastate crops.

In the aftermath of the Babylonian exile, the author of Lamentations expresses the deep pain and anguish that he has over all that has befallen his people and the city, and at one point he draws attention to the experience of the children. The author describes how they "faint in the streets of the city" (Lam 2:11) and ask their mothers "where is bread [Heb. "grain"] and wine [*yayin*]?" (2:12). Small children talking and asking about wine may seem hyperbolic,[1] but as Adele Berlin points out, since both grain and wine could be stored away, the children were probably asking whether there were any stored rations to save their family.[2]

Having rations in the face of destruction comes to the fore particularly in scenes of siege leading up to the Assyrian exile. When Samaria was under siege by Ben-Hadad and the Arameans, King Jehoram of the northern kingdom lamented to a woman begging him for help that he could not provide anything from the threshing floor or the winepress (2 Kgs 6:27). Under siege there would be no processing grain for bread, no pressing grapes for wine. Later when Sennacherib and the Assyrians were preparing to besiege Jerusalem, the Assyrians taunted them, saying that Jerusalem will soon lack resources and so need to "eat their own excrement and drink their own urine" (2 Kgs 18:27; Isa 36:12). The Assyrians continued by calling upon Jerusalem to trust Sennacherib instead of the king of Judah, Hezekiah. If Jerusalem listened, they declared, this would alleviate their distress, leading them to be able to eat from their own vine once again (2 Kgs 18:31; Isa 36:16).[3] This promise would only be realized if they agreed to be exiled to Assyria—a land described as producing "grain and new wine [*tirosh*], a land of bread and vineyards, a land of olive trees and honey" (2 Kgs 18:32; Isa 36:17).

These lush and fertile images are reminiscent of the descriptions of the land that God originally promised them, the one they already possessed. Yet, in an ironic reversal of these motifs, they were about to be exiled away from that land because of their covenantal unfaithfulness. The irony of the Assyrian invitation is capped off with a command all too reminiscent of the famous Deuteronomic injunction to the people of Israel before entering the land: "choose life and not death!" (2 Kgs 18:32; cf. Deut 30:19). In stunning fashion, then, the Deuteronomic promises of fertility in the land were being conflated with the covenantal curses of exile. Yet YHWH gave Hezekiah a sign regarding the fortune that awaited the people despite the threat of siege. Hezekiah was told to eat "what grows by itself" in the first year, and then "what springs from that." Following this in the third year, vineyards would be planted and the fruit would be enjoyed (2 Kgs 19:29; Isa 37:30). The prospect of a siege, in this case, gives way to abundance on the other side, symbolized by the vineyard—there is always hope that God would be merciful.

Yet the prophets regularly warned about various disasters that awaited the people prior to, during, and after the experiences of exile and displacement. Accordingly, they critiqued covenantal violations, announced what disobedience would lead to, and tried to incite repentance. For example, the preexilic prophet Micah proclaimed agricultural consequences because the people did not pursue justice, kindness, and

---

1. Alter, *Hebrew Bible*, 3:655.
2. Adele Berlin, *Lamentations: A Commentary*, OTL (Louisville: Westminster John Knox, 2002), 72.
3. In 2 Kgs 18:31 LXX, the text mentions "drinking" from the vine again rather than "eating" from it.

mercy and instead practiced their rituals without attention to the world around them (Mic 6:6–8). They will sow but not reap (6:14), press olives but not use the oil, and produce new wine (*tirosh*) but not drink proper *yayin* (6:15).[4] At the time that Micah was prophesying, he states that he felt alone in the pursuit of righteousness, describing his relationship with his compatriots as if it were like fruit that was left all alone after a grape harvest and gleaning (7:1). As he says earlier, no one wanted him to proclaim the things he was prophesying (2:6), because they believed that they were protected from judgment (2:7) because of YHWH's presence among them in the temple (Mic 3:11; cf. Jer 7:4). The kind of prophet that the people wanted, Micah mockingly asserts, is the kind of prophet who pronounces lies (*sheqar*) that an abundance of wine (*yayin*) and beer (*shekar*) will be coming (Mic 2:11).[5] This comment highlights how the people only wanted to receive good news of covenantal blessing, expressed as copious amounts of alcohol, rather than hearing the announcement of privation as covenantal curses. The prophets do regularly speak of God's restorative activity in terms of providing an abundance of alcohol (cf. chs. 13–14), so it is not random that the people want to hear this kind of prophetic message. Yet YHWH's message for them at this time was devastating judgment that even included the destruction of the temple (Mic 3:12).

Elsewhere in the prophets it is common to anticipate judgment for disobedience meted out against the land, rendering it incapable of producing anything (e.g., Jer 7:20; Ezek 12:19–20; Hos 5:7; Amos 7:1–4). Hosea declared that the land and all of its creatures were in mourning (Hos 4:3), because Israel's idolatry (4:12, 17), cultic practices (4:13–14, 19), and even cultic prostitution (4:14) made them like a sex worker drunk on *yayin* and *tirosh* (4:10–11) and forgetful of YHWH's laws (4:1–2, 5–6, 14c). Even when their drinks (*sobe*) run out, Hosea decried, they turn right back to sex workers (4:18). Thus, they will eat but not be satisfied (4:10), and so become desolate (5:9).

In some instances of this broad prophetic expectation of judgment, the land will become a desert wasteland, incapable of cultivation (Hos 2:3; Jer 50:38–40). Isaiah and Hosea anticipated that the land will be covered by thorns and thistles (Isa 7:24; Hos 9:6), with Isaiah emphasizing that this includes "every place where there were a thousand vines worth a thousand silver shekels" (Isa 7:23). Clearly, the coming agricultural devastation would result in huge economic losses.

It is notable that Hosea can depict Israel's idolatry as a form of cultic drunkenness, and yet Isaiah can depict apostasy on the other end of the spectrum as a diluted drink (Isa 1:22).

As a wrinkle on this prophetic image of the land's devastation, Micah prophesied that YHWH would decimate Samaria, reducing it to a field that is no longer thriving

---

4. Most translations obscure the new wine reference.
5. Welton (*"He Is a Glutton"*, 190–91) notes the play on words between lies (*sheqar*) and beer (*shekar*).

for humans. Yet the land will still be usable for viticulture (Mic 1:6). Though the land of Samaria will be decimated, others will come and cultivate it as a vineyard—a picture similar to what Babylon did to Judah, leaving behind some of the poor to work the vineyards (2 Kgs 25:12; Jer 39:10; 52:16).

> In Jeremiah, idolatry corrupts God's people and so the covenantal land suffers as a result (e.g., Jer 3:1–2, 9; 16:18; 23:10). Although YHWH brought Israel out of Egypt (2:6) and brought them "into a fertile land to eat its fruit and rich produce," Jeremiah tells the people that "you came and defiled my land and made my inheritance detestable" (2:7).

In some prophetic visions, vineyards will be consumed by various animals and insects. Beasts will come along to devour the vines and fig trees (Hos 2:12b; Jer 50:39), leading to their withering (Hos 2:12a). Another threat to vineyards were locusts (Amos 4:9), which Joel most notably emphasizes, describing a level of destruction comparable to the day of the Lord. Because locusts devastated the vines (Joel 1:7, 12), Joel declares that "new wine" (*asis*) "has been snatched from [the] lips" of the consumers of wine (*yayin*) and the drunkards (1:5), and that the "new wine" (*tirosh*) has dried up (1:10). Joel therefore calls upon the people to mourn this loss. There could be a sense that Joel viewed the people drinking *yayin* and getting drunk as failing to recognize divine involvement in the devastation.[6] This would fit the themes we saw in chapter 10, but as John Barton notes, Joel is not here providing a prophetic critique of drunkenness. Rather he is announcing that devastation has already begun through the locust plague[7]—an announcement to which he hopes the farmers and vintners will respond mournfully as well (Joel 1:11; cf. Amos 5:17).

Other prophets speak of God rescinding the grape harvest in similar ways. Jeremiah describes the utter destruction that will come upon the people of Judah, stating, "I will take away their harvest, declares the Lord. There will be no grapes on the vine. There will be no figs on the tree, and their leaves will wither. What I have given them will be taken from them" (Jer 8:13). Habakkuk also anticipates that there will be no fruit on the vine when the Babylonians invade (Hab 3:17). Hosea even says that the threshing floor and winepress will not feed Israel, and the new wine (*tirosh*) will fail them (Hos 9:2). As such, this judgment scene imagines the new wine and the winepress almost like agents who will turn their backs on Israel, in agreement with God's judgment against them. This is because the people lament the lack of grain and "new wine" (*tirosh*) instead of calling out to God, the giver of these good gifts, in repentance (7:14; cf. 2:8–9 [2:10–11 MT]). Consequently, Ezekiel prophesies that there will be "panic" instead of joy on the mountains (Ezek 7:7); the latter likely referring to the joy of the grape harvest, since mountains and hills were commonly where vines were grown.[8] Isaiah, too, envisions that YHWH

---

6. So James L. Crenshaw, *Joel: A New Translation with Introduction and Commentary*, AB (New York: Doubleday, 1995), 94.

7. John Barton, *Joel and Obadiah: A Commentary*, OTL (Louisville: Westminster John Knox, 2001), 50–51.

8. Alter, *Hebrew Bible*, 2:1068; Daniel I. Block, *The Book of Ezekiel: Chapters 1–24*, NICOT (Grand Rapids: Eerdmans, 1997), 253; Moshe Greenberg, *Ezekiel 1–20: A New Translation with Introduction and Commentary*, AB (Garden City: Doubleday, 1983), 148.

will take away the "grape harvest" (Isa 32:10), and so he summons women to weep for the "fruitful vines" (32:12), the "houses of merriment," and "this city of revelry" (32:13). The lack of harvest means that there will not be any merrymaking in the city because the joy of harvest and the anticipation of new wine are gone.

The prophet Jeremiah also addresses the loss of merriment, specifically calling for the postponement of drinking in the face of coming devastation and illness (Jer 16:4). This includes, unsurprisingly, not participating in feasts (*mishteh* in 16:8), which will be brought to silence (16:9). But it also includes not attending funerary meals (*marzeakh* in 16:5) or even performing the rituals of mourning, like drinking "a cup of consolation" (16:7; my trans.). It is easy to see how Jeremiah's admonishment here applies to feasting, but it is less obvious for rituals of mourning. The funeral meal mentioned here (*marzeakh* at 16:5) is often associated with the wealthy and their religious consumption of alcohol,[9] but here in Jeremiah it clearly refers to a place of mourning.[10] Jeremiah's rejection of mourning rituals involving alcohol seems to be rooted in two ideas: (1) there is enough mourning to come, so reserve those rituals for later;[11] and (2) even the consumption of wine to console one during a time of mourning—an attempt to "drown one's sorrows," perhaps—is too uplifting, given the horrors that await them. The sorrows they try to drown will soon learn how to swim.[12]

As we have seen, the prophets closely associate thriving viticulture with a thriving temple cult (cf. chs. 5–6, 13), but the corollary exists also, where devastation results from neglecting the cult. For example, Ezekiel proclaims how profaning the sanctuary and participating in pagan cultic sites will lead to famine and pestilence (Ezek 5:11; 6:11–14). One of the most prominent instances of this theme in the prophets comes in the writings of the postexilic prophet Haggai, who addresses the neglect of the restored temple throughout his oracles. After the return from exile, the rich were neglecting to rebuild God's house even though they themselves had finished their own homes (Hag 1:4; cf. 1:8–9). To these people, Haggai declares:

> You have planted much, but harvested little. You eat, but never have enough. You drink, but never have your fill [*shakar*; i.e., "get drunk"]. You put on clothes, but are not warm. You earn wages, only to put them in a purse with holes in it. (Hag 1:6)

Haggai's point here is that the rich never have enough, and yet they continue to neglect YHWH's house to their shame.

This is a similar message to what Amos and Zephaniah declare in their judgments against the rich who have manipulated the poor. Such people will go on and plant

---

9. McLaughlin, *Marzēaḥ*, 70–79.
10. McLaughlin, *Marzēaḥ*, 194; Dubach, *Trunkenheit*, 248.
11. McLaughlin, *Marzēaḥ*, 216.
12. Paraphrasing a quote attributed to the Mexican painter, Frida Kahlo (1907–1954).

their vineyards, but as a punishment for their sins they will not be able to enjoy the wine (*yayin*) that results (Amos 5:11; Zeph 1:13). Because the rich have neglected God's house, as Haggai declares, there will be a lack of rain (Hag 1:10), and thus a lack of "new wine" (*tirosh*), among other things (1:11). Likewise, because of their idolatry God will take away the good gifts that he gave them, including grain and new wine (*tirosh*), which they have misidentified as coming from other gods (Hos 2:8 [2:10 MT]; cf. 2:5 [2:7 MT]).

In a circular way, part of the devastation that a lack of viticulture entails affects the people's ability to participate fully in the temple cult. The prophet Joel calls on the priests to mourn the devastation of the locust plague upon local viticulture (Joel 1:9), not least because it impacts their own diets and well-being since they are dependent on regular offerings.[13] Yet cultic and festival participation will be affected as well, both by the lack of libations of *yayin* to offer (Hos 9:4–5; Joel 1:9) as well as the lack of alcohol to consume at the festivals, thus removing joy from their observances (Hos 2:11). After the Babylonian destruction of the first temple, the author of Lamentations mourns that there is no one on the road making pilgrimage to Jerusalem for the festivals (Lam 1:4). Yet with devastating irony, the author speaks of a raucous noise of people heading to the temple as on a festival day, but what was mistaken for sounds of festive celebration turned out to be the din of the temple's destruction (2:7, 22).

God's judgment as the devastation of Israel's vineyards also applies to the nations, showing the significance of viticulture to the surrounding agrarian societies. For example, God destroyed the vines and fig trees of Egypt at the exodus (Pss 78:47; 105:33). With respect to Moab, God will cause their vines and grapes to wither and be trampled (Isa 16:8–9; Jer 48:32b). There will be no rejoicing or shouting at their vineyard harvests (Isa 16:9–10; Jer 48:33a), and no one will be pressing wine (*yayin*) or shouting at the winepresses while treading grapes (Isa 16:10; Jer 48:33). Indeed, Moab is personified as a vineyard in these oracles, being called "vines of Sibmah." As we will see, Israel is often personified as a vineyard in contexts of judgment as well.

ISRAEL AS GOD'S VINEYARD

A well-known biblical metaphor for God's relationship with Israel presents God as a vintner who cares for a vineyard. Surprisingly, this theme primarily occurs in contexts that focus on Israel's disobedience and the consequent judgment of the vineyard. There are some notable exceptions to this, but one common nuance is that Israel has not lived up to her viticultural potential of producing the best wine. The component

---

13. Barton, *Joel and Obadiah*, 53.

parts of the imagery can be found fully or partially in a handful of passages, which include: (a) God the vintner plants and cultivates the Israel-vineyard carefully; (b) the vineyard grows prominent; (c) the vineyard's quality is compromised; (d) the vineyard becomes exposed, either to the elements, creatures, or thieves; and (e) the vineyard is destroyed. In the following sections we will look at the way in which this theme is articulated in Psalm 80, Hosea, Jeremiah, Ezekiel, and Isaiah, before turning to see how Jesus employs it in the Gospels.

Israel as God's Vineyard in Psalm 80

Psalm 80 provides a succinct overview of most of the key subthemes just noted. The psalmist depicts Israel as a vine that God took from Egypt and planted elsewhere (Ps 80:8), even with his right hand (80:15a). Like a good vintner, God "cleared the ground" first, and once the vine took root it "filled the land" (80:9). The vine became so prominent that all the "mountains were covered with its shade" (80:10), reinforcing the relationship between vineyards and mountainsides. The psalm then shifts to acknowledge that this vineyard received ill-treatment. Without explaining what changed so drastically, the psalmist laments, "Why have you broken down its walls so that all who pass by pick its grapes?" (80:12). The lack of a fortified boundary left the vine and its fruit exposed to wild animals (80:13), which conveys the experience of exile, though without mentioning the disobedience that caused it. Given the precarious situation for the vineyard, the psalmist asks God to "watch over this vine" (80:14). Instead, the vine is "cut down" and burned by fire (80:16), and so the psalm ends with a prayer for God to change the current state of affairs (80:17–19).

> Fourth Ezra (1st c. CE) addresses the destruction of the Jerusalem temple in 70 CE, asking why God has chosen "one vine" and "one region" (5.23), only to allow it to be "given over," "dishonored," "scattered," and "trodden down" by "those who opposed your promises" (5.28–29).[14] In this way, 4 Ezra resembles Psalm 80, since the author does not fixate on the reasons for the demise but simply laments it.

Israel as God's Vineyard in Hosea and Jeremiah

The prophets Hosea and Jeremiah focus primarily on the subthemes of the corruption of the vine and its destruction in a few scattered allusions. Hosea looks back to the origins of Israel by referring to a time when they were merely like grapes in the wilderness (Hos 9:10). Sadly, they were quickly given to idolatry and so did not

---

14. B. M. Metzger, "The Fourth Book of Ezra," *OTP* 1:533.

bear fruit (9:11–17). Instead of worshiping God for the abundance of the vine, they turned to foreign gods (10:1). As a result, God will destroy their cultic sites (10:2).

Jeremiah describes how Israel was like a "choice vine" (*soreq*), being of "sound and reliable stock," that turned into a "corrupt, wild vine" after it was planted (Jer 2:21). Elsewhere Jeremiah attributes the corruption of "my vineyard" to its leadership (12:10). As judgment, Jeremiah declares that the remnant of Israel will be gleaned like a vine (6:9) and be devastated by military action, metaphorically referring to lions, wolves, and leopards wreaking havoc on the land (5:6). These beasts are given the injunction: "Go through her vineyards[15] and ravage them, but do not destroy them completely. Strip off her branches, for these people do not belong to the LORD" (5:10). The language implies that although devastation is coming, there will be a remnant that will be spared. Despite the fact that Israel and Judah believed that they were immune from these threats (5:12), Jeremiah prophesied against Israel that a great nation will overtake them (5:15), such that their family, livestock, and agricultural produce (including "vines and fig trees") will be devoured (5:17).

Israel as God's Vineyard in Ezekiel

As with Hosea and Jeremiah, Ezekiel's use of the vineyard metaphor is mostly related to the subthemes of the vineyard's demise and destruction. There are allusions to this throughout Ezekiel, such as when he speaks of Israel's production of bad fruit (Ezek 18:2). This is also in view when he compares Jerusalem to the uselessness of the wood of the vine, which cannot be used for construction or anything else (15:1–5). Consequently, it will be discarded into the fire like vine branches (15:4–5), imagining the downfall of Jerusalem and the desolation of the land (15:6–8). Ezekiel's primary development of the vineyard theme, though, occurs in Ezekiel 17 and 19.

Ezekiel refers to Judah's experience of Babylonian exile symbolically in Ezekiel 17:1–24, comparing Judah-in-exile to a thriving vine. As part of a larger parable, an eagle took twigs from the top of cedar trees in Lebanon and carried them off and planted them in a land of merchants (Ezek 17:3–4). Then the eagle planted a seedling that became a prominent vine (17:5), spreading all around and producing branches and "leafy boughs" (17:6). But the vine reached out its branches to another eagle flying overhead in the hope of gaining access to water (17:7), even though it was planted in rich soil near a good source of water with the ability to bear fruit (17:5, 8). Yet this second eagle ripped up the ground and exposed the vine's roots, making it vulnerable to the sun, the east wind, and the threat of being ripped out of the ground completely (17:9–10).

The image is convoluted, but the explanation is provided in the text (17:11–15).

---

15. The Hebrew says "rows" (*sharah*), which probably referred to rows of a cultivated vineyard.

The first eagle is Nebuchadnezzar, the king of Babylon, who took from the top of the cedars of Lebanon when Babylon snatched away the royalty in Jerusalem (17:12), referring to Jehoiachin, the king of Judah. The land of merchants where the royal cedar twig was brought is Babylon (cf. 16:29). The seedling that became a vine with roots and branches, though, refers to Zedekiah, the king that Nebuchadnezzar put in charge of the land of Judah just prior to the exile (Ezek 17:13–14; cf. 2 Kgs 24:17). The attempts of this vine to receive support from the second eagle refer to how Zedekiah sought aid from Egypt (Ezek 17:15). As a result, God declares that he will destroy Zedekiah for governing Judah in this way (cf. 2 Kgs 25:1–7), both for breaking off the agreement with Babylon, and for seeking to receive support from Egypt instead of relying upon God (Ezek 17:16–21). This then leads to the explanation that the parable prefigures the destruction of Jerusalem and the deportation of Judah to Babylon (cf. 2 Kgs 25:8–21). The oracle culminates in an expectation that yet another "shoot" from a cedar will be replanted in the land, with all other trees sitting under its shade (Ezek 17:22–24), likely anticipating a messianic ruler.[16] This final image is one of restoration, but it is notable that what is restored is a "cedar tree," supplanting the "vineyard" theme.

A few chapters later, Ezekiel compares Judah's regal figures to branches of a vine (Ezek 19:10–14), as part of a larger tapestry of poetic images that also compares them to lion cubs (19:1–9). The poem begins with a summons to lament "the princes of Israel" (19:1) and describes how a mother lion raised two particular cubs to be strong lions. Yet when the first one became strong it was bound by the nations in a net and taken to Egypt (19:2–4). Then, when the second one became strong, it was similarly captured and taken to Babylon (19:5–9). The text does not explain the imagery, as in Ezekiel 17, and so scholars are divided on the identities of the two regal figures and the mother lion.[17] Regardless, however, regal figures are in view and so is the exile.

From here the poem shifts to depict the same mother as a fruitful vine planted near water (Ezek 19:10–14).[18] The vine then rose high off the ground with great branches "fit for a ruler's scepter" (19:11), suggesting that the branches represent regal figures. Yet this great vine was uprooted, and so it withered from the east wind (19:12) and was consumed by fire. As an extension of the imagery of exile, the vine was then planted "in a dry and thirsty land" (19:13), where it was further consumed by fire, leaving no fruit and no branches to be used as a ruler's scepter (19:14). The juxtaposition of these two sets of images—that of the lion cubs being taken away and the vine with its royal branches being uprooted—present the same story of the Babylonian exile poetically.

---

16. Block, *Ezekiel*, 548–53.
17. Cf. Block, *Ezekiel*, 603–7.
18. The Hebrew says, "like a vine in your blood" (Ezek 19:10), which most translators regard as a scribal error. Cf. Julius A. Bewer, "Textual and Exegetical Notes on the Book of Ezekiel," *JBL* 72.3 (1953): 159.

Israel as God's Vineyard in Isaiah

The most extensive depiction of the vineyard metaphor appears in Isaiah's song of the vineyard (Isa 5:1–7). In this poetic section, a vintner plants a new vineyard that is taken from "the choicest vines" (*soreq* in 5:2). He provides it with everything needed to thrive and flourish, which includes placing the vineyard on a hillside with great soil (5:1), cultivating the ground for proper irrigation and removing the stones (5:2), installing physical infrastructure in the vineyard like a tower and a winepress (5:2), and protecting it by fencing and hedging it (5:5). This imagery is explained explicitly in the following way: "the vineyard of the Lord Almighty is the nation of Israel, and the people of Judah are the vines he delighted in" (5:7a).

Despite the vintner's oversight and care for his vineyard (Isa 5:4), however, he only found "bad fruit" when he looked for "good grapes" (5:2), making the vineyard unfit for wine. The bad fruit that YHWH found in his vineyard was "bloodshed" and "cries of distress" instead of "justice" and "righteousness" (5:7). Because the vineyard was unfit, YHWH says that he will remove the protective barriers around the vineyard so that it will be trampled and destroyed (5:5). The destruction of the wall here is similar to the imagery in Psalm 80:12–13, although Isaiah does provide the rationale for the wall's destruction. Additionally, God will withhold rain, and the land will become a "wasteland" full of thorns, lacking in proper upkeep and maintenance (Isa 5:6).

Although the song of the vineyard only includes Isaiah 5:1–7, the text continues with a series of woes (5:8–30) that are best read as developing the sorry state of God's vineyard and as pronouncing corresponding judgments to follow.[19] The specific indictments against God's vineyard in the woe section include a socioeconomic critique of excess (cf. ch. 4). The people are indulgently consuming alcohol—from the early morning they "run after" beer (*shekar*) and late at night "they are inflamed with wine [*yayin*]" (5:11). Clearly this depicts people constantly drinking alcohol, but it may be the case that there is an additional nuance. Instead of being "inflamed" by wine at night, these people may be *chased by wine*, mirroring their hasty pursuit of beer in the morning, and personifying the control of alcohol over them.[20] If so, wine is being depicted here as a kind of puppet master.[21]

Yet this is not merely a general indictment of excess. Those who have the leisure to consume alcohol all day are the wealthy, who have enough resources to do so and who can afford the time because they do not need to work. These people leave no space for the poor, but instead "add house to house" and "join field to field" (Isa 5:8). Their feasts (*mishteh*) include all sorts of festive musical accompaniment, as well as wine (*yayin* in 5:12a), pointing further to their opulence and contrasting sharply

---

19. Even if much of Isaiah 5–10 was originally produced in a different order (i.e., the *Denkschriften* hypothesis), its present canonical form deserves its own account. So Childs, *Isaiah*, 37–49.

20. Roberts, *First Isaiah*, 80.

21. The famous heavy-metal song "Master of Puppets" by Metallica (1986) is about substance addiction.

with their lack of acknowledgment of YHWH (5:12b). They are also called "heroes at drinking wine [*yayin*] and champions at mixing drinks [*shekar*]" (5:22). These excessive drinkers are, once again, the elite who "acquit the guilty for a bribe" and "deny justice to the innocent" (5:23). We might say that one of the faults of God's vineyard is that its resources are not equitably accessible to all.

As a judgment against God's vineyard, and specifically the rich who consume alcohol excessively, Isaiah declares that "a ten-acre vineyard will produce only a bath of wine" (Isa 5:10). Technically there is no word for wine in the Hebrew text, but since a bath is a liquid measurement, wine is clearly implied. A bath would only amount to five and a half gallons,[22] or a little over twenty liters.[23] This would be like saying that vineyard could only produce 26–28 bottles of wine, whereas a single acre (in a modern setting) should be able to produce hundreds of gallons. This showcases the meagre results after a year's worth of work. The judgments in the woe section culminate at the end of the chapter with a summons to the nations, whose warriors are compared to lions, to bring about God's judgment upon his people (5:26–30). As Oswalt comments, "The wild animals are called and now come to trample the vineyard."[24]

This focus on socioeconomic inequality in the woe section of Isaiah 5:8–30 is strengthened by looking closely at the first brief instance of the vineyard motif in Isaiah. In Isaiah 3, the prophet announces that YHWH is directing judgment "against the elders and leaders" of the people because they "have ruined my vineyard" (Isa 3:14). Specifically, these leaders have stolen from the poor (3:14), which Isaiah describes as "crushing" and "grinding" their faces (3:15). As depictions of injustice against God's vineyard, these terms could be suggestive of the winemaking process, although they are not standard vinicultural terms. Regardless, it still may be the case that this imagery is directed at inequities within literal vineyards, where the rich were benefiting and the poor were not. Either way, together Isaiah 3 and Isaiah 5 depict Israel as a vineyard and utilize that metaphor to call out the disparities between the rich and the poor.

Allusions to the vineyard motif occur elsewhere in Isaiah, primarily through the theme of God preserving and restoring a remnant of Israel.[25] The entire oracle of Isaiah begins with

Pseudo-Philo (1st–2nd c. CE), which is, broadly speaking, a rewriting of the Old Testament's storyline from Adam to the death of King Saul, is replete with images of Israel as God's vineyard (LAB 18.10–11; 23.11–12). The first expression of the theme is found in the account of the golden calf, where Moses intercedes to God to continue caring for his vine instead of burning it and creating a new one despite its lack of fruit (12.8–10). God decides to be merciful, which entails withholding judgment rather than bringing about restoration, and the remaining examples of the vine imagery are deployed to appeal to God's mercy to withhold judgment (30.4; 39.7).

---

22. Roberts, *First Isaiah*, 79.
23. H. G. M. Williamson, *A Critical Commentary on Isaiah 1–27, Volume 1: Commentary on Isaiah 1–5*, ICC (London: T&T Clark, 2006), 355.
24. Oswalt, *Isaiah*, 168.
25. References to branches and shoots in Isaiah might refer to vine branches within the vineyard motif (cf., e.g., 4:2; 11:1; 60:21). On the preservation of a remnant in Isaiah, see, e.g., 6:11–13; 10:20–22.

an announcement of the land's desolation (Isa 1:7). Yet Isaiah compares "daughter Zion" to a "shelter in a vineyard" (1:8), imagining the survival of a remnant instead of a complete destruction like what befell Sodom and Gomorrah (1:9). This theme of a surviving remnant is also depicted at the end of Isaiah through an ancient saying regarding the treatment of grapes:

> As when juice [*tirosh*] is still found in a cluster of grapes
>   and people say, "Don't destroy it,
>   there is still a blessing in it,"
> so will I do in behalf of my servants;
>   I will not destroy them all. (Isa 65:8)

The potential for grapes to produce the blessing of *tirosh* is itself a strong indication of Israel's attitude toward wine and illustrates here that God intends to preserve his vineyard by bringing Judah back from exile (65:9).

Yet these allusions to the vineyard motif that anticipate preservation and even restoration are found elsewhere only in Isaiah 27:1–6. This brief section alludes back to Isaiah 5 and imbues the metaphor with hope. Given that this scene is part of a larger apocalyptic section of Isaiah concerned with the eschatological banquet (Isa 24–27), this passage will be explored at greater length in chapter 14. As we have seen from this survey of the image in the Old Testament, it is in fact the only place where the element of restoration is overtly incorporated. With that in mind, we shift to how Jesus utilized this theme in his teachings.

Israel as God's Vineyard in Jesus's Teachings

The vineyard motif appears throughout the Gospels, not least through the recurring setting of vineyards in Jesus's parables. But the most prominent instances are the parable of the wicked tenants and Jesus's declarations in John 15 that he is the true vine. We will look at each in turn.

The parable of the wicked tenants is the most thorough expression of the vineyard motif in the Gospels, and it seems to be directly dependent on the song of the vineyard in Isaiah 5. The parable, which occurs in the passion narratives of all three Synoptic Gospels after Jesus cleansed the temple (Matt 21:33–46; Mark 12:1–12; Luke 20:9–18), is about a vineyard owner who plants a vineyard and rents it out to farmers to care for it while he is away. Before the vintner departs, though, he sets the vineyard up for success: "he put a wall around it, dug a pit for the winepress and built a watchtower" (Mark 12:1b; cf. Matt 21:33).[26] These elements share some

---

26. The infrastructural details are lacking in Luke 20:9. Cf. Gos. Thom. 65.

verbal agreement with the description of the vintner's preparation in Isaiah 5:2 LXX and recall God's care and attention to the vineyard.

The key plot of the parable is that while the owner is away, he sent servants to gather fruit at harvest time. But each one in turn is mistreated, and some are even killed (Matt 21:34–36; Mark 12:2–5; Luke 20:10–12). The vineyard owner reasons that if he finally sent his son the farmers would honor him (Matt 21:37; Mark 12:6; Luke 12:13). But instead, the farmers devised a plan to kill the son and take his inheritance by force, making the vineyard theirs (Matt 21:38–39; Mark 12:7–8; Luke 20:14–15). Because of this mistreatment, Jesus concludes the parable by saying that the vineyard owner will kill the farmers and give "the vineyard to others" (Mark 12:9; Luke 20:16; cf. Matt 21:40–41). To ground this judgment, Jesus quotes from Psalm 118:22–23, which includes the line, "The stone the builders rejected has become the cornerstone" (Mark 12:10–11; Matt 21:42; Luke 20:17).

The parable departs from the broader vineyard motif by not addressing the subthemes of the vineyard's corrupt fruit or subsequent destruction. Instead, the focus is on the unruly supervisors of the vineyard, leading to the need for new oversight. The vineyard motif singles out Jerusalem's leadership elsewhere, especially in Isaiah 5, Jeremiah 12, and Ezekiel 17, but in those instances the corrupt leadership partially explains the production of bad fruit. This is not the case in Jesus's parable. It is instead the leaders who are hindering the vineyard from producing fruit. This is confirmed by the fact that all of the scribes, chief priests, Pharisees, and elders recognize that the parable was directed at them (Matt 21:45–46; Mark 12:12; Luke 20:19; cf. Mark 11:27).[27]

Other elements in this context imply not just a critique of leadership but specifically an indictment of Jerusalem's *cultic* leaders. This is suggested in part by the timing of the parable, since it appears *after* the event when Jesus cleansed the temple during his final week in Jerusalem, and just *before* the Olivet Discourse when he predicted the temple's demise.[28] The prophetic sign act, coupled with his prophetic pronouncement, highlights Jesus's fraught relationship with the temple administration. A cultic connotation to the parable is also suggested by the "stone" imagery from Psalm 118:22–23 (Matt 21:42; Mark 12:10–11; Luke 20:17). As such, the psalmist may be mixing this metaphor with the metaphor of the rejection of the vintner's son. But it is probably relevant to the parable in two ways. First, there is likely an original wordplay in Hebrew that is obscured in translation—the Hebrew word for "son" (*ben*) sounds like the word for "stone" (*eben*), linking the son's rejection in the parable to the stone's rejection in the

---

27. Similarly, the Qumran sectarians believed Isa 5 was about contemporary leaders in Jerusalem, called "scoffing men" (4QIsaiahPesher[b] [4Q162] I–II).

28. Rightly, M. Eugene Boring, *Mark: A Commentary*, NTL (Louisville: Westminster John Knox), 329.

psalm.²⁹ Second, and related to the cultic nature of the parable, the rejected stone becomes a cornerstone, suggesting that a new temple is being constructed around the vintner's son—Jesus.³⁰ Additionally, the theme of Israel as a vineyard developed into an image of the temple in rabbinic Judaism (cf. Tg. Isa. 5:2, 5; Song Rab. 2:16 [§1]; 7:13 [§1]; t. Sukkah 3:5; b. Sukkah 49a).³¹ These traditions are quite late, but there is some Second Temple evidence, albeit fragmentary, that the sectarians at Qumran may have already begun to make this association (cf. 4Q500).³² If this background informed Jesus's parable, it would help to reinforce that the critique primarily concerns Jerusalem's cultic leaders (which is already implied by the parable's literary placement and use of Ps 118).

> Josephus records how King Herod the Great renovated the second temple (late 1st c. BCE) and added an impressive sculpture of a golden vine (*Ant.* 15.11.3). This highlights the obvious role of wine in the temple, but it also suggests Israel's identity as God's vineyard, which may have already begun to be connected to the temple itself.

This focus on the leaders is clear even though Matthew uniquely ends his version of the parable with Jesus declaring that the implication is that "the kingdom of God will be taken away from you and given to a people [*ethnos*] who will produce its fruit" (Matt 21:43). The closest Mark and Luke get to saying this is Jesus's line that the vineyard will be given to "others" (Mark 12:9; Luke 20:16), suggesting new leadership of the vineyard since there is not a brand-new vineyard created to replace the old one. In Matthew, the shift from "you" to "a people" who will produce fruit seems to go beyond whatever leadership has hindered the production of fruit and may suggest a movement away from Israel to the church.³³ More likely, however, this is an intra-Jewish dispute that defines those who belong to this *ethnos* as those who produce fruit. As Ulrich Luz says, Jesus's statement includes "an appeal to those who thus far did not belong to Israel to bring fruits."³⁴ This means that even those who are the most unlikely to produce such fruit are being summoned. Gentiles are not strictly in focus, although they would be included. More immediately, inclusion is extended to those internal to Israel, who were often regarded as outsiders, such as tax collectors and sex workers.

Matthew's version of the parable of the wicked tenants is embedded within a larger sequence of parables, including others involving vineyards, which provide further support for this interpretation. In the parable of the workers in the vineyard (Matt 20:1–16), the workers receive the same wage at the end of the day, regardless of how many hours they worked. This suggests that everyone will enjoy the kingdom

---

29. See Matthew Black, "The Christological Use of the Old Testament in the New Testament," *NTS* 18.1 (1971): 11–14; Klyne Snodgrass, *The Parable of the Wicked Tenants*, WUNT 27 (Tübingen: Mohr Siebeck, 1983), 113–18.

30. Adela Yarbro Collins, *Mark: A Commentary*, Hermeneia (Minneapolis: Fortress, 2007), 548.

31. See G. K. Beale, *The Temple and the Church's Mission: A Biblical Theology of the Dwelling Place of God*, NSBT (Downers Grove, IL: InterVarsity Press, 2004), 183–88; C. A. Evans, "How Septuagintal Is Isa. 5:1–7 in Mark 12:1–9?," *NovT* 45.2 (2003): 105–10.

32. George J. Brooke, "4Q500 1 and the Use of Scripture in the Parable of the Vineyard," *DSD* 2.3 (1995): 268–94.

33. E.g., Davies and Allison, *Matthew*, 3:189–90.

34. Ulrich Luz, *Matthew 21–28: A Commentary*, trans. Wilhelm C. Linss, Hermeneia (Minneapolis: Fortress, 2005), 43.

equally, regardless of when they join, showcasing that it is not too late for outsiders to join. In the parable of the two sons (21:28–32), a father directs his two sons to go work in the vineyard. The first one does so, though only after initially refusing. By contrast, the second one decides not to go, even though he initially promised he would. Jesus uses this story to convey the point that despite the first son's reluctance, he ultimately did what the father wanted. This depicts the way in which the kingdom is open to those who appear the least likely to join, but who are "entering the kingdom of God ahead of" the Jerusalem leadership (21:31b–32). Strengthening this is the observation that this parable comes right before Jesus tells the parable of the wicked tenants, which addresses the leadership specifically rather than the people generally (21:45–46). This particular idea is further developed in the immediately following parable of the wedding banquet (22:1–14), where those who were originally invited not only refuse to show up but even mistreat those inviting them. This then leads to new and unlikely guests being invited, resulting in a full party (22:10). These parables reinforce the point that many people regarded as outcasts will surprisingly participate in the kingdom, and—as the parable of the wicked tenants contributes to this bigger picture that Matthew is painting—they will produce fruit fit for God's vineyard.

Jesus teaches elsewhere about the importance of producing good fruit and being known by one's fruit (Matt 7:16; Luke 6:44; cf. Jas 3:12), which may allude to the vineyard theme. But the most extensive image of bearing fruit that does seem to connect here is Jesus's statement that he is the true vine in John 15. Just as with the parable of the wicked tenants, God is portrayed as the vintner. However, the difference here is that Jesus is part of the vineyard, "the true vine," rather than the son of the vintner (though God is called "my Father"; John 15:1, 8). Consistent with the broader vineyard theme, Jesus says that a lack of fruit will lead to destruction. But here the focus is more so on individual disciples, depicted as branches, and their connection to the vine. In a play on words in Greek, Jesus says that a branch that does not bear fruit is taken away (*airō*), but if a branch does bear fruit, then it is pruned (*kathairō*) so that it might bear even more fruit (15:2). The fate of the branches that were taken away (15:2) is the same as those branches that do not remain in the vine—they are cast aside to dry up and then be consumed by the fire (15:6).

The key difference that John 15 has with the vineyard theme is that this passage does not fixate on the lack of fruit or the production of corrupt fruit but instead highlights how the vineyard can be productive—if the branches remain in the true vine (John 15:4–5, 8, 16). Indeed, Jesus tells his disciples that they are already "clean [*katharos*]" (15:3) in another play on words with the term used for pruning (*kathairō* in 15:2). The significance of the play on words with pruning and cleaning is

Sirach (2nd c. CE) personifies wisdom as being like various trees and plants, including a vine: "Like the vine I bud forth delights, and my blossoms become glorious and abundant fruit" (Sir 24:17 NRSVue). This is part of a summons for people to come to wisdom and enjoy what she has to offer (24:19), though Jesus is promising in John 15 to produce fruit in those who remain in him.

that the passage evokes ritual purity, implying fruit fit for cultic use in sacred space.[35] This not only suggests further corroboration that the vineyard theme came to take on cultic connotations in the Second Temple period but also that Jesus's words here in John ought to have some implication for John's theology of the Eucharist (cf. ch. 15).

Given the broader background of the vineyard theme that we have seen in this chapter, it may seem as if Jesus is claiming to create an alternative vineyard through his use of the *true* vine—that is, one that is fruitful and productive, over and against Israel, which has not produced desirable fruit. Yet there seems to be discernible influence from Jeremiah's use of the broader vineyard theme, which sheds some light on this issue. Jeremiah 2:21 is the only place in the LXX where a vine (*ampelos*) is described as being "true" (*alēthinē*) in any way, and it is the only verse where these two terms appear together. For Jeremiah, speaking of Israel as a true vine is intended to contrast with the corrupt vine that it became.[36] In this sense, Jesus is a true vine because the branches connected to him will not grow corrupt, but will bear much fruit.

But there seems to be more behind the notion of being a true vine in the background in Ezekiel, which is much more prominently connected to John 15.[37] In the LXX, Ezekiel 15:2, 17:6–7, and 19:10–12 are the only vineyard-theme passages where the same Greek terms in John 15 for vines (*ampelos*) and branches (*klēma*) appear together, and they rarely occur together elsewhere in the LXX (cf. Jer 31:32 [48:32 MT]; Joel 1:7). As we saw earlier, Ezekiel 15:2 refers to the uselessness of the wood and branches of vines beyond burning them for fuel (15:4–5)—an image of the fate of Jerusalem (15:6–8). The LXX translation of Ezekiel 15:4 adds that the reason for the discarded branches was the annual pruning process (*katharsis*): "the fire consumes the yearly cleansing of it" (Ezek 15:4 NETS). Significantly, this is the only place in the LXX where a cognate of *kathairō* (cf. John 15:2) is used for pruning.[38] In Ezekiel 17:6–7, the relationship of the vine to its branches represents King Zedekiah and the people of Judah living in the land, where it had come to *bear fruit* (17:8). This was before Zedekiah fraternized with Egypt, leading to the vine drying up (17:9–10) and the exile coming about in full. Ezekiel 19, likewise, depicts a vine in terms of the royal family of Judah and describes how prominent the vine became with its regal branches (19:11), before it was plucked up, left to dry out, planted in a desert, and destroyed in the fire (19:12–14).

John 15 therefore carries a clear parallel with Ezekiel, depicting the fate of the branches drying up and being consumed by fire (cf. John 15:6 with Ezek 15:4–6;

---

35. Grant Macaskill, *Union with Christ in the New Testament* (Oxford: Oxford University Press, 2013), 263.

36. See Gary T. Manning Jr., *Echoes of a Prophet: The Use of Ezekiel in the Gospel of John and in Literature of the Second Temple Period*, JSNTSup 270 (London: T&T Clark, 2004), 135.

37. For an overview, see Manning, *Echoes*, 135–49.

38. See also Manning, *Echoes*, 140–41.

17:9–10; 19:12–14).[39] Additionally, John 15 is similar to Ezekiel 17 and 19 in the fact that these are the only passages in the broader vineyard theme within biblical and broader Second Temple literature that portray an individual leader as the vine/vineyard (Ezek 17), and which describe the relationship between the vine and branches (Ezek 17, 19). In Ezekiel 17, Zedekiah is the vine that fails to keep his covenant with Nebuchadnezzar in hopes of receiving aid from Egypt, which is a precursor for the vine's exile. And in Ezekiel 19, the prominent branches of the vine of Judah's royal dynasty are no more.

Undoubtedly there is a broader matrix of the vineyard theme informing the imagery in John 15, but given some of the specific terminology and thematic overlap just noted, Ezekiel appears to play a distinctive role and contributes to the notion of Jesus being the *true* vine. He is not like other false vines, like Zedekiah, who represent the failed leadership of Judah.[40] Tying together vine imagery and regality is something that we see elsewhere in the Didache, for example, which refers to Jesus as "the holy vine of David" (Did. 9.1).[41] Of course, within John's Gospel, Jesus's self-identification as the true vine must mean that he is the only source of life.[42] But the background of Ezekiel 17 adds the nuance that Jesus is the leader—indeed the vine, who can make God's vineyard flourish. That is, so long as the branches abide in him and receive the vitality that he offers to produce good fruit.

CONCLUSION

As we have seen in this chapter, judgment as privation reinforces how alcohol was understood to be a great blessing, since its absence is associated with the curses of the covenant and the judgment of God. The symbolic varietal in this chapter helps us appreciate the nuances of another one. The notion of privation includes how Israel's disobedience jeopardizes their presence within God's vineyard. The vineyard metaphor is thus primarily utilized rhetorically to critique Israel for not living up to the intentions of God the vintner and not producing the exceptional wine that she could. At times this critique is focused collectively on the people, and at other times the focus is on Israel's corrupt leaders.

These images of judgment—the loss of the land and the goodness that it can provide in the form of blessings like wine and beer—will be rounded out by the material discussed in the following chapter. There we will find further images of

---

39. See also Manning, *Echoes*, 142.

40. So similarly, Manning, *Echoes*, 145, yet he emphasizes the faithlessness of Israel more than I think is implied in John 15. Manning also connects the messianic expectation of the new cedar in Ezekiel 17:22–24 to the notion of the true vine in John 15 (*Echoes*, 142–45), which is not persuasive, not least because Jesus is not "the true cedar."

41. Michael W. Holmes, *The Apostolic Fathers: Greek Texts and English Translations*, 3rd ed. (Grand Rapids: Baker, 2007), 357.

42. Raymond E. Brown, *The Gospel According to John (XIII–XXI): Introduction, Translation, and Notes*, AB (New York: Doubleday, 1970), 674.

judgment and associations with exile. But whereas this chapter was primarily focused on privation and loss, the following chapter highlights the themes that turn alcohol into a parody in the theme of the cup of wrath.

RELEVANT QUESTIONS

1. To what degree, if any, does the privation of alcoholic beverages in judgment scenes in the Old Testament speak to God's displeasure with alcohol itself?
2. What does the representation of Israel as a vineyard suggest about the importance of winemaking for ancient Israelites?
3. As a member of God's vineyard, what characteristics would best describe the wine of your own life?

CHAPTER 12

THE CUP OF WRATH

The privation of covenantal blessings explored in the previous chapter presented us primarily with the sting of loss: the loss of harvests and the happy treading of grapes in anticipation of fresh wine; the loss of joy that comes from consuming intoxicating beverages; and the loss of stability, security, and income that comes with owning vineyards. In each of these instances of privation, the concrete realities of winemaking were threatened. But judgment imagery in the Bible also utilizes aspects of winemaking symbolically. When this occurs, viticulture and wine are not the targets of God's judgment, but they become part of a set of metaphors for what God's judgment is like (and what it feels like). It is as if each element of the winemaking process, including harvesting, grape treading, wine drinking, and being intoxicated is inverted into a horrifying counterpart of the real thing. If the previous chapter presented us with the *privation* of blessing, the present chapter focuses on its *parody*.[1] By parody, I do not mean that any of this is humorous—far from it. Parody suggests the inversion of what something is normally meant to symbolize.

A helpful point of comparison for the variety of ways in which winemaking is deployed symbolically in Scripture is to look at how leaven functions metaphorically in the New Testament. As a reminder from chapter 1, leaven can be used as a negative image, conveying the growth of something undesirable. For instance, leaven can refer to the influence of Herod, the Pharisees, and the Sadducees (Matt 16:6, 11; Mark 8:15; Luke 12:1), the teaching of Paul's opponents in Galatia (Gal 5:9), or the immorality of a man in Corinth (1 Cor 5:6–8). But leaven can also be used metaphorically to refer positively to the expanse of the kingdom of God in Jesus's parables (Matt 13:33; Luke 13:20–21). These two uses reflect the roles that actual leaven played in the lives of ancient Israelites. On the one hand, leaven is obviously valuable for making bread, which ancient Israelites regularly enjoyed. And yet, during Passover, they were to abstain from using it, possibly eventually giving rise to its negative connotations. Thus, its symbolic value as a metaphor depends on what leaven is being used to depict. So also all of the processes associated with grapevine cultivation and wine production were integral blessings in the life of ancient Israel, but the symbolism deployed is not always positive, as we will see.

---

1. I borrow this language of parody from MacDonald, *Not Bread Alone*, 189.

HARVESTING AND TREADING

Harvest time for any produce marks a climactic end point to a season of hard work and preparation. Thus, harvesting grain and grapes became metaphors for the culmination of one's life and the end of the age. Job describes how the wicked will experience a premature downfall, similar to a vintner who shakes off unripe grapes from the vine before the harvest (Job 15:33). Furthermore, the particulars of gleaning grapes became symbolic of complete and total judgment. One particularly devastating example from the prophet Jeremiah targets the remnant of Israel. Whereas the theme of the remnant often serves as an image of God's preservation of some within Israel through devastating events, Jeremiah declares, "Let them glean the remnant of Israel as thoroughly as a vine; pass your hand over the branches again, like one gathering grapes" (Jer 6:9). Going back over the vine to pluck the grapes that were missed during harvest (i.e., the remnant) makes "gleaning" a profound picture of total judgment. Similarly, in two separate oracles against Edom in Obadiah and in Jeremiah, the prophets anticipate the complete judgment of the enemy nation in contrast to what grape harvests are like (Jer 49:9; Obad 5). But as they do so, they each ask a pair of rhetorical questions about thieves and grape-gatherers, respectively. In each case, thieves and grape-gatherers can only take what they can carry, and so they must be selective. But Obadiah and Jeremiah mention thieves and grape-gatherers as a warning to Edom that their own experience of judgment will not be so selective—there will not be anything left to scavenge or glean when God's judgment arrives.[2]

After grapes are harvested, they are trodden or pressed to create grape must—a blood-like juice that became a graphic image of judgment. We see representations of this image in the narratives of the Old Testament. In the story of Gideon in Judges, harvesting and treading symbolizes militaristic victory and gathering the spoils of war. While Gideon, who is from the clan of Abiezer, was off on a military campaign against the Midianites, some men from Ephraim stayed behind because Gideon went off to battle without them. Even though they were away from the action, however, they did take out two Midianite generals, Oreb and Zeeb—the latter of which they killed by crushing him at a winepress (Judg 7:25). The grisly demise of Zeeb evokes how winepresses normally extract "blood," albeit "the blood of the grape," and the scene is given greater metaphorical resonance when Gideon returns to meet the Ephraimites. Although the Ephraimites were disappointed that Gideon left for war without them, Gideon reassures them with the following rhetorical question: "Aren't the gleanings of Ephraim's grapes better than the full grape harvest of Abiezer?" (8:2). The point is that Abiezer's "harvest" (i.e., Gideon's military victory over the

---

2. Barton, *Joel and Obadiah*, 140–42; Paul R. Raabe, *Obadiah: A New Translation with Introduction and Commentary*, AB (New York: Doubleday, 1996), 142–43.

Midianites) is not greater than the "gleanings" of the harvest (i.e., the Ephraimites overtaking the two Midianite generals).³ Gideon's descriptive representation of these victories illustrates these metaphors of judgment.

This metaphorical image of treading is developed further as a divine punishment in other texts. Lamentations describes the Babylonian exile and the destruction of the temple as if God was treading out Judah in a winepress (Lam 1:15). The prophet Joel prophesies that when God sits in judgment over all the nations at the Valley of Jehoshaphat, he commands the sickle to begin the harvest, and those who tread the winepress to begin their work (Joel 3:12–13). Both of these images evoke the time of the harvest, but the focus of the passage is especially on the grapes. The gruesome result of the treading is that the vats of wine will overflow because of the wickedness of the nations (3:13). What is remarkable about Joel's image of vats overflowing in a scene of judgment is that the exact image of an overflowing vat is used in Joel 2:24 to describe the bounty associated with God's acts of restoration (as we will see in the next chapter). Significantly, the same image is being used to describe both God's blessing and his judgment, even in the same short book!

The description of Jezebel's demise may also symbolize grape treading. If so, this would be poetic justice for killing a man named Naboth and stealing his family vineyard for royal use (cf. 1 Kgs 21:1–16). When Jezebel dies, her blood splattered as she fell from a window and was trampled by horses (2 Kgs 9:33). The Hebrew verb for trampling here (*ramas*) is not a specialized term from viniculture, but it is used similarly as a violent metaphor for treading the winepress in Isaiah 63:3 (as noted below).

In Revelation, the prophecy in Joel 3:13 is utilized and developed further in a vision in chapter 14 as two separate harvests: a grain harvest (Rev 14:14–16) and a grape harvest (14:17–20). It could be that John the Seer recognized that the sickle in Joel 3:13 was intended for a grain harvest and so interpreted Joel as presenting two separate harvests. But in John's vision, both harvests involve sickles, alluding directly to the wording of Joel (cf. Rev 14:15, 18). When the grain is harvested, we are not told what happens next. But with the grape harvest, a violent judgment scene ensues, as the grapes are put "into the great winepress of God's wrath" and trampled (14:19–20). The result is not an abundance of wine because the metaphor shifts from the symbol to its referent: "and blood flowed out of the press" (14:20b). The text graphically describes the quantity of blood as reaching up to the bridle of the horse for nearly two hundred miles long (cf. 4 Ezra 15.35–36).

There is some debate among scholars over how to understand the relationship between these two harvests in Revelation 14. A minority of scholars propose that both harvests are harvests of the elect, taking the winepress imagery as an expression of the blood of the martyrs.⁴ But this interpretation fails to recognize that the theme of trampling the winepress is always an image of divine judgment in the Bible.

---

3. See Webb, *Judges*, 251.
4. E.g., G. B. Caird, *A Commentary on the Revelation of St. John the Divine* (New York: Harper & Row, 1966), 188–95.

Other scholars regard both harvests as divine judgment, contending that nothing is actually stated either way with regard to the harvested grain, and the allusions to Joel 3:13 for each harvest suggests judgment in each case.[5] Yet most scholars convincingly argue that the grain harvest should be interpreted as the positive one of the two.[6] In other contexts, grain harvests can include the harvest of the elect, even where it differentiates the wheat from the weeds (Matt 3:12; 13:24–30, 36–43; Luke 3:17). Additionally, just a few verses earlier in Revelation, in a vision of the 144,000 with the Lamb, they are described as being the "firstfruits," which anticipates a full harvest of the elect (Rev 14:4).[7] Furthermore, there seems to be a distinction between the harvesters in each case. It is clear that the one conducting the grape harvest is an angel (14:17). But the one conducting the grain harvest is "seated on the cloud," referred to as being "like a son of man," and wearing "a crown of gold on his head" (14:14). This apocalyptic image of Jesus is rooted in Daniel 7,[8] which could suggest that the different harvesters point to different destinies: Jesus harvests the elect (i.e., the grain), and an angel harvests the wicked (i.e., the grapes for the treading).

Related to the imagery of a bloody winepress, both Isaiah and Revelation use this trope with a focus on the one treading the grapes as having blood-stained garments. The prophet Isaiah describes a terrifying judgment scene in which YHWH returns from Edom and Bozrah, an Edomite city, with red all over his garments (Isa 63:1–2). This is a play on words because Edom means "red" (cf. Esau as the "red" one in Gen 25:25) and Bozrah is reminiscent of the Hebrew word for the grape harvest.[9] YHWH announces that he was treading the winepress in his anger (Isa 63:3–4), but instead of juice staining his robes, it is blood (63:3).[10]

Similarly, in the vision of Jesus's eschatological return in Revelation 19, the text describes Jesus as wearing "a robe dipped in blood" (Rev 19:13), because "he treads the winepress of the fury of the wrath of God Almighty" (19:15b). Clearly, this verse is dependent on Isaiah 63 here, but there is more to the comparison that is worth noting. The threefold repetition of the word "of" in the translation may seem clunky. But there is actually another "of" phrase (i.e., genitive construction) in the Greek that is often omitted in our translations because of

> "The Battle Hymn of the Republic" (Julia Ward Howe, 1861) draws explicitly upon the judgment imagery in Revelation 19:15 of Christ treading in the winepress (alongside his use of a violent sword):
>
> *Mine eyes have seen the glory*
> *Of the coming of the Lord;*
> *He is trampling out the vintage*
> *Where grapes of wrath are stored;*
> *He hath loosed the fateful lightning*
> *Of His terrible swift sword;*
> *His truth is marching on.*

---

5. David E. Aune, *Revelation 17–22*, WBC 52C (Nashville: Thomas Nelson, 1998), 844–45; G. K. Beale, *The Book of Revelation*, NIGTC (Grand Rapids: Eerdmans, 1998), 773–78.

6. E.g., Richard Bauckham, *The Climax of Prophecy: Studies on the Book of Revelation* (Edinburgh: T&T Clark, 1993), 283–96; Craig R. Koester, *Revelation: A New Translation with Introduction and Commentary*, AB (New Haven: Yale University Press, 2014), 627–29.

7. Brian K. Blount, *Revelation: A Commentary*, NTL (Louisville: Westminster John Knox, 2009), 280.

8. Blount, *Revelation*, 279–80; Koester, *Revelation*, 623; Bauckham, *Climax*, 294–96.

9. Childs, *Isaiah*, 516.

10. Targum Isaiah expands the viticultural metaphor to include more overt militaristic images (cf. Tg. Isa. 63:3–4).

its redundancy. The text refers to "the winepress *of the wine* (*oinos*) of the fury . . ." The reason these extra words are important is because they suggest that the "wine" that Jesus produces is also part of God's punishment.[11] Indeed, in this vision in Revelation, it will be consumed by the birds of the air at "the great supper of God" (19:17–21).

This vision in Revelation is taken directly from the sacrificial-feast scene after the battle of Gog and Magog in Ezekiel 39:17–20, in which the avian guests to the meal are commanded to drink "till you are drunk" (39:19). The depiction of blood causing drunkenness in judgment scenes occurs elsewhere with reference to the weapons used to implement YHWH's judgment—such as the "arrows" and "swords" of warfare (Deut 32:42; Isa 34:6–7; Jer 46:10; cf. 1 En. 62.12).[12] These types of images seem to be developments of the idea that defeating an enemy in battle can be compared to drinking their blood (cf. Num 23:24), with the main development being that the blood is explicitly intoxicating.

> Judith describes the mountains, where blood is spilled in battle, as themselves becoming drunk (Jdt 6:4).

The combination of judgment images in Revelation 19—treading and making bloody "wine"—is also mirrored in Isaiah 63, which uniquely imagines that the "wine" that YHWH produces will be used to make the nations drunk (Isa 63:6). Both of these passages in Revelation 19 and Isaiah 63 present divine judgment as being like pressing grapes, but they also extend the judgment to include the "alcoholic beverage" that is produced. Revelation 19, therefore, alludes to Isaiah 63, where the trampling judgment sets up the theme of the cup of wrath for the consumption of the nations.

THE CUP OF WRATH

The cup-of-wrath theme imagines God's judgment to be like consuming an overwhelmingly potent beverage. The main features of this theme include: (a) a cup that administers divine judgment (b) directly from God, and (c) the drunkenness of those who drink it. We could constrain this theme to only those passages where each of those features are present. But it seems best to place all instances of a cup meting out divine judgment, or divine judgment described as drunkenness, under the broad umbrella of the cup-of-wrath theme. Sometimes a cup of judgment is mentioned without reference to its effects (Ps 11:6 NRSVue: "a scorching wind shall be the portion of their cup"). At other times, there is no mention of a cup at all, or some

---

11. R. H. Charles, *Critical and Exegetical Commentary on the Revelation of St. John*, 2 vols., ICC (1920; repr., Edinburgh: T&T Clark, 1966), 2:136–37.

12. I would add the "slingstones" in Zech 9:15 to this list, but doing so requires emending the Hebrew text. See, e.g., Carol L. Meyers and Eric M. Meyers, *Zechariah 9–14: A New Translation with Introduction and Commentary*, AB (New York: Doubleday, 1993), 154; James D. Nogalski, *Micah–Malachi: The Book of the Twelve*, SHBC (Macon: Smyth & Helwys, 2011), 910–11.

other means of consuming judgment is used (i.e., jars/wineskins in Jer 13). Thus, it is not the case that each element of the broader theme is always present. To be clear, the cup-of-wrath theme never involves the consumer becoming angry or wrathful, although one passage imagines God's judgment against wrongdoing as being like a soldier's response to waking up from "the stupor of wine" (*yayin* in Ps 78:65) to defeat his enemies (78:66). Because most of the examples involve *drinking*, we may assume that the contents are imagined to be a beverage. The idea of wrath being a kind of liquid is presumed, cognitively at least, in those instances in which God *pours out* his wrath (cf., e.g., Ps 79:6; Jer 6:11; 10:25; 14:16; Lam 2:4; 4:11). This explains how Job can refer to the wicked who will "drink of the wrath of the Almighty" (Job 21:20 NRSVue).[13] In fact, Hosea says straightforwardly that YHWH will pour out his wrath like water (Hos 5:10). But the contents of the cup do not seem to be a consistent feature of the cup-of-wrath theme.

The Contents of the Cup

In a few places, the contents could be blood. As we saw above, the bloody wine of Isaiah 63:6 can make the nations drunk. Similarly, Isaiah and Zephaniah both depict judgment scenes in which the guests invited to a feast turn out to be the meal themselves (Isa 49:26; Zeph 1:7–8). In Isaiah the vile feast is even worse because the guests are compelled to eat themselves and become drunk on their own blood, as if drinking fermenting must (*asis* in Isa 49:26). The associations with blood are disturbing for many reasons, not least because of the gruesome violence it evokes, but also because of the ritual taboo associated with consuming blood (cf. Lev 17:13–14; Acts 15:20b, 29; 21:25). As we will see, however, the broader "cup of wrath" motif does not seem to assume that the contents are blood, and it may be noteworthy that in Isaiah 49:26 and 63:6 there is no reference to a cup.

In Revelation, however, human blood is consumed by Babylon from a golden cup (Rev 17:4–6). Babylon in Revelation is a representation of first-century Rome, the city of seven hills (17:9) that oppresses God's people (17:6) and rules over the kings of the earth (17:18). As part of the text's vilification of Rome—and an undignified portrayal of the goddess Roma, who personifies Rome—Babylon is described like a drunk sex worker (cf. 18:24; 19:2),[14] who consumes the blood of God's people to the point of drunkenness. Drinking the blood of the martyrs is what Babylon will be punished for doing, and paradoxically is the means of that punishment. As we will see, there is more than just blood symbolized as the contents of the cup.

It is also possible that the contents of the cup could be poisoned water. Jeremiah describes the experience of agricultural devastation as being like receiving "poisoned

---

13. The NIV adds "the cup," but that is missing from the Hebrew.

14. Babylon is a cipher for Rome, who reenacted the role of the archetypal enemy of God by destroying the temple (70 CE) just as Babylon did (586 BCE). To use an acting metaphor, a character from the original film has been recast by a different actor for the sequel.

water" from YHWH (Jer 8:13–14). Later he declares that God will feed his disobedient people "bitter food" and "poisoned water" in exile (9:15–16; 23:15). Yet there is no mention of a cup or of drunkenness in these passages, and nowhere else is water mentioned as something consumed from the cup of wrath. Thus, these likely comprise a separate set of judgment images.

Some scholars also wonder if poison is assumed in the broader motif on the basis of Numbers 5, which describes the infamous *Sotah*—or trial by drinking. Numbers 5 legislates that if a man suspects that his wife committed adultery (and so may be pregnant), he should bring her to the tabernacle along with a special grain offering (Num 5:11–15). Then, to see if she is being truthful (5:19–22), the priest will give her "bitter water that brings a curse" (5:18), which is holy water with "dust from the tabernacle floor" (5:17). If the woman is lying, she will experience harm and miscarry. If she is telling the truth, nothing will happen to her. The bitter water is thus a trial to determine guilt.

> Nowhere else in Scripture do we see any overt reference to the trial of Numbers 5. But an early apocryphal Gospel, the Protevangelium of James (2nd c. CE), describes Mary the mother of Jesus undertaking the *Sotah* while pregnant in order to determine if her story is true. She survives the test, and in a twist of the procedure, Joseph does too (Prot. Jas. 16).

McKane famously argued that the *Sotah* is the background for the cup of wrath, and thus we should recognize that the cup similarly functions as a trial to determine guilt.[15] According to this view, whether it is water or wine, the contents will turn into poison if the consumer is guilty. Yet there are three main problems with this argument: (a) the *Sotah* is a process for humans to determine guilt, but with the cup God already knows who is guilty and who is not; (b) consuming the cup is a metaphor for a judgment that is *certain* to come to pass; and (c) there is never any suggestion that the contents might not cause harm to the consumer. Nowhere is the cup of wrath ever suggested to be a trial like the *Sotah* in Numbers 5.[16]

Yet this does not entirely rule out the possibility that the contents of the cup are poisoned from the start. In fact, the words for "wrath" and "venom" in Hebrew are homonyms (*khamah*), making the comparison of God's wrath to a poisoned chalice very direct.[17] This could be related to the possibility that the theme originated in the context of a regal feast, in which poisoned wine is used to assassinate unsuspecting dignitaries. This may be the meaning of Hosea 7:5, which says that something happened on "the day of the festival of our king," likely referring to his birthday. But because of the ambiguity of wrath/venom (*khamah*), it is not entirely clear. Either

---

15. William McKane, "Poison, Trial by Ordeal and the Cup of Wrath," *VT* 30.4 (1980): 474–92; idem, *A Critical and Exegetical Commentary on Jeremiah*, 2 vols., ICC (Edinburgh: T&T Clark, 1986), 1:634–36.

16. Holladay, *Jeremiah 1*, 673; Raabe, *Obadiah*, 240–41; Dubach, *Trunkenheit*, 254. Micha Roi agrees with this (167), but he contends that McKane was "inversely correct" (179). This is because in his view the *Sotah* was designed to regulate the kinds of practices to which the cup of wrath alludes, since they are mostly combined, as we will see, with adultery and sex work as images for spiritual unfaithfulness. See Micha Roi, "The Law of the Sotah and the Cup of Wrath: Substantive and Adjective Law in the Hebrew Bible," *RB* 124.2 (2017): 161–79.

17. Cf. *HALOT* 1:326.

the princes *poisoned* the wine (*yayin*) of the king (7:5) as part of a conspiracy against him (7:6–7),[18] or the princes became *inflamed* by the wine (7:5) and thus conspired against him (7:6–7).[19] The latter seems the most convincing, but the point for our purposes here is to highlight the Hebrew homonym, since some scholars contend that poisoning is assumed in the "cup of wrath" passages.

One passage that provides some potential evidence for this theory comes in the Song of Moses in Deuteronomy 32. In this song, the enemies of God are described as having vines from Sodom and Gomorrah, which bring forth poisonous and bitter grapes that produce wine like snake venom (Deut 32:32–33). After this description, God asks the rhetorical question, "Have I not kept this in reserve and sealed it in my vaults?" (32:34). What is reserved and sealed away must be the poisonous wine, suggesting that he intends to use it to mete out judgment.[20] The very next verse describes how God will repay and avenge, suggesting that the poisonous wine is the means of doing so (32:35).

Clearly we have here in Deuteronomy 32 an image of God using poisoned wine to enact judgment. But the problem with poisoned wine as an explanation for all of the other passages is that, other than the poisoned water from Jeremiah and this instance in Deuteronomy, poison is nowhere a feature of the cup-of-wrath theme. As we will see, the staggering and other effects from drinking the cup are best understood as imagery depicting drunkenness, rather than being poisoned. For example, in Jeremiah, YHWH commands Moab to be made drunk because of her pride and haughtiness, and so she will "wallow in her vomit" and become "an object of ridicule" (Jer 48:26). Sometimes it is simply stated that God causes the drunkenness of those he is judging, as in Nahum 3:11, without utilizing other aspects of the cup-of-wrath theme. Occasionally the effects of severe intoxication are used to depict judgment, like groping "in the darkness" and staggering "like drunkards" in Job 12:24–25.

Thus, we ought to imagine that the contents of the cup of wrath are a kind of extremely intoxicating beverage. The punishment, then, is the ensuing drunkenness, which often arises in a context of militaristic destruction similar to the vulnerability-to-violence theme for literal drunkenness explored in chapter 10. In some cases the cup of wrath is a metaphor for that militaristic defeat, such as when Zechariah describes how God will use Jerusalem as a cup to make the nations go away "reeling" when they try to attack and besiege it (Zech 12:2). Similarly, Jeremiah 51 expands this to include a festive setting, in which Babylon is overtaken by YHWH's cup and thus overtaken. The oracle states: "while they are aroused, I will set out a feast for them and make them drunk, so that they shout with laughter—then sleep forever

---

18. Alter, *Hebrew Bible*, 2:1220.
19. This view is supported by the LXX and most modern translations (so, e.g., NIV).

20. So, e.g., Richard D. Nelson, *Deuteronomy: A Commentary*, OTL (Louisville: Westminster John Knox, 2002), 376.

and not awake" (Jer 51:39, cf. 51:57). Consuming the cup is itself the punishment, but their incapacitation means that no one will be able to stop the city from being destroyed (51:58).

Yet intoxication within this metaphor implies alcohol, and sometimes there is additional imagery that suggests as much. Isaiah envisions YHWH mixing together (*masak*) "a spirit of dizziness" that causes stumbling like "a drunkard" that "staggers around in his vomit" (Isa 19:14), suggesting that the image relates to a wine or some other alcoholic beverage. Isaiah appears to refer to YHWH's use of this spirit once more, calling it "a spirit of deep sleep" that causes severe intoxication in Ariel. The result is self-inflicted blindness and staggering as if from wine (*yayin*) or beer (*shekar*), but not actually (29:9–10; cf. 51:21). In other words, in these two passages from Isaiah, the "spirit" is *compared to* alcohol.

In other cases, though, it is explicit that the contents are a kind of wine. For example, the psalmist writes, "You have shown your people desperate times; you have given us wine [*yayin*] that makes us stagger" (Ps 60:3). In a similar example, the psalmist announces that "in the hand of the LORD is a cup full of foaming [*khamar*] wine [*yayin*] mixed with spices [*mesek*]; he pours it out, and all the wicked of the earth drink it down to its very dregs" (75:8).

> Second Baruch also imagines God's judgment as a wine to be consumed to the dregs: "you who have drunk the clarified wine, you now drink its dregs, for the judgment of the Most High is impartial." (2 Bar. 13.8)[21]

The foaming wine in Psalm 75 could provide some explanatory value for the origin of the theme, if we recognize how the foaming and bubbling of the fermenting must could be perceived as a kind of agitation. However, this is not clear in other cup-of-wrath passages, and ongoing fermentation might imply that the judgment is not as strong as it could be (see ch. 2 for carbonation-based foam).

A similar image appears in Jeremiah 13, when Jeremiah recites a well-known proverb at a banquet that every jar should be full of wine (*yayin* in Jer 13:12).[22] Jeremiah flips the proverb on its head, however, informing everyone present that the full wine jars now symbolize that the whole land will be filled with drunkenness (13:13), ominously heralding impending judgment (13:14). Jeremiah also explicitly makes use of wine in the *cup*-of-wrath imagery in subsequent oracles (25:15; 51:7), which will be explored later in this chapter.

---

21. A. F. J. Klijn, "2 (Syriac Apocalypse of) Baruch," *OTP* 1:625.
22. For the proverbial nature of the statement, see McKane, *Jeremiah*, 1:292, 296. For *nebel* as jars rather than wineskins here, see McKane, *Jeremiah*, 1:293–95, especially because they are "smashed" in v. 14.

In many passages in Revelation, the cup of wrath clearly contains wine (Rev 14:10; 16:19; cf. 18:6), which is also suggested by the development of the winepress judgment scenes that we analyzed earlier (14:19–20; 19:15). It also seems to be assumed in the "bowl" judgments (Rev 15–16), which follow after the "seal" and "trumpet" judgments, and which appear to develop the cup-of-wrath theme further.[23] At the start of the bowl sequence, we read that "one of the four living creatures gave to the seven angels seven golden bowls *filled* with the wrath of God" (15:7). These seven angels then are commanded to "*pour out* the seven bowls of God's wrath on the earth" (16:1), which they then do in turn (16:2, 3, 4, 8, 10, 12, 17). The language of filling and pouring suggests a liquid, and wine is probably in view. This is especially the case given the association of wine and wrath throughout Revelation and because the culminating bowl judgment is the wine-filled cup of wrath given to Babylon (16:19). Furthermore, these bowls come from the heavenly temple (15:5–8), and the kinds of bowls mentioned here are *phialai*, which were used for libations.[24] This suggests that pouring out the bowls in judgment is a kind of libationary act,[25] further suggesting that wine is in view.

> Meredith J. C. Warren suggests that John the Seer was most likely opposed to using wine ritually in the Eucharist.[26] I do not find this persuasive because Revelation does not overtly refer to the Eucharist (though see Rev 3:20), and further the use of wine to depict God's judgment is common throughout Scripture, and nowhere is it deployed to critique wine itself.

Although the cup-of-wrath passages convey the potency of God's judgment, we need not imagine that all of them share the same imagined contents, especially since these are all symbolic metaphors. As Dubach affirms, the cup-of-wrath theme is more focused on the effects of the cup, rather than on its contents.[27] Regardless of what the contents are symbolically portrayed to be, the cup of wrath theme is surely a parody of the good cup that God provides his people, as MacDonald suggests.[28] In the place of the cup that provides joy and blessing (cf. Pss 16:5; 23:5), he offers a cup that brings judgment (cf. Pss 11:6; 75:8). And when he offers the cup, it is often passed around to multiple consumers, which is a subtheme that I will now explore with the remaining cup-of-wrath passages.

---

23. E.g., Koester, *Revelation*, 645; Beale, *Revelation*, 788, 806; S. H. Travis, "Wrath of God (NT)," *ABD* 6:997.

24. See esp. Gaifman, *Art of Libation*.

25. David E. Aune, *Revelation 6–16*, WBC 52B (Nashville: Thomas Nelson, 1998), 879.

26. Meredith J. C. Warren, "The Cup of God's Wrath: Libation and Early Christian Meal Practice in Revelation," *Religions* 9 (2018): 1–13.

27. Dubach, *Trunkenheit*, 253.

28. MacDonald, *Not Bread Alone*, 189.

Passing the Cup

The subtheme of passing the cup of wrath around can be seen in a handful of places, most of which are the exemplary expressions of the theme itself. As we will see, the cup is sometimes passed to Jerusalem, or more often away from Jerusalem and given to another nation (or nations). The main focus here in this section is on the movement of the cup and its use for multiple recipients.

In an oracle by the prophet Ezekiel, we see the cup of wrath being passed from Samaria to Jerusalem, who are depicted as two sisters named Oholah and Oholibah (Ezek 23:4). Ezekiel declares that Jerusalem has been idolatrous like her sister—an idolatry portrayed as a kind of prostitution, which is later depicted as drunkards who traveled from afar to visit a sex worker (23:40–45). Because of these sorts of things, Jerusalem will experience the same fate as Samaria: "I will put her cup into your hand" (23:31). This corresponds to the Assyrian exile for Samaria and the Babylonian exile for Jerusalem (cf. 23:9–10). The cup is described as "large and deep," something that "holds so much" (23:32), and which is "a cup of ruin and desolation" (23:33). Consuming the contents of the cup "will bring scorn and derision" (23:32), and the consumer "will be filled with drunkenness and sorrow" (23:33). Significantly, the cup will be consumed entirely, until the cup is dry and the consumers "chew on its pieces" (23:34). The "pieces" here could refer to the dregs and grape particles at the bottom of a cup of wine, but it is also possible that the cup itself will be consumed along with its contents.[29] This latter view would serve to explain the graphic imagery of self-harm that follows upon consuming the cup (cf. "you will tear your breasts" in 23:34b). Either way, the point of chewing on the pieces stresses that every bit of God's judgment will be experienced, as the cup passes from Samaria to Jerusalem.

Within a vision from Jeremiah (Jer 25:15–38), the prophet is portrayed as a cupbearer,[30] whom YHWH commands to take around a cup from YHWH's hand (25:15, 17) that is "filled with the wine [*yayin*] of my wrath," to each of the nations that God has chosen to punish (25:15). At the end of the vision, YHWH roars from the temple (25:30a), which sounds like the shouts of "those who tread the grapes" (25:30b).[31] This once again connects to the imagery of treading the winepress as divine judgment. The result of drinking this wine of YHWH's wrath is that those who consume it "will stagger and go mad because of the sword I will send among them" (25:16). The addition of the sword here appears to mix metaphors a bit. But most likely drunkenness from the cup is the metaphorical "vehicle" to describe destruction by the sword.[32] The sword makes explicit that the cup often stands as a

---

29. Block, *Ezekiel*, 754, 756.
30. Holladay, *Jeremiah 1*, 673–74.
31. The Hebrew does not mention grapes, but the "shouts" of people "treading" suggests grape treading.
32. Else K. Holt, "King Nebuchadnezzar of Babylon, My Servant, and the Cup of Wrath: Jeremiah's Fantasies and the Hope of Violence," *Jeremiah (Dis)Placed: New Directions in Writing/Reading Jeremiah*, ed. A. R. Pete Diamond and Louis Stulman, LHBOTS 529 (New York: T&T Clark International, 2011), 215.

metaphor for militaristic demise, as noted earlier. It also suggests that the wine was not poisoned, because if it was the use of the sword would be superfluous.³³ Instead, inebriation from the cup of wrath leads to being susceptible to the sword, invoking the vulnerability theme from chapter 10.

As Jeremiah narrates this visionary experience of taking the cup around (Jer 25:17), he administers it to various cities and nations, beginning with Jerusalem and Judah and extending beyond to Egypt and many others (25:17–26). The last to drink from the cup is the king of Babylon (25:26). Then YHWH tells Jeremiah to say to these nations: "drink, get drunk and vomit, and fall to rise no more because of the sword I will send among you" (25:27). Despite how dreadful the cup is, no one can refuse to drink it (25:28b). As Jeremiah goes around with the cup, he also declares that since YHWH will do this against his own beloved Jerusalem, he will surely bring devastation to the other nations for their sins as well (25:29).

Jeremiah makes a similar, though inverted, point to Edom in another example of this subtheme, when YHWH declares: "If those who do not deserve to drink the cup must drink it, why should you go unpunished? You will not go unpunished, but must drink it" (Jer 49:12). Jeremiah's reference to the "undeserving" probably does not refer to Jerusalem or Judah, because Jeremiah would never assess them this way.³⁴ Thus, the idea that some who consume the cup might not be guilty probably reflects the fact that the recipients of the cup are always groups of people, whether cities or nations. So, this likely refers to those individuals within the group who will experience the corporate judgment, even though they do not deserve it.³⁵

In a few passages from Lamentations and Obadiah, the cup also passes from Jerusalem to Edom, who is personified as looking on the devastation of Jerusalem after she consumed the cup of wrath. Lamentations declares to "Daughter Edom" that "to you also the cup will be passed; you will be drunk and stripped naked" (Lam 4:21). The point is that "Daughter Zion" will no longer be punished by the cup; instead, Edom will be judged (4:22). Obadiah prophesies similarly against Edom for standing idle and watching Jerusalem be conquered (Obad 11). He declares, "just as you [Jacob] drank on my holy hill, so all the nations will drink continually" (16).³⁶ These opaque references probably refer to consuming the cup of wrath; Judah did so in the experience of the exile, and other nations will as well, including Edom, until it would "be as if they had never been" (16). As Raabe notes, there seems to be an intensification to the imagery since the nations will drink the cup *continuously*, and there will be no recovery from consuming it.³⁷

---

33. Jack R. Lundbom, *Jeremiah 21–36: A New Translation with Introduction and Commentary*, AB (New York: Doubleday, 2004), 259–60, 266.

34. For this reason, some scholars view the passage as a later interpolation. See, e.g., McKane, *Jeremiah*, 2:1220–21; Holladay, *Jeremiah 1*, 373.

35. Similarly, F. B. Huey Jr., *Jeremiah and Lamentations*, NAC 16 (Nashville: Broadman & Holman, 1993), 402.

36. The "you" of v. 16 is probably a reference to Jacob/Judah rather than Edom because it is plural, whereas Edom is addressed in the singular elsewhere. See Raabe, *Obadiah*, 203–4.

37. Raabe, *Obadiah*, 204–5.

The subtheme of the cup of wrath being passed away from Jerusalem also appears in an oracle about Jerusalem's experience of exile in Isaiah 51. After Jerusalem consumes the cup of wrath "from the hand of the Lord"—which is also called "the goblet that makes people stagger" (51:17)—she is portrayed as a drunk woman awaking from the stupor of being "made drunk, but not with wine [*yayin*]" (51:21). Once she awakens, YHWH declares to her that she will not drink again from "the cup that made you stagger" and "the goblet of my wrath" (51:22). Instead, the cup will be removed from her hands and put "into the hands of your tormentors" (51:23), implying the restoration of Jerusalem and the demise of her enemies.

Because of what Babylon did to Jerusalem and the rest of the nations they subdued, she will also be judged. Habakkuk prophesies to Babylon, stating, "The cup from the Lord's right hand is coming around to you" (Hab 2:16). This will lead to their downfall because of the way they exploited others (2:15). Interestingly, in an oracle from Jeremiah, Babylon is herself presented as "a gold cup in the Lord's hand" (Jer 51:7a). This alludes to Babylon's role as an instrument of divine judgment against the nations, which is comparable to how Zechariah depicts Jerusalem as a cup used against would-be attackers (Zech 12:2). Babylon was used to make "the whole earth drunk" (Jer 51:7b), because "the nations drank her wine [*yayin*]" and "they have now gone mad" (51:7c). Yet in the end Babylon will meet her demise, not from receiving the cup of wrath herself (in this oracle at least; cf. 25:26), but from falling and breaking (51:8), presumably as the gold cup smashes when it is dropped from YHWH's hand.

Revelation adapts this imagery of Babylon as a golden cup in YHWH's hand in its portrait of Babylon as a drunk sex worker, *who herself has a gold cup* full of immorality (Rev 17:4). As noted earlier in this chapter, Babylon becomes drunk with the blood of the martyrs (17:6). But she also uses the gold cup[38] to make the nations "drink the wine [*oinos*]" that *incites* immorality with her (14:8), by causing them to become drunk (17:2) and to commit immorality (18:3).[39] As a symbolic metaphor, this set of images develops the theme of sexual vulnerability from alcohol that we saw in chapter 10. But the fraternizing of the nations with Babylon is part of an economic critique of those who benefit from the unjust empire (cf. 18:3).[40]

The way that Babylon uses the gold cup to make the nations drunk mirrors Jeremiah's vision, but in Revelation this image appears to be further nuanced. Another cup is given to Babylon (Rev 16:19), distinct from Babylon's golden cup, called the cup of wrath (14:10). And yet, in the final vision of Babylon's demise, we read that a "double portion" has been poured into *Babylon's own cup* (18:6), the cup

---

38. The gold cup is not mentioned in Rev 14:8, 17:2, or 18:3, but it is implied by the connection to immorality.

39. The wine could be the symbol for sexual immorality in these passages, but it is probably better to understand the genitive strings in the sense that the wine causes immorality with Babylon. See Beale, *Revelation*, 755–56.

40. See Beale, *Revelation*, 895–97, cf. 849–50.

from which she drinks, and by which the nations were supremely intoxicated. This "double portion" is not twice the amount of wine but twice the strength of the wine. This alludes to Roman practices of wine dilution within one's own glass, just as the reference to "full strength" does in Revelation 14:10 (cf. Ps. Sol. 8.14; cf. ch. 3 for dilution). The use of Babylon's cup to execute God's judgment means, as Brian Blount states, that God has "commandeered" it and has "deployed it now against her."[41]

In fact, a deeper connection between Babylon's cup and the cup of wrath is suggested by the use of the Greek word for wrath/fury (*thymos*) for both cups. Babylon's cup contains the wine of the passion (*thymos*) of her immorality (Rev 14:8; 18:3), which is variously translated in modern translations. But the cup also contains the wine of God's wrath/fury (*thymos* in 14:10; 16:19), which is taken from the winepress of God's wrath/fury (*thymos* in 14:19; 19:15). The use of *thymos* for each cup suggests that the one leads to the other; drinking from Babylon's cup will inexorably cause one to drink from the cup of wrath.[42] It is only in the final expression of this theme, when the double portion is poured into Babylon's gold cup (18:6; cf. 17:4), that we see how the gold cup from Jeremiah 51 metes out God's judgment directly. This highlights how "evil is self-destructive,"[43] and showcases that Babylon, to use a common expression, was "hoisted by her own petard."

The Cup of Gethsemane

Just prior to his arrest, in what could be another instance of the cup-of-wrath theme, Jesus prays in the garden of Gethsemane, wrestling greatly over the "cup" he is about to drink—namely, his impending crucifixion (Matt 26:36–46; Mark 14:32–43; Luke 22:39–46). Most scholars, however, insist that the cup Jesus mentions is a separate cup—the cup of suffering.[44] This cup is not developed in the Old Testament, but it is mentioned in some extracanonical Jewish and Christian sources. In the Testament of Abraham (1st–2nd c. CE), death is personified as being and having a bitter/poisonous cup (T. Ab. 16.12; 17.16; 19.6). In second-century CE martyrdom texts, the martyr's death is specifically likened to receiving a cup that God mixes for the martyr (Mart. Ascen. Isa. 5.13), which is also called "the cup of your Christ" (Mart. Pol. 14.2). In later rabbinic sources there are references to a "cup of death" (e.g., Tg. Neof. Gen 40:23; Frg. Tg. Gen 40:23; Tg. Neof. Deut 32:1). Essentially, in these passages the cup is a symbol for an individual's fate. The key distinction, then, is that the cup of wrath implies divine judgment, whereas the cup of suffering does not.

---

41. Blount, *Revelation*, 329, cf. 315.

42. Rightly, Grant R. Osborne, *Matthew*, ZECNT (Grand Rapids: Zondervan, 2010), 539–40.

43. Travis, "Wrath," 997. So similarly, e.g., Koester, *Revelation*, 673.

44. So, e.g., M. Black, "The Cup Metaphor in Mark xiv. 36," *ExpTim* 59 (1947–48): 195; Raymond E. Brown, *The Death of the Messiah, From Gethsemane to the Grave*, 2 vols., AYBRL (New Haven: Yale University Press, 1998), 169–70; François Bovon, *Luke 3: A Commentary on the Gospel of Luke 19:28–24:53*, trans. James E. Crouch, Hermeneia (Minneapolis: Fortress, 2012), 200–201.

The argument in favor of the cup of suffering in Gethsemane builds upon Jesus's earlier reference to a cup. In context, James and John assumed that Jesus is about to claim his throne upon arrival in Jerusalem, and so they asked (or their mother did for them; cf. Matt 20:20–21) to be seated on either side of Jesus in his "glory" (Mark 10:37) or "kingdom" (Matt 20:21). Jesus asked in response if they were able to drink the cup that he was about to drink, and he affirmed that they would drink it (Matt 20:22–23; Mark 10:38–39).[45] The argument goes that this must refer to each of their respective deaths by martyrdom, signposting that what will happen to Jesus on the cross will also happen to the two of them. According to this interpretation, if James and John will drink the same cup as Jesus, then both references to the cup assume a cup of suffering rather than the cup of wrath.

It seems preferable, however, to regard both cups as expressions of the cup of wrath.[46] For one, texts about the cup of suffering postdate the Gospels, whereas the background of the cup of wrath is quite extensive. Moreover, the fact that James and John will drink the same cup that Jesus drinks does not rule out the cup of wrath, because that dreadful cup is always given to groups as it moves from recipient to recipient.[47] None of them is immune to the "messianic woes," the suffering that precipitates the full arrival of the coming messianic age (e.g., Dan 7:21–22; 12:1; Mark 13:1–37; 2 Bar. 70.2–10; 1QH^a XI, 3–18; 4QFlor [4Q174]; Apoc. Abr. 29.14–15).[48] So suffering is entailed by the cup of wrath, but the notion of a distinct cup of suffering is a later development. Most strikingly of all, Jesus prays in Gethsemane that the cup could be taken away from him or moved along (Matt 26:39, 42; Mark 14:36; Luke 22:42), which alludes to the theme of the cup of wrath being passed around, surveyed earlier in this chapter.[49] In particular, the words of YHWH to Jerusalem in Isaiah 51:22–23 seem noteworthy here, as YHWH takes the cup from her hand so that she no longer has to drink it, and gives it to her enemies.[50]

> John is quite unique because instead of reporting the same Gethsemane scene, Jesus *affirms that he will drink the cup from the Father* (John 18:11; cf. 12:27; 17:11). In other words, there is no wavering in John's representation of the cup.

---

45. Mark also records Jesus asking if they can be baptized with the same baptism that he will experience, which Matthew omits (20:22–23). The pairing of the cup and baptism, at the very least, is evocative of early Christian ritual practices, suggesting that these rituals are rooted in early Christian theologies of solidarity with Jesus's suffering and death. See my forthcoming book: John Anthony Dunne, *Suffering and the Sacraments: An Early Christian Theology of Ritual Solidarity* (Bellingham, WA: Lexham).

46. So, e.g., Collins, *Mark*, 496, 680; Davies and Allison, *Matthew*, 3:89–90, 497.

47. Further, to the degree that the cup in Matthew 20:22–23 and Mark 10:38–39 also anticipates the Eucharist (perhaps especially in Mark), it speaks to how consuming the Eucharist itself is a recognition that the people of God will suffer in the messianic age, and confronts one with divine judgment (cf. 1 Cor 11:28–32). See also C. F. D. Moule, "The Judgment Theme in the Sacraments," in *The Background of the New Testament and Its Eschatology*, ed. W. D. Davies and D. Daube, FS C. H. Dodd (Cambridge: Cambridge University Press, 1956), 468–76.

48. Davies and Allison, *Matthew*, 3:497. Cf. Dale C. Allison Jr., *The End of the Ages Has Come: An Early Interpretation of the Passion and Resurrection of Jesus* (Philadelphia: Fortress, 1985), 5–25.

49. Intriguingly, the place-name Gethsemane combines the Hebrew words for winepress (*gat*) and oil (*shemen*), suggesting that oil and possibly wine were pressed there.

50. Richard B. Hays notes the probable allusion without further development. See *Echoes of Scripture in the Gospels* (Waco, TX: Baylor University Press, 2016), 161.

Thinking theologically about the implications of this reading, though, the cup of Gethsemane does not support penal substitutionary atonement—the idea that Jesus takes on punishment in place of other people.[51] Such an atonement theory may be established elsewhere. For our purposes here, however, it should be stated that the cup-of-wrath background neither conveys sacrifice nor atonement, and nowhere is the cup consumed vicariously for anyone else. The cup of wrath, instead, is about divine judgment, which Jesus recognizes in Gethsemane as beginning with God's Messiah. The time of the great tribulation was therefore inaugurated by Jesus's death.[52]

From a canonical standpoint, Revelation underscores that early Christians believed that they were participants in both the kingdom *and the tribulation* (Rev 1:9), highlighting clearly that what is included in the "not yet" of inaugurated eschatology is the persistence of trials and suffering alongside the signs of the kingdom. Revelation further highlights how the cup of wrath extends to include all the nations complicit with the beast and Babylon, and paradoxically shows how the suffering and tribulation of God's persecuted people ensures the judgment of the nations, since one of the symbolic contents contained in the cup of wrath is the blood of the martyrs (Rev 17:6). Revelation also reveals how Jesus, who was vindicated after drinking the cup of wrath, will return as the agent of God's judgment, treading the great winepress himself, signaling both the end of oppression and the vindication of God's people when the tribulation has ceased and the kingdom has arrived in full.

CONCLUSION

In this chapter we have seen how God's judgment is compared to the production and consumption of wine, including harvesting and treading imagery, as well as to consuming God's wrath in the form of an intoxicating beverage to the point of drunkenness. These terrifying images constitute another major symbolic varietal of wine in the Bible, but they are not to be taken literally. They reflect, as all judgment texts in Scripture do, the utter seriousness with which the God of justice approaches sin and injustice in the world. The previous two chapters together, and certainly the present chapter, may seem the most at odds with the commonly held view that wine symbolizes joy and blessing in the Bible. To be sure, it is worth sitting with the seriousness of this imagery and to recognize that wine—and alcohol more broadly—does not have the same connotations in every text. Nevertheless, even the privation and parody of wine serve to reinforce the estimation of wine as a blessing, but from

---

51. Some scholars who think that the cup of Gethsemane is the cup of wrath argue that this means that Jesus has vicariously taken on the sins of humanity, which in my view is based on an abstraction of the cup-of-wrath passages. See, e.g., C. E. B. Cranfield, "The Cup Metaphor in Mark xiv. 36 and Parallels," *ExpTim* 59 (1947–48): 137–38; Craig L. Blomberg, *Matthew*, NAC 22 (Nashville: Broadman, 1992), 395.

52. Allison, *End of the Ages*, 115–41.

a different angle. God's judgment can include a rescinding of his good gifts, and metaphorically those gifts can be replaced with a bitter draught.

Yet despite this thoroughgoing set of images, when the prophets wanted to talk about the restoration of Israel, whether from the exile or some other disaster, they communicated that restoration with visions of an abundance of wine. This abundance is one that comes even after the cup of wrath has been passed around. More on that in the next chapter.

RELEVANT QUESTIONS

1. If the cup of wrath is a parody, what elements of wine production and consumption seem to be the most inverted, and which ones seem underdeveloped?
2. To what extent should we understand the cup-of-wrath theme as an image of self-inflicted judgment that God allows rather than administers?
3. Since the cup of the martyr's blood that Babylon consumes in Revelation is the means of her own downfall, highlighting that those who persecute the church are doomed to fail, how might wine stir our thoughts and actions in relation to the suffering of the church around the world?

CHAPTER 13

ESCHATOLOGICAL ABUNDANCE OF WINE

When the prophets of Israel and Judah imagined what it would be like for God to restore God's people from calamity and to rebuild the Jerusalem temple, they anticipated an abundance of alcohol. As we saw in the previous two chapters, the chief calamity—exile from the land—was often presented as a *privation* of wine and viticulture due to the curses of the covenant (ch. 11). And divine judgment is frequently depicted as a *parody* of wine consumption, through the broader theme of the cup of wrath (ch. 12). Yet the prophets dared to look beyond the privation and parody of wine to a time of plenty, trusting in the mercy of God to bring about blessing once more, with alcoholic beverages as constitutive elements of that future blessing.

Perhaps the most extreme version of this prophetic longing for restitution depicted by an abundance of alcohol is the set of images found in the final oracles of both Joel and Amos, who envision the mountains dripping with sweet wine (*asis*). Beyond these prophetic texts, the most astonishing portrayal of abundance in biblical literature is Jesus's miracle at a wedding in Cana in which he turned water into wine (*oinos*). These remarkable passages will receive their own focus in this chapter, after first highlighting the broader prophetic hope of alcohol production and consumption reappearing on the other side of catastrophe. The return of wine and viticulture, in particular, are conjoined with the restoration of the people to the land, the renewal of the covenant, and the revitalization of the temple system. These associations will amplify the significance of the prophetic visions of sweet wine dripping down mountains and the miracle of large jars at a small wedding full to the brim with the best wine.

VITICULTURE AND RESTORING THE PEOPLE

After the harsh experience of foreign invasion and forced removal from the land, the prophets believed that God would bring the exiles back from their displacement. The prophets Jeremiah and Ezekiel declare that people will no longer say the sad proverb that resonates with the generational trauma of the exile: "the parents have eaten sour grapes, and the children's teeth are set on edge" (Jer 31:29; see also Ezek 18:2–3). The proverb reflects how successive generations deal with the consequences of former ones. It is as if parents bit into a sour grape and doing so dulled *their children's teeth*.

Many scholars regard the proverb as generally unclear.[1] Alter contends that the proverb is actually about unripe fruit (*boser*), which are denser and more likely to blunt teeth.[2] But blunting could just as likely occur from the fruit's acidity, causing a person to pucker and grind their teeth. Regardless, Jeremiah anticipates that this proverb will one day be *forgotten*, implying the restoration of viticulture. But it also anticipates the end of social injustices from one generation being passed on to the next one (cf. Lam 5:7), and it holds each individual accountable for their own sin (Jer 31:30; Ezek 18:4). God will act to bring about restorative justice. One of the effects of this will be renewed viticulture, which has as its chief aim the enjoyment of alcohol.

Because the covenant has been broken by disobedience, it must be renewed if a covenantal relationship will endure. Jeremiah and Ezekiel connect viticulture to their respective visions of a new covenant when God will inscribe the law on people's hearts (Jer 31:31–34), and even give them a new heart and his own Spirit (Ezek 36:25–28). According to Jeremiah, after those who are scattered are brought back (Jer 31:10), they will become like a "well-watered garden" instead of a wasteland (31:12). The term "well-watered" is used again in the immediate context in Jeremiah 31:25 to speak of the reality of the people living in the land again: "I will refresh the weary and satisfy the faint" (31:25).[3] Vineyards will be planted on the hillsides (31:5) for the people to enjoy "the bounty of the Lord," including new wine (*tirosh* in 31:12). As a prophetic sign-act of this forthcoming reality, Jeremiah buys a field (32:7), foreshadowing, among other things, that the people would return from Babylonian captivity (32:43–44) to cultivate vineyards in their land (32:15). Ezekiel describes the transition from desolation to abundance in terms of becoming like the garden of Eden (Ezek 36:35; cf. 28:13–16). When the exiles are brought back into the land (36:24), there will be agricultural abundance rather than famine (36:29–30). In that garden-like setting, the people themselves will be fruitful and multiply (36:11, cf. 36:37–38), evoking the creation mandate of Genesis 1:28.

The land's physical transformation at the time of Israel's restoration occurs elsewhere too (e.g., Isa 4:2; 55:10–13; 58:11; Ezek 34:23–31). Isaiah envisions God pouring out his Spirit to enact this revitalization like Ezekiel does (Isa 32:15–17), even similarly comparing Zion to the primeval garden (51:3). In order to bring the exiles back to their homeland safely, Isaiah also imagines God reshaping the topography into a highway (35:1–10; 40:3–4; 49:11–12; 51:10–11; 57:14; 62:10) and causing the desert places along that highway to be fruitful (41:18–20; 43:19–21; 44:1–5).[4] The psalmist likewise speaks of desert places turning lush (Ps 107:35) and changing into fields and

---

1. See Gerald L. Keown, Pamela J. Scalise, Thomas G. Smothers, *Jeremiah 26–52*, WBC 27 (Dallas: Word, 1995), 130.

2. *Hebrew Bible*, 2:966.

3. In the LXX, this is expressed as: "I intoxicated (*methyskō*) every thirsty soul" (Jer 38:25 NETS).

4. Inversely, increased desiccation expresses judgment (see, e.g., Ps 107:33–34; Isa 42:15; 50:2; 59:18; 64:19).

vineyards with "a fruitful harvest" (107:37). God's restorative actions toward the land even lead the psalmist to recall aspects of the Abrahamic covenant: "he blessed them, and their numbers greatly increased, and he did not let their herds diminish" (107:38).

God's renewal of Israel's lot in the world will include removing the threat of foreign oppression and its impact on viticulture. Zechariah envisions God's protection of the people in the midst of an enemy attack (Zech 9:14–15) as not only resulting in deliverance from harm (9:16), but also in the provision of new grain for young men and new wine (*tirosh*) for young women (9:17).[5] Further, the joy that comes from being gathered by God from the diaspora is like the joy of a warrior intoxicated by wine (10:7). Once gathered back to the land, foreign armies will no longer oppress the people or the land, nor will they steal produce from them. As Isaiah announces, "Never again will I give your grain as food for your enemies, and never again will foreigners drink the new wine [*tirosh*] for which you have toiled" (Isa 62:8b). In the new creation, God's people will no longer start viticultural projects and building endeavors only to have them thwarted: "they will plant vineyards and eat their fruit" (65:21). Ezekiel also stresses that the people will dwell in security and be able to plant their vineyards in safety (Ezek 28:26). Additionally, Isaiah envisages that the tables will be turned; the former oppressive nations will become shepherds and even vinedressers on Israel's behalf, working in their fields and vineyards (Isa 61:5).

When foreign enemies are no longer a threat, the weapons of warfare can be reappropriated into utensils of viticulture. Both Isaiah and Micah anticipate an era in which the nations will essentially unlearn war and will have no need for their swords or spears any longer (Isa 2:4; Mic 4:3).[6] Swords will become plowshares, and spears will become pruning hooks (i.e., vintner knives)—utensils used to prune grapevines in the offseason in preparation for new growth. Repurposing weapons suggests the ideal political situation for viticultural activity, leading to the need for vintner knives to promote robust harvests.

In addition to imagining that flourishing viticulture will accompany Israel's restoration to the land, Hosea describes that restoration as a viticultural process. The connection seems to arise from the metaphor of Israel as God's vineyard. As a possible allusion to this imagery, Hosea asserts that God will restore Israel by "sow[ing]" her back into the land (Hos 2:23 NRSVue), taking her from the wilderness and giving back her vineyards (2:14–15). Within the expectations of the vision, this activity has the effect of bringing nature back into harmony, resulting in the land producing grain, oil, and wine (*tirosh*) once more (2:22). Indeed, what God "sowed" in the land will reap a great harvest. The people will "flourish like the grain,"[7] and they

---

5. Alter contends that the virgins are compared with new wine, rather than given it. See *Hebrew Bible*, 2:1374.

6. Joel 3:10 inverts the imagery into a call for arms for a final battle before restoration (Joel 3:17–21).

7. The LXX suggests inebriation from beer: "they shall live and be intoxicated on grain" (Hos 14:8 NETS).

will blossom like the vine, with their newfound fame being compared to the highly prized wine (*yayin*) of Lebanon (14:7).

Isaiah extends this imagery a bit further, configuring restoration itself as an offer of great food and wine. In particular, Isaiah envisions God as a gracious merchant summoning everyone to buy wine, but surprisingly without a financial transaction.[8] As he proclaims:

> Come, all you who are thirsty,
> > come to the waters;
> and you who have no money,
> > come, buy and eat!
> Come, buy wine (*yayin*) and milk
> > without money and without cost. (Isa 55:1)

The people who come, Isaiah tells us, will "delight in the richest of fare" (55:2). This vision is notably distinct from the apocryphal Apocalypse of Thomas (5th c. CE), where there is an abundance of wine in the eschaton, but it will all be taxed.[9] In Isaiah, God will provide more than everyone's needs and lavishly offer good wine. This goes beyond the visions of restored viticultural activity and enjoyment of wine as the work of their hands. Here is the gracious offer of wine without cost and without the effort needed to make it.

VITICULTURE AND REVITALIZING THE TEMPLE

As the people return to their land and enjoy its abundance in this era of restoration, the temple will also be thriving once more. When the prophets describe this reality, they often highlight the close association between agricultural success and a flourishing temple system. If agricultural production is high, then more offerings and tithes will be sent to the temple. But furthermore, the prophets speak of the directionality going the other way as well (cf. Jer 33:11)—rightly ordered worship in the temple positively impacts the fertility of the land (cf. ch. 6).

The prophet Haggai provides a clear expression of this broader pattern. He was prophesying after the exile when people were renovating their own homes while neglecting to revitalize the temple. This had a direct impact on the declining agriculture (Hag 1:10–11). Despite the neglectful attitude of the people, the prophet declared that the new temple will be even more glorious than the previous one

---

8. On God as a merchant rather than a banquet host, see Andrew T. Abernethy, *Eating in Isaiah: Approaching the Role of Food and Drink in Isaiah's Structure and Message*, BIS 131 (Leiden: Brill, 2014), 120–23.

9. See J. K. Elliott, *The Apocryphal New Testament: A Collection of Apocryphal Christian Literature in an English Translation Based on M. R. James* (1993; repr., Oxford: Oxford University Press, 2009), 648.

(2:1–9), leading to an agricultural increase. Yet, amid their neglect, the disobedience of the people is likened to contagious impurity that attaches to their offerings, including wine, rendering them unworthy of inclusion in the temple cult (2:12–14). Consequently, plagues were corrupting their crops (2:17), so that someone intending to retrieve fifty measures of wine from the wine vats would only find twenty (2:16). The people remained in that precarious situation agriculturally when they began work on the temple, which Haggai acknowledges by noting that the vine and fig tree lack fruit. But Haggai points to the promise of future blessing at the time when the temple project was complete (2:19).

We see similar pictures in Zechariah and Malachi, but to a lesser degree. Zechariah foresees an era of people sitting under their fig trees and vines (Zech 3:10), and the heavens sending their rains so that vines yield their fruit (8:12). This is an era that will arrive when the high priest Joshua works to remove the guilt from the land (3:9), and a figure called the Branch restores the temple cult (cf. 6:12–14) so that YHWH returns to it (8:1–8). Malachi proclaims that the devouring locusts will not destroy the vine (Mal 3:11) once the messenger of YHWH appears in the temple (3:1) to purify the sons of Levi (3:3) and to restore the cultic system (3:4).

A restored temple means that festivals will return once more, which includes feasting and wine. As Isaiah pronounces:

> Those who harvest it will eat it
>   and praise the Lord,
> and those who gather the grapes will drink it
>   in the courts of my sanctuary. (Isa 62:9)

In context, this passage highlights not just that people will be able to consume the wine that they produced (cf. Isa 62:8), but that they will be able to do so during ritual celebrations in the temple. This is not a contradiction of the priestly prohibition from drinking while serving in the temple (cf. Lev 10:9–10; Ezek 44:21), since the temple courts are a large part of the complex, and the priests can carry out their duties during the festivities. In the future that the prophets anticipate, the festivals that were turned into mourning during the exile will be turned back to joy when YHWH returns (Zeph 3:14–19; Zech 8:1–8). Pilgrims will make their journeys to the temple in safety (Nah 1:15; 2:1), and the nations will likewise participate in the festival worship at the temple (e.g., Mic 4:2; Zech 8:19–21). In fact, for Zechariah, participation in the Feast of Tabernacles will be the basis upon which the nations receive rain or plagues (Zech 14:16–19).

The revitalized temple is also portrayed as a fertile place in and of itself. When the prophets describe the future temple, they often include the symbolism of rivers issuing from it (cf. Zech 14:8), reminiscent of the first temple (cf. ch. 6). In Ezekiel's extended vision of the future (Ezek 40–48), the temple is called a house on the mountain (43:12), and from it flows a life-giving river with lush gardens growing along the sides of the riverbanks (47:1–12). Earlier in his prophetic oracles, Ezekiel asserts that the garden of Eden is set on "the mountain of God" (28:13–14, 16; cf. 20:40).

In these passages the mountain is a synecdoche for the temple, since ANE temples were set on hills and other high places in order to be closer to the gods.[10] The connection to the garden of Eden highlights how some early interpreters of Genesis understood the garden to be a holy space (Jub. 3.12; 4Q265 7 II, 14), even like the holy of holies (Jub. 8.19) within the temple of the cosmos (Philo, *Planting* 50).[11] Isaiah and Micah both prophesy of the restored temple's prominence in terms of the mountain of YHWH being elevated above all others (Isa 2:1–4; Mic 4:1–5). Micah's version is most likely dependent on Isaiah, and he expands the imagery of blessing to include an abundance of vines and people living beneath their vines and fig trees (4:4).

> Jubilees records Abram making offerings (Jub. 13.8–9) on a mountain near vines, rivers, and other images of fertility (13.6).

MOUNTAINS DRIPPING SWEET WINE IN JOEL AND AMOS

As noted at the outset, the final prophetic oracles in Joel and Amos provide the most extreme versions of this prophetic theme of eschatological abundance, when they foresee "sweet wine" (*asis*) dripping down the mountains (Joel 3:18 [4:18 MT]; Amos 9:13).[12] In each oracle, the catalyst for this particular image of abundance is likely revitalizing the temple system, which stands in line with some of the themes from the previous section. This reading is relatively clear in the ending of Joel, given the multiple references to Jerusalem, the holy mountain, YHWH's house, and Zion in Joel 3:17–21. It is less clear, however, in Amos 9:11–15, where the explicit stimulant of viticultural abundance is rebuilding "David's tent." In my view, the referent for this unique phrase is the future messianic temple. Whereas it is undoubtedly clear that both Joel and Amos anticipate that God's restoring power will cause "sweet wine" to drip from the mountains, I simply want to extend this one step further and suggest that the image is conjoined, in each case, with a return of God's presence and the reordering of the temple system specifically.

In Joel's oracles, his vision of viticultural abundance is associated with God's presence, as God pours out the Spirit *on all flesh* (Joel 2:28–32) and returns to make

---

10. On the theme of the cosmic mountain, see Richard J. Clifford, *The Cosmic Mountain in Canaan and the Old Testament* (Cambridge: Harvard University Press, 1972).

11. For more on this theme of the garden of Eden as sacred space, see, e.g., Jon D. Levenson, "The Temple and the World," *JR* 64.3 (1984): 275–98; Beale, *Temple*, 29–80.

12. On *asis* as freshly pressed juice beginning to ferment, cf. ch. 2.

a dwelling place in Zion (3:17–21). Joel's prophecy was either written during the exilic period after the temple was destroyed, or in the postexilic period shortly after the temple was rebuilt,[13] when God's enduring presence was an open question. Joel's prophetic message concerns a devastating locust plague that had ravaged local crops and produce, but which is cast as a signpost of the climactic judgment day—the day of the Lord.

When the priests and the people petition God through public lament (Joel 1:9b, 13; 2:17), fasting (1:14; 2:15), and genuine repentance (2:12–13), viticultural processes will resume. God promises to bring back the fertility of the land, including the vine (2:22), by providing early and late rain in the growth cycle (2:23). The land will then give the people grain, oil, and "new wine [*tirosh*]" (2:19). Indeed, the threshing floor will fill with grain, and the vats will overflow from excessive production, bursting with oil and "new wine [*tirosh*]" (2:24). God will bring reparations, paying back the years taken by the locusts (2:25), and this agricultural abundance will resound in worship: "and you will praise the name of the LORD your God" (2:26). Indeed, accompanying that worship will be libations, which will be made possible once more (2:14).

> In the Acts of the Apostles, Peter connects the events of Pentecost to Joel's expectation of God pouring out the Spirit (Acts 2:16–21). Given the abundance of wine that accompanies that reality for Joel, the wrongful accusation from bystanders that those filled with the Spirit at Pentecost were actually drunk with "new wine [*gleukos*]" (Acts 2:13), takes on a layer of irony, since there was no wine present at Pentecost.

Joel envisions further that the blessings of fertility will continue to flow back into the land as a result of God's renewed presence in Zion.

> In that day the mountains will drip new wine [*asis*],
>   and the hills will flow with milk;
> all the ravines of Judah will run with water.
> A fountain will flow out of the LORD's house
>   and will water the valley of acacias. (Joel 3:18 [4:18 MT])

This passage directly inverts the previous threats in Joel's prophecies: rather than the absence of "sweet wine" (*asis*; 1:5 NRSVue), there will be more than is comprehensible, and the dry ravines (1:20) will once more flow as they should.[14] The reason for this is ultimately cultic restoration. Elie Assis notes that the sequence of liquids here—wine, milk, and water—moves from most expensive to least expensive, and that the river flowing from the temple reverses the order, flowing up and in the opposite direction. This suggests that each of these blessings come from the temple, which figuratively supplies the water to make them all possible.[15]

---

13. Most opt for a postexilic dating, but for an exilic dating, see especially Elie Assis, *The Book of Joel: A Prophet between Calamity and Hope*, LHBOTS 581 (London: Bloomsbury, 2013).

14. See James D. Nogalski, *Redactional Processes in the Book of the Twelve*, BZAW 218 (Berlin: de Gruyter, 1993), 26.

15. Assis, *Joel*, 251.

> 1 Enoch 10.18–19 (3rd–1st c. BCE) speaks to the great abundance that vines will produce in the era of restoration: "And in those days the whole earth will be worked in righteousness, all of her planted with trees, and will find blessing. And they shall plant pleasant trees upon her—vines. And he who plants a vine upon her will produce wine for plenitude."[16]

Turning to Amos 9:11–15, *asis* also drips down from the mountains when "David's tent" is rebuilt (NIV: "David's fallen shelter"). Most scholars regard this oracle as a later interpolation to the message of the preexilic prophet, which imagines the restoration of the Davidic empire to its former place of prominence.[17] In other words, the "house" of David has metaphorically become a dilapidated shack because of the splintering of the northern and southern kingdoms, and therefore it is no longer worthy to be called a house. But there are good reasons for viewing "David's tent" in cultic terms rather than strictly regal ones.[18] My view is that Amos's final vision, despite differences in details, is not fundamentally different from Joel's final vision in its stress on God's presence in the temple bringing about viticultural and agricultural abundance.[19]

Within the epilogue of Amos, when the "tent of David" is rebuilt and restored (Amos 9:11), there will be intense viticultural activity. Prosperity will be characterized by a fast forwarding of the agricultural cycle: "the reaper will be overtaken by the plowman and the planter by the one treading grapes" (9:13a). In other words, the whole viticultural cycle, which produces a single harvest each year, *will now occur several times a year*, even yielding more in just one of those harvests than could ever be consumed! This is envisioned by the overwhelming abundance of *asis*: "new wine [*asis*] will drip from the mountains and flow from all the hills" (9:13b). This *asis*, freshly pressed and flowing down into collecting vats right on the mountainside, will quickly ferment and be enjoyed as proper wine (*yayin*, 9:14) because there is far too much *asis* to consume (or even pasteurize, to be anachronistic) before it ferments. Additionally, given the fast-forwarding nature of the viticultural cycle, in just a few months there will be even more on the way! When David's tent is rebuilt, there will also no longer be any concern that their hard work will be thwarted by war or pestilence, because Edom and all the nations who are "called" by the name of the

---

16. E. Isaac, "1 (Ethiopic Apocalypse of) Enoch," *OTP* 1:18.
17. See, e.g., Paul, *Amos*, 289–92; Francis I. Andersen and David N. Freedman, *Amos*, AB (New Haven: Yale University Press, 1989), 889–90, 903–4, 912–18. For the regal interpretation coupled with the epilogue's originality, see, e.g., JoAnna M. Hoyt, *Amos, Jonah, and Micah*, EEC (Bellingham, WA: Lexham, 2019), 316–19.
18. For more on this, see John Anthony Dunne, "David's Tent as Temple in Amos 9:11–15: Understanding the Epilogue of Amos and Considering Implications for the Unity of the Book," *WTJ* 73.2 (2011): 363–74.
19. I argue further that Joel's final vision interprets Amos's epilogue this way. See John Anthony Dunne, "Mountains Shall Drip Sweet Wine from the Temple: Joel's Interpretation of the Epilogue of Amos," *JSOT* 47.4 (2023): 473–89.

Lord will be "possessed" (9:12). Whether we understand this militaristically (so most), or in terms of salvific inclusion,[20] the nations will neither threaten the people nor undermine their viticultural activity. In the end of the vision, the people and the villages themselves are metaphorically described as something YHWH plants into the land (cf. Hos 2:23), underscoring the agricultural focus of the entire epilogue. Towns will be rebuilt and restored, and the people will never again be "uprooted" from their land, extending the agricultural metaphor further (Amos 9:14–15).

In my view, the viticultural activity that accompanies the rebuilding of David's tent is best understood as the result of the restoration of the temple. As we have seen in this chapter, this fits a prophetic emphasis on the common connection between agricultural abundance and a thriving temple cult, and it also specifically mirrors the ending of Joel, which uses similar imagery to describe what happens when YHWH returns to the temple. The main argument is that the final vision of David's tent being rebuilt is the only instance of hope in all of Amos, and thus it must provide a solution to the extensive plight that precedes it—disorderly and unjust cultic practices.

An ancient Sumerian inscription by Gudea, king of Lagash (22nd c. BCE) commemorating the construction of the temple of Ningirsu contains the following:

> Its [i.e., the shrine's] first
> offering
> is a mountain dripping with wine. (Cylinder A, col. 28, lines 10–11)[21]

Here the mountains drip with wine because of cultic libations that issue from the temple of Ningirsu. Then a few lines later the inscription states:

> Its Mledin-garden which fills the
> temple
> is (like) a mountain dripping with
> wine; it is a place where radiant
> awesomeness grows. (Cylinder A, col. 28, lines 23–24)[22]

In this second instance the mountain drips with wine because of the viticultural activity in the temple complex.

---

20. Amos 9:12 LXX refers to the remnant of humanity seeking the Lord. Cf. Acts 15:16–18.

21. Taken from appendix A in Richard E. Averbeck, "A Preliminary Study of Ritual and Structure in the Cylinders of Gudea" (PhD diss., The Dropsie College, 1987), 675.

22. Averbeck, "Preliminary Study," 676.

Cultic worship is a major theme for Amos, stirring up his prophetic ire from the beginning to the end. Amos begins by announcing that YHWH roars from the temple in Zion (Amos 1:2). From there he critiques the cultic activity of the northerners (4:4–5; 5:7, 21–27; 8:10), confronts a northern priest (Amos 7), and declares that their cultic sites will be destroyed (3:14; 5:5–6; 7:9) and their festivals will cease (8:9). The final chapter of Amos even begins with YHWH standing by "the altar" (9:1), without specifying its location, and announcing its terrible destruction (9:1–5). The death and devastation that comes upon the people and the land because of the destruction of the altar in Amos 9:1 is overturned by the life and abundance that comes from rebuilding David's tent in Amos 9:11. This suggests that David's tent is also a cultic site and that its restoration is designed to correct the cultic issues that Amos addresses.[23]

Rebuilding David's tent thus redresses cultic problems, but so does the abundance of wine that David's tent brings about. The expectation in this final vision that people will plant their vineyards and drink their own wine once again (Amos 9:14), directly reverses the viticultural futility of planting vineyards and not enjoying wine (*yayin* in 5:11). It also remedies the devastation against vineyards that is due to corrupt participation in the cult (4:8–9). Indeed, because there is more wine presented in the epilogue than anyone could hope to drink on their own, the vision also redresses the economic disparity associated with the abuse of wine by the rich (5:11; 6:6).[24] Further, the abundance of wine from David's tent rectifies the inappropriate cultic use of wine, since the rich consume wine (*yayin*) out of basins (*mizraq* in 6:6)[25] and at "every altar" in the house of "their g/God" (2:7–8; cf. ch. 4).

The Hebrew term that is used for "tent" in Amos 9:11 is *sukkah* rather than the typical term for the tabernacle (*ohel*), although on at least one occasion the tabernacle is called a *sukkah* (2 Sam 11:11).[26] A *sukkah* is a makeshift hut used during the Feast of Tabernacles to commemorate Israel's wilderness wanderings when they traveled around with the tabernacle (cf. ch. 5). Over time, this feast came to be especially associated with the Jerusalem temple as "the Temple festival *par excellence*," with celebrants making their pilgrimages to Jerusalem in order to observe the festival and to make daily processionals to the temple.[27] The festival itself occurs in the fall around harvest time, when vintners would set up *sukkoth* in the vineyards to keep an eye on the grapes so that they could begin harvest at the most opportune time.[28]

---

23. Aaron Schart, "The Fifth Vision of Amos in Context," in *Thematic Threads in the Book of the Twelve*, ed. Paul L. Redditt and Aaron Schart, BZAW 325 (Berlin: de Gruyter, 2003), 62.

24. Rightly Green, "Vineyards," 306.

25. These are basins used in sacred space; cf., e.g., Exod 27:3; 38:3; Num 4:14; 1 Kgs 7:45; Jer 52:18–19; Zech 14:20.

26. Gregory R. Goswell, "David in the Prophecy of Amos," *VT* 61.2 (2011): 253.

27. Daniel K. Falk, "Festivals and Holy Days," *EDEJ* 640.

28. Walsh, *Fruit*, 139–40; McGovern, *Ancient Wine*, 217.

The use of *sukkah* in Amos 9:11 likely evokes this Feast of Tabernacles context and the grape harvest, given the emphasis on viticulture in the epilogue and indeed the abundance of wine. Jerusalem is called a tent by Isaiah on a few occasions (*sukkah* in Isa 1:8; *ohel* in 16:5), and there is some additional evidence to support the connection of *sukkah* with sacred space.[29] Thus, viewing the Jerusalem temple as a *sukkah* evokes the idea that Jerusalem is surrounded by vineyards.

Lastly, there is good reason to associate David with a vision of the restored temple. Within Amos itself, David is mentioned one other time, where his role as a cultic songwriter is acknowledged, not his regal office (Amos 6:5).[30]

> David is remembered for contributing to temple worship through the psalter as well as through composing songs, creating instruments, and instructing priests and Levites in their performance (e.g., 1 Chr 6:31–32; 15:16; 16:1–36; 23:2–6; 2 Chr 8:14–15; 23:18; cf. 1 Esd 5:59–62; 8:49; 11QPsalms^a [11Q5] XXVII, 2–11; Josephus, *Ant.* 7.12.3; 7.14.7).[31] In later Christian tradition, David even becomes a heavenly worship leader (Apoc. Paul 29).

Although David did not build the temple, his son Solomon did (1 Kgs 8). The temple is thus rightly associated with his line, as the Davidic covenant establishes (2 Sam 7:12–17). Chronicles even ascribes much of the logistics for the temple's construction to David (1 Chr 15:1; 22:1, 5–7; cf. Josephus, *Ant.* 9.7.2), and Jerusalem is often remembered as the city of David. Moreover, David's association with the tabernacle during his lifetime likely has something to do with the choice of the language of "tent" in Amos 9:11.

> The strong association of David and the temple led Josephus to say accidentally that David built it (*Ant.* 1.13.2). David is associated with temple imagery in later pseudepigraphical works as well; the Apocalypse of Sedrach 1.17–18 (2nd–5th c. CE) says that divine love "made David the dwelling place of the Holy Spirit."[32]

---

29. Cognate evidence includes *sok* (with a samekh) in Pss 27:5; 76:2 [76:3 MT] and *sok* (with a sin) in Lam 2:6. Additionally, *sukkah* is used elsewhere to refer to God's sheltering presence (Pss 31:20 [31:21 MT]), and the pillar of fire covering Zion (Isa 4:5–6). See Goswell, "David," 252.

30. Rightly pointed out by Goswell, "David," though I disagree that the epilogue is non-messianic.

31. On this see esp. Eckhard J. Schnabel, "Singing and Instrumental Music in the Early Church," in *Sprache lieben—Gottes Wort verstehen*, ed. Walter Hilbrands, FS Heinrich von Siebenthal, BBE (Giessen: Brunnen, 2011), 307–39.

32. S. Agourides, "Apocalypse of Sedrach," *OTP* 1:609.

Thus, the restoration of this "tent" is part of the era of the restoration of the kingdom. This dual connotation of regal and cultic significance is paralleled by the reference to Bethel as "the king's sanctuary" and "the temple of the kingdom" (Amos 7:13).

It seems, therefore, that the eschatological rebuilding of David's tent and the abundance of wine are cultic solutions to the cultic plights recorded in Amos. Contrary to those who view the epilogue of Amos 9:11–15 as a later addition to the text,[33] it is best to see that a cultic interpretation of David's tent and viticultural production is centrally connected. When this passage is quoted in Luke's account of the so-called Jerusalem Council (Acts 15:16–18), the citation of Amos 9:11–12 is best read along the lines offered here, but refracted in the light of the resurrection and the pneumatology of Luke-Acts.

> The implication of citing Amos 9 in Acts 15 is that the community indwelt by the Spirit of the resurrected Christ constitutes the rebuilding of David's tent—the eschatological temple. This reading fits the narrative of Acts because: (a) Christ-followers are indwelt by God's presence at Pentecost (Acts 2); (b) Jesus is the "cornerstone" of this temple (4:11); (c) God's presence is not confined to a building in Jerusalem (Acts 7); and (d) gentiles receive the same Spirit (15:8).[34]

Recognizing David's tent as the temple in Amos strengthens the association in prophetic literature between viticultural abundance and the temple cult, and further connects wine to rightly ordered worship. In other words, the prophets understood that enjoyment of wine and satisfaction in God are best paired together.

THE WEDDING AT CANA

Building off of the restorative abundance that Joel and Amos predicted, the Gospel of John records that Jesus's first "sign" was to miraculously transform 120–180 gallons of water into wine at a wedding (John 2:1–10). Just as the prophets anticipate an abundance of wine in response to a lack of it, so too Jesus provides wine where there is none.

In 2 Baruch (1st–2nd c. CE), there will be great viticultural abundance when "the Anointed One will begin to be revealed" (2 Bar. 29.2). As it says: "The earth will also yield fruits ten thousandfold. And on one vine will be a thousand branches, and one branch will produce a thousand clusters, and one cluster will produce a thousand grapes, and one grape will produce a cor of wine" (29.5).[35] A cor equates to nearly sixty gallons.

---

33. See Julius Wellhausen, *Die kleinen Propheten* (1898; repr., Berlin: de Gruyter, 1963), 95.

34. For more on this, see, e.g., Richard J. Bauckham, "James and the Jerusalem Church," in *The Book of Acts in Its Palestinian Setting*, ed. Richard J. Bauckham, vol. 4 of *The Book of Acts in Its First Century Setting*, Bruce W. Winter (Grand Rapids: Eerdmans, 1995), 415–80; Beale, *Temple*, 232–44.

35. Klijn, "2 (Syriac Apocalypse of) Baruch," *OTP* 1:630.

Water was often undrinkable and inaccessible in the ancient world, but Jesus did not make something undrinkable drinkable. Instead, he made something remarkable, which goes beyond the sheer quantity of wine. As the master of the feast states, it was customary to serve the better wine at the start of an event and then bring out the inferior wine as the party goes on (John 2:10). This is because one's taste buds grow increasingly dull while drinking alcohol, rendering a person less capable of appreciating nuance and subtlety. In many ways that custom still exists. No dinner party host today would pull out a nice bottle of Chateau Lafite Rothschild after serving their guests several cheap bottles of Charles Shaw from Trader Joe's (i.e., "Two-Buck Chuck"). Yet Jesus had completely inverted the custom, providing an abundance of great wine late in the celebration (perhaps even after multiple days of celebrating). Jesus could have produced inferior wine, which would still have been miraculous and in keeping with banqueting customs, but he produced something exceptional.

> Pliny the Elder (*Nat.* 14.14.91) refers to the custom of swapping out lesser wines over the course of a meal: "moreover Cato, when sailing on his expedition to Spain, whence he returned with a triumph, drank no other wine [Lat. *vinum*] than what was drunk by the crew of his galley, so little did he resemble the gentlemen who give even their guests other wines than those served to themselves, or else substitute inferior wines as the meal progresses" (Rackham, LCL).

Jesus performed this miracle after the guests had consumed plenty already—so much so that they ran out. In fact, when the master of the feast explains that better wine is normally served first, he says that the inferior wine comes after the guests are drunk (*methyskō* in John 2:10). Many English translations euphemistically render this with something like "after they have had their fill," but the Greek is not so ambiguous. The sheer quantity of wine at Cana builds upon and develops the theme of this chapter, and I maintain further that it does so with its own set of temple imagery, where once again a revitalized temple system leads to an *abundance* of wine.

The most pronounced visions of abundant wine surveyed so far include the references to mountains dripping sweet wine in Joel 3 and Amos 9, which I have argued are ultimately about the impact of a revitalized temple system on viticulture. Given that these scenes provide the most profound vision of abundance and that the wedding at Cana vividly portrays abundance unlike any other biblical text, it is likely that the visions of Joel and Amos contributed to John's understanding and portrayal of the wedding. Ronald Feenstra, for example, argues that Amos 9 is part of the intertextual background of John 2, but because he reads Amos 9 as signaling the restoration of the Davidic kingdom, he does not develop the temple imagery that I will.[36]

> Lucian, in his satire *Saturnalia* (§22), addresses how wine would be distributed inequitably to guests, with *gleukos* contrasted with superior wine: "let the wine [*oinos*] be one and the same for all the guests—where is it laid down that [the master] should get drunk on wine with a fine bouquet (*anthosmias*) while I must burst my belly on new stuff [*gleukos*]?" (Kilburn, LCL).

---

36. Ronald Feenstra, "Hills Flowing with Wine: A Meditation on John 2:1–11," *RJ* (April 1988): 9–10.

Further, the background of temple imagery also informs this passage through the fact that the *best* wine in ancient Israel was meant to be stored at the temple, as we saw in chapter 6. Thus, the biblical background of the temple is relevant for both the quality and the quantity of wine at Cana.

Several factors suggest that the sign at Cana is imbued with temple imagery. This is conveyed by two elements in the immediate context of the pericope of the wedding itself, but these elements take on greater cultic connotations in the surrounding context. The first element of temple imagery in the wedding pericope is that the water was initially poured into six stone water jars that accord with customs of ritual purification (John 2:6). The note about ritual purification either suggests that the 120–180 gallons of water were used *to provide ritual purification* (i.e., through handwashing), or that the jars were made of stone in accordance with Jewish beliefs that stone vessels *were insusceptible to impurity* like other vessels were.[37] Regardless of which option is more likely, the host family was clearly concerned about purity. While ritual purity was not exclusively a concern for priests,[38] or anyone else going to the holy temple (this scene takes place in Galilee, after all), one could not be ritually impure and enter into sacred space, which may have been symbolically significant for John. In fact, linking the wine at Cana with purity is also reflected in Jesus's teaching on the vine and the branches, where, as part of a broader discourse about the coming of God's holy presence through the Spirit, he declares that the disciples who were with him were already pure (15:3).[39]

The second element of temple imagery at Cana comes from the narrator's conclusion, which states that Jesus displayed his "glory" through this sign (John 2:11). Glory is a term often used to designate God's presence in sacred space (e.g., Exod 40:34–35; 1 Kgs 8:10–11; Isa 6:1; Ezek 10:4; 43:5; 44:4; Hag 2:7). The prologue of John explicitly makes this connection, stating that "we have seen his glory" when the Word became flesh and "made his dwelling among us" (John 1:14). The significance of the term "glory" here is accentuated by the verb for "dwelling" (*skēnoō*). This comes from the Greek noun for "tent" and is the term used to refer to God's presence in the tabernacle in the LXX (e.g., Exod 25:9; Lev 16:20; Num 19:13; Deut 31:14–15; Josh 22:29; 2 Sam 6:17; 1 Kgs 1:39; 1 Chr 16:1). In other words, in the incarnation the Word's presence revealed a glory comparable to the tabernacle of old, and that same glory was discernable in the abundance of wine at Cana.

By themselves, references to glory and purity in the Cana episode do not

---

37. For the latter view, see Yonatan Adler, *The Origins of Judaism: An Archaeological-Historical Reappraisal*, AYBRL (New Haven: Yale University Press, 2022), 57, 66–71. Cf. Wil Rogan, *Purity in the Gospel of John: Early Jewish Tradition, Christology, and Ethics*, LNTS 679 (London: T&T Clark, 2023), 12–13, 55–58.

38. John C. Poirier, "Purity beyond the Temple in the Second Temple Era," *JBL* 122.2 (2003): 247–65.

39. So Macaskill, *Union*, 263. See also Rogan, *Purity*, 107–46, for a treatment of how this statement, and the earlier declaration in John 13:10 after Jesus washes the disciples' feet, relates to both moral and ritual purity.

necessarily suggest temple imagery, but those connotations are further enhanced by the surrounding context, specifically the scene of the temple cleansing that immediately follows (John 2:13–22). The majority of scholars recognize that, historically speaking, this scene is out of place. Most likely the temple cleansing is one of the last things that Jesus did, being the main thing that got him crucified as a criminal. This is how the Synoptic Gospels situate the event chronologically (cf. Matt 21:12–17; Mark 11:15–19; Luke 19:45–48). Some scholars have suggested that the details between John and the Synoptics are different enough to suggest that Jesus performed similar actions in the temple twice, bracketing the beginning and ending of his ministry.[40] A few others suggest that perhaps John's chronology is to be preferred over the Synoptics.[41] From a historical perspective, I find it quite implausible that such an event could have occurred without Jesus being punished for it shortly thereafter.

I suggest, instead, that John has moved the temple cleansing forward in order to connect it with the wedding at Cana. There are two main effects that this has in the narrative. The first is how the temple-cleansing episode makes explicit what is already evoked in the wedding at Cana in terms of temple imagery. When Jesus performs this prophetic sign act in the temple, it portends the temple's judgment due to economic corruption (cf. John 2:14–17). Jesus even speaks explicitly of destroying the temple in this scene, but when he does so he says, "Destroy this temple, and I will raise it again in three days" (2:19). As the narrator tells us plainly, this saying refers to his body (2:21), thus drawing our attention to seeing Jesus as a new temple, which is a theme that John will go on to develop (cf. 4:21–24; 7:37–39). Thus, the juxtaposition of these two scenes brings out the cultic significance of the six stone water jars and the reference to glory in the Cana episode.[42]

The second major effect of bringing these two scenes together is that they function as prophetic sign acts of Jesus's death and resurrection, respectively. The two pericopae are even linked by an *inclusio*: the wedding took place "on the third day" (John 2:1), and the rebuilding of the temple (i.e., Jesus's resurrection) will take place "in three days" (2:19). The significance of this reference to the third day is much debated. It could also refer to: (1) Tuesday, as the third day of the week in Jewish reckoning and a common day for Jewish weddings;[43] (2) the symbolic end of a week of new creation, since John 1:1 opens with allusions to Genesis 1:1—"in the beginning"—and the amount of days that follow would make Cana occur on the seventh day (cf. references to "the next day" in John 1:29, 35, 43);[44] or (3) a mundane

---

40. E.g., D. A. Carson, *The Gospel according to John*, PNTC (Grand Rapids: Eerdmans, 1991), 176–78.

41. E.g., Paul N. Anderson, "Jesus in Johannine Perspective: Inviting A Fourth Quest for Jesus," *Conspectus* 32.1 (2021): 13.

42. So, e.g., Macaskill, *Union*, 174–75, though without connecting this to the abundant wine.

43. See John A. T. Robinson, *The Priority of John* (London: SCM, 1985), 166–67.

44. So, e.g., Leon Morris, *The Gospel according to John*, rev. ed., NICNT (Grand Rapids: Eerdmans, 1995), 156.

reference to three days after meeting Nathanael without any added significance (1:43–51).⁴⁵ But I contend that "the third day" is best read as tying the wedding more closely to the temple cleansing, forming an *inclusio* by reference to three days.⁴⁶

What makes the abundance of wine a sign act of Jesus's death is clear from his response to his mother when she brings the matter to his attention. Jesus is initially reluctant to do anything about the absence of wine because his "hour" had not yet come (John 2:4), referring to his death on the cross (cf. 7:6, 8, 30; 8:20; 12:23, 27–28; 13:1). This suggests that either performing a sign in general would initiate the road to the cross, or perhaps, as is more likely, *that a sign involving wine would do so*. E. Ray Clendenen rightly connects the hour reference to Jesus's death rather than to the hour of restoration, but he wrongly stresses that this scene also develops imagery pertaining to the cup of wrath.⁴⁷ A connection between wine and Jesus's death would immediately signify the role of wine in commemorating that death.⁴⁸ This is just one of a few ways that John prefigures the celebration of the Eucharist without narrating the Last Supper itself (i.e., the bread-of-life discourse in John 6; cf. ch. 15 in this volume). Thus, in the two episodes we see sign acts for Jesus's death (the wedding at Cana) and resurrection (the temple cleansing) paired side by side.

Moreover, if it is specifically wine that evokes Jesus's hour, the scene points us forward to John's narrative portrayal of the crucifixion, in which water and blood flow from Jesus's side (John 19:34), and also to the representation of Jesus as the Passover lamb. John the Baptist calls Jesus "the Lamb of God" (1:29), and in the crucifixion account the narrator highlights several elements of the crucifixion that evoke the sacrificial slaughter of the Passover lamb. First, John explicitly situates Jesus's crucifixion on "the day of Preparation," just before the start of the Sabbath when the Passover lambs would be slaughtered (19:14, 31, 42). Second, John emphasizes the fact that Jesus's bones were not broken (19:31–37), paralleling the prohibition regarding the bones of the Passover lamb (Exod 12:46; Num 9:12). Finally, the fact that sour wine was offered to Jesus on the cross by means of a *hyssop* branch specifically (John 19:29), rather than a generic reed as in Matthew and Mark (Matt 27:48; Mark 15:36), evokes the use of hyssop to wipe blood on the doorposts of the original Passover (Exod 12:22). All of this imagery then suggests that Jesus's death is portrayed as a Passover sacrifice in John.⁴⁹

Therefore, if Jesus's miraculous production of wine anticipates his "hour" as a forward-pointing sign, then the significance of that "hour" also serves to inform the

---

45. So, e.g., Ernst Haenchen, *John: A Commentary on the Gospel of John*, trans. Robert W. Funk, Hermeneia (Philadelphia: Fortress, 1984), 172.

46. Craig S. Keener, *The Gospel of John: A Commentary*, 2 vols. (Peabody: Hendrickson, 2003), 1:496.

47. E. Ray Clendenen, "Jesus's Blood at the Wedding in Cana?," *JETS* 63.3 (2020): 491–503.

48. So also Becker, *Rebe*, 189.

49. Another support is the allusion to the death of the firstborn son, since Mary's *firstborn* (Jesus) entrusts her to the Beloved Disciple, her new "surrogate firstborn." See Jonathan M. Lunde, "Jesus' Entrustment of His Mother as Passover Imagery (John 19:25–27)," *WTJ* 84 (2022): 1–17.

meaning of the sign. Even the language of "sign" speaks to the miraculous deeds of God at the time of the exodus from Egypt, which are often called "signs" or "signs and wonders" (e.g., Exod 7:3; Num 14:22; Deut 7:19; 11:3; 29:3; 34:11; Josh 24:17; Judg 6:13; Neh 9:10; Pss 78:12, 43; 105:27; 106:7; 135:9; Jer 32:20–21; Mic 7:15). In the case of Jesus's sign at Cana, it might also remind us of the exodus plague in which water was turned into blood (Exod 7:20). The connections being drawn between Cana and blood could suggest that the wine was red, but it must be reiterated that there is no indication that the sign was visually discernable (cf. ch. 2). Regardless, the Passover imagery instills the wedding at Cana with further temple imagery, since the Passover lambs were to be sacrificed in sacred space.

When all of this is considered, it highlights a significance to the wedding at Cana that has largely gone unappreciated. To be sure, the amount of wine produced by Jesus evokes the broader background of abundance in the era of restoration. But I suggest that it does so by specifically developing the prophetic imagery of the role of the temple in that process, highlighting Jesus's identity as the temple of God and extending God's presence through the abundance of wine.[50] The quality and the quantity of wine at Cana are both sheer grace that accompany God's act to restore—a restoration that we now see canonically as being accomplished through the death of Jesus.

CONCLUSION

In this chapter we have seen how integral viticulture is to the prophetic expectation of restoration from tragedy, including exile. When God acts to make the wrong things right, the prophets consistently expect that this will include greater viticultural output than what was previously possible. As the prophets do this, the connotations of God providing for dietary needs and bringing enjoyment to the people is certainly there. This strongly reinforces how wine was believed to be a blessing from God (cf. ch. 5), but here the added characteristic that sets this symbolic varietal apart is restoration and renewal. Much of this imagery may well be symbolic of what God's restoration will *feel like* (just like the cup of wrath symbolizes what divine judgment feels like), but I suspect that prophets of an agrarian society that spoke of a coming day with abundant wine and feasting truly imagined that wine was part of God's good future. Certainly, the abundance depicted in Joel and Amos as well as in Jesus's first sign highlight this better than anything else. When God acts to bring restoration, he does

---

50. Many argue that this episode is inspired by the legends of Dionysus, the god of wine. If this scene invokes Dionysus, the temple imagery would buttress a strategy to present Jesus as greater than Dionysus. On the background of Dionysus, see Courtney J. P. Friesen, *Reading Dionysus: Euripides' Bacchae and the Cultural Contestations of Greeks, Jews, Romans, and Christians*, STAC 95 (Tübingen: Mohr Siebeck, 2015).

not do so apart from reorienting the hearts of his people to worship, as signified by the association of an abundance of wine with the renewal of the temple.

It is important to recognize further that an abundance of wine would signal bliss for everyone in society, *even those who had no taste for it*. Wine's presence—indeed, its abundance—signaled good news for everyone, because such production also heralds stability from war, the end of inclement weather, and the prospect of tremendous economic return. In the case of the wedding at Cana, the blessing extends to the host family and the newly married couple in particular, since they were saved from the embarrassment of not being able to continue to provide for their guests. All this further demonstrates that wine's role as a blessing is not limited to the effects of consuming it. Wine's symbolic value goes beyond personal consumption to include the flourishing of familial, societal, and international relations, as well as one's relationship to the land and to God.

When God acts to restore all things and bring about an era of abundance, he does so with an inaugural banquet in which everyone is invited, regardless of class, culture, gender, or any other barriers that might typically make finer foods and wines inaccessible to people. It is to that banqueting table that we now turn.

RELEVANT QUESTIONS

1. How much of the prophetic imagery should we interpret as literal depictions?
2. How are we to understand the seemingly cause-and-effect relationship in the prophets between obedience and abundance? Can this be contextualized for our day?
3. If you have ever felt alcohol provoke deep longings in your heart, what would it look like to direct those longings to their ultimate destination, making each glass or bottle an eschatological opportunity to contemplate the inauguration of the restoration that the prophets foresaw and that began with an abundance of wine at the start of Jesus's ministry?

CHAPTER 14

THE ESCHATOLOGICAL BANQUET

Celebratory meals often commemorate a special occasion or a special relationship, like when a romantic couple celebrates their anniversary with a meal at a nice restaurant. But celebratory meals can also inaugurate new relationships, such as when that romantic couple eats a special dinner with close friends and family on their wedding day. As we saw in the previous chapter, when God acts to restore all things, the prophets anticipate thriving viticulture and a lot of wine. This grand vision concerns a reality that will carry on perpetually, but the initiating event that introduces that era of abundance is sometimes depicted as a great banquet. In some ways, this banquet theme could be folded into the theme of abundance explored in the previous chapter, and certainly they should not be separated sharply from each other. In many ways a lot of overlap exists, not least because both themes concern the same reality of future restoration. Nevertheless, the imagery of the eschatological banquet is distinct enough to warrant its own treatment.

The chief account of this celebratory feast in the Old Testament comes from Isaiah 25. By the time of the New Testament, the expectations for this meal developed further, and we see its influence on the actions and teachings of Jesus, climaxing in the final meal that he shared with his disciples. The end-time banquet is also explicitly depicted in Revelation as a wedding dinner, which provides the culminating vision of this overarching biblical theme, though in a highly idiosyncratic, and indeed disturbing, way. This chapter thus explores the climatic meal as the inauguration of the era of abundance from Isaiah to Jesus, and on to Revelation.

A FEAST CELEBRATING THE DEATH OF DEATH

The eschatological banquet depicted in Isaiah 25 is part of a literary unit often referred to as "the little apocalypse of Isaiah," because of its distinctive apocalyptic features (Isa 24–27).[1] Prior to describing the feast, the text opens with a pronouncement of

---

1. For literary connections between this passage and the rest of Isaiah, despite scholarly emphasis on its independence, see Childs, *Isaiah*, 171–74.

judgments against the whole earth, and one area of impact that the text chooses to focus on is feasting. The devastating judgments are due to the disobedience of the nations (24:5), which causes all the land to be cursed (24:6) and is described with imagery reminiscent of what we saw in chapter 10. In particular, the vines have withered up, causing the new wine (*tirosh*) itself to become sad,[2] along with those who would wish to rejoice in heart from it (24:7). The celebratory songs that normally accompany the consumption of wine (*yayin*) have been silenced (24:8–9a). Additionally, the alcohol that they do have does not taste very good; their beer (*shekar*) turns bitter to the taste (24:9b). The scene is one of deep mourning, expressed in terms of the lack of wine: "in the streets they cry out for wine [*yayin*]; all joy turns to gloom, all joyful sounds are banished from the earth" (24:11). The total devastation is likened to the end of the grape harvest after it has been fully gleaned (24:13). In other words, the desolation will be total. The damage to the earth ironically makes it so that the earth "reels like a drunkard" (24:20), despite the complete absence of alcohol.

Yet the destruction leads to an apocalyptic vision of hope, in which feasting resumes in a profound way. As YHWH takes his position as king of the earth (Isa 24:23), he defeats his enemies (25:1–5) and commemorates his victory and enthronement with a banquet *for everyone* (25:6).[3] This celebratory meal will center alcohol consumption, since it is called a *mishteh*. It is "a feast [*mishteh*] of rich food for all peoples, a banquet [*mishteh*] of aged wine [*shemer*]—the best of meats and the finest of wines [*shemer*]" (25:6). The term for wine here technically designates the sediment of wine (called dregs or lees; cf. ch. 2), which means that the dregs were kept in the wine as it aged before it was strained and filtered, and contextually it must refer to the best kind of wine fit to celebrate YHWH's victory and enthronement.[4]

> The wine in Isaiah 25:6 should be distinguished from two cheap forms of wine made from grape refuse. The first involves taking the dregs out of fermented wine and then pressing them to extract residual wine.[5] The second is made from grape particles that had already been pressed (i.e., pomace) by soaking them in water and pressing them again. This method produces what was often called "after wine" or "seconds" (Cato, *Agr.* 25; 57; Pliny, *Nat.* 14.12.86).

---

2. The metaphor could mean that the *tirosh* is running out ("dries up" in NIV), or that it is "flat" (Alter, *Hebrew Bible*, 2:696).

3. On the scene's regal dimension, see Andrew T. Abernethy, *The Book of Isaiah and God's Kingdom: A Thematic-Theological Approach*, NSBT (Downers Grove, IL: IVP Academic, 2016), 35–36.

4. See, e.g., Becker, *Rebe*, 125; Walsh, *Fruit*, 214–15.

5. Frankel, *Wine and Oil*, 43.

As everyone is feasting on a spread of great food with this great wine, the meal that is placed before YHWH is, shockingly, death itself. Indeed, YHWH "will swallow up death forever" (Isa 25:8), lifting the shroud and veil of death that covers *the nations*—not just Israel—so that there are no more tears (25:7–8). The references to mourning likely imply that the shroud and veil are clothing items used for ritual mourning of bereavement.[6] Part of the surprise here is that death and Sheol, the realm of the dead, are often portrayed as swallowers themselves who cannot stop consuming (e.g., Num 16:30, 32–34; Prov 1:12; 30:15–16; Isa 5:14; Hab 2:5).[7] But in Isaiah's vision, they get a taste of their own medicine.

The death of death at this meal extends the theme of militaristic vulnerability during feasting that we saw in chapter 10, but it does so to the most unlikely of victims. As Isaiah's apocalyptic vision continues on beyond the description of the meal, it anticipates not simply that death will be no more, but that it will be reversed as well: "Your dead shall live; their corpses shall rise" (Isa 26:19 NRSVue). The end-time banquet, then, ultimately celebrates the defeat of death, the transcendence of mortality. When death dies, God is quite literally the life of the party.

The role of that future feast in kickstarting the era of abundance is highlighted by what takes place afterward within Isaiah's apocalyptic vision. At the end of it, YHWH will destroy Leviathan (Isa 27:1), the chaos monster of the sea, and then turn to protect "a fruitful vineyard" (27:2). In later Jewish tradition, the food served at the future banquet is a feast of Leviathan, likely due to this image in the surrounding context of Isaiah 25 (cf. 4 Ezra 6.52; 2 Bar. 29.4; b. Bava Batra 75). Most scholars, however, tend to read the defeat of Leviathan in Isaiah 27 as an apocalyptic symbol for the demise of an oppressive power (e.g., Tyre, Assyria, Babylon, or Egypt). The vineyard, though, is a clear reference to Israel, an intentional allusion back to the song of the vineyard in Isaiah 5.[8]

But now that same image is developed for the era of restoration on the other side of the judgment—a judgment that the original song was designed to anticipate (cf. ch. 11). YHWH will watch over this vineyard, water it, and care for it (Isa 27:3), and this will lead to Jacob and Israel being able to "bud and blossom and fill all the world with fruit" (27:6), blessing the nations through viticultural productivity. If the vineyard were to produce "briers and thorns," those nuisances would be destroyed (27:4), but, in fact, none can be found in this vineyard, unlike the lament of the original song (5:6). In fact, YHWH has *no more wrath* (27:4), signaling that this vision of Israel as God's vineyard is fundamentally different than Isaiah 5.

---

6. Blenkinsopp, *Isaiah 1–39*, 359.

7. This imagery recalls the Ugaritic god of death, Mot, who is a voracious eater in *The Baal Cycle* (cf. *KTU* 1.5–6). See Paul Kang-Kul Cho and Janling Fu, "Death and Feasting in the Isaiah Apocalypse (Isaiah 25:6–8)," in *Formation and Intertextuality in Isaiah 24–27*, ed. J. Todd Hibbard and Hyun Chul Paul Kim, AIL 17 (Atlanta: SBL, 2013), 117–42.

8. See, e.g., Roberts, *First Isaiah*, 338; Blenkinsopp, *Isaiah 1–39*, 374.

Importantly, however, it is not a cancellation of the former song, because Isaiah 27's vision addresses the other side of judgment and restoration. The apocalypse then ends with an agricultural motif of gathering grain at harvest time, symbolizing how the people will be brought back to Zion to worship YHWH (27:12–13). All of these realities of abundance are inaugurated by the eschatological banquet of Isaiah 25, which sets off a new era of blessing in which there is no more judgment.

THE TEACHINGS OF JESUS

The theme of the eschatological banquet continued to develop within Jewish thinking and influenced Jesus's actions and teachings in a number of ways.[9] As we saw in the previous chapter, Jesus's initial miracle at Cana, where he turns water into wine (John 2:1–11), prefigures the era of abundance. To be sure, it also evokes the final banquet, given that Jesus provides this abundant amount of wine at a banquet. Jesus's reputation for being a drunkard (cf. ch. 8) points to how the eschatological reality of feasting, which would be characteristic of the kingdom of God, was already present in his ministry. We can see that Jesus is mindful of this dynamic when we look at a handful of his parables, as well as his words to the disciples at the Last Supper.

The Question about Fasting

The first instance where Jesus anticipates the eschatological banquet is in his parable of the new wineskins, which occurs in each of the Synoptic Gospels. Jesus tells this parable in response to a question about why his disciples do not fast, unlike John the Baptist, his disciples, and the Pharisees (Mark 2:18; cf. Matt 9:14). As we saw in chapter 8, John the Baptist fasted because the kingdom is *near*, whereas Jesus feasted because the kingdom is *here*. Jesus's response to this question includes three main analogies; one is from the example of weddings (Mark 2:19–20), and the others are from the domestic sphere, including clothing (2:21) and wineskins (2:22). Together, they allude to the eschatological banquet.

In the wedding analogy, Jesus says that nobody fasts with a bridegroom; instead, they celebrate with him (Mark 2:19). Since Jesus is the bridegroom, the disciples ought to feast with him, just like guests at a wedding. The banqueting stops, in the analogy, when the bridegroom is gone, foreshadowing Jesus's death. "On that day" the disciples will fast (2:20), as they mourn his death (cf. "days" in Matt 9:15 [NRSVue]). The parables themselves do not explicitly mention a subsequent return of the bridegroom that would bring the fasting to an end. But within the context of

---

9. See, e.g., Dennis E. Smith, "The Messianic Banquet Reconsidered," in *The Future of Early Christianity: Essays in Honor of Helmut Koester*, ed. Birger A. Pearson (Minneapolis: Fortress, 1991), 64–73.

the rest of the Gospel narratives, it is probably correct to sense a hint that feasting will follow the bridegroom wherever he goes.

With the clothing and the wineskin parables that follow, the main point of the wedding analogy is carried over: appropriate actions are determined by the circumstances. It is neither appropriate to use new fabric to cover a hole in an old article of clothing (Mark 2:21), nor to put new wine (*oinos neos*) into old wineskins (2:22).[10] The rationale for both is to avoid a rupture. With respect to old wineskins, Jesus says that "the wine [*oinos*] will burst the skins, and both the wine [*oinos*] and the wineskins will be ruined" (2:22b). Matthew and Luke both clarify that the wine is destroyed because it will spill from the torn wineskin (Matt 9:17; Luke 5:37). An old wineskin will rupture because new wine is still fermenting, and old wineskins have already been weakened from the wear and tear of storing previous wines that had not completed fermentation. Both the clothing and the wineskin analogies further reinforce the need to put together what ought to go together, which is also the point of the wedding analogy. But as the question about fasting itself implies, some people will find this approach uncomfortable. In Luke's version of the event, Jesus concludes the parable of the wineskins with an additional line laced with irony, "And no one after drinking old wine wants the new, for they say, 'The old is better'" (Luke 5:39; cf. Gos. Thom. 47).

The irony here is multilayered. In part, the irony pertains to the new wine that Jesus brings. Although old wine is generally preferable to new wine (ask any connoisseur), it is not the case that Jesus's new wine is somehow mediocre. Rather, the point is that not everyone will be convinced of that.[11] The other layer of irony is that Jesus delivers this line in response to an original question about fasting. Accentuating this further is how Luke explicitly places the question about fasting in a context in which Jesus enjoys a "great banquet" with tax collectors and receives interrogation about that too (Luke 5:27–32). Both episodes involve a line of questioning that stems in part from abstemious sentiments, which Jesus ironically aligns *with a preference for old wine*. Taking all three analogies together, the ultimate point of Jesus's response to the question about fasting is that it is inappropriate to fast with the one who is ushering in an era of renewal, characterized by feasting.

Feasting in Jesus's Lukan Parables

In Luke's travel narrative of Jesus's approach to Jerusalem, he records several unique parables that notably emphasize the theme of feasting and even offer hints about the future climactic feast (Luke 13–16). Together they stress that, although the eschatological feast is open to everyone, there will come a time in which it will be

---

10. Matthew adds that by doing so it preserves both the new wine and the new wineskin (Matt 9:17).

11. See J. Andrew Cowan, *The Writings of Luke and the Jewish Roots of the Christian Way: An Examination of the Aims of the First Christian Historian in the Light of Ancient Politics, Ethnography, and Historiography*, LNTS 599 (London: T&T Clark, 2019), 122–24.

too late to join. As a result, the final makeup of those feasting at the banquet will overturn expectations.

In the parable of the narrow door (Luke 13:22–30), the titular door leads to the place where the banquet is held, but it will eventually be shut by the host (13:25). Those left outside will try to remind the host that they previously "ate and drank" with him, but to no avail (13:26–27). Instead, they will mourn when they see the patriarchs—Abraham, Isaac, and Jacob—and the prophets (13:28) *reclining* next to foreign gentiles in the kingdom of God (13:29). The Greek term for reclining (*anaklinō*) is used to refer to the act of lying on one's side at a table for a meal in the New Testament (Matt 8:11; Luke 12:37) and is one of several related words that can function that way.[12] Thus, the parable speaks of a future scene of an end-time banquet that is inclusive of all kinds of people. But the rhetorical thrust is that the door to the banquet will only stay open for so long.

> Third Enoch 48A.10 (5th–6th c. CE) anticipates that the eschatological banquet with the Messiah will include the nations: "the kingdom of Israel, gathered from the four quarters of the world, shall eat with the Messiah, and the gentiles shall eat with them."[13]

In Luke 14, Jesus tells two parables—the parable of the wedding feast (Luke 14:7–11) and the parable of the great banquet (14:12–24)—while eating "in the house of a prominent Pharisee" (14:1). The first parable is prompted "when he noticed how the guests picked the places of honor [*prōtoklisia*] at the table" (14:7). The term for a place of honor refers to seats designated for special guests reclining at the table (Matt 23:6; Mark 12:39; Luke 20:46). Jesus tells those feasting with him not to concern themselves with reclining (*kataklinō*) at such a seat when invited to a wedding feast (Luke 14:8). The reason is because they may have to give up their seat to someone with a higher status and so embarrass themselves (14:9). Rather, he says that they should take a lower spot, so that if the one who invited them chooses to elevate them to a better position, all those who are there reclining (*sunanakeimai*) will see them exalted (14:10).

Then Jesus turns to the host and tells him that whenever he might have a "luncheon or dinner" (Luke 14:12), or even a "banquet" (14:13), he should not invite the wealthy but rather the poor and other disenfranchised people, even though they

---

12. E.g., *kataklinō* (Luke 7:36; 14:8; 24:30), *katakeimai* (Mark 2:15; 14:3; Luke 5:29; 7:37; 1 Cor 8:10), *anakeimai* (Matt 9:10; 22:10–11; 26:7, 20; Mark 6:26; 14:18; 16:14; Luke 22:27 [x2]; John 12:2; 13:23, 28), *sunanakeimai* (Matt 9:10; 14:9; Mark 2:15; 6:22; Luke 7:49; 14:10, 15), and *anapiptō* (Luke 11:37; 14:10; 17:7; 22:14; John 13:25; 21:20).

13. P. Alexander, "3 (Hebrew Apocalypse of) Enoch," *OTP* 1:301–2.

cannot repay the host through a reciprocal invitation. The second-century satirist Lucian addresses inviting poor people to banquets in *Saturnalia* (§22), painting it as a foolish decision for the host, given poor people's large appetites and lack of etiquette. Instead of being repaid, Jesus says, "you will be repaid at the resurrection of the righteous" (Luke 14:14). This final line places the host's hospitality in an eschatological light, alluding to the final judgment as well as the eschatological banquet, where the host will be repaid in kind. Jesus is reorienting the values of banqueting and upending its common associations regarding class and status, *as an imitation in the present of what the future banquet will be like*. This is made particularly clear in the parable of the great banquet that immediately follows.

> The Rule of the Congregation from Qumran describes the messianic meal, noting the inclusion of new wine (*tirosh*), with each person seated and arranged according to their "dignity," which is the pattern for all meals thereafter in the messianic age (1QSa [1Q28a] II, 11–22).[14] This account of the messianic banquet stands in stark contrast to what we see in the banqueting texts in Luke.

The parable of the great banquet is prompted by someone reclining (*sunanakeimai*) at that same meal saying, "Blessed is the one who will eat at the feast in the kingdom of God" (Luke 14:15). This places the entire discussion on feasting in Luke 14 within the realm of the eschaton. In response to that comment, Jesus tells the parable of a man who puts on a "great banquet" (*deipnon mega*). Once the banquet is ready, the host sends out his servants to summon all of his guests (14:16–17). Yet, despite the host's generosity, the guests decline the offer (14:18–20). In response, the host tells one of his servants to invite new guests from among the poor and marginalized to come to the banquet that is already prepared (14:21). When the servant says that he has done so, and that there's still plenty of room (14:22), the host tells the servant to continue searching unlikely places, "roads and country lanes," to make sure the house is full (14:23). As for those who were initially invited, they will not "get a taste of my banquet" (14:24). Just like the parable of the narrow door in Luke 13, this showcases the countercultural inclusion of those deemed beyond consideration for a banquet. Furthermore, within these two parables there is also a sense that the invitation should not be taken for granted; with the parable of the narrow door, the opportunity to participate is limited by time, and in the parable of the great banquet, there are consequences for declining the invitation.

---

14. See *DSSSE* 1:102–3.

A surprising reversal of expectations and destinies in relation to the eschatological banquet is also stressed once more in the parable of the rich man and Lazarus (Luke 16:19–31).[15] The story begins with a poor man named Lazarus begging to eat scraps that fall from the rich man's table like a dog (16:21). This situation is reversed in the afterlife, however, after they have both died, when the rich man begs for "scraps" from Lazarus in the form of a drop of water from his finger (16:24). Rejecting Lazarus's desire for scraps stands as representative of the kind of character that the rich man was, leading to his miserable fate. In the parable, their respective destinies are both reversed and fixed, being separated by a great chasm (16:26), with the rich man on one side in Hades (16:23), and Lazarus at "Abraham's side" (*kolpos* in 16:22, 23; "bosom" in the KJV).

Despite what some readers assume, "Abraham's side" is not a name for a geographical realm in the afterlife, but a reference to Lazarus's position next to Abraham. If Abraham's name was merely used to designate a place, rather than a person, it would be strange for him to be an active character in this parable. Being in Abraham's "bosom," or even "bosoms" (cf. the plural *kolpois* in Luke 16:23), could be a paternal image of Abraham comforting Lazarus.[16] But whatever paternal notions may be intended, Lazarus is here seated at the table, reclining beside Abraham and leaning into him.[17] The reversal of the previously desired "scraps" suggests that Lazarus is now feasting with Abraham. Additionally, being at "Abraham's side" is very similar to the description of the beloved disciple's position next to Jesus at the meal in John 13 (13:23, 25, 28; cf. 21:20), where the same Greek word expresses that he was at the "side" (*kolpos*) of Jesus (13:23).

Within the context of Luke 13–16, the turn of events that lead to Lazarus being seated next to the chief patriarch recalls the parable of the wedding feast, where Jesus mentions how wonderful it is to receive an unlikely elevation to a position of honor at a feast (Luke 14:10). Furthermore, the parable of the narrow door, as noted already, anticipates a time of feasting with the patriarchs in the kingdom of God, including Abraham (Luke 13:28–29). Thus, all of this imagery suggests that the parable presents Lazarus feasting next to Abraham in the eschatological banquet, as a representative of the other unlikely participants at the feast mentioned previously.

---

15. Although this story is not called a parable, it should be recognized as one. See, e.g., Craig L. Blomberg, *Interpreting the Parables*, 2nd ed. (Downers Grove, IL: IVP Academic, 2012), 254–61.

16. So, e.g., François Bovon, *Luke 2: A Commentary on the Gospel of Luke 9:51–19:27*, Hermeneia (Minneapolis: Fortress, 2016), 481–82.

17. So, e.g., Marshall, *Luke*, 636; John Paul Heil, *The Meal Scenes in Luke-Acts: An Audience-Oriented Approach*, SBLMS 52 (Atlanta: SBL, 1999), 136–40.

> The Apocalypse of Paul 27.1–2a (4th c. CE) anticipates that Israel's patriarchs will be feasting in paradise near a river of wine: "again he took me up and brought me to the north of the city and led me where there was a river of wine, and there I saw Abraham and Isaac and Jacob, Lot and Job and other saints, and they greeted me."[18]

Jesus's feasting parables in Luke 13–16 offer glimpses of his expectations of what the future feast will be like. Beyond that, they also work backward from that future meal to cast a vision for what feasting ought to look like now in anticipation. Accordingly, our banqueting ought to be characterized by radical hospitality, because that is the value that informs the eschatological banquet. Moreover, these parables are clear that participation in the messianic banquet is open to all, but not for all time. Insofar as there is still time to do so, those who turn back in repentance will be welcomed, just as the parable of the prodigal son (Luke 15:11–32) demonstrates with the celebration of a great feast (15:22–24). Even though this parable is not overtly about the eschatological banquet, the broader context and thematic parallels with other parables in this portion of Luke suggests that it should be read in that light. Additionally, Jesus tells this parable in response to yet another set of concerns about why he eats with sinners (15:1–2). Thus, the parable of the prodigal son further underscores that everyone is indeed invited to the banquet and that there will be many unlikely participants—a theme that runs through this whole section of Luke.

The Last Supper

The influence of the eschatological banquet on Jesus is also seen in the final meal that he shares with his disciples. Not only does Jesus refer to the future banquet during the meal, but the meal itself is intended as a foretaste of that feast.[19] There are a few aspects of the Last Supper that are worth noting in this regard, although we will return to the Last Supper in the next chapter for a closer look at other details of the incident, like the so-called words of institution over the bread and the cup and the background of the Passover.

The first allusion to the eschatological banquet is when Jesus claims that he will no longer drink from the "fruit of the vine" until he drinks it "new" (*kainos*) in the kingdom (Matt 26:29; Mark 14:25).[20] Drinking the fruit of the vine is

---

18. Elliott, *Apocryphal New Testament*, 631.
19. So, e.g., Albert Schweitzer, *The Mysticism of Paul the Apostle*, trans. William Montgomery (1953; repr., Baltimore: Johns Hopkins University Press, 1998), 237–57.

20. Drinking wine "new" is omitted from Luke 22:18.

a metonymy for drinking wine, not least—once again—because no one would be drinking grape juice in the spring, several months after harvest (cf. ch. 2). In chapter 8, we looked at whether Jesus took on a vow of abstinence from wine at the Last Supper, and I argued instead that with his claim he both demonstrated his embrace of the cross and also predicted his vindication. But what did Jesus mean about drinking wine "new" in the coming kingdom? It could be that Jesus was referring to new wine, as some scholars have asserted. This would take "new" adjectivally, modifying the neuter pronoun "it" (*auto*), which refers back to the word for fruit (*genēma*).[21] Yet nowhere in the New Testament does *kainos* ever modify wine.

More likely, the word "new" is modifying something about how Jesus will drink wine.[22] If so, it could mean that Jesus will drink it as a renewed person,[23] or within the future state of newness,[24] or perhaps most simply, and most likely, that he will simply drink it once more (i.e., "anew").[25] Regardless of what the precise nuance is, it is clear that Jesus anticipates that his death will not be the final word for him,[26] and that whatever vindication comes, it will be accompanied by wine. This clearly signals his expectation of future feasting at the end-time banquet.

"New wine" only appears a handful of times in the New Testament, usually with *oinos* modified by *neos*, as in the new wineskin parable (Matt 9:17; Mark 2:22; Luke 5:37–38). *Kainos* also appears in those texts, but in each case, it modifies the wineskins (*askos*), not the wine. Acts 2:13 mentions "new wine" (NRSVue), but it is a different Greek term that is used (*gleukos*). In the LXX, *kainos* never modifies *oinos*, though in one instance it modifies wineskins (Josh 9:13 LXX), whereas *oinos* with *neos* occurs in Isaiah 49:26 LXX and Sirach 9:10. Within broader Koine Greek literature there are likewise no instances of *kainos* modifying *oinos* (cf., e.g., Josephus, Philo, the Pseudepigrapha, and the Apostolic Fathers).

In Luke's version of the Last Supper, we see two additional reflections on the eschatological-banquet theme. The first is when Jesus adds that not only will he not drink wine again until he does so when the kingdom comes (Luke 22:18), but that he will also not eat the Passover again until it is "fulfilled" in the kingdom of God (22:15–16). This comment further reinforces the expectation of feasting in the age to come. But there is more to say about the implications that this particular Lukan comment has for considering the background of the Passover on the Last Supper, which will be addressed in the following chapter of this book.

The second addition in Luke's version that points to the eschatological banquet is fairly overt. In context, a dispute breaks out among the disciples during the Last Supper regarding who might be the greatest among them (Luke 22:24). This would

---

21. So, e.g., Casey, *Aramaic Sources*, 220–21.
22. On the adverbial function of the accusative, see, e.g., Daniel B. Wallace, *Greek Grammar Beyond the Basics: An Exegetical Syntax of the New Testament* (Grand Rapids: Zondervan, 1996), 293.
23. So, e.g., Evans, *Mark 8:27–16:20*, 395.
24. So, e.g., Donald A. Hagner, *Matthew 14–28*, WBC 33B (1995; repr., Grand Rapids: Zondervan Academic, 2018), 774.
25. So, e.g., Marcus, *Mark 8–16*, 959.
26. So, e.g., Davies and Allison, *Matthew*, 3:475.

seem to be a strange time for such a conversation, unless we recognize how this meal has provoked reflection on the future banquet, and how Luke has previously emphasized the notion of the position of honor at a meal in earlier parables. In response, Jesus asks whether someone is greater if they recline at the table (*anakeimai*) or if they serve the table (22:27a). The assumption, of course, is that the one reclining at the table is greater.

But Jesus upends their expectations by identifying himself, whom they regard as the host of that future banquet, as someone who actually serves the table (Luke 22:27b). This ironic inversion of greatness defies all of their expectations and is a signature of the "upside down" kingdom. It recalls the parables of the wedding feast and the great banquet in Luke 14, in which the expectations of who should be invited to a feast are overturned. Jesus does this here at the Last Supper with an irony reminiscent of the earlier Lukan saying that old wine is better than new wine in the parable of the new wineskins (5:39). Everyone knows that old wine is better than new wine, and that being seated at the host's table is a great honor. But in Jesus's kingdom there is a strikingly different value system. Yet, as Jesus goes on to say in Luke's version of the Last Supper, because the disciples have been with Jesus during his trials (22:28), they will join him in the kingdom at the table of the eschatological banquet, where they will "eat and drink" with him (22:29–30). They will even have such great positions of honor and authority that they will judge the twelve tribes of Israel (22:30). This exaltation, however, cannot be divorced from Jesus's emphasis on service and enduring Jesus's trials alongside him. Just as Jesus will be vindicated, so will they, which means that such vindication comes through embodying his service and enduring his trials. It is a reversal of expectations to positions of honor at the table, just as the parable of the wedding feast describes.

The Lukan nuances to the Last Supper highlight a recurring thread to Jesus's teachings regarding the eschatological banquet. Whereas the influence of the end-time meal is clear in each of the Synoptic Gospels, it is most prominent and most developed in Luke. In particular, there is an emphasis on how the banquet will reverse previous expectations. Similarly, we also see how Jesus believed that the future banquet ought to inform present banqueting and present living. This is demonstrated not least in Jesus's posture of eating with tax collectors and sinners, but also how he undercut banqueting customs. Banqueting was a setting in which people flaunted their status; this was true both for hosts, who showed off their wealth and ability to draw in great guests, and for guests themselves, who not only took pride in being invited to such dinner parties but who also wanted to be bestowed with the highest honors at the table. Instead, Jesus called hosts to be radically inclusive (Luke 14:12–14, 21–23), and called guests to be deferential (14:10), and even to pursue service (22:24–27).

THE MARRIAGE SUPPER OF THE LAMB

In Revelation, John the Seer records a vision of the eschatological banquet. Yet in many respects, it differs wildly from what we have seen so far in this chapter. With an appreciation of John's unique use of symbolism in his apocalypse, however, we can detect some important commonalities with the overarching theme.

The final banquet for John is specifically part of a wedding celebration between the Lamb, referring to Jesus, and his bride, a symbol for God's people (Rev 19:7–8). The banquet is clearly a great celebration, since an angel tells John to write about what a great blessing it is to receive an invitation to the marriage supper (19:9). There is no reference to an angel in Greek, but in the light of verse 10 it is clear that an angel is the one speaking. Previously in this chapter we saw that everyone is invited to the end-time banquet; Isaiah tells us that the feast is for "all peoples" (Isa 25:6), and Luke highlights the presence of gentiles (Luke 13:29) as well as the poor and marginalized (Luke 14:13, 21, 23; 16:19–31). Rather than contradicting those iterations of the theme, however, the command from the angel here in Revelation to write about the blessing of being invited further underscores that it will be devastating for those not attending the banquet, as Jesus also makes clear (cf. Luke 13:27–28; 14:24; 16:22–26).

Just how devastating it will be is apparent in the next few sections, when Jesus returns to the earth as the rider on a white horse and defeats his enemies in violent fashion (Rev 19:11–21). As we saw in chapter 12, when Jesus returns his robe will be "dipped in blood" (19:13). The scene is reminiscent of the vision in Isaiah 63:1–6, when YHWH returns from the winepress in judgment, because Revelation says that he "treads the winepress of the fury of the wrath of God Almighty" (Rev 19:15).

> It is tempting to interpret this image as a symbolic expression of what Jesus accomplished on the cross for salvation and what Christians celebrate in the Eucharist. Gisela Kreglinger reflects powerfully on the Christian art and iconography in the churches of Franconia that portray Christ in this way.[27] Such is a beautiful development of this tradition, but insofar as Christ is portrayed as being in the winepress in Revelation, it is strictly an image of judgment against the enemies of God (cf. ch. 12).[28]

---

27. See *Spirituality of Wine*, 51–52, 75, 82, 99, 125, 127, 220; idem, *Soul of Wine*, 73–79.

28. Cf. Becker, *Rebe*, 212.

In the aftermath of this war, the birds of the air come to participate in "the great supper of God" (Rev 19:17), drawing from Ezekiel 39:17–18, where the birds feast on the flesh of those who were slain in battle (Rev 19:18; cf. 19:21).

This development to the eschatological banquet theme is striking and unsettling. Within the dualism of Revelation, God's people are invited to the marriage supper of the Lamb, and their oppressive enemies are present in a very different way altogether. These two scenes are meant to be read together, not least because the feasting of the birds is called a *deipnon* or "supper" (Rev 19:17), just like the wedding feast (19:9)[29]—but also because there is no mention of wine at the marriage supper of the Lamb. In the descriptions of the millennium (20:1–10) and the new creation (Rev 21–22) that follow, there is also no mention of wine. In fact, there are no positive references to wine in the whole apocalypse. John even alludes to the eschatological banquet scene from Isaiah 25:6–8, which was addressed at the start of this chapter, by stating that in the new creation every tear will be wiped away when death exists no more (Rev 21:4). And yet John does so without mentioning the occasion of feasting.

As we saw in chapter 12, in Revelation wine either symbolizes God's wrath against the oppressive enemies of God's people (Rev 14:10, 19; 16:19; 18:6; 19:15) or the sins of Rome, described as physical and sexual abuse (14:8; 17:2; 18:3).[30] The only exception to John's symbolic use of wine is when wine is viewed as an economic commodity threatened by the outpouring of judgment (6:6; 18:13). This means that the wine of the great eschatological banquet in Revelation 19 is not the wine of celebratory consumption (which again is not mentioned), but the wine of judgment that is produced by the one who treads the dreadful winepress (19:15).

> These references in Revelation are part of a larger economic critique of the nations and merchants who were financially complicit with the beastly power of Rome through using their currency (cf. Rev 13:16–18) and trading with them (18:11–13, 15, 17, 19, 23)—a connection that is symbolically depicted as a sexual union (17:1–2; 18:3, 9). While undeniably in a unique apocalyptic register, Revelation's critique of the corrupt wine trade resembles the economic concerns in the parables of Luke earlier in this chapter, not least those in Luke 14, but especially the parable of the rich man and Lazarus (Luke 16:19–31).

As divergent as it seems at first, there are commonalities between Revelation's vision of the marriage supper with other instances of the eschatological-banquet theme. It appears that John has transposed the images of an abundance of wine at the eschaton, and specifically the theme of the great banquet, into an expression of the violent arrival of the kingdom of God as it overtakes the kingdoms of the earth. Whereas that transposition adds unique elements to the theme, it carries over some similarities. For one, the marriage supper in Revelation 19 inaugurates the era of restoration, just as the other texts anticipate. Furthermore, the judgment against

---

29. Pierre Prigent, *Commentary on the Apocalypse of St. John*, trans. Wendy Pradels (Tübingen: Mohr Siebeck, 2001), 548–49.

30. Later apocalyptic traditions associate the work of the antichrist with an eschatological abundance of wine (Apoc. Dan. 10.1–7), even turning water into wine (Gk. Apoc. Ezra 4.27).

enemies in Revelation 19 fits how Isaiah, who provides the first iteration of this theme, views the banquet as arriving after a devastating judgment against the whole earth (Isa 24), leading to the defeat of the greatest enemy of all—death itself (25:7–8). Related to this, although Jesus does not speak of warfare in relation to the eschatological banquet in the Gospels, judgment is still conveyed through the limited opportunity to join (Luke 13:24–28), the consequences for declining the offer (14:24), and the inability to reverse the outcome of not participating in it (16:26).

But what about the lack of drinking wine in Revelation's vision of the marriage supper and the restoration that follows? I think there is value in looking at this question from the other way around. The theme of the eschatological banquet must be appreciated within the light of John's symbolic universe. Within that set of symbolism, other things are explicitly said to be absent from John's vision of new creation, including the sea (Rev 21:1), the temple (21:22), the sun and moon (21:23; 22:5), the night (21:25; 22:5), things that are unclean and people who do what is "shameful or deceitful" (21:27), and curses (22:3). Each of these is missing (or reimagined) because of what they represent and because of what the new creation represents. Revelation does not outright say that there is no wine, but its absence is conspicuous, especially in the light of the Old Testament background that it draws upon so heavily. The Sibylline Oracles claim that there will not be vine branches in the new creation (Sib. Or. 7.148–49), but Revelation is not that direct.

Yet the lack of celebratory wine in John's visions should not be viewed as a total aberration of the banqueting theme, because wine for John symbolizes God's wrath. If that is what wine represents in Revelation, then no one should want it. Within the set of apocalyptic symbols that John uses, it is therefore precisely *the lack of wine itself* that is good news! Whereas the prophets anticipate an abundance of wine and feasting in the era of restoration, John's apocalyptic symbols do not work that way. There is no wine for the saints in John's final visions, because there is no *wrath* for the saints. The saints will never have to drink *that wine*, because wrath is not part of God's new creation. This resembles how Isaiah speaks of God having no wrath against his vineyard, Israel (Isa 27:4), in the era of abundance after the great banquet. Celebratory wine is not consumed in Revelation 19, but the "wine" that is mentioned does signal the end of oppression. As we saw in chapter 13 of this book, the prophetic visions of an abundance of wine would communicate to an ancient agrarian society that the future era of restoration will not be characterized by oppression, which would stifle their viticultural productivity. In a different, though related, way, John also signals that an abundance of wine means the end of oppression, because John's abundant wine overtly signals the judgment that is coming against the enemies of God's people when God restores all things.

CONCLUSION

As we have seen, the eschatological banquet, which is first portrayed in Isaiah 25, is a unique expression of the symbolic varietal of abundant wine when God restores everything. Revelation, which provides the final canonical reflection on this theme, does not utilize the imagery of abundance in the same way. But it does so for a good reason, given John's apocalyptic symbolism.

Even though Revelation's final visions do not mention wine, that does not mean that wine will be absent from the future kingdom; it is merely absent from those apocalyptic visions. Isaiah, for one, anticipates the presence of vineyards in the new creation (Isa 65:21), and Jesus implies, in some of his parables and his comments at the Last Supper, that a future banquet awaits God's people. That future banquet ought to inform our lives in the present, reorienting our values and widening our sense of whom we deem "worthy" of our lavish hospitality. In the meantime, as we await the end-time banquet, we get a foretaste of it every time we participate in the Eucharist. In order to better understand that dynamic, the next chapter explores the remaining aspects of the Last Supper that await to be addressed in this book.

RELEVANT QUESTIONS

1. How should the nature of salvation as the acceptance of God's invitation to a future banquet shape our mindset around feasting in the present?
2. What can the practice of radical banqueting look like in your life when you host dinners and parties?
3. What might pursuing service and deference as a guest look like when you are invited to meals and festive gatherings?

CHAPTER 15

THE LAST SUPPER AND THE BLOOD OF CHRIST

Although the eschatological abundance anticipated by the prophets has not yet arrived in human history, we live in a time of anticipation—a time in which we participate in the future banquet proleptically, when we meet at the Lord's table to celebrate the Eucharist. The anticipatory nature of the Last Supper has already been addressed (cf. chs. 8 and 14), and in this chapter we turn to focus on how Jesus asks his followers to replicate that meal to commemorate it in perpetuity, which includes the wine that they consume.

Most notably, Jesus connects the wine at the Last Supper to the new covenant, which is a renewal of the covenant relationship. As he does so, he draws upon the background of the Passover, the festival that celebrates Israel's exodus from Egypt before the ratification of the Mosaic covenant. Yet, there is debate about whether the Last Supper was celebrated as a Passover meal specifically, and—if it was—the degree to which certain Passover traditions, like the use of four cups of wine, were known in Jesus's day. Part of the debate revolves around John's unique portrayal of the final meal and the timing of Jesus's death. Famously, John does not narrate the Last Supper, but his Gospel nevertheless appears to present its own eucharistic allusions that deserve our attention to round out our understanding.

WAS THE LAST SUPPER A PASSOVER MEAL?

The Last Supper is commonly associated with the celebration of the Passover, but this is not an entirely straightforward matter. The initial question is whether Jesus's final meal with his disciples was actually a Passover meal, and then another question concerns the extent to which the background of the Passover influenced what Jesus said and did that night. For our purposes, how we answer these questions impacts the interpretation of Jesus's "words of institution" about the cup of wine—specifically how the cup connects to covenant renewal and whether it was one of multiple cups consumed during the Passover.

The Last Supper is only recorded in the Synoptic Gospels, and it appears to be presented as a typical Passover meal, yet this is complicated by the chronology of events portrayed in the Gospel of John. Taking Mark as a representative example of how the Synoptics situate the Last Supper in relation to Passover, the account opens by stating that the Passover was near (Mark 14:1). From there Mark recounts how Jesus and the disciples planned where they would have the meal and prepared for it on the first day of the Feast of Unleavened Bread (14:12–16), and then consumed the bread and the wine after evening came that night (14:17). Although John does not narrate the Last Supper per se, the text does place Jesus's final night with his disciples "before the Passover" (John 13:1), and it puts the death of Jesus on the day of preparation (the 14th of Nisan), when the lambs were slaughtered for the Passover meal later that evening on the 15th of Nisan (19:14, 31; cf. 18:28). Thus, the apparent discrepancy is that John has Jesus crucified in the afternoon before the official start of Passover, whereas the Synoptics have Jesus eating the Last Supper on the first night of Passover. This raises several questions. Were John and the Synoptics working with different calendars?[1] Did John shift the timing of events for his theological purposes?[2] Or were the Synoptics depicting a pre-Passover meal that imitates the Passover?[3] Each of these questions have been variously answered in the affirmative from time to time by different scholars. Those who insist that the Last Supper occurred before the Passover meal during the evening of the day of preparation (to harmonize with John's chronology), highlight that the Synoptics never mention that Jesus and his disciples ate lamb with bitter herbs alongside the bread and wine, which would have been integral to a first-century Passover meal.[4] Yet the Greek term *pascha*, which is the word for the Passover festival itself, is often specifically the word used for the lamb that is slaughtered and consumed at the festival (cf. 1 Cor 5:7). Thus, the references to eating the *pascha* in the Synoptics may imply the presence of lamb (cf. Matt 26:17; Mark 14:12, 14; Luke 22:15).[5] Regardless of whether or not the meal took place on the night when the Passover meal was supposed to be consumed, the background of the Passover was certainly relevant to the meaning of the Synoptic presentation of the Last Supper. Thus, we will explore the influence of the Passover on the Synoptic accounts of the Last Supper, before turning to the Gospel of John to see its unique use of eucharistic imagery.

COVENANTAL BLOOD

At the Last Supper, Jesus draws attention to the components of his final meal—the bread and the wine—using them as a means to speak of his imminent death. This itself can be seen to be influenced by the context of Passover, since the various elements of the Passover meal were chosen precisely for their symbolic value in

---

1. E.g., I. Howard Marshall, *Last Supper and Lord's Supper* (Grand Rapids: Eerdmans, 1981), 57–75.

2. E.g., Jeremias, *Eucharistic Words*, 15–88.

3. E.g., Brown, *Death*, 2:1361–69.

4. E.g., N. T. Wright, *Jesus and the Victory of God*, COQG 2 (Minneapolis: Fortress, 1996), 556.

5. E.g., John Nolland, *Luke 18:35–24:53*, WBC 35C (Dallas: Word, 1993), 1050.

commemorating the original events of the exodus (e.g., Exod 12:7–12).[6] Indeed, the notion of *remembrance*—which Luke exclusively associates with the bread (Luke 22:19) and Paul links to both the cup and the bread (1 Cor 11:24–25)—is rooted in the Passover tradition itself (cf. Deut 16:3).[7]

One of the clearest ways in which the Synoptics present Jesus as drawing on the Passover is how his words of institution allude to Exodus 24:8 (Matt 26:28; Mark 14:24; Luke 22:20; cf. 1 Cor 11:25). In Exodus 24:8, Moses ratifies the national covenant with Israel after the exodus from Egypt by sprinkling the blood of sacrificed animals on the people and declaring, "This is the blood of the covenant that the Lord has made with you in accordance with all these words." Indeed, in the context of Exodus 24, Israel consumed a meal from the sacrificed animals that ratified the covenant (Exod 24:11). Meals commonly functioned this way, as with the festive drinking (*mishteh*) that calmed the feud between King Abimelech and Isaac (Gen 26:30), and the meal that made amends between Jacob and Laban (31:43–54), and, as a negative example, when the people of Israel ate and drank during the golden-calf incident (Exod 32:6) just after the covenant meal in Exodus 24. Jesus's words thus suggest that the Last Supper was a covenant meal, but specifically one that was inspired by the meal in Exodus 24. As such, Jesus's words seem designed to showcase how he was both ratifying a covenant with blood and leading a second "exodus" like Moses did at the first Passover.[8] Note the representation of Jesus's words in the various accounts that we have from the Synoptics and also from Paul's letter to the Corinthians:

This is my blood of the covenant, which is poured out for many. (Mark 14:24)

This is my blood of the covenant, which is poured out for many for the forgiveness of sins. (Matt 26:28)

This cup is the new covenant in my blood, which is poured out for you. (Luke 22:20)

This cup is the new covenant in my blood; do this, whenever you drink it, in remembrance of me. (1 Cor 11:25)

Jesus's words about the cup have been variously interpreted, not least because of the notable variation between accounts. Yet the allusion to Exodus 24:8 is fairly

---

6. E.g., Roy E. Ciampa and Brian S. Rosner, *The First Letter to the Corinthians*, PNTC (Grand Rapids: Eerdmans, 2010), 550–51.

7. E.g., Joseph A. Fitzmyer, *The Gospel According to Luke X–XXIV: Introduction, Translation, and Notes*, AB (New Haven: Yale University Press, 1985), 1401.

8. Davies and Allison, *Matthew*, 3:477–78.

straightforward. Despite the difference in wording, in each account Jesus connects the cup to "my blood," suggesting that the wine at the Last Supper was red wine.

Unique nuances also exist in the various accounts of Jesus's words regarding the cup of wine. Matthew, for example, clarifies that the vicarious and beneficial nature of Jesus's blood (that Mark affirms) was specifically poured out to provide forgiveness of sins. Each account refers to the "covenant," but Luke and Paul specify that the covenant ratified and represented by the cup was, in fact, the "new covenant." Furthermore, in each version except Luke, it is clearly stated that the cup that was blessed was consumed, though only Paul explicitly ritualized this action for future occasions ("whenever you drink it") and specifically commended this in remembrance of Jesus. Because Luke does not record that the wine was consumed, some scholars have even suggested that the cup in Luke 22:20 was actually a libationary offering "poured out" for the disciples.[9]

Those scholars who regard the cup of wine as libationary in Luke contend further that the background of Greco-Roman banqueting is more significant to interpreting the Last Supper than the Passover. Such banquets consisted of a two-part event that included a meal (*deipnon*) and a subsequent drinking party (*symposium*), which were punctuated ritually by a ceremonial libation after which the drinking would commence.[10] This would then lead to various festivities, like singing hymns, playing games, discussing philosophy, and engaging in sexual exploits.[11] According to this perspective, not only does there appear to be a libationary offering, but it is notable that Jesus blessed the cup *after the meal* (*deipnon*; Luke 22:20; cf. 1 Cor 11:25),[12] which is when the drinking would commence.

Yet these suggestions do not work when the details are examined more closely. Although Jesus blesses a cup of wine after the meal in Luke 22:20, the disciples have already passed around and taken from a cup *previously* (Luke 22:17). Moreover, in Matthew and Mark, Jesus appears to bless the cup "while they were eating," not after (Matt 26:26; Mark 14:22).[13] As such, none of the Synoptic Gospels present a strict boundary between eating the meal and drinking wine.

With regard to the alleged libation, one implication of this association would be that the "blood" that Jesus spoke of would not relate to his imminent death, but specifically to the libationary act and the ritual consumption of wine in that Last Supper setting. As Christina Risch has argued, however, when blood is "poured out" in the Bible, it tends to refer to the violent spilling of blood,[14] which would then

---

9. Matthias Klinghardt, "A Typology of the Communal Meal," in *Meals in the Early Christian World: Social Formation, Experimentation, and Conflict at the Table*, ed. Dennis E. Smith and Hal E. Taussig (New York: Palgrave Macmillan, 2012), 12.

10. For the full schema, see, e.g., Dennis E. Smith, *From Symposium to Eucharist: The Banquet in the Early Christian World* (Minneapolis: Fortress, 2003), 13–46.

11. Cf., e.g., Faas, *Roman Table*, 94–96.

12. Smith, *From Symposium*, 178.

13. I take the present participle as temporal.

14. Christina Risch, "The Wine-Symbolism in the Old Testament and Jewish Tradition and Its Relevance for the Interpretation of the Lord's Supper," in *Feasts and Festivals*, ed. Christopher Tuckett, CBET 53 (Leuven: Peeters, 2009), 92.

point to Jesus's death rather than to a libation.[15] In other words, the text by no means confines the sacrificial ritual to what took place at the meal but instead ritualizes in advance what would take place later on the cross. Thus, Jesus did not pour out a wine libation at the Last Supper, and the importance of blessing the cup in terms of timing was not where it may have occurred within the putative structure of the meal, but rather that it occurred near the start of the Passover festival.

THE THIRD CUP OF THE PASSOVER MEAL?

As we have seen, contrary to the idea that Greco-Roman banqueting best explains the Last Supper, Jesus and his disciples clearly consumed more than one glass of wine during the meal. But how many glasses did they consume, and which one did Jesus use to proclaim the words of institution? The traditional Passover seder calls for four cups of wine (m. Pesahim 10), though another stream of the tradition calls for *at least* four cups to be consumed (t. Pesahim 10). Each cup is given its own symbolic interpretation, though even this is not a stable tradition in antiquity, since both the meaning of each cup of wine and the rationale behind the number four are diversely understood (cf. Gen Rab. 88:5; y. Pesahim 10:7–8 [23–34]). Each cup is also accompanied by its own blessing, with the last one also accompanied by a hymn. These variegated traditions were preserved in writing several centuries after the time of Jesus, but many scholars contend that they were practiced in the first century and thus inform Jesus's words and actions at the Last Supper.

Turning to the Gospels to see if there is any representation of this tradition, it is intriguing to note that after Jesus blesses the cup of wine in Matthew and Mark, he sang a hymn with his disciples (Matt 26:30; Mark 14:26). This could fit the rabbinic background, but notably *only if that cup was the fourth cup of the evening, since the hymn concludes their meal.* Further corroboration of this could be seen in Luke's portrayal of a cup before and after the bread (Luke 22:17, 20), possibly corresponding to the Mishnah's description of cups blessed before and after the meal (m. Pesahim 10:7). Scholars who find the background of the four cups relevant to the Last Supper tend to argue that Jesus blessed the third cup of the evening with the words of institution.[16] Indeed, some extend this into Jesus's comments about fasting from "the fruit of the vine," contending that Jesus was signaling that he would not drink the fourth and final cup of the seder, the cup traditionally associated with the *hallel* psalms of praise (Pss 113–118), since the disciples sang a hymn after Jesus made that statement.[17]

Brant Pitre argues that Jesus intentionally did not finish the Passover meal, abstaining from the fourth cup until he consumed it *on the cross*—"the cup" that

---

15. Risch, "Wine-Symbolism," 87–96.
16. E.g., Jeremias, *Eucharistic Words*, 84–88.
17. David Daube, *The New Testament and Rabbinic Judaism*, rev. ed. (Peabody: Hendrickson, 1998), 330–31.

he prayed about in Gethsemane (Matt 26:39, 42)—when Jesus literally consumed sour wine to complete the Passover meal.[18] This is an ingenious proposal, but it is ultimately unpersuasive. It is quite a stretch to regard the offerings of sour wine during the crucifixion as the fourth cup of the Passover, not least because of the lack of cups involved (cf. sponges on a reed/hyssop in Matt 27:48; Mark 15:36; Luke 23:36; John 19:29). Furthermore, the broader passion tradition also records that Jesus was offered mixed wine *prior to the crucifixion* (with gall in Matt 27:34; with myrrh in Mark 15:23). But because Jesus did not consume it, Pitre contends that these offerings were not part of the fourth cup. Yet Matthew does mention that *Jesus tasted the wine first before he rejected it* (Matt 27:34), which at the very least would suggest, extending the logic of the view, that Jesus partook of two cups during the passion rather than just one. Furthermore, this view smooths over the variation in the accounts of mixed and sour-wine offerings, which are not easily harmonized, raising additional questions about the legitimacy of reading the sour-wine offering as the fourth cup of the Passover seder.[19]

More importantly, rather than try to discern which of the four cups was blessed at the Last Supper, the whole tradition is likely too late to be relevant.[20] As we saw in chapter 5, it was not until Jubilees and the Gospels that we find any evidence of wine consumption during the Passover celebration (cf. Jub. 49.6). Clearly wine must have been customary for Passover, at least by the New Testament era, but the notion of four highly symbolic cups of wine seems foreign to the Gospels. The most likely explanation is that the four-cups tradition developed in the aftermath of the destruction of the temple in 70 CE, since we do not find any unequivocal examples of this tradition that predate it. If this is the case, the four cups likely developed as a way to compensate for the inability to offer the required sacrifices for the Passover meal.[21] Undoubtedly elements of the later Passover tradition do have antiquity, especially the general notion of interpreting the elements of the meal.[22] But the four-cup tradition likely does not.[23] By attempting to distance the Last Supper from the four-cups tradition, however, I am not trying to undermine the importance of the Passover festival for interpreting this meal. Indeed, the Last Supper should be understood as a Passover meal, even if it was celebrated early (see above), but it was

---

18. Brant Pitre, *Jesus and the Jewish Roots of the Eucharist: Unlocking the Secrets of the Last Supper* (New York: Doubleday, 2011), 147–70.

19. For the difficulties here, and how early Christians harmonized the accounts based on intertextuality with Psalm 69, see Dunne, "Souring of the Ways."

20. Contrary to comments in Kreglinger, *Spirituality of Wine*, 70–71; idem, "Bible," in *The Oxford Companion to Wine*, ed. Julia Harding and Jancis Robinson with Tara Q. Thomas, 5th ed. (Oxford: Oxford University Press, 2023), 80.

21. E.g., Bokser, *Origins*.

22. Joel Marcus, "Passover and Last Supper Revisited," *NTS* 59.3 (2013): 303–24.

23. David Instone-Brewer's detailed commentary on the Mishnah argues that some of the tradition in m. Pesahim postdates 70 CE, including the fourth cup specifically (on largely redaction-critical grounds). Nevertheless, he does posit (unpersuasively in my view) that in Jesus's time there was a three-cup tradition. See his *Traditions of the Rabbis from the Era of the New Testament, Volume 2A: Feasts and Sabbaths: Passover and Atonement* (Grand Rapids: Eerdmans, 2011), 185–88.

precisely a *first-century* Passover meal. So it must be interpreted in that historical light, prior to the development of the four-cups tradition.

When the temple was still standing, the Passover celebration was closely associated with it, not least due to the sacrifice of the Passover lambs. Indeed, Passover was one of the main pilgrimage festivals for this reason. The fact that the Passover seder tradition did not continue the ritual of Passover sacrifice highlights the centrality of the temple and also the pressure to rethink the Passover celebration in its absence.[24] By associating his own death with the elements taken from the Passover meal, Jesus was giving his death a sacrificial significance and giving their final meal together a cultic connotation. Multiple cups of wine were consumed that night, as the Synoptics indicate, but the significance of the cup that Jesus blessed is precisely the significance that he attributed to it: his blood ratifies a new covenant with his followers.

THE UPPER ROOM DISCOURSE

As noted already, the Gospel of John does not record the words of institution at the Last Supper, but it does give attention to the final meal that Jesus had with his disciples within the so-called Upper Room Discourse (John 13–17). John clearly presents this meal as taking place at the same time as the Last Supper. This is seen not least through the chronological placement of the meal before Jesus's arrest but also in the record of similar moments, such as when Jesus announced that his betrayer was someone dipping into the same dish as him (John 13:26; see Matt 26:23; Mark 14:20; cf. Luke 22:21). As noted earlier, this meal occurs just before Passover, and so is not technically a Passover meal in John, but John does associate the significance of Jesus's death with the Passover more than the other Gospels (cf. ch. 13). The synchronicity of Jesus's death with the slaughter of the Passover lambs, at least, demonstrates this point (John 19:14). Clearly the Passover is significant for John's Christology, and it is still relevant for Jesus's Upper Room Discourse given its proximity to the start of the festival.

Lacking the words of institution, the Upper Room Discourse instead records a unique incident of Jesus washing his disciples' feet (John 13:1–19) and a few lengthy monologues. The most significant of those monologues, for our purposes, is Jesus's discourse on the true vine (15:1–11). Without repeating what has already been said about this passage (cf. ch. 11), it is significant that Jesus addresses his close connection with his followers in terms of viticulture around the same time in which we would expect him to provide the words of institution for the cup of wine (although Jesus's discourse on the true vine occurs as they leave the meal rather than at the meal; cf. John 14:31c).

---

24. See Bokser, *Origins*, 76–106.

> Didache 9.1–2 (1st–2nd c. CE) states, "Now concerning the Eucharist, give thanks as follows. First, concerning the cup: We give you thanks, our Father, for the holy vine of David your servant, which you have made known to us through Jesus, your servant; to you be the glory forever."[25] Using vine imagery to speak of Jesus's ancestral heritage to King David is intriguing enough, but depicting Jesus as a vine is clearly reminiscent of John 15, and it is notable that the Didache connects this to eucharistic wine.

In my view, we cannot divorce Jesus's claim to be the true vine from the use of wine in the celebration of the Eucharist in the communities who originally received the Gospel of John (John 15:1, 5). As we have seen already (cf. ch. 11), the imagery has cultic significance since the disciples-as-branches are called "clean" (John 15:3). Additionally, the image of branches being connected to the vine (15:2, 5), and remaining in him in order to bear fruit (15:4–7), describes how the Eucharist ritually signifies union with Christ. This "remaining" is also reciprocated; as Jesus's disciples abide in him, he abides in them ("remain in me, and I in you"). Mutual abiding highlights that the love and joy shared between Christ and the participants in the Eucharist are the fruits of this union (15:9–11). To be sure, to abide in Christ is part of a call to continual discipleship, but the ritual that undergirds and upholds that reality is the Eucharist, here alluding specifically to the role of wine. Far from being anti-sacramental, as scholars like Rudolf Bultmann have famously proposed, John's Gospel is thoroughly invested in highlighting how Jesus's ministry and message symbolically anticipate the rituals of the early Christian community.

> Unlike John, which does allude to the Eucharist, Hebrews only hints at it (Heb 13:10). The omission is striking because there appears to be potential for a typological connection between the bread and wine that Melchizedek uses to bless Abraham (Gen 14:18) and the bread and wine that Jesus offers in the Eucharist. This is especially curious given the author's interest in Jesus's role as a priest after the order of Melchizedek (Heb 7:1–28), who perpetually offers his life—that is, his blood, to God in the heavenly temple (cf. 9:12–14; 10:19; 12:24; 13:11–12, 20).[26]

---

25. Holmes, *Apostolic Fathers*, 357.
26. On the significance of Jesus's life in Hebrews, see David M. Moffitt, *Atonement and the Logic of Resurrection in the Epistle to the Hebrews*, NovTSup 141 (Leiden: Brill, 2010).

Instead of recording the words of institution, John preserves claims and theologically loaded incidents that evoke the ritual, such as the provision of an abundance of wine at the wedding at Cana (see ch. 13). The true-vine discourse in John 15, in particular, showcases a participatory interpretation of eucharistic wine, which is seen even more clearly in the bread-of-life discourse as part of the feeding of the five thousand in John 6.

"DRINK MY BLOOD"

As noted already, each account of the words of institution in the Synoptics and Paul includes the words "my blood." Even though John never records the words of institution, Jesus alludes to them through his injunction to "drink my blood" within the bread-of-life discourse (John 6:53–56). Notably, this moment is also situated near the time of Passover (6:4), which already evokes the timing of the Last Supper. It also comes before Jesus "gave thanks [*eucharisteō*]" (6:11; cf. 6:23) at the distribution of the bread and fish to the thousands who had gathered to hear him. Then, after performing this "sign" (6:14), Jesus identifies himself as the "bread of life" (6:35, 48; cf. 6:41), directly connecting God's provision of manna for the wilderness generation that experienced the original Passover to God's provision of himself (6:32–33, 49–51, 58). As Jesus states most directly:

> I am the living bread that came down from heaven. Whoever eats this bread will live forever. This bread is my flesh, which I will give for the life of the world. (John 6:51)

In response to the negative reaction that Jesus receives from his words (6:52), Jesus doubles down on the imagery and extends it further with reference to his flesh and blood: "Very truly I tell you, unless you eat the flesh of the Son of Man and drink his blood, you have no life in you" (6:53). Then Jesus continues this imagery even further, making the eucharistic associations with the bread and wine unmistakable:

> Whoever eats my flesh and drinks my blood has eternal life, and I will raise them up at the last day. For my flesh is real food and my blood is real drink. Whoever eats my flesh and drinks my blood remains in me, and I in them. (John 6:54–56)

Drinking blood is repeated multiple times in this passage, and Jesus calls his blood "real drink," alluding to consuming eucharistic wine (John 6:55). With reference to his flesh, Jesus's phrasing for eating becomes more visceral as the discourse develops, shifting from the general term for "eating" his flesh (*esthiō* in 6:51, 53) to the term for "munching" (*trōgō* in 6:54, 56–58), suggesting that genuine eating is in view.²⁷ One need not affirm transubstantiation in order to recognize that this passage provides theological insight into the practice of the Eucharist and that a strict memorial interpretation does not do justice to Jesus's words. It is highly unlikely to me that language of "eating" Jesus's flesh and "drinking" his blood could be recorded and then circulate in early Christian contexts in which eucharistic bread and wine was consumed ritually without at least implying a connection.²⁸

> Rudolf Bultmann, who argued that the Gospel of John was anti-sacramental, believed that John 6:51–58 was about the Eucharist, and so he contended that the passage must have been a later addition to the text.²⁹

Furthermore, within the Gospel of John itself, there are other clues to support a eucharistic reading of the bread-of-life discourse on John's own terms. The language of "remaining" in Jesus by virtue of eating and drinking his flesh and blood in John 6:56 is reminiscent of John 15, and so is the notion of *reciprocal* abiding with Christ ("remain in me, and I in you"). As I argued with reference to the true-vine discourse, this same imagery here should likewise be interpreted as underscoring that consuming eucharistic bread and wine ritually signifies union with Christ. Both passages are also prominently framed as weighty "I am" statements that Jesus makes about himself, further connecting the bread and the vine as a eucharistic pair.³⁰

A eucharistic reading of the bread-of-life discourse is also suggested by the references to manna from heaven. Paul overtly connected manna with the Eucharist in 1 Corinthians 10:1–5, which shows that early Christians were making the association, and so it is likely that John was too. Indeed, Paul does not merely make this connection but also develops the participatory nature of the Eucharist as a fellowship with the body and blood of the Messiah through consuming bread and wine (1 Cor 10:14–22), which will be addressed further in the following chapter.

The bulk of interpreters who downplay a eucharistic reading of John 6 stress that consuming Christ is a symbolic way of speaking about embracing him in faith.³¹ To be sure, the broader passage does indeed stress the priority of faith (6:29, 35). The context even uses similar language to convey the benefits of both believing in Jesus

---

27. Edwyn C. Hoskyns, *The Fourth Gospel* (London: Faber and Faber, 1947), 298–99.
28. Even Meredith J. C. Warren's intriguing reading of John 6—connecting it to Greco-Roman literary representations of cultic meals honoring fallen heroes and associating them with the divine—does not rule out the eucharistic implications of the text, in my view. See his *My Flesh Is Meat Indeed: A Nonsacramental Reading of John 6:51–58* (Minneapolis: Fortress, 2015).
29. *Das Evangelium des Johannes*, KEK (Göttingen: Vandenhoeck & Ruprecht, 1957), 174–77.
30. Brown, *John*, 673.
31. See, e.g., Carson, *John*, 294–99, though he is open to secondary eucharistic allusions.

and receiving his flesh and blood as food and drink, such as having eternal life and partaking in the resurrection (6:40). But the eucharistic imagery must mean that what Jesus says cannot be reduced to *merely* an extended metaphor for faith. It must also mean that the one who believes in him continues to commune with him through eucharistic practices. To be sure, faith is given priority in the bread-of-life discourse, but faith does not merely believe in Christ; it "feeds" on him. The Eucharist ritualizes the provision of life through the ingestion of bread and wine that believers receive by faith.

CONCLUSION

At the Last Supper, Jesus renewed the covenant, drawing on the backdrop of the Passover, in which Moses originally ratified the Mosaic covenant with the nation of Israel. Those who participate in the Eucharist are members of the new covenant, having received the benefits of Jesus's life offered up for them. This includes, of course, the forgiveness of sins, which is specifically associated with the cup of wine blessed at the Last Supper, drawing our attention to the shed blood of Christ on the cross. This blood, John tells us, offers life for those who drink it, showcasing that the Eucharist is not an incidental Christian practice, or purely a symbol. It offers us life because it ritualizes our union with the one who is "the resurrection and the life" (John 11:25). As we abide in him and he abides in us, we participate in his ongoing life that sustains us, in the same way as the vine sustains the branches. The result of this eucharistic communion between Christ and the community is a deepening of love and unity (John 15:9–11), which early Christian shared meals were meant to foster. This is yet another discrete varietal of what wine represents in the Bible.

After the Last Supper, Jesus's final meal with his disciples developed into one of the central Christian rituals, imitated regularly at corporate gatherings. In this meal, the bread and wine were consumed to commemorate the inauguration of the new covenant, to proclaim the death that made it possible, and to experience the ongoing presence of Christ with us until he returns. The early development of eucharistic practices in shared meals and the theologizing that accompanied it will be explored in the next chapter, highlighting how the participatory nature of the Eucharist, implicit in the Synoptics and overt in John, is strengthened and developed further.

RELEVANT QUESTIONS

1. How might the notion that blood represents life rather than death in ancient Jewish reckoning impact our perspectives on the wine of the Eucharist?
2. What do we learn about the significance of participation in Christ by ingesting the wine of the Eucharist?

CHAPTER 16

THE EUCHARIST AND EARLY CHRISTIAN MEALS

An ancient graffito on the walls of Pompeii, a city that was destroyed by Mt. Vesuvius in 79 CE, reads, "the man with whom I do not dine is a barbarian to me" (*CIL* IV.1880).[1] This statement captures the ethos of what a shared meal meant to many people in the ancient world, and it speaks to both the tension and the promise at the heart of those meals. For early Christians, this unity was expressed during meals, not by consuming the same things but through belief in a deeper spiritual union that existed regardless of what was on their plates or poured into their glasses. As an exploration of this spiritual unity that meals represented and reinforced, the present chapter will address how their unity was threatened by excess alcohol consumption in the ongoing ritual celebration of the Lord's Supper. After first considering some elements of early Christian meals more broadly that underscore the depth of their spiritual union, we will turn to the problem of drunkenness in early Christian eucharistic gatherings, with special attention given to 1 Corinthians 10–11 and Ephesians 5:18.

IDENTITY AND ETHOS AT EARLY CHRISTIAN MEALS

Previously we explored how early Christians ate and drank together as a continuation and commemoration of the Last Supper (cf. ch. 15). It is perhaps not an exaggeration to say that the table was the locus of nascent Christian identity formation. The table afforded a space for early Christ-followers to innovate with unique social experiments that ran counter to society, as Hal Taussig has argued, such as eating and drinking with guests that were diverse in ethnicity, social status, gender, and economic means.[2] Central Christian symbols that marked out insiders and outsiders such as faith and baptism, Michael Wolter reminds us, were not consistently visible and discernible. What could be discerned by outsiders, and what could reinforce identity for insiders, however, was the meal.[3]

---

1. Cf. Emily Gowers, *The Loaded Table: Representations of Food in Roman Literature* (Oxford: Oxford University Press, 1993), 26.

2. See Hal Taussig, *In the Beginning Was the Meal: Social Experimentation & Early Christian Identity* (Minneapolis: Fortress, 2009).

3. Michael Wolter, "Primitive Christianity as a Feast," in Tuckett, *Feasts and Festivals*, 171–82.

In the beginning of Acts, we see an ideal portrait of early Christian gatherings in the immediate aftermath of the outpouring of the Spirit at Pentecost (Acts 2:1–41). Filled with the Spirit, early Christian believers shared their goods and gathered together to worship, pray, and break bread (2:42–47). There are no overt references to the Eucharist in Acts, but many scholars suspect that the references to "breaking bread" are allusions to the ritual (cf. 2:42, 46; 16:34; 20:7; 27:33–36). This is especially the case when the post-resurrection scene at Emmaus in Luke 24 is factored into the equation, since it was only after Jesus broke bread that the disciples recognized who he was (Luke 24:30–31). The significance of that recognition is twofold: it points back to Jesus breaking bread at the Last Supper (Luke 22:19), and it reflects the way in which Christ could continue to be "seen" in the ongoing commemoration of that meal in the Eucharist. Some insist that the breaking-bread scenes in Acts are not eucharistic because wine is never mentioned.[4] But it is possible that "breaking bread" was Luke's shorthand reference to shared Christian meals, which were often commemorative of Christ's death. Regardless, the ethos of the shared meal in Acts is one of tremendous cohesion, characterized by love and support.

As the Christian movement became more diverse in various respects, meals were the place where identity was contested, and meals provided the impetus for further identity formation. When matters of food and drink came up in the early Christian gatherings, there was no systematic explanation that everyone should have the same diet or the same set of beliefs on dieting. As Romans 14–15 makes clear (cf. ch. 8), what is most important for Paul is that everyone is able to be together at meals to reinforce their shared ethos. This is true of all shared meals, even the Eucharist, which, if not overtly mentioned in the passage, would nevertheless be relevant, since Paul is not addressing private habits of consumption. No matter one's diet, everyone should be able to eat together. To insist otherwise would be to suggest that the kingdom of God is primarily concerned with matters of eating and drinking (Rom 14:17a). Indeed, as Paul says, to be divided over food and drink directly undermines the "righteousness, peace and joy in the Holy Spirit" with which the kingdom of God is chiefly concerned (14:17b).

What is striking about this claim, however, given the expectation of an eschatological banquet (cf. ch. 14), is that the future realization of the kingdom is, in fact, characterized by eating and drinking! Yet Paul's letters are often focused on the present manifestation of the kingdom. It is not as if Paul is arguing that Christians should be unconcerned with food and drink presently because the future kingdom will not include any of that. Instead, he is arguing that righteousness, peace, and joy in the Holy Spirit ought to be present within the community rather than divisions

---

4. E.g., Grimm, *From Feasting to Fasting*, 79–81.

over food and drink. He is pointing to the deeper spiritual reality that constitutes the unity of diverse believers around the table.

Describing the role of food in early Christian gatherings, Pliny the Younger (1st–2nd c. CE) notes that "after this ceremony [of singing and oath taking] it had been their custom to disperse and reassemble later to take food of an ordinary, harmless kind" (*Ep. Tra.* 10.96.7 [Radice, LCL]).

Paul's belief that believers should not be segregated when they eat contributes to his critique of Peter in Antioch for withdrawing from gentiles when representatives from Jerusalem arrived during a meal (Gal 2:11–14). Paul's response highlights that what is egregious here is that Peter's actions suggest that gentiles are not welcomed at the family meal, even though they all have the same faith (2:16–17), the indwelling presence of Christ (2:19–20), and the gift of the Spirit (3:1–5). This commonality makes division at the table exceedingly troubling, and this is especially so if the shared meal was a eucharistic celebration.[5]

Yet certain people and certain behaviors could not be tolerated at these shared meals. The author of Jude warns against the presence of false teachers at "love feasts" (*agapais*; Jude 12). The label "love feasts" underscores how the meal reinforced the community ethos of love, even as it celebrates the love of God in Christ.[6] Thus, these "love feasts" were most likely eucharistic meals, as later tradition attests (cf. Ign. *Smyrn.* 8.2; Ep. Apos. 15).[7] The point of mentioning the "love feasts," however, is to warn against the presence of false teachers, whom Jude compared to submerged reefs in the ocean (Jude 12; NIV "blemishes"). The imagery suggests that the community should avoid them, lest these teachers cause their faith to shipwreck.[8]

Second Peter uses this verse from Jude in its own renunciation of false teachers at early Christian meals, describing how they "carouse in broad daylight" and revel "in their pleasures [*apatais*] while they feast with you" (2 Pet 2:13). In this passage, it is not just the false teachers' presence at the meals that is problematic (as in Jude), but also the indulgent manner in which they feasted. There is possibly a play on words here since Jude's term for "love feasts" (*agapais*) is replaced by a term for pleasure (*apatais*), which looks and sounds similar.[9] If such a wordplay exists, the point would likely be that the false teachers have twisted the love feasts into something entirely different altogether, distorting the ethos of love that they were intended to foster.[10]

It is possible that all of these instances of shared meals—the breaking-bread scenes in Acts, the food scruples in Romans 14–15, the Antioch incident in Galatians, the "love feasts" in Jude, and the feasting in 2 Peter—concern eucharistic meals. Even if some or all of them do not do so directly, they still provide insight into early Christian concerns and values for any kind of shared meal, eucharistic or otherwise.

---

5. So, e.g., Smith, *From Symposium*, 173–74.
6. See Richard J. Bauckham, *Jude, 2 Peter*, WBC 50 (Waco, TX: Word, 1983), 85.
7. So, e.g., Bauckham, *Jude, 2 Peter*, 84.
8. The NIV renders *spilades* as "blemishes," but it is commonly used for oceanic rocks or reefs, which are more fitting because of references to other natural objects like clouds, trees, waves, and stars (Jude 12b–13). See, e.g., Bauckham, *Jude, 2 Peter*, 85–86.
9. Some manuscripts of 2 Peter 2:13 read *agapais* ("love feasts"), as in Alexandrinus, but that variant probably stems from harmonization with Jude 12.
10. See, e.g., Bauckham, *Jude, 2 Peter*, 266.

They all underscore the importance of a spiritual union and a shared ethos that binds all the participants together. The unity that these passages either convey, as in Acts, or strive to maintain, as in Romans, Galatians, Jude, and 2 Peter, is also addressed in 1 Corinthians 10–11 and Ephesians 5:18. These texts deserve to be addressed at greater length because of the ways in which excess alcohol consumption is singled out as a particular threat to the community's identity and ethos.

PARTICIPATION AND THE EUCHARIST IN 1 CORINTHIANS 10–11

When Paul speaks overtly about eucharistic meals in 1 Corinthians 10–11, it is in direct response to two controversial matters affecting the community. The first instance appears at the end of a discussion on whether believers should eat food offered to idols (1 Cor 8–10), when Paul appeals to the elements of the Eucharist to make his case (10:14–22). The other instance is when Paul addresses the drunkenness that would ensue during the eucharistic celebration in Corinth (11:17–34). With both of these controversial matters, Paul appeals to the unity that believers ought to have during their shared meals.[11] This unity is a spiritual bond made possible by the work of the Spirit, uniting believers to Christ and to each other. As such, this union is not merely symbolic or figurative but is a reality that eucharistic meals mediate. Yet, it is a unity that is obscured and indeed threatened by the divisive matters of consumption. I will address the way in which this spiritual connection informs how Paul addresses both of these topics, taking them in reverse order, since 1 Corinthians 11 provides the most sustained treatment on the topic of the Eucharist in the Pauline corpus.

The incidence of drunkenness at the eucharistic gathering reflects division and disunity. The underlying issue seems to be socioeconomic disparity, although this should not be overstated since it was probably the case that most of the Corinthians lived at or near the subsistence level.[12] Nevertheless, those with more means would consume food and wine at their eucharistic gatherings to the point of excess, and those who did not have as much would end up hungry (1 Cor 11:21). As far as Paul is concerned, this nullifies the Eucharist, making it no longer "the Lord's Supper" (*kyriakon deipnon*, 11:20). Rather, it has become a "private supper [*idion deipnon*]" (11:21), which they should eat and drink in their own homes so as not to ostracize those with less (11:22). In order for the meal to be *the Lord's Supper*, it must be corporate and communal. Division should not characterize *how* it is celebrated in part because of *what* it is celebrating.

---

11. Cf. my "Food Laws and Customs, Jewish and Roman," in *DPL*², 319–24.

12. See Bruce W. Longenecker, *Remember the Poor: Paul, Poverty, and the Greco-Roman World* (Grand Rapids: Eerdmans, 2010).

As part of Paul's ad hoc response to Corinthian disunity at eucharistic meals, he cites the tradition of the Last Supper and the so-called words of institution (1 Cor 11:23–26). A few notable differences occur in the wording of Paul's version, and it is worth addressing the two most unique features here. First, with each element of the Eucharist, the tradition dictates that it be consumed "in remembrance of me." Luke's tradition includes remembrance also, but only in relation to the bread, not the cup (Luke 22:19–20), which is intriguing for the breaking-bread passages in Acts noted earlier. Second, Paul's version includes the unique line at the end: "for whenever you eat this bread and drink this cup, you proclaim the Lord's death until he comes" (1 Cor 11:26). Some scholars have suggested that the reference to the cup in 11:26 refers to any time that wine is consumed.[13] In other words, for Christians, the consumption of wine is always a ritual act in relation to the Lord's death. The NIV's translation, "this cup," is an attempt to clarify that only the eucharistic cup is in view—a focus that is reflected in some variants in the manuscript tradition.[14] The eucharistic cup is most likely in view because of the reference to "the cup of the Lord" (11:27), but also because of the earlier reference in the letter to "the cup of thanksgiving" (10:16). Thus, Paul has in mind the cup that becomes ritually significant through the blessing, not just any cup of wine (although every glass of wine should be approached contemplatively). This second element adds additional emphasis to the idea that the Last Supper was interpreted as a proleptic and anticipatory meal (cf. chs. 8 and 14). Paul must have cited this tradition in part to showcase how the Corinthian customs were not aligned with the purpose of the Eucharist—which is to remember and to proclaim *Jesus's death in the past*, and to do so with the expectation that *Jesus will return in the future*. This was meant to be a regular occurrence, taking place much more frequently than the annual Passover upon which this tradition was based.[15] The remembering, proclaiming, and expecting are what the Corinthians ought to do *presently*, rather than divide among themselves as some splurge and others go hungry. Yet Paul believes that there is more going on *presently* when they participate in the eucharistic bread and wine that is also being undermined, as the subsequent paragraph makes clear (11:27–32).

Because the Corinthians were conducting the Lord's Supper "in an unworthy manner" (1 Cor 11:27)—referring to the type of divisive behavior noted in verses 17–22—Paul had dire warnings for them. Celebrating the Eucharist this way makes one "guilty of sinning against" the body and blood of the Lord (1 Cor 11:27), and so one eats and drinks "judgment" on oneself (11:29). Paul even explains

---

13. So, e.g., C. K. Barrett, *The First Epistle to the Corinthians*, BNTC (Peabody, MA: Hendrickson, 1968), 269–70.

14. See Anthony C. Thiselton, *The First Epistle to the Corinthians: A Commentary on the Greek Text*, NIGTC (Grand Rapids: Eerdmans, 2000), 886.

15. Gordon D. Fee, *The First Epistle to the Corinthians*, NICNT (Grand Rapids: Eerdmans, 1987), 614.

that such unworthy participation is why some in the community became sick and even died (11:30).

To avoid this, Paul commands the Corinthians to examine themselves beforehand (11:28) and to see if they are able to *discern the body* (11:29). The latter charge most likely refers to discerning the significance of each celebrant as a member of the single body of Christ.[16] This is because Paul is still addressing divisive behavior in this section, and moreover he immediately transitions to provide an extended reflection on the body of Christ afterward (1 Cor 12). Indeed, Paul ends his warnings of judgment by again stressing that everyone should eat together (11:33–34). The passage therefore assumes that the unity affected by the Eucharist is not metaphorical, as the judgment language clearly suggests. Paul reveals the same logic about eucharistic bread and wine in the earlier discussion on food offered to idols (1 Cor 10), which demonstrates that it was not merely a symbolic ritual.

With the matter of food offered to idols, Paul appeals to the Eucharist in two ways. The first is when Paul compares Israel's historical temptations to idolatry after the exodus with similar temptations facing Jesus-followers. Just as Israel came out of Egypt by passing through the sea, and then received "spiritual food and drink" from God in the form of manna from heaven and water from the traveling rock,[17] so also early Jesus-followers have been baptized and participate in the spiritual food and drink of the Eucharist (1 Cor 10:1–4). Paul connects the Eucharist and the exodus earlier in the letter as well when he calls Christ "our Passover lamb" (5:7) in a context calling for the Corinthians to celebrate "the Festival" with "unleavened bread" and without any vices plaguing the community (5:6, 8). Most scholars view "the Festival" as a reference to life in general,[18] but I agree with Gordon Fee that the regular celebration of the Eucharist is more likely,[19] which anticipates the communal ethics of the Eucharist that Paul addresses in 1 Corinthians 10–11. This suggests, among other things, that Paul is operating with a typological, and indeed highly symbolic, interpretation of eucharistic bread and wine. Indeed, for Paul, the details of Israel's history within that typology contain an important lesson for Paul's own generation (10:6, 11). Israel's proclivity to idolatry in the face of God's provision, in which they "sat down to eat and drink and got up to indulge in revelry" (10:7, citing Exod 32:6), relates to the Corinthian temptation to participate in idolatry (and no doubt promiscuity; cf. 1 Cor 5:1–13). Both communities participated in the "sacraments" of baptism and the Eucharist in their respective ways, and both were tempted to idolatry. So, Paul calls the Corinthians to flee from idolatry to ensure that history does not repeat itself (10:15). Yet furthermore, this historical

---

16. So, e.g., Fee, *First Epistle*, 623–24; Ciampa and Rosner, *First Letter*, 555; Macaskill, *Union*, 212.

17. John 6:25–59 also brings together manna and eucharistic imagery (cf. ch. 15).

18. E.g., Ciampa and Rosner, *First Letter*, 215; Thiselton, *First Epistle*, 406.

19. See Fee, *First Epistle*, 239.

connection also relates to the issue of drunkenness at the eucharistic gatherings in 1 Corinthians 11. Indeed, Paul highlights how the ancient Israelite community had members who died because of sexual immorality, for "testing Christ," and for grumbling about God's provision (10:8–10). This behavior anticipates the death of those in Corinth who have died as well, because they participated in the Lord's Supper "in an unworthy manner."

The second way that Paul addresses food offered to idols to unpack the theological meaning of eucharistic bread and wine is when he highlights the spiritual union that occurs when one shares a meal dedicated to Christ or demons, respectively (1 Cor 10:16–22). Each element of the Eucharist, the cup of blessing and the broken bread, constitute fellowship (*koinōnia*) with the blood and body of Christ (10:16). Since the bread comes from a single loaf, it showcases for Paul the ecclesial unity that this *koinōnia* bolsters (10:17).

> To restate some conclusions from chapter 15 with reference to 1 Corinthians 10:16, the "cup of blessing" is neither a libation of wine separating the two portions of the Greco-Roman banquet,[20] since Paul never even mentions libations in the discussion on food offered to idols,[21] nor is it the third of the four cups consumed during the traditional Passover seder,[22] which is anachronistic. Instead, it is most naturally taken as the cup of eucharistic wine mentioned in 1 Corinthians 11:25–27.

Paul then highlights how a similar fellowship was constituted when ancient Israel participated in their own "sacramental" rites, since they were participants in the altar by virtue of the fact that they ate sacrifices offered to God (1 Cor 10:18). For Paul's broader purposes in 1 Corinthians 8–10, it is not merely the case that divine fellowship occurs when food is offered to God and to Christ, but it also occurs when food is offered to other divine beings or demons (10:20–21). Shared meals constitute a partnership with a divine entity who is the host at the head of the table—either Christ or a demon.[23] Because of this dynamic, Paul affirms that one cannot be in fellowship (*koinōnia*) with both Christ and demons by drinking from their respective cups or by sharing in their tables (10:21). This notion builds on ancient Jewish notions of social contagion: "to be in the presence of another is to be susceptible, to some extent at least, to the communication of their status and properties, particularly

---

20. Klinghardt, "Typology," 12.

21. So Charles H. Cosgrove, "Banquet Ceremonies Involving Wine in the Greco-Roman World and Early Christianity," *CBQ* 79.2 (2017): 299–316.

22. E.g., Thiselton, *First Epistle*, 756–60, 883–84.

23. Joseph A. Fitzmyer, *First Corinthians: A New Translation with Introduction and Commentary*, AYB (New Haven: Yale University Press, 2008), 434.

in a ritual sense."[24] Furthermore, the language of the "table" connotes the altar in the temple, further solidifying the connection between the Eucharist and ancient Israelite participation in sacrificial meals (10:18).[25] Thus, Paul's broader discussion in 1 Corinthians 10 about participating in the blood and body of Christ through eucharistic bread and wine provide additional explanation for why partaking of the Eucharist "in an unworthy manner" could lead to judgment (11:27–32). At the very least, it shows that the Eucharist must be more than a symbolic memorial.[26]

Real participation in the blood and body of Christ through eucharistic bread and wine is best understood as mediated through the Spirit. This is most clearly seen in 1 Corinthians 12, where Paul emphasizes how the Spirit constitutes Christ-followers as the body of Christ. The Spirit is operative in both baptism, baptizing believers into one body, and the Eucharist, since believers "drink" of the same Spirit (1 Cor 12:13). The idea of "drinking" from the same Spirit here, as a reference to eucharistic wine, typologically connects back to "the spiritual drink" of Israel's wilderness wanderings (10:2–4). The mediation of the Spirit to constitute union with Christ in 1 Corinthians 12 is anticipated when Paul speaks of the bodies of believers being "members" of Christ (6:15a) and becoming one spirit with him (6:17). This is achieved through the indwelling of the Spirit, which makes them like temples (6:19–20). Additionally, the same logic, which says that believers cannot have *koinōnia* with both demons and Christ through participating in sacred meals (10:20–21), is also operative in this context, since Paul's prerogative is to stress that sexual union with a sex worker is contrary to union with Christ (6:15–18). The significance of this connection further underscores that it is the work of the Spirit that brings about the reality of our union with Christ and each other.

> Paul's arguments about sexuality in 1 Corinthians 6 begins with a Corinthian slogan that says, "Food for the stomach and the stomach for food, and God will destroy them both" (1 Cor 6:13). Some scholars contend that none of it,[27] or perhaps part of it (e.g., ESV, CSB, NRSVue), comes from the Corinthians. Others argue that the saying is their slogan, but Paul disagrees with the *application* of it.[28] If any of these are correct, then it would seem that Paul does not anticipate that resurrected bodies will have stomachs, constituting yet another instance where he seems to downplay the theme of eschatological banqueting (cf. Rom 14:17). Yet, most

---

24. Macaskill, *Union*, 207.
25. So too Ciampa and Rosner, *First Letter*, 482.
26. Rightly Ben Witherington III, *Conflict and Community in Corinth: A Socio-Rhetorical Commentary on 1 and 2 Corinthians* (Grand Rapids: Eerdmans, 1995), 225.

27. So, e.g., David E. Garland, *1 Corinthians*, BECNT (Grand Rapids: Baker, 2003), 229–32.
28. So, e.g., Fee, *First Epistle*, 280–83.

> likely Paul disagrees with both the logic and the application, which is that God only cares about our souls, not our bodies.[29] Although Paul could have a unique conception of resurrected bodies as lacking stomachs, the resurrected Jesus ate food (Luke 24:30, 41–43; John 21:9–13), and Revelation contains a vision of the tree of life producing fruit each month in the new creation (Rev 22:1–2).

Paul's discussion of eucharistic bread and wine is clearly designed to buttress the unity of the church, and his arguments reveal that this unity is rooted in a union with Christ that is mediated by the Spirit through rites like the Eucharist. Drunkenness, then, is one particular kind of disruption to unity, taking a central element of early Christian worship and using it to drive a wedge in the community. As such, excessive consumption of wine in eucharistic settings is a distortion of corporate worship, which Ephesians 5:18 also addresses.

DRUNKENNESS AND THE SPIRIT-FILLED COMMUNITY IN EPHESIANS 5:18

Ephesians 5:18, with its prohibition against drunkenness, is often understood to pertain to one's personal or private consumption of alcohol.[30] But as we have seen, this passage is focused on the corporate gathering of the church (cf. ch. 7). In what follows, then, I will explore how the passage is rooted in a similar understanding of corporate spiritual union as in 1 Corinthians 10–11. Here is the passage cited in full:

> Do not get drunk on wine, which leads to debauchery. Instead, be filled with the Spirit, *speaking* to one another with psalms, hymns, and songs from the Spirit. *Sing* and *make music* from your heart to the Lord, always *giving thanks* to God the Father for everything, in the name of our Lord Jesus Christ. *Submit* to one another out of reverence for Christ. (Eph 5:18–21; emphases added)

Grammatically, the italicized words above, including the references to corporate worship (e.g., *speaking, sing, make music, giving thanks*) and to corporate submission, are participles in Greek that are all subordinate to the command, "be filled with the Spirit." This is obscured by the NIV translation, which treats three of these participles as independent, and so translates them like imperatives. Though this is

---

29. So also Ciampa and Rosner, *First Letter*, 254 (see n37); Thiselton, *First Epistle*, 462–63.

30. The present section is a summary of John Anthony Dunne, "Filled with the Spirit: Wine and Worship in Levitical Light (Ephesians 5.18–21)," *BPT* 11.4 (2018): 407–43.

possible in certain contexts, it is not likely here.³¹ The emphasis on wine, worship, and the inclusion of the participle "giving thanks" (*eucharisteō*) suggests that the passage envisions a eucharistic gathering. Furthermore, the fact that early Christians often gathered for worship and eucharistic meals in house churches helps to explain why this passage about corporate worship leads directly into a household code (Eph 5:22–6:9). It transitions there through the fifth and final participle about mutual submission in verse 21. This connection further highlights, then, the corporate nature of the drunkenness prohibition and the Spirit-filling command. Thus, we should read all five of these participles as either conveying the *means* of Spirit-filling,³² or the *result* of that filling.³³ Either way there is an important connection that these references to the corporate gathering have to both the prohibition to avoid drunkenness and the command to be filled with the Spirit. We will not understand either aspect of the verse unless we know how they pertain to corporate worship in house churches.

Part of making sense of this passage is determining whether Paul is addressing a specific problem in the churches or not. There is no evidence to suggest that the matter of drunkenness in Ephesians was caused by socioeconomic issues, similar to what we saw in 1 Corinthians. Another suggested background for Paul's command is the audience's adoption of Greco-Roman banqueting customs,³⁴ including possibly those customs commemorating Dionysus with frenzied, orgiastic celebrations of wine.³⁵ Yet one of the problems that interpreters of Ephesians face more broadly is a lack of an obvious exigency. In fact, given how general the letter of Ephesians is and how ubiquitous drunkenness is, some suggest that Paul is simply making a more proverbial appeal to avoid drunkenness.³⁶

Whether or not there was a specific problem behind the drunkenness prohibition, Paul seems to be presenting an *offensive*, rather than a *defensive* posture. Instead of determining what specifically Paul may be opposing with this passage, it is the theological rationale that informs what he says here that is most important. Specifically, what ties the details of this passage together—the command to be filled with the Spirit, the prohibition against drunken debauchery, and the references to corporate worship—is temple theology. Each of these elements will be addressed in turn.

Second Maccabees 6:4 (NRSVue) combines the language of debauchery and filling when talking about the temple: "For the temple was *filled* with *debauchery* and *reveling* by the nations, who dallied with prostitutes and had intercourse with women within the sacred precincts and besides brought in things for sacrifice that were unfit" (emphases added).

---

31. On the independent use of participles, see Wallace, *Greek Grammar*, 650–52.

32. Clinton E. Arnold, *Ephesians*, ZECNT (Grand Rapids: Zondervan, 2010), 350.

33. Wallace, *Greek Grammar*, 639.

34. E.g., Taussig, *In the Beginning*, 47; Richard A. Wright, "Drinking, Teaching, and Singing: Ephesians 5:18–19 and the Challenges of Moral Instruction at Greco-Roman Banquets," *LTQ* 47.3–4 (2017): 85–104.

35. E.g., Cleon L. Rogers Jr., "The Dionysian Background of Ephesians 5:18," *BSac* 136.543 (1979): 249–57.

36. E.g., Frank Thielman, *Ephesians*, BECNT (Grand Rapids: Baker Academic, 2010), 358.

Starting with the command to be Spirit-filled, this injunction is best understood in relation to the rich temple theology in Ephesians.[37] Ephesians 2:11–22 is the most explicit passage in this regard, with its description of Jews and gentiles becoming a temple indwelt by God's Spirit; indeed, even a new person. This brings together the temple and the imagery of the body of Christ, as we saw in 1 Corinthians.[38] Additionally, the language of "filling" and "fullness," so pervasive in Ephesians (1:23; 3:14–19; 4:8–10; cf. Col 1:19; 2:9), likely stems from descriptions of the temple in the Old Testament being full of God's glory (cf. Exod 40:34–35; 1 Kgs 8:10–11; 2 Chr 5:13–14; 7:1–2; Isa 6:1; Ezek 10:4; 43:5; 44:4; Hag 2:7).[39] Thus, being "filled with the Spirit" in Ephesians 5:18 suggests that the Spirit is the *content* of the filling,[40] which further underscores that those indwelt with the Spirit constitute a temple.[41] Some scholars have argued instead that the Spirit is more likely the *means* of filling,[42] or the *sphere* in which the filling takes place,[43] contending that *content* is unlikely on grammatical grounds.[44] But the problem with these other suggestions is that they leave the content of filling unspecified—*filled with what*? In my view, recognizing that the Spirit is the content of the filling reinforces the temple imagery of Ephesians 5:18, which is consistent with the temple theology of the letter and with broader Pauline reflection on the church as a temple (cf. 1 Cor 3:16; 6:19).

With the temple association of Spirit-filling in mind, the prohibition against drunkenness can be understood in this light. On the face of it, the contrast between drunkenness and the temple presence of the Spirit is paralleled in the story of Pentecost in Acts 2. As that event unfolded, some people thought that those who were "filled" with the Spirit (Acts 2:4) and speaking in tongues were actually "filled" with new wine (*gleukos* in 2:13). But whereas the narrative of Acts implicitly *compares* the work of the Spirit with drunkenness by virtue of the crowd's misconception, Ephesians explicitly *contrasts* Spirit-filling with drunkenness, and the logic of the temple seems to be at work in both instances. As we saw in chapter 7, priests were prohibited from drinking alcohol while they served in the temple so that they did not make any mistakes in the administration of cultic worship (cf. Lev 10:8–9; Ezek 44:21). In the same way, the community indwelt with the Spirit of God should likewise avoid the negative influence of excess alcohol on their gatherings. Though drinking alcohol in sacred space was completely prohibited for the priests, such

---

37. See, e.g., Beale, *Temple*, 259–63; Robert L. Foster, "'A Temple in the Lord Filled to the Fullness of God': Context and Intertextuality (Eph. 3:19)," *NovT* 49.1 (2007): 85–96.

38. On how the temple and the body are connected in Paul, see Macaskill, *Union*, 147–59.

39. So Andreas J. Köstenberger, "What Does It Mean to Be Filled with the Spirit? A Biblical Investigation," *JETS* 40.2 (1997): 230.

40. See, e.g., ESV; KJV; NASB; NIV; NLT; NRSVue; Arnold, *Ephesians*, 341, 349–50; Köstenberger, "What Does," 231.

41. So, e.g., Arnold, *Ephesians*, 341, 350.

42. See, e.g., CSB; NET; T. K. Abbott, *A Critical and Exegetical Commentary on the Epistles to the Ephesians and to the Colossians*, ICC (Edinburgh: T&T Clark, 1897), 161; Wallace, *Greek Grammar*, 375.

43. See, e.g., John Paul Heil, "Ephesians 5:18b: 'But Be Filled in the Spirit," *CBQ* 69.3 (2007): 506–16; Thielman, *Ephesians*, 360.

44. For a defense of the dative of content as a category with multiple examples, see Dunne, "Filled with the Spirit," 414–24.

did not apply to early Christian meals, because eucharistic meals characteristically included wine. Nevertheless, the sacredness of the space is underscored by the prohibition of drunkenness. Priestly purity in the Eucharist here in Ephesians 5:18–21 is also fittingly connected to priestly cleansing in baptism a few verses later (Eph 5:26), where Paul says that Christ *cleansed* the church by "washing with water through the word."[45]

The corporate worship that ensues in this passage can also be explained by the background of the temple. Eckhard J. Schnabel's study on singing in Second Temple Judaism and early Christianity maintains that early Christian singing developed out of temple theology.[46] Schnabel notes that there are no sources that unambiguously refer to corporate singing in the synagogue until the fifth to sixth centuries CE (cf. Acts Pil. 16.7–8).[47] Instead, in Second Temple Judaism there were really only two spheres in which singing regularly took place—the cultic and the domestic. Of these two, the primary one was the cult. In the cult, singing hymns and playing appropriate instruments was a priestly, and specifically a Levitical, responsibility while serving in sacred space.[48]

Outside of cultic settings, singing occurred in the home, especially during the celebration of Passover (m. Pesahim 9:3). In fact, Philo says that the home during Passover takes on "the character and dignity of a temple" (*Spec. Laws* 2.148),[49] presumably due in part to the power of singing (cf. *Planting* 126). What Ephesians depicts, then, in its broader context of corporate eucharistic worship and the ensuing household codes, is how the house church, filled with the Spirit, combines the two spheres of singing—the domestic and the cultic—and makes them one and the same. Singing at eucharistic gatherings is partly due to the Eucharist's roots in the Passover, since Jesus and his disciples sang hymns at the Last Supper (Matt 26:30; Mark 14:26), but also due to early Christian conceptions of themselves as the temple of God. The Levitical and priestly connotations that this gives to early Christian worship further supports the suggestion that the prohibition against drunkenness is rooted in the comparison of Spirit-indwelled Christians with ancient priests serving in the temple.

The association of the temple with singing is even expressed by how those under foreign rule and exile could not sing the Lord's song in a foreign land (Ps 137:3–4; Lam 3:14; 5:14; cf. 4 Ezra 10.19–22).

Thus, Ephesians 5:18–21 conveys temple imagery through (1) Spirit-filling, (2) the prohibition against drunkenness, and (3) corporate singing. These three

---

45. Isaac Augustine Morales, *The Bible and Baptism: The Fountain of Salvation*, CBTS (Grand Rapids: Baker Academic, 2022), 180.

46. See Schnabel, "Singing," 312–13. Schnabel's essay is helpful on the theology and background of singing, but he does not make the connections proposed here with Eph 5:19.

47. Schnabel, "Singing," 319.

48. Cf., e.g., 1 Chr 15:22; 25:6–7; 2 Chr 5:12–13; 7:6; 23:12–13; 29:27–30; 34:12; Ezra 2:70; 3:10–13; 7:7, 24; 8:17; Neh 7:1, 43–45, 73; 10:28, 39; 11:22; 12:24, 27–37, 45–47; 13:5, 10; cf. 1 Esd 5:56–62; 1 Macc 13:47; 2 Macc 1:30; Josephus, *Ant.* 9.13.3; 11.3.8; 11.4.2; Philo, *Drunkenness* 94; m. Bikkurim 3:4; m. Middot 2:5; m. Pesahim 5:7; m. Sukkah 5:4; m. Tamid 7:4.

49. C. D. Yonge, *The Complete Works of Philo*, rev. ed. (Peabody, MA: Hendrickson, 2013), 582. Elsewhere, Philo refers to the songs of praise sung at the temple during Passover (*Contempl. Life* 79–89).

elements together highlight the significance that early Christians placed on their eucharistic gatherings in house churches as constituting themselves as sacred practitioners in sacred space.[50] The prohibition against drunkenness, therefore, must be understood in the context of public worship—a context that regularly included wine as part of its eucharistic celebration of Christ's death and ongoing presence in the community. Christ's presence was communicated to them by means of the Spirit's filling, which consecrated their domestic spaces into sacred spaces in which appropriate worship was to be offered to God. Not only that, but the Jews and gentiles indwelt with the Spirit become a new family too (cf. Eph 2:11–22), because a temple, after all, is God's home, and those who belong to God are part of God's family. Drunkenness therefore threatens the unity and sacredness of the community and distorts worship. The ancient priests and Levites were required to completely avoid drunkenness while worshiping in God's presence. How much more, then, should Christians do so, since they are both priests of God and the temple of God, indwelt with God's Spirit?

> Pliny the Younger reports how early Christian gatherings included singing: "they had met regularly before dawn on a fixed day to chant verses alternately among themselves in honour of Christ as if to a god" (*Ep. Tra.* 10.96.7 [Radice, LCL]).

CONCLUSION

Shared meals were meant to reflect the identity and ethos of the church as a unified gathering of diverse people. Further, shared meals were intended to shape and constitute that identity and ethos. With the Eucharist itself, the Spirit is active in bringing about the unity of the participants with the host of the meal—Jesus the Messiah. The wine of the Eucharist, then, is part of the means that God uses to establish and maintain our spiritual bond with Christ and each other. Yet the excessive consumption of that same wine in communal gatherings disrupts the communal instantiation of that deeper reality, as we saw in both 1 Corinthians and Ephesians. Drunkenness should be avoided because it divides the community along socioeconomic lines (1 Cor 11:17–22), and because it is unfitting for a community indwelt by God's Spirit (Eph 5:18–21). Although wine was integral to early Christian worship, drunkenness distorted that worship. This insight about the nature of drunkenness in contexts of worship does not mean that private drunkenness is appropriate or that corporate drunkenness in other contexts is either. Instead, this nuance helps us recognize the ways that drunkenness affects communities, not just individuals, and how it fundamentally distorts our ability to worship God.

As Christians today, we are in the same basic position of early Christians with

---

50. Similar to how Ephesians combines temple and priestly imagery for the church, 1 Peter also portrays early Christians as both a temple built on Christ the cornerstone (1 Pet 2:5–8) and as a priesthood that offers "spiritual sacrifices" (2:5, 9).

their shared meals and eucharistic celebrations. We too are indwelt by God's Spirit and continue to practice the Eucharist as an expression of our union with Christ and each other. We do so as we await the Lord's return, when all things will be restored and the great end-time feast begins—the feast for which the Eucharist is but an appetizer. This means that the issues of alcohol that concerned early Christians apply to us today, and the ways we choose to navigate them roughly two thousand years later are not fundamentally different for us (even as the paths that we choose regarding alcohol can actually be *quite different* for each of us personally). With that in mind, we have at last arrived at a place where it is time to reflect on the relevance of the biblical portrayals of alcohol in the next and final chapter.

RELEVANT QUESTIONS

1. How can contemporary eucharistic practice promote the kind of unity in the body of Christ symbolized in early Christian expression and also make space for fellow believers with distinct scruples and dietary restrictions?
2. Given the role of wine in the Eucharist, what can alcohol teach us about distorted worship?
3. What would it look like to proclaim the Lord's death "as often as you drink" wine, and not simply when partaking of communion?

PART 3

REFLECTING ON RELEVANCE

CHAPTER 17

ALCOHOL FOR TODAY

Throughout this book we have seen how integral alcohol is to Scripture, appearing in nearly every biblical book in some form or another—whether it pertains to production, consumption, medicinal use, ritual offerings, or intoxication. Strikingly, it is absent in only a handful of New Testament epistles—2 Thessalonians, Philemon, and 1–3 John. Because of the sheer prevalence of wine in the Bible, Hanneke Wilson can even assert, one assumes with tongue in cheek, that "the Bible is not suitable reading for teetotalers."[1]

Furthermore, rather than being literary adornment to weightier topics, alcoholic beverages are deployed in different ways and for various purposes (which I grouped together into discrete symbolic varietals). In some cases, the nuances differ vastly from what can be found elsewhere in the Bible, even within the same biblical book or corpus. Proverbs, for example, frequently warns about the dangers of drunkenness (e.g., Prov 23:29–35; 31:4), while also celebrating the proper use of intoxicants (e.g., 3:9–10; 9:1–6). The prophets notably display some of the greatest diversity. Wine in particular is often portrayed as a divine blessing, symbolizing restoration from devastation, including that which came as a result of divine judgment (e.g., Isa 25:6; 55:1–2; Jer 31:5, 12). Yet in other texts, wine symbolizes the divine judgment itself, especially with the cup-of-wrath theme (e.g., Isa 51:17–23; 63:1–6; Jer 25:15–29; 51:7). Joel is a great example, especially for its size, because it gives varied connotations to the same element of viniculture—wine vats that overflow after treading the winepress. Such vats are a sign of God's restorative blessing (Joel 2:24) and an image of God's devastating judgment (3:13), but before the oracle ends Joel envisions God's restorative blessings once more when the mountains drip sweet wine (*asis* in 3:18 [4:18 MT]).

The Bible also contains books that are fairly univocal in their emphasis on alcohol, but which are on polar ends of the spectrum. Revelation and Song of Songs are great examples of this. The connotations they give to wine differ greatly, and they also deploy the imagery of wine to address similar subject matter in different ways. In Revelation wine never has connotations of blessing or restoration. Rather, it is associated with the "sexual deviance" of Babylon, either by way of her performance of that deviance or her punishment for it. But in Song of Songs, wine is only associated with pleasure, and it does so as part of a vibrant portrayal of sexuality.

---

1. Wilson, "Bible," 81.

Indeed, biblical texts do many diverse things with wine, which evoke distinctive senses for the careful reader attentive to nuance.

Within the diversity of biblical images, we can also see canonical development of various themes. The imagery of wine being part of God's covenantal blessing extends from the original promise of the land to Abraham (ch. 5) into the anticipation of a future banquet (ch. 14) that introduces the era of eschatological abundance (ch. 13). This notion of blessing is reinforced through the themes of privation (ch. 11) and parody (ch. 12), where God's good gifts are taken away in judgment and even deployed as judgment for failure to uphold the covenant. The latter notion of wine implemented as judgment develops themes of vulnerability to drunkenness throughout Scripture, which becomes even more pronounced in the New Testament (ch. 10). Furthermore, the ritual use of alcoholic beverages in the worship of ancient Israel within the temple and during sacred festivals (ch. 6) extends into early Christian use of wine in eucharistic meals (ch. 16), modeled after Jesus's Last Supper with his disciples (ch. 15). The Eucharist—which proclaims Christ's death and celebrates his ongoing life in communities united by the Spirit in a world of suffering—is in fact the most robust image of them all. This is because the Eucharist develops the themes of ritual and covenant, including the nuances of blessing and judgment, and it points forward to the promises of abundance. Thus, eucharistic wine is the thematic culmination of a biblical theology of alcohol—a robust blend of all the biblical varietals.

Indeed, alcoholic beverages are not only predominant in our sacred texts, but they continue to be integral to our sacred practices. Judaism is not a teetotaling religion and, as Mark Forsyth states, the Eucharist ensured that the same is true of Christianity.[2] To be sure, plenty of Christians and even entire Protestant denominations abstain completely, but the significance of the Eucharist throughout church history shows that teetotaling is the exception. With the advent of pasteurization in the nineteenth century, it is also a modern phenomenon, despite what Two-Wine theorists would have us believe (cf. ch. 2) and even those who teach that ancient wines were typically quite diluted (cf. ch. 3).

Yet what I take very seriously about the fact that Christian Scripture integrates alcoholic beverages throughout its pages, and that our most central religious practice involves the consumption of wine, is not simply the *compatibility* of alcohol with Christianity. Rather it is that any discussion of the biblical-theological implications of alcohol cannot be reserved for those who personally consume it. A biblical theology of alcohol must be for all Christians—even teetotalers. In this final chapter, then, I will explicate some principles about what the Bible has to say to all contemporary Christians about alcohol.

---

2. Forsyth, *Drunkenness*, 80.

THE GIVER OF ALL GOOD GIFTS

A biblical theology of alcohol underscores the fact that all good things ultimately come from God. Wine and beer are just some of the ways that God blesses creation (see ch. 5). Biblical figures believed this, not simply because they thought that God was responsible for the weather conducive for agricultural growth, but also because they did not understand how fermentation worked. Throughout the ancient world, fermentation was believed to be a supernatural transformation attributable to divine activity. In chapters 2–4 of this book, I sketched out what alcoholic beverages were like in ancient Israel and the surrounding cultures, based primarily on the biblical record. At times I highlighted the major differences in ancient vineyard cultivation and wine production from contemporary trends. But, as Paul Lukacs rightly asserts, the greatest divergence between ancient wines and their modern counterparts is not how they are made, or how they taste, but how we *perceive* them.[3] Due to modern science, we have lost the ancient enchantment with wine and beer in which they were not simply recognized as divine gifts but also as miracles.

Thus, the biblical account of wine and beer as blessings ought to reorient our perspective toward the entirety of creation as God-given. Anyone who does not enjoy adult beverages is not depriving themselves of divine blessing, however, because there are many ways in which God lavishes us with his kindness. A celibate Christian, for example, who voluntarily refrains from the divine gift of sex, can still know countless other blessings. The same is certainly true for those who abstain from alcohol.

Furthermore, a person does not need to enjoy alcohol in order to appreciate the gift that it can be. Imagine a wedding guest at Cana undertaking a Nazirite vow. This person would not have consumed the superior wine that Jesus produced, but they would have surely welcomed the increase in conviviality among the guests and the decrease in shame among the families of the bride and groom for running out of wine. Even while abstaining, these things would inevitably have a positive effect on that person. Indeed, the wine at Cana was a gift to all who were present, regardless of whether they tasted it.

What the theme of wine and beer in the Bible teaches all of us is that we should not grow complacent about God's gifts, especially since they can quickly be taken away (see ch. 11). Instead, we should foster gratitude for the God-given things that we regularly enjoy, whatever they may be. Like Paul said, "whether you eat or drink or whatever you do, do it all for the glory of God" (1 Cor 10:31). As God's covenant people, then, we should consume alcoholic drinks, if we do so, *theologically*, being mindful of what it declares about the goodness of God and also what it demands from us as God's people.

---

3. Lukacs, *Inventing Wine*, 31.

A DIVERSITY OF CONSUMPTIVE HABITS

A biblical theology of alcohol inherently relates to people with diverse consumptive habits, because the Bible itself reflects such a variety (see ch. 8). A handful of biblical characters abstain completely from wine and beer, like John the Baptist and the Rekabites, and a few others fast from it temporarily, such as Daniel, priests, and Nazirites. Yet plenty more characters can be found consuming alcoholic drinks, including Abraham, David, and even Jesus. There is also no real reason to assume that any of the biblical *authors* completely abstained from alcohol. If any did, it would probably have been John the Seer, who wrote Revelation (especially if he did not write the Gospel of John). The only evidence that could suggest this is that Revelation never mentions wine positively (although it never prohibits it either). This is admittedly speculative. But even if we thought it was a reasonable observation, it would only bolster the point that the Bible does not reflect a consistent set of consumptive habits for Christians. Given the biblical witness, we should expect a similar diversity within biblical limits in the church.[4]

> A 2017 study by Barna Group found that 60 percent of "practicing Christians" and 46 percent of evangelicals in America answered yes to the question: "Do you ever drink alcoholic beverages of any kind?"[5]

Yet the rationale underlying much of Christian abstinence from intoxicants does not often map on to the way that the biblical characters chose to abstain. Biblical characters might have fasted or abstained because they were committed to a vow or a particular responsibility, had entered into a time of prayer or mourning, had a concern about contracting ritual impurity through contamination with idols, or wanted to accommodate those people in their community who had qualms about it. No one abstained in the Bible, however, because they believed that consuming alcoholic beverages was always morally wrong, which is perhaps the most common reason for Christian abstinence today. As we have seen (cf. ch. 7), the Bible nowhere prohibits the consumption of alcohol for all people at all times. If I have any interest in changing anyone's mind on this, it is only with regard to how we read the Bible, not one's choice to abstain.

---

4. The church should not be a difficult place to be sober, as Erin Jean Warde laments from her own experience with alcohol addiction as an Episcopal priest. See *Sober Spirituality: The Joy of a Mindful Relationship with Alcohol* (Grand Rapids: Brazos, 2023), 11–25.

5. "The Buzz about Alcohol: America's Views on Booze," *Barna*, October 17, 2017, www.barna.com/research/buzz-alcohol-americas-views-booze.

Christians can commit to abstinence, however, without resorting to inaccurate claims about what the Bible says. To be clear, biblical justification is not needed to support one's decision to remain abstinent. A vegan Christian, for example, neither needs to justify their abstinence from meat with Scripture nor interpret biblical texts about sacrificial meals in the Old Testament in a distinctively vegan way. Vegans can simply choose to abstain, and the same goes for teetotalers.

There are, in fact, plenty of legitimate reasons to abstain from alcohol that have nothing to do with the Bible. These can include rather mundane preferences, such as disliking the taste or the feelings of intoxication. Some abstain out of obedience to local laws, to respect the drinking age, to care for an unborn child during pregnancy, to avoid weight gain, or to exercise caution when operating motor vehicles. Others have serious concerns and conditions related to traumatic experiences involving alcohol abuse, family history of alcoholism, a genetic predisposition to addiction,[6] a medical condition that is provoked by alcohol, or a concern about the health and safety risks related to alcohol use—including such conditions as cancer, cirrhosis of the liver, and strokes.[7]

In the light of some of these associated risks, I. Howard Marshall argued that contemporary Christians need to go "beyond the Bible" and "be 'tighter' than Scripture in view of changed circumstances."[8] Even though the biblical authors do express concerns about the risks of excess consumption, the point is that we now have an even greater knowledge of the hazards of alcohol consumption because of the advent of modern medical science. We have also seen some of those biblical risks compounded by modern technology, as with drunk driving.

It does seem that the purported health benefits of moderate alcohol consumption (i.e., one to two drinks a day) have been overblown,[9] and are increasingly shown to be negligible in the light of new studies.[10] The benefits of moderate alcohol consumption are not physiological, it seems, but rather emotional, mental, and interpersonal. Moderate alcohol consumption stimulates the emotional and cognitive centers of the brain,[11] produces serotonin in the nervous system to dull negative emotions and increase happiness,[12] slightly reduces the chances of being diagnosed

---

6. Theologically speaking, neither a strictly medical model of addiction (purely genetic), nor a strictly moral model of addiction (purely human responsibility), is helpful for understanding addiction holistically. See Stephen R. Haynes, *Why Can't Church Be More Like an AA Meeting? And Other Questions Christians Ask about Recovery* (Grand Rapids: Eerdmans, 2021), 143, cf. 79–89, 143–53.

7. "Alcohol's Effects on the Body," National Institute on Alcohol Abuse and Alcoholism, www.niaaa.nih.gov/alcohols-effects-health/alcohols-effects-body.

8. I. Howard Marshall, "The Gospel Does Not Change but Our Perception of It May Need Revision," in *How I Changed My Mind About Women in Leadership: Compelling Stories from Prominent Evangelicals*, ed. Alan F. Johnson (Grand Rapids: Zondervan, 2010), 147.

9. Contrary to Kreglinger, *Spirituality of Wine*, 164–79; idem, *Soul of Wine*, 97–104.

10. E.g., David Nutt, *Drink? The New Science of Alcohol and Your Health* (New York: Go Hachette, 2020); Samantha Raphelson, "No Amount of Alcohol Is Good for Your Health, Global Study Says," *NPR*, August 24, 2018, www.npr.org/2018/08/24/641618937/no-amount-of-alcohol-is-good-for-your-health-global-study-claims.

11. Miles Thomas, "On Vines and Minds," *The Psychologist* 21.5 (2008): 378–81.

12. David M. Lovinger, "Serotonin's Role in Alcohol's Effects on the Brain," *AHRW* 21.2 (1997): 114–20.

with depression,[13] causes one to experience a cognitive form of myopia that narrows one's focus to connect better with the present situation,[14] fosters a deeper intimacy with loved ones, and promotes creativity and social collaboration.[15]

Yet, even with these benefits, it must be stressed that there are emotional, mental, and interpersonal risks as well, especially when coupled with abuse, where depression is more likely and the interpersonal dangers of myopia increase. Moreover, in situations where the reward centers of the brain are more greatly stimulated, addiction cycles are propelled.[16] Thus, the dangers should be evaluated seriously, and one's decision to consume alcoholic beverages should be part of one's risk calculus and ongoing assessment of the immediate environment.

A Christian might also choose to abstain for other legitimate reasons that are rooted in biblical principles, such as warnings against drunkenness. For example, the official statement on abstinence put out by the Assemblies of God (AGUSA) stresses that it is ultimately unwise for Christians to consume alcohol.[17] We might describe this approach as "creating a hedge around the law." If the "law" in this case is a prohibition against drunkenness, then calling for abstinence—even though the Bible does not—functions like a hedge that keeps people far away from "breaking the law." Such is a legitimate position to hold as people enter membership in the AGUSA, even though a prohibition against excess does not necessitate abstinence from the thing itself.

AGUSA's statement on abstinence, however, does more than just create a "hedge" around drunkenness, since it begins with summative claims about wine and "strong drink" in the Bible that are outdated and inaccurate. That is, it relies at times on an account of ancient wine as excessively diluted (cf. ch. 3), and at other times implicitly on the Two-Wine theory (cf. ch. 2). This is seen, for instance, when they claim that the nature of the *oinos* at the wedding at Cana is unclear, and that "the larger contextual interpretation" of the passage favors the idea that Jesus did not produce something "detrimental." Yet the *context* makes the intoxicating nature of the wine straightforward, given the master of the banquet's comments about drunkenness (John 2:10).[18] Thus, the AGUSA could concede ground exegetically, while still maintaining their same approach to biblical application by "hedging" its requirements.

---

13. Nader Nekvasil and Diana Liu, "In U.S., Moderate Drinkers Have Edge in Emotional Health," *Gallup*, January 25, 2016, https://news.gallup.com/poll/188816/moderate-drinkers-edge-emotional-health.aspx.

14. Malcolm Gladwell, "Case Study: The Fraternity Party," in *Talking to Strangers: What We Should Know about the People We Don't Know* (New York: Little, Brown, and Co., 2019), 187–232.

15. See esp. Slingerland, *Drunk*.

16. "The Cycle of Alcohol Addiction," National Institute on Alcohol Abuse and Alcoholism, www.niaaa.nih.gov/publications/cycle-alcohol-addiction.

17. "Abstinence from Alcohol," Assemblies of God, August 2–3, 2016, https://ag.org/Beliefs/Position-Papers/Abstinence-from-Alcohol.

18. "Abstinence," 7. Cf. also their comments on *yayin* and *tirosh* (p. 5), and their hermeneutically disingenuous harmonization of *shekar* in Deut 14:26 with Num 28:7 (p. 4).

> It is one thing for Christian denominations to promote abstinence, but it is an overreach to actively sponsor legislation imposing abstinence on broader society. Famously, the Women's Christian Temperance Union of the late nineteenth century and early twentieth century helped to propel the era of Prohibition, as codified in the 18th Amendment to the US Constitution. This was then clarified in the Volstead Act, which made the production, importation, purchase, and consumption of beverages with an ABV above 0.5 percent illegal beginning in January, 1920.[19] This was eventually repealed on December 5th, 1933, and the legality of alcohol use in the US was enshrined into law with the 21st Amendment.[20] Despite the fact that the majority of Americans today claim to consume alcohol (60% in 2021),[21] and an even higher percentage claim that consuming alcohol is not morally wrong (78% in 2018),[22] some Christian organizations, like the Southern Baptist Convention (SBC), have expressed an ongoing desire to promote legislation that limits the sale and consumption of alcohol.[23]

Another set of legitimate biblical reasons to abstain can be derived directly from Romans 14–15 (cf. chs. 8, 16). In those texts, Paul speaks into the controversy surrounding diet and other practical ecclesial matters, characterizing the stakeholders on both sides as the "weak" and the "strong." Fundamentally, he declares that whatever does not "come from faith is sin" (Rom 14:23). In other words, if a person does not believe that they have the liberty to consume alcoholic beverages for whatever reason—even if that reason is based on problematic exegetical or theological reasoning—that person should not drink. Only if they can do so in good faith, believing that it is not a sin, should they partake. Additionally, even those who do believe that it is within their Christian freedom to consume alcohol (i.e., the "strong") may choose to abstain for the sake of those who struggle with it—as Paul calls the "strong" to do in certain situations. As a variation on this, one might abstain from alcoholic drinks as a missional or evangelistic strategy among teetotaling populations in order to avoid placing an undue obstacle to faith.[24]

---

19. Forsyth, *Drunkenness*, 217.

20. Although Mississippi did not change their laws until 1966. See Forsyth, *Drunkenness*, 224.

21. See Megan Brenan, "U.S. Alcohol Consumption on Low End of Recent Readings," *Gallup*, August 19, 2021, https://news.gallup.com/poll/353858/alcohol-consumption-low-end-recent-readings/aspx.

22. Jeffrey M. Jones, "Most in U.S. Say Consuming Alcohol, Marijuana Morally OK," *Gallup*, June 4, 2018, https://news.gallup.com/poll/235250/say-consuming-alcohol-marijuana-morally.aspx.

23. SBC, "Resolutions Concerning The Liquor Flood," May 1, 1941, www.sbc.net/resource-library/resolutions/resolutions-concerning-the-liquor-flood. Cf. SBC, "Resolution on Alcohol," June 1, 1988, www.sbc.net/resource-library/resolutions/resolution-on-alcohol-7; idem, "On Alcohol Use in America," June 1, 2006, www.sbc.net/resource-library/resolutions/on-alcohol-use-in-america.

24. Cf. Jayson Casper, "They Will Know We Are Christians by Our Drinks," *CT* (April 2017): 20–21.

Other appeals to biblical principles to support abstinence might be well-intentioned, but they are not usually good places to turn. For example, Christians will sometimes refrain from alcohol because they want to avoid the "appearance of evil" (1 Thess 5:22 KJV) or looking like the world (cf. Rom 12:2; 1 John 2:15–17). Others will abstain because their "bodies are temples" (1 Cor 6:19). Insofar as these sentiments reflect a desire to avoid drunkenness, they are good principles to follow—but not for mere alcohol consumption. The simplest reason for this is because alcoholic beverages were stored and ritually libated at the temple (cf. ch. 6), not to mention that these concerns never seemed to keep Jesus, the temple of God (John 2:18–22; cf. 1:14), from consuming or even producing wine. As he did these things he even gained a reputation, appearing to be "a glutton and a drunkard" (Matt 11:19; Luke 7:34).

> I often wonder why Appalachian snake-handling Pentecostals, who are willing to drink poison in church (cf. Mark 16:18), would not countenance the idea of swapping their strychnine for red wine.

If Christian teetotalers are eager to root their abstinence in biblical patterns, there are a few that they can resource. Norman Geisler, for example, contends that Christians should be like Nazirites and voluntarily choose to abstain from alcohol.[25] Setting aside the fact that Nazirite abstinence is temporary in Numbers 6, Christians certainly *could* (not should) vow to completely abstain. Additionally, Christians who do drink definitely should consider how they might resource the example of Nazirites and other biblical figures who fasted from wine and beer for periods of time, even for shorter durations as with Daniel and the priests. Both feasting and fasting within Christianity highlight the tension of the "already" and the "not yet" presence of the inaugurated kingdom of God, with both expressions pointing forward to the coming arrival of the kingdom in its fullness. Individual Christians can experience both in their own lives, including (but not limited to) observing the liturgical cycle of feasting (i.e., Christmas and Easter) and fasting (i.e., Lent), and whole groups of Christians can commit to fasting from things like alcohol right alongside other groups of Christians who do not, modeled after Jesus and John the Baptist. Another pattern for complete abstinence is expressed by one of my very good friends, Andrew, who is also a biblical scholar. He made a promise to God at a very young age, because of his parents' encouragement, that he would never touch alcohol, resembling the promise of the Rekabites to their father (Jer 35:1–19). Andrew has kept his word, even though he does not believe that he is bound to that lifestyle for any other reason than the promise itself. Another pattern of abstinence that can be resourced from Scripture is displayed by one of my students, Lissa, who explained in a seminary course I taught, "Wine and Meals in the Bible,"

> The "appearance of evil" is not the best translation of 1 Thessalonians 5:22 (KJV), because Paul is not prohibiting everything that might *appear* to be evil, but rather every particular *form* in which evil manifests itself.

---

25. Geisler, "Wine-Drinking," 54.

that she abstains from alcoholic drinks except for her ritual use of eucharistic wine. Her own self-reflection on this led her to connect her experience to the story of Hannah, who is someone who abstained from alcohol (1 Sam 1:12–18; cf. 1:9), and yet nevertheless recognized the ritual role of wine in sacred space (1:24).

THE RITUAL USE OF ALCOHOL

A biblical theology of alcohol affirms the importance of Christian rituals, not least because wine is incorporated into one of the main rituals of the church. As Christians, we are a covenant people with rituals, just like ancient Israel, even though our rituals do not include libations or tithes of wine or the same kind of festive consumption of wine on holy days. Yet the New Testament's use of temple imagery in relation to wine deepens its ritual significance for us (cf. chs. 13–16). Furthermore, the new covenant that Christ inaugurated is celebrated in the ritual practice of consuming bread and wine, as he taught his disciples at the Last Supper. The new covenant, then, does not entail a different approach to alcoholic drinks than the covenants that preceded it. In fact, when Jeremiah envisioned the new covenant (Jer 31:31–34), he spoke of thriving viticulture (31:5, 12).

We should recognize, as well, that the ritual use of alcoholic beverages across the covenantal scheme of Scripture sheds light on their value for God's covenant people. As we have seen, wine and beer were gifts of God's blessing and signposts of restoration from devastation. So the ritual use of an alcoholic drink reminds the consumer of the blessings associated with our covenant relationship with God. It reminds us of the covenantal demands placed upon us as well, and that our lives are just as dependent on God's grace and love, even in the twenty-first century. Since we are covenant people who consume wine ritually, therefore, drunkenness is the distortion of worship.

When compared to baptism, the repetition of the Eucharist singles it out as "the central Christian action."[26] This appreciation of the centrality of the Eucharist is often lost within churches where wine is no longer used in the service, though admittedly not always. The churches that preserve the use of wine in the Eucharist, however, maintain a strong appreciation of the role of ritual and Christian precedent. These churches usually regard the Eucharist as a means of grace, or a sacrament. Churches that use grape juice exclusively (or dealcoholized wine) are usually the ones who tend to practice the Eucharist in a nonweekly format. These churches tend to regard the Eucharist as an ordinance instead of a sacrament, meaning that it is a ritual commanded by Jesus, but is not effectually a means of grace. To be sure, there are

---

26. N. T. Wright, *The Meal Jesus Gave Us: Understanding Holy Communion*, rev. ed. (Louisville: Westminster John Knox, 2015), 37.

good reasons why many churches have adopted the use of grape juice,[27] regardless of one's sacramentalism, or at least incorporate grape juice as an option alongside wine (just as gluten-free bread is often an option), especially for those who struggle with alcohol or are deemed too young. Since the Eucharist is all about unity, we certainly should not divide over the use of wine in the ritual.

But whether we use wine or juice, more important in my view is the frequency of the practice. Often people will say the infrequency of their congregational celebration of the Eucharist is designed to ensure the special place of the ritual. This argument lacks consistency, however, since we do not make the same sorts of claims about musical worship or the sermon. These things are incorporated into our weekly patterns of church life *because* they are so important, and we would not consider that their great significance means that we should only include them on a monthly, quarterly, or semiannual basis.

Using grape juice for the Eucharist, though, can hinder our experience of it (and sometimes, if this move is not safeguarded, it can inadvertently make space for other adjustments to eucharistic norms, like when my youth group used Nutter Butter™ cookies and orange soda). The use of a common cup, where the congregation receives the wine from a single source, is consistent with biblical descriptions (cf. Matt 26:27–29; Mark 14:23–25; Luke 22:17–18; 1 Cor 10:16, 21; 11:25–26) and reinforces the point of the ritual, which is to underscore our unity as the body of Christ (cf. 1 Cor 12:12–13). Yet outside of certain traditions, it is not commonly used. Now that we know more about bacteria and other microbes, the common cup can be achieved in a more sanitary fashion through the use of a fortified wine, which can be as high as 20 percent ABV.[28] The practice that retains the common cup in the most sanitary fashion is intinction, when congregants dip the bread into the wine before consuming it, as we did at my local church prior to the COVID-19 pandemic. But drinking directly from the common cup, which I have only experienced once in my life while at an Anglican church in Sydney, was profoundly moving for me.

The eucharistic experience, though, that convinced me the most that I had been missing something was an earlier time in which I visited a small Baptist church in Paris. I was living there one summer, studying at L'Institut Catholique de Paris to improve my French for my doctoral studies. At one point during the church service, I was able to track with enough of what was going on to know that we were about to take communion. When the silver communion tray was being passed around with individualized communion cups, it was a familiar sight. My low-church background in the States prepared me well for this. I would grab one of the thimble-sized cups,

---

27. On the development and rationale behind this shift within Methodism specifically, see Jennifer L. Woodruff Tait, *The Poisoned Chalice: Eucharistic Grape Juice and Common-Sense Realism in Victorian Methodism* (Tuscaloosa: University of Alabama Press, 2011).

28. Fortified wines are stronger and sweeter than normal wines, achieved by adding a grape-based spirit before full fermentation to kill the yeast and retain the wine's sugar content.

pass the tray along to the next person, and quickly down the grape juice in one gulp. Except I was not at all prepared for the fact that what I drank was not grape juice. It was wine. Apparently, my French was not that great after all. This was the first time that I had ever had wine with communion, and I was so startled by it, particularly because I did not drink it like it was wine, that it *burned* going down. As I was disoriented by the fact that I had just consumed wine at nine o'clock in the morning and had a burning sensation in my throat and chest, I was suddenly overwhelmed by a thought that I had never had before while taking communion—*Where, O Death, is your sting?* For the first time in my eucharistic experience, the Eucharist actually made me think of death, Jesus's death to be sure, but also the death of death itself. The cloying grape juice that I normally consume in the Eucharist never provided me with that kind of experiential knowledge before. As I sat there in that Baptist church, the eucharistic wine suddenly compelled me to think of the eschatological banquet that will celebrate the defeat of death, when everyone at the table has the best food and wine placed before them (Isa 25:6–8). Indeed, the wine in that Baptist church was truly a foretaste of that banquet, as the Eucharist is intended to be, just like the grape clusters brought by those scouting out the promised land signified the inheritance that the Israelites would soon receive.[29]

I want to be abundantly clear: we do not need the sting of wine to know or to believe that death will die because of Christ's shed blood, and we do not necessarily need a common cup to affirm the unity that the Eucharist provides. Even if we were not willing to adopt a common cup or the use of wine for communion in our local churches, we should remind our congregations about the kind of *experiential knowledge* that they might be missing. These ritual practices can provide beautiful experiences to help us *remember* what we ought to remember, as Jesus taught us to do with the Eucharist.

CREATION AND EMBODIMENT

A biblical theology of alcohol affirms the goodness of the *physical* world. Indeed, it supports our environmental concerns in the present day, not least because vintners experience the ecological effects of climate change since so much of their work comes down to regional weather patterns.[30] To plant a vineyard is to be rooted in a place, and to consume wine is to ingest part of that place—*terroir*. For a vineyard to thrive, certain ecological conditions must exist, or else the grapes will not grow properly or the finished project will be diminished. One does not need to appreciate wine in order to recognize how ecological stewardship, which directly impacts wine production,

---

29. Wright, *Meal*, 60; cf. 57–61.
30. Cf. Lee Hannah et al., "Climate Change, Wine, and Conservation," *PNAS* 110.17 (2013): 6907–12.

is part of our call as humanity to steward the world that God has given us. Indeed, for those of us who imbibe, we should consider what stewardship looks like with our consumer choices, including the producers that we enjoy and the merchants from whom we purchase. Mindfulness in this area looks like many things, not least supporting regenerative practices in areas of agriculture and sustainability in terms of production, bottling, and distribution.

Alcohol in the Bible is in fact great medicine against the ills of Gnosticism that continue to infect Christianity, with its insistence on a dualism that prioritizes our souls over our bodies and heaven over earth.[31] The biblical account is much more integrated than this framework imagines, and alcoholic beverages serve to bolster this fact. We do not need to consume alcohol personally to appreciate this integration, but the repetitive references to alcoholic drinks throughout Scripture affirm that our bodily appetites are not wrong or gross, and neither are they ever going away. Furthermore, it confirms that the material nature of creation will be part of the eschaton, not just the present state of things. Given the role of wine in this regard in biblical literature, we can see how it represents the physical world since, as Peter Green says, "Every sip of wine is a sip of the earth, sky, and sun—it is a microcosm of creation."[32] Insofar as it brings us pleasure, wine is "the *telos* of creation,"[33] an experience of "the blessings of God's final consummation offered to us in history."[34] The full biblical account of wine and beer thus encourages our delight in God's creation, and it establishes that our bodily pleasures are part of God's design for human existence, even for redeemed humanity in the new creation.

ART AND CREATIVITY

A biblical theology of alcohol affirms the breadth of human artistry. A delightful beverage, whether a well-structured wine from Bordeaux, a hoppy IPA from San Diego, or a single malt scotch from Islay reflects God's goodness to us. But it also reflects a craft that humans have cultivated. Human creativity in the realm of alcoholic drinks is just one expression of the *imago Dei*, not least because God is frequently portrayed as a vintner, or wine producer (e.g., Isa 5:1–7; John 15:1–2). As divine image-bearers, we are called to steward creation (Gen 1:26–28), and there are many ways in which that stewardship can open us up to artistic expression through the natural world. This does not have to be the production of alcoholic beverages, obviously, but it can include it. In fact, Christians have been some of the best artisans within the alcohol industry of the last several centuries. In the Catholic tradition, alcohol has been vital to the work of several monastic orders, such as the wine of

---

31. Rightly Kreglinger, *Spirituality of Wine*, 82.
32. Green, "Vineyards," 357.
33. Green, "Vineyards," 124.
34. Green, "Vineyards," 360.

the Benedictines and Cistercians, the beer of the Trappists, and the liqueur of the Carthusians (Chartreuse). In the Protestant tradition, the most notable example is the world-famous stout produced in Dublin—Guinness.[35]

However, the artistry of wine and beer in the ancient world is often obscured by the common misunderstanding that they were consumed simply as a necessity due to the inaccessibility of clean water (cf. ch. 3). As we saw in chapter 4, wine was more accessible to the elite, and so the average person would have consumed it during times of increased celebration, such as holy days and religious festivals. Thus, wine had particular religious associations for many people, in keeping with its ritual function discussed above. This in itself pushes past the notion that it was strictly a necessity (both for the elite and the commoners). Furthermore, the artistry of wine is seen in multiple places in Scripture. The addition of various ingredients reflects a desire to enhance the wine or to create new flavor combinations (e.g., Song 7:2; 8:2). Language regarding superior kinds of wine reflects a refined appreciation on the part of ancient consumers—such as when the young woman in the Song of Songs says that the "best wine [*yayin*]" is in the mouth of her lover (7:9 [7:10 MT]), or when Jesus says that people know that old wine is preferable to new wine (Luke 5:39), or indeed when the great wine that Jesus made at Cana is distinguished from inferior ones (John 2:10).

Thus, Scripture's witness to alcoholic beverages affirms our creative efforts and our artistic expression in general, and specifically in the culinary realm. What we consume nourishes us and helps us survive. But it can also be savored and made to be even more pleasing. When it comes to consuming alcoholic drinks today, the last thing it should be is a necessity. We do not need alcoholic beverages in order to survive, obviously, but it can enhance our appreciation of life. If it does not enhance life, we should not drink it. There are plenty of other ways for one's life to be enhanced. But if we feel like we *need* alcohol in order to feel good, or to cope with a situation, or to transform into a particular version of ourselves, these can be warning signs that we are *using* alcohol, rather than cultivating an enjoyment of it. Any kind of approach to alcoholic drinks that is strictly pragmatic—drinking alcohol for alcohol's sake—is dangerous.

If you are a coffee drinker like me, you may have a pragmatic approach in the morning—*just give me some caffeine!* I am a bit of a coffee snob, so I love to make single-origin pour-overs in the morning (and then again at my office with my duplicate setup). But sometimes when I am in my office I can be pressed for time and decide instead to use the community Keurig machine, because I would like a little boost before a meeting or class. When I do this, I know I am being fairly utilitarian

---

35. Cf. Stephen Mansfield, *The Search for God and Guinness: A Biography of the Beer That Changed the World* (Nashville: Thomas Nelson, 2014).

because I do not enjoy Keurig coffee at all. In the world of alcoholic beverages, however, I have no interest in several brands or styles of beer, wine, or whiskey, etc., even if they are the only things on offer. Choosing to drink rubbish because we would rather have some alcohol rather than none is a dangerously pragmatic outlook that we should avoid (not least because pragmatism with alcohol can lead to drunkenness, unlike coffee). When alcoholic beverages strictly become a means to something else, rather than artistic expressions to be savored on their own, we can be susceptible to abusing them.

THE ABUSE OF GOD'S GIFTS

A biblical theology of alcohol recognizes that alcoholic beverages can be misused and abused like any of God's good gifts. In many circles today, alcohol carries with it a stigma for ripping families apart and inciting violence. Sin is a distorting power that can cause us to be unable to see the beauty in God's design or to incite us to skew it. The kinds of theological associations that we see with wine and beer in Scripture are often lost on people, and for many, unfortunately, they may not even be retrievable.

The Bible itself warns about drunkenness, so it is not naive about the potential for misuse. Scripture portrays many instances of drunkenness causing vulnerability that makes one susceptible to harm and exploitation (ch. 10), which is presented symbolically in the form of the cup of wrath (ch. 12). These can certainly function as implicit warnings about drunkenness. Yet when Scripture is overtly critical of drunkenness, it is highly nuanced. To start, it is critical of the kinds of things that one might do when drunk (i.e., sins of commission), which would constitute a sin against God. It is also concerned about what one might be incapable of doing while drunk (i.e., sins of omission). Hence, those with great responsibility, like priests, kings, and pastors, receive special attention with regard to alcohol consumption. Biblical texts likewise denounce habitual drunkenness in particular, which provides ample opportunity for all sorts of sins of commission and omission. The Bible also condemns drunkenness that arises from the worship of a foreign deity. Yet Scripture's overt critique of drunkenness is primarily directed at the elite, who have more resources than everyone else (cf. ch. 4).[36] For people struggling to survive, abundance is a blessing. But for people who have more than they need, excess is morally problematic.[37] For those of us in affluent societies, this is something we should reflect on critically. There is space in Scripture for instances of heightened intoxication in safe and celebratory settings (cf. John 2:10). But habitual drunkenness, and drunkenness that leads to sins of omission or commission, the ritual worship

---

36. Dubach, *Trunkenheit*, 285–86.

37. Welton, "Too Much Food," 358.

of gods other than YHWH, or the neglect or exploitation of the poor receive ample critique in the biblical material.

Scripture thus provides us with a general principle regarding drunkenness that should guide us on the issue of consumption. All Christians, whether we drink or abstain, should adhere to the biblical warnings about drunkenness. In fact, abstinence from drunkenness is an abstinence that all Christians can pursue.[38] This is true regardless of the kind of alcoholic drink in view. Paul says that we should not get drunk on wine (Eph 5:18), which of course does not mean that drunkenness by another means is permitted. But it also does not suggest that we should abstain from anything stronger in ABV than wine. The strength is not the issue; the issue is how much and how quickly. This is why the concept of a "standard drink" today is so important (defined as containing 0.6 ounces of pure ethanol).[39] Just because a beverage is stronger than another one does not necessarily mean that more alcohol is being consumed when you factor in proportions. For example, 12 ounces of 5 percent ABV beer is roughly equivalent to 5 ounces of 12 percent wine or 1.5 ounces of a 40 percent whiskey.[40] Thus, although distilled spirits did not exist in the ancient world, they are not off-limits to Christians, biblically speaking, if the principle of drunkenness is upheld.[41] Most people at a Scottish pub, for example, can easily enjoy a dram or two of scotch over the course of a delightful conversation without even getting tipsy—which is not at all the same thing as taking shots in quick succession.

As Christians, we should strive to ensure that drunkenness does not characterize our lives, whether that is through moderation or abstinence. In Galatians, drunkenness is one of the vices that will keep a person from inheriting the kingdom of God (Gal 5:21), which is set in contrast to the fruit of the Spirit (5:22–23). Among the ninefold fruit of the Spirit, like a single cluster of grapes,[42] is the virtue of self-control. Virtues are habits that we embody, which are empowered by the work of the Spirit. Self-control in the area of alcohol consumption will look different for various Christians, but in context it is set against the vice of drunkenness, which pertains to the realm of the flesh that has been crucified with Christ (5:24).

Self-control is thus only attainable, even if imperfectly expressed, through repeated reliance on the Spirit. Unlike an approach to ethics that might insist on universal applicability, the Spirit may lead us to personally approach alcohol in different ways, but all toward that same goal of producing the fruit of self-control. As Jesus said with reference to his own feasting relative to John the Baptist's abstinence, "wisdom is proved right by her deeds" (Matt 11:18–19). This means that the fruit of

---

38. Rightly Kreglinger, *Spirituality of Wine*, 42.

39. "Understanding the Dangers of Alcohol Overdose," National Institute on Alcohol Abuse and Alcoholism, www.niaaa.nih.gov/publications/brochures-and-fact-sheets/understanding-dangers-of-alcohol-overdose.

40. "Understanding the Dangers."

41. The principle of drunkenness applies to the recreational use of mind-altering drugs.

42. Butler and Heskett, *Divine Vintage*, 125.

their personal practices, if you like, is what will vindicate how they have both chosen to live. To paraphrase Paul, neither abstinence nor feasting is anything, but a new creation is everything (Gal 6:15).

GOD IS EAGER TO RESTORE

Although the divine gifts of alcoholic beverages can be seriously abused, a biblical theology of alcohol suggests that this is not the last word on the matter. Not only is God eager to restore the damage caused by alcohol, but additionally the Bible reveals that God will restore *with alcohol*. The prophets anticipate an abundance of wine associated with the restoration of creation, which will be marked off with a great festive celebration (cf. chs. 13–14).

> There are a few wineries in Israel-Palestine that claim their wines fulfill biblical prophecy like Amos 9:13–14. This, of course, increases their marketability, but it misses the fact that these passages imagine the consummation of creation. They look forward to a time beyond us when all things are restored and forgiven, which is signaled by an unprecedented volume of wine.

This is all the more striking when we recognize that an abundance of wine is how God chooses to respond to a people that had broken the covenant in multiple ways. Thus, rather than always being a sin from which God's people need to be forgiven, alcohol can actually be seen to represent God's forgiveness, grace, and mercy. As Christians today, we can choose to live in the light of where redemption is headed by consuming alcohol as a foretaste of that restoration, or we can choose to save up our appetites. Either way, if we belong to God, regardless of our approach to alcohol, we will all have a seat at his banqueting table. But not only can we consume alcohol in an anticipatory fashion that is consistent with God's purposes for his people and his world, we can also begin to flip the script now and see the redemptive role of alcohol realized in small ways, even if incompletely, prior to Christ's return.

As an illustration of this to close out this book, my dad, John Joseph, is a teetotaler. He has no moral or biblical objection to alcohol, but he refuses to drink it. He has told me on a few occasions that he can count on one hand all of the times that he ever tried to drink a beer or a daiquiri; it's just not for him. The most colorful story involves him puking in the bushes after drinking just a few sips of a Heineken at a bar somewhere in Oklahoma. He usually says that he just dislikes the flavor, if anyone asks. But there is actually a deeper reason.

The reason for my dad's abstinence stems from a traumatic experience that he had as a kid. He is the oldest of five children, and his father was an alcoholic. On top of that, his father chose to leave my grandmother when my dad was only nine years old. In one of our old family scrapbooks, which is full of pictures of Dad and his siblings back in the 1960s and early 1970s, there is a note that my grandfather left for my dad, whom he called "Jack." He wrote, "You're the man of the house now." I have no idea why my dad kept it or why we still have it. But needless to say,

Dad grew up resentful and bitter toward his father, and so his disgust with alcohol is actually a visceral reaction to his father and how he abandoned their family. Alcohol destroyed my dad's relationship with his father, and he has never been able to gain a personal appreciation for the taste of it since.

But that is not where the story ends. Believe it or not, although my dad does not drink alcohol, he actually brews beer and knows quite a bit about it. He can tell you the names of head brewmasters of several breweries around the country, explain the differences between various styles of beer, and describe to you, with delight, what every beer smells like—he *loves* to smell everyone's beer. On the one hand, this is not strange at all within our family dynamic. My dad is a craps dealer in Las Vegas, but he is a dealer who does not gamble himself. Before that he was a chef, and cooking has remained a passion of his. But he does not need to consume any of it to derive happiness from cooking. My mom is a vegan, and even though Dad would make a rubbish vegan himself, he cooks special meals for my mom nearly every day. So, the idea of my dad being a homebrewer who does not drink alcohol—like a beer version of Walter White—makes total sense, if you got to know him.

On the other hand, why would he bother to take up the pastime of brewing, especially given his background? The answer is simple—he did it because he loves me. It was his idea to buy me a homebrewer kit for my birthday, and it was his idea then to buy more equipment, try new techniques, sift through homebrewing forums online, use different ingredients, and make different styles. My dad has never tried anything that we made—not even the incredible stout that my *Doktorvater*, Prof. N. T. Wright (who is a Guinness man through and through), said was "three or four notches past Guinness!" But Dad loves making beer because, unlike his father, he loves his family. What ruined his relationship with his father has only bolstered his relationship with me. My dad has experienced how alcohol can bring people together, and he has never needed to consume it to do so. At family holidays and get-togethers, my dad continues to be genuinely interested in learning all about the beers and wines we share and the cocktails we make—especially how they smell—and he is always eager to participate in every ritual "cheers" that we do. He usually does so with his water bottle, because he, too, wants to partake of the joys that alcohol can bring.

That is one of the small signposts that I have experienced pointing to the powerful way in which alcohol's destructive power, though very real, will not dictate how this story ends.

SCRIPTURE AND OTHER ANCIENT LITERATURE INDEX

Old Testament

Genesis

Reference	Page
1–3	65
1:1	190
1:2	126
1:9	126
1:26–28	126, 248
1:28	177
2:7	126
2:25	126
3:7, 10–11, 21	126
3:17–19	61, 126
3:19	119
5:29	126
6	127
6:1–4	127
7:19	126
8:1–5	126
8:4	126
8:21	83
9:1, 7	126
9:20	126
9:20–21	126
9:24–27	127
11:30	57
12:1–2	57
12:1–9	58
12:4	57
12:4–9	57
14:18	58, 216
15:1–6	57
15:12–16	57
15:17–21	57
16–25	58
16:1	57
17:1–7, 16	57
17:8	57
17:19–21	58
19:2–3	130
19:5	130
19:8a	130
19:8b	130
19:30	130
19:31	128
19:32–35	128
19:33, 35	128
19:36–38	128
20:6, 10, 13	130
21:8	58
22:17	57
24:1–9	58
25:25	162
25:29–34	58
26:30	211
27:25	58
27:28	58
27:29	58
27:37	58
27:39–40	58
27:41	59
29:22	128
31:43–54	211
37–50	59
38:12–13	128
38:14–15	129
38:24–26	130
40:1–3	51
40:9–13	51
40:20	51
43:34	125
44:1–2, 5, 12, 16–17	125
49:1–27	59
49:8–10	59
49:11	14
49:11–12	14, 59
49:11a	59
49:11b	59
49:12	14, 59

Exodus

Reference	Page
4:25	129
7:3	192
7:20	192
12:7–12	211
12:22	191
12:46	191
13:5	59
22:4	43
22:28–29	43, 76
22:29 [22:28 MT]	21
23:8–13	43
24:8	211–212
24:11	211
25:9	189
25:29	78
27:3	185
29:40	79
29:40–41	78
30:9	78
32:6	211, 225
34:21	43
34:26	43, 76
37:16	78
38:3	185
40:34–35	189, 230

Leviticus

Reference	Page
2:11	80
10:8–9	230
10:9	24, 80, 88, 106
10:9–10	180
10:10	88
11	87
11:7	87
16:20	189
17:13–14	87, 164
19:9–10	43
19:23	42
19:23–25	126
19:24	42, 76
19:25	42
23:13	79
23:22	43
23:23–25	66
23:24	66
23:34	68
23:36	68
23:37	78
25:1–4	43

25:10–12 43	18:27, 30 77	14. 87
25:19–23 63	19:13 189	14:8 87
26:3–5 63	20:5a 61	14:22–23 .... 43, 76, 77
26:5 63	20:5b 61	14:23 77
26:9 63	20:17 43	14:24–26 77
26:16–17 64	21:22 43	14:26 ... 24, 25, 77, 80, 86, 87, 242
26:20 64	22:24 43	14:28–29 77
26:25 64	23:24 163	15:4–5 63
26:30–31 64	28:1–8 79	15:14 43
26:32–33 64	28:7 ...... 24, 28, 79, 80, 87, 242	16:3 211
26:34–35 64	28:7–10 .... 25, 86	16:13 68
26:42–44 64	28:9–10 79	16:20 63
26:44 64	28:14 .... 79, 87	18:1–5 77
27:30 76	28:14–15 80	18:4 .... 43, 76, 77
	28:16–25 78	20:6 42–43
Numbers	28:24 78	21. 124
4:7 78	28:26–31 78	21:18–21 89
4:14 185	29:6 78	21:20 89
5:11–15 165	29:11 78	21:21 89
5:17 165	29:16, 18–19, 21–22, 24–25, 27–28,	22:9 42
5:18 165	30–31, 33–34, 37–39 78	23:24–25 43
5:19–22 165	29:24, 27, 30, 33, 37 79	24:18–22 43
6. .... 98, 99, 244	29:35 68	25:15 63
6:1–2 88	32:9 60	26:1–2 .... 43, 76
6:3 .... 21, 24, 25, 26, 27, 80		26:1–11 77
6:3–4 88	**Deuteronomy**	26:12–13 77
6:4, 8, 12 89	1:8, 16–17, 31–32 63	27–32. 141
6:5 .... 43, 88, 106	1:24–25 60	27:3 63
6:6–8 88	4:25–26, 40 63	28:1–2, 9, 11, 13–14 63
6:13 89	4:27 64	28:3–5, 9, 11 63
6:15, 17 89	4:30–31 64	28:7 63
6:18 89	6:2–3,18. 63	28:12 63
6:20 89	6:11 60	28:15 64
6:21 88	7:9–11 64	28:18, 20–21, 38–39, 42, 59–61.. 64
9:12 191	7:12–13 63	28:24 64
13. 61	7:13 63	28:30 .... 43, 64
13:20 60	7:14 63	28:33 64
13:23–24 60	7:15 63	28:39 64
14. 61	7:16 63	28:45, 58–59 64
14:22 192	7:19 192	28:47–50, 63–64 64
15:4–5 79	8:1, 6–7, 11–20 63	28:51 64
15:5 79	8:7–9 60	29:3 192
15:7 79	11:3 192	29:6 .... 61, 80
15:9–10 79	11:13–14 63	29:6 [29:5 LXX]. 24
15:24 79	11:14 .... 20, 63	29:20–28 64
16:14 61	11:17 64	30:9–10 64
16:30, 32–34 196	11:26–28 63	30:18 63
18:1–32 77	12:1 63	30:19 142
18:12 77	12:13–19 118	31:14–15 189
18:12–13 .... 43, 76	12:17–18 .... 43, 76	32:8 127
18:25–32 77	12:17–19 77	32:14 .... 14, 19, 85

SCRIPTURE AND OTHER ANCIENT LITERATURE INDEX

32:32–33 166	14:9 98	25:36 . . . . 50, 132
32:34 166	14:10 98	25:36–37 18
32:35 166	14:12, 17 98	25:37 132
32:37–38 81	14:19 99	25:38 132
32:42 . . . . 14, 163	15:4–5 73	30:1 133
32:46–47 63	15:5 99	30:16 133
33 64–65	15:15–17 98	31:13 103
33:28 65	16:1 98	
34:11 192	16:4 14	*2 Samuel*
	16:17 98	1:12 103
Joshua	16:23–24 82	3:20, 27 133
5:10–12 69	16:25 . . . . 19, 133	6:17 189
9:4, 13 46	17:5 82	6:19 41
9:13 LXX 203	18:24, 31 82	7:12–17 186
22:29 189	19:3–9 130	11:11 . . . . 100, 129, 185
24:13 60	19:6 . . . . 19, 130	11:13 . . . . 100, 129
24:17 192	19:9 19	11:15–17 130
	19:19 130	13:1–22 133
Judges	19:21–22 130	13:23 . . . . 128, 133
2:3 82	19:22 . . . . 19, 130	13:28 . . . . 18, 133
2:12 82	19:23 130	16:1–2 46
2:17, 19 82	19:24 130	
3:6 82	19:25–30 130	*1 Kings*
3:7 82	21:15–24 129	1:5 133
3:24 129	21:19–21 129	1:9–10, 19, 25 133
6:10 82	21:20–21 42	1:32–35 133
6:11 44		1:39 189
6:13 192	*Ruth*	1:41 133
6:31 82	2:14 23	2:13–25 133
7:25 160	3:2–3 129	3:5–9 63
8:2 160	3:4 129	3:15 63
8:33 82	3:7 . . . . 19, 129	4:20 63
8:34 82		4:25 . . . . 42, 63
9 81–83	*1 Samuel*	4:29–34 63
9:1–5 81	1:1 100	6–8 63
9:7 83	1:9 100	7:45 185
9:13 . . . . 20, 82, 83	1:11 . . . . 100, 101	8 186
9:15 82	1:12–18 245	8:10–11 . . . . 189, 230
9:27 . . . . 44, 82, 83	1:13–14 100	8:35–38 84
9:49 83	1:15 . . . . 27, 80, 100	9:1–9 63
9:52–55 83	1:19 245	9:7–8 63
10:6 82	1:20 100	10:5, 21 50
10:13–14 82	1:22 100	13:8–9 99
10:16 82	1:24 . . . . 79, 100, 101, 245	13:20–25 99
11:24 82	10:3 46	16:9 133
13:2–3 98	15 68	17:1 64
13:4 . . . . 24, 80, 98	16:20 46	17:14–16 53
13:5 . . . . 98, 99	22:7 48	17:18 LXX 53
13:7 . . . . 24, 80, 98	25:5–11 132	18:41–42 64
13:14 . . . . 24, 25, 80, 98	25:8 . . . . 128, 132	19:6–8 100
14:5, 8 98	25:18 . . . . 46, 132	20:12 . . . . 100, 133

20:16 . . . . 100, 133	7:10 19	12:44 78
20:20 133	7:12–14 84	13:4–9 78
21:1–2 48	8:14–15 186	13:5 . . . . 78, 231
21:1–16 161	9:4, 20 50	13:10 231
21:3–4 48	20:9 84	13:12 78
21:7 19	23:12–13 231	13:13 78
21:9, 12 103	23:18 186	13:15 43
	26:10 . . . . 41, 48	
2 Kings	29:27–30 231	***Esther***
5:26 48	29:35a 78	1:3 67
6:27 142	31:5 . . . . 43, 76	1:5 67
7:8 133	32:27–29 50	1:7 . . . . 50, 67
9:33 161	32:28 50	1:7, 10 67
16:13, 15 81	34:12 231	1:8a 67
18:27 142	35:1–19 69	1:8b 67
18:31 142		1:9 67
18:31 LXX 142	***Ezra***	1:10 . . . . 18, 67
18:32 142	2:70 231	1:11 67
19:29 142	3:10–13 231	1:12 67
23:21–22 69	6:9 80	2:18 67
24:17 149	6:9–10 79	2:19 67
25:1–7 149	7:7, 24 231	3:1–2 67
25:8–21 149	7:17 79	3:6, 13 . . . . 66, 104
25:12 . . . . 48, 144	7:22 . . . . 43, 76	3:7 66
	8:17 231	3:12 103
1 Chronicles		3:15 . . . . 68, 131
6:31–32 186	***Nehemiah***	4:11 104
9:29 78	1:11 52	4:16 . . . . 68, 103
10:12 103	2:1 52	4:17 LXX 103
11:18 81	5:3 49	5:4–5 131
12:39–40 [12:40–41 MT] 50	5:4 49	5:4–6 67
15:1 186	5:5 49	5:6 . . . . 67, 131
15:16 186	5:11 49	5:8 . . . . 67, 131
15:22 231	5:13–14 49	5:9 . . . . 19, 131
16:1 189	5:15 52	6:14 131–132
16:1–36 186	5:17–18a 52	7:1 131–132
16:3 41	5:18 18	7:2 132
22:1, 5–7 186	7:1, 43–45, 73 231	7:2, 7–8 67
23:2–6 186	8:1–8 66	7:4 104
25:6–7 231	8:9–10 66	7:4 Alpha Text 104
27:27 . . . . 16, 48	8:10 . . . . 22, 66, 72	7:4 LXX 104
29:21 79	8:12 66	7:7 132
	8:18 68	7:8 132
2 Chronicles	9:10 192	8:3 68
2:10 [2:9 MT] 47	9:25 60	8:17 132
5:12–13 231	9:35–37 49	9:1 66
5:13–14 230	10:28, 39 231	9:17, 19, 22 67
6:26–30 84	10:37 78	9:31 97
7:1–2 230	10:37, 39 [10:38, 40 MT] . . . 43, 76	
7:6 231	11:22 231	***Job***
7:8–10 69	12:24, 27–37, 45–47 231	1:4 101

1:5 . . . . 101, 124
1:6 127
1:13, 18 101
1:18–19 131
1:19 101
8:4 102
12:24–25 166
15:33 160
21:20 164
24:6, 18 48
24:11 48
32:18–19 . . . . 22, 46
32:19 22
38:7 127

Psalms

4:7 [4:8 MT] 62, 85
11:6 . . . . 163, 168
16:4 81
16:5 . . . . 133, 168
23:1–4 133
23:4 134
23:5 . . . . 84, 133, 168
23:5–6 133
23:5 [22:5 LXX] 133
23:6 84
27:5 186
31:20 [31:21 MT] 186
35:9 NETS 85
36:5–6 84
36:7 84
36:8 [36:9 MT] 85
46:3 85
46:6 [46:5 MT] 85
50:12–14 83
60:3 167
63:1–5 84
65:4b 84
65:9–13 84
69:21 . . . . 23, 32
75:8 . . . . . . 31, 35, 36, 85, 167, 168
75:8 [75:9 MT] 19, 35
76:2 [76:3 MT] 186
78:12, 43 192
78:47 146
78:65 164
78:66 164
79:6 164
80 147
80:8 147
80:9 . . . . 41, 147
80:10 . . . . 41, 42, 147
80:12 147
80:12–13 . . . . 43, 150
80:13 147
80:14 147
80:15a 147
80:16 147
80:17–19 147
102:9 . . . . 31, 36
102:9 [102:10 MT] 36
104:14–15 62
104:15 . . . . 18, 82, 85
105:27 192
105:33 146
106:7 192
107 124
107:27 124
107:33–34 177
107:35 177
107:37 178
107:38 178
113–118 213
118 154
118:22–23 153
128:3 . . . . 42, 63
135:9 192
137:3–4 231
141:4 105

Proverbs

1:12 196
2:16–22 91
3:9–10 . . . . 4, 62, 76, 116, 237
4:17 117
4:17 LXX 117
5:1–23 91
6:6–11 91
6:24–35 91
7:1–27 117
7:5–27 91
7:13–14 117–118
7:18 . . . . 118, 123
9:1 118
9:1–6 . . . . 118, 237
9:2 . . . . 31, 35, 36, 118
9:3–4 118
9:5 . . . . 31, 35, 36, 118
9:5–6 118
9:13–18 117
9:17 119
10:5 91
10:26 . . . . 23, 91
13:4 91
15:15 . . . . 19, 118
15:17 92
15:19 91
17:1 92
19:15, 24 91
20:1 . . . 4, 26, 27, 80, 116, 123, 124
20:4, 13a 91
21:17 . . . . 51, 116, 123
22:13 91
22:14 91
23 90
23:2–3, 20–21 91–92
23:3, 6 92
23:19–21 . . . . 51, 91, 116, 123
23:21 91
23:27–28 91
23:29 . . . . 117, 123, 131
23:29–35 . . . . 90–91, 237
23:30 . . . . 31, 35, 36
23:31 . . . . 14, 93, 94, 115, 117
23:31 LXX 91, 94, 124
23:33 117
23:35 . . . . 117, 123, 131
24:31 . . . . 41, 43
24:33–34 91
25:20 23
26:4–5 116
26:9 116
26:13–16 91
28:8, 22 91
29:3 91
30:15–16 196
30:19–20 91
31 90
31:3 92
31:4 . . . . . 27, 80, 92, 115, 117, 237
31:4–5 . . . . 119, 123
31:4–7 50
31:5 . . . . 92, 117
31:6 . . . . 25, 27, 32, 80
31:6–7 92
31:16 . . . . 47–48, 73, 92

Ecclesiastes

1:3, 9, 14 119
1:17 120
2:1 120
2:1–3 123
2:2 120

2:3a 120
2:3b 120
2:4 121
2:10a 121
2:11 . . . . 119, 121
2:13 123
2:14b–16 120
2:17–20 119
2:24–25 120
3:10 121
3:11 121
3:12–13 121
3:16 119
3:17 122
3:18–21 121
3:22b 121
4:1, 3, 7, 15 119
5:9 121
5:10 121
5:13–15 121
5:18 . . . . 119, 121
5:19 122
6:1, 12 119
7:1 120
7:1–4 123
7:2 120
7:2–3 19
7:2b 120
7:3 120
7:4 120
8:9, 15, 17 119
8:15 . . . . 119, 120
9:3, 6, 9, 11, 13 119
9:5 121
9:7 . . . . 18, 121
10:5 119
10:16–17 . . . . 51, 119, 123
10:17 119
10:19 . . . . 18, 85, 122
11:1 122
11:1–2 . . . . 54, 122
11:2 122
11:9 122
12:9–14 122
12:13 122
12:14 122

Song of Songs
1:2 . . . . 71, 72
1:4 . . . . 71, 72
1:5–6 74

1:14 73
1:16 73
2:4 71
2:13 73
2:15 . . . . 43, 73
4:5 73
4:10 72
4:10b 71
4:16 . . . . 72, 73
5:1 . . . . 31, 72
5:1b 71
5:16 22
5:16a 72
6:11 . . . . 42, 73
7:1–5 72
7:2 . . . . 31, 36, 249
7:2 [7:3 MT] 35, 72
7:3 73
7:8 . . . . 42, 72, 73
7:9 [7:10 MT] 72, 249
7:11 73
7:12 [7:13 MT] 73
8:2 . . . . 21, 31, 72, 249
8:4 73
8:11–12 74

Isaiah
1:7 152
1:8 . . . . 44, 152, 186
1:9 152
1:19 62
1:22 . . . . 24, 31, 36, 81, 143
2:1–4 181
2:4 . . . . 42, 178
3:14 151
3:14–15 53
3:15 151
4:2 . . . . 151, 177
4:5–6 186
5. . . . . 152, 153
5:1 . . . . 41, 150
5:1–7 . . . . 150, 248
5:2 . . . . 14, 41, 43, 44, 150
5:2 LXX 153
5:4 150
5:5 150
5:6 . . . . 41, 150, 196
5:7a 150
5:8 150
5:8–30 . . . . 150, 151
5:10 151

5:11 . . . . 24, 27, 80, 150
5:11–12, 22 53
5:12a 150
5:12b 151
5:14 196
5:22 . . . . 24, 27, 31, 35–36, 80, 151
5:23 . . . . 36, 151
5:26–30 151
6:1 . . . . 189, 230
6:11–13 151
7:23 . . . . 48, 143
7:24 143
8:6 84
10:20–22 151
11:1 . . . . 108, 151
16:5 186
16:8 14
16:8–9 146
16:9–10 146
16:10 . . . . 20, 44, 146
18:5 42
18:6 42
19:10 27
19:14 . . . . 31, 36, 167
21:5a 132
21:5b 132
22:12 138
22:13 138
24. 207
24–27 . . . . 152, 194
24:5 195
24:6 195
24:7 . . . . 20, 85, 195
24:8–9a 195
24:9 . . . . 20, 24, 25, 27, 80
24:9b 195
24:11 195
24:13 195
24:20 195
24:23 195
25. 194
25:1–5 195
25:6 . . . . 6, 19, 45, 205, 237
25:6–8 . . . . 206, 247
25:7–8 . . . . 196, 207
25:8 196
26:19 196
27:1 196
27:1–6 152
27:2 196
27:3 196

SCRIPTURE AND OTHER ANCIENT LITERATURE INDEX

Reference	Pages
27:4	41, 196, 207
27:6	196
27:12–13	197
28	134
28:1	134
28:3	134
28:7	24, 27, 80
28:7a	134
28:7b	134
28:8	134
28:9	134
28:10	134–135
28:11	135
28:13	134, 136
28:15	136
28:18–19	136
29:9	24, 27, 80
29:9–10	167
32:10	145
32:12	145
32:13	145
32:15–17	177
34:5	14
34:6–7	163
35:1–10	177
36:12	142
36:16	142
36:17	142
37:30	142
40:3–4	177
41:18–20	177
42:15	177
43:19–21	177
44:1–2	237
44:1–5	177
49:11–12	177
49:26	14, 21, 22, 164
49:26 LXX	203
50:2	177
51;21	171
51:3	177
51:10–11	177
51:17	171
51:17–23	237
51:21	167
51:22	171
51:22–23	173
51:23	171
53:12	78
55:1	179
55:1–2	53
55:2	179
55:10–13	177
56:9	134
56:12	27, 80, 134
57:6	81
57:14	177
58:11	177
59:18	177
60:21	151
61:5	178
62:8	180
62:8–9	20
62:8b	178
62:9	180
62:10	177
63:1–2	162
63:1–6	205, 237
63:3	161, 162
63:3–4	162
63:6	163, 164
64:19	177
65:8	19, 152
65:8 [LXX]	20
65:9	152
65:11	31, 35, 36, 81
65:11–12	90
65:17–25	65
65:21	178, 208

Jeremiah

Reference	Pages
2:6	144
2:7	144
2:21	14, 148, 156
3:1–2, 9	144
5:6	148
5:10	148
5:12	148
5:17	148
6:9	148, 160
6:11	164
7:4	143
7:18	81
7:20	143
8:13	144
8:13–14	165
9:15–16	165
10:25	164
12	153
12:10	148
13	164
13:12	46, 167
13:13	167
13:14	167
14:16	164
15:16	102
15:17	102
16:4	145
16:5	53, 145
16:7	145
16:9	145
16:18	144
19:13	81
23:5	108
23:10	144
23:15	165
25:15	167, 169
25:15–29	237
25:15–38	169
25:16	169
25:17	169, 170
25:17–26	170
25:26	170, 171
25:27	170
25:28b	170
25:29	170
25:30a	169
25:30b	169
29:5	103
31:5	41, 177, 237, 245
31:10	177
31:11 LXX	45
31:12	177, 237, 245
31:25	177
31:29	176
31:30	177
31:31–34	177, 245
31:32 [48:32 MT]	156
32:7	177
32:15	177
32:20–21	192
32:29	81
32:43–44	177
33:11	179
33:15	108
35:1–19	244
35:2	102
35:5	102
35:6, 8, 14	102
35:7, 9	102
35:10	102
35:11–17	103
35:14	102, 103

35:18–19 103
38:25 NETS 177
39:9 48
39:10 .... 48, 144
40:7 48
40:10 .... 46, 49
40:12 49
44:17–19, 25 81
46:10 163
48:11 .... 19, 45
48:12 46
48:26 166
48:32b 146
48:33 .... 20, 44, 146
48:33a 146
49:9 160
49:12 170
50:38–40 143
50:39 144
51 .... 166–167, 172
51:7 .... 167, 237
51:7a 171
51:7b 171
51:7c 171
51:8 171
51:39 167
51:57 167
51:58 167
52:16 .... 48, 144
52:18–19 185
52:19 78

Lamentations
1:4 146
1:15 161
2:4 164
2:6 186
2:7, 22 146
2:11 141
2:12 141
3:14 231
4:11 164
4:21 .... 128, 170
4:22 170
5:7 177
5:14 231

Ezekiel
5:11 145
6:11–14 145
7:7 144

10:4 .... 189, 230
12:19–20 143
15:1–5 148
15:2 156
15:4 156
15:4–5 .... 148, 156
15:4–6 156
15:6–8 .... 148, 156
16:29 149
17 .... 148, 153, 157
17:1–24 148
17:3–4 148
17:5 148
17:6 .... 41, 148
17:6–7 156
17:7 .... 41, 148
17:8 148
17:9–10 .... 148, 156, 157
17:11–15 148
17:12 149
17:13–14 149
17:15 149
17:16–21 149
17:22–24 .... 149, 157
18:2 148
18:2–3 176
18:4 177
19 .... 148, 157
19:1 149
19:1–9 149
19:2–4 149
19:5–9 149
19:10–12 156
19:10–14 149
19:11 .... 42, 149, 156
19:12 149
19:12–14 .... 156, 157
19:13 149
19:14 149
20:28 81
20:40 181
23:4 169
23:9–10 169
23:31 169
23:32 169
23:33 .... 45, 169
23:34 169
23:34b 169
23:40–45 169
27:18 .... 14, 47
27:18–19 46

28:6 178
28:13–14, 16 181
28:13–16 177
34:23–31 177
36:11 177
36:24 177
36:25–28 177
36:29–30 177
36:35 177
36:37–38 177
39:17–18 206
39:17–20 .... 14, 163
39:19 163
40–48 .... 78, 181
43:5 .... 189, 230
43:12 181
44:4 .... 189, 230
44:21 .... 88, 180, 230
45:17 78
45:21–25 69
47:1–12 .... 84, 181

Daniel
1 114
1:3–4 105
1:5, 8 104
1:10 105
1:12 LXX 112
1:15 105
1:16 105
3:25 127
5:1 131
5:2 131
5:4 131
5:23 131
5:25 131
6:18 103
7 162
7:21–22 173
10 114
10:1–3 105
10:3 105
12:1 173

Hosea
2:3 143
2:5 [2:7 MT] 146
2:8, 22 [2:10, 24 MT] 20
2:8–9 [2:10–11 MT] 144
2:8 [2:10 MT] 146
2:11 146

2:12a 144	3:10 .... 42, 178	***Micah***
2:12b 144	3:12–13 161	1:6 144
2:14–15 178	3:13 ...... 14, 161, 162, 237	2:6 143
2:22 178	3:17–21 .... 178, 181, 182	2:7 143
2:23 .... 178, 184	3:18 .... 41, 84	2:11 .... 27, 143
4:1–2, 5–6, 14c 143	3:18 [4:18 MT] .. 21, 181, 182, 237	3:11 143
4:3 143		3:12 143
4:10 143	***Amos***	4:1–5 181
4:10–11 143	1–2 52	4:2 180
4:11 20	1:2 185	4:3 .... 42, 178
4:11 [LXX] 20	2:7–8 185	4:4 42
4:12, 17 143	2:8 52	6:6–8 143
4:18 .... 24, 143	2:12 89	6:7 85
5:7 143	3:14 185	6:14 143
5:9 143	4:1 53	6:15 .... 20, 143
5:10 164	4:4–5 185	7:1 143
7:5 .... 165, 166	4:8–9 185	7:15 192
7:6–7 166	4:9 144	
7:14 144	5:5–6 185	***Nahum***
9:2 144	5:7, 21–27 185	1:10 24
9:4 79	5:11 .... 52, 146, 185	1:15 180
9:4–5 146	5:17 144	2:1 180
9:6 143	5:21–24 52	3:11 166
9:10 147	6:4 53	
9:11–17 148	6:5 186	***Habakkuk***
10:1 148	6:6 .... 53, 185	2:5 196
10:2 148	6:6b 53	2:15 .... 128, 171
14:7 .... 14, 47, 179	6:7 53	2:16 171
14:8 178	7 185	3:17 144
	7:1–4 143	
Joel	7:9 185	***Zephaniah***
1:5 .... 21, 144, 182	7:13 187	1:7–8 164
1:7 .... 144, 156	8:9 185	1:13 .... 52, 146
1:9 .... 79, 146	8:10 185	3:14–19 180
1:9b, 13 182	9:1 185	
1:10 144	9:1–5 185	***Haggai***
1:11 144	9:11 .... 69, 183, 185, 186	1:4 145
1:12 144	9:11–12 .... 93, 187	1:6 .... 52, 145
1:14 182	9:11–15 .... 69, 181, 183, 187	1:8–9 145
2:12–13 182	9:12 184	1:10 146
2:14 .... 79, 182	9:13 .... 21, 41, 93, 181	1:10–11 179
2:15 182	9:13–14 252	1:11 146
2:17 182	9:13a 183	2:1–9 180
2:19 182	9:13b 183	2:7 .... 189, 230
2:22 182	9:14 .... 183, 185	2:12–14 180
2:23 182	9:14–15 184	2:16 180
2:24 .... 20, 161, 182, 237		2:17 180
2:25 182	***Obadiah***	2:19 180
2:26 182	5 160	
2:28–32 181	11 170	***Zechariah***
3:3 [4:3 MT] 52	16 170	3:9 180

3:10 . . . . 42, 180
6:12 108
6:12–14 180
8:1–8 180
8:12 180
8:19 97
8:19–21 180
9:14–15 . . . . 14, 178
9:15 . . . . 78, 163
9:16 178
9:17 . . . . 20, 178
10:7 178
12:2 . . . . 166, 171
14:8 . . . . 84, 180
14:10 48
14:16–19 180
14:20 185

Malachi
3:1 180
3:3 180
3:4 180
3:11 180
4:3 [3:21 MT] 21

Old Testament Apocrypha
1 Esdras
3–4 116
3:17b–24 116
5:56–62 231
5:59–62 186
6:30–31 79
8:49 186
9:50–55 66
9:54 66

1 Maccabees
1:47 87
3:49 89
6:34 14
13:47 231
16:16 131

2 Maccabees
1:30 231
6:5 229
15:39 . . . . 37, 113

3 Maccabees
5.2, 10, 45 111

4 Ezra
5.23 147
5.28–29 147
6.52 196
10.19–22 231
15:35–36 161

Judith
6:4 163
11:13 77
12:1–4 110
13:2 131
16:20 84

Sirach
1:16 118
6:28–30 108
9:10 . . . . 45, 203
19:2 116
24 118
24:17 155
24:19 155
31:27–29 92
33:16 43
39:26 14
39:26–27 115
40:20 18
50:15 . . . . 14, 79

Tobit
1:7 77
4:15–16 53

Old Testament Pseudepigrapha
Apocalypse of Abraham
5.13 31
23.6 126
29.14–15 173

Apocalypse of Daniel
10.1–7 206

Apocalypse of Ezra
4.27 206

Apocalypse of Sedrach
1.17–18 186

2 Baruch
10.10 79

13.8 167
29:4 196
29.2 187
29.5 187
70.2–10 173

3 Baruch
4.7, 15 126
4.17 95
8.5 95
13.4 95

1 Enoch
10.18–19 183
32.1–6 126
62.12 163

2 Enoch
8.5–6 85

3 Enoch
48A. 10 199

Jubilees
3.12 181
6.3 79
7.1–6 126
7.7–13 127
8.19 181
13.6 181
13.8–9 181
32.10–15 77
32.27–29 68
49.6 . . . . 70, 214

LAB (Pseudo-Philo)
12.8–10 151
18.10–11 151
23.11 60
23.11–12 151
30.4 151
39.7 151
37.2 83

Letter of Aristeas
89–90 84
112 60

Martyrdom and Ascension of Isaiah
5.13 172

Odes of Solomon
6.8 85
6.10–18 85
11.6–7 85
11.8–10 85

Pseudo-Hecataeus
199 88

Psalms of Solomon
8.14 172

Sibylline Oracles
2.141–42 116
2.318 85
7.148–49 207
8.209–12 85
8.493–94 81
14.292 14

Testaments of the Twelve Patriarchs
Testament of Judah
14.1 94
16.1 94
16.2 94

Testament of Levi
8:5 77

Testament of Abraham
16.12 172
17.16 172
19.6 172

Testament of Solomon
18.31 111

Dead Sea Scrolls
1QH^a
XI, 3–18 173

1QS (Community Rule)
VI, 4–6 97
VI 20–VII, 25 97

1QSa [1Q28a]
II, 11–22 200

4Q252
II, 7 127

4Q265
7 II, 14 181

4QIsa Pesher^b [4Q162]
1–11 153

4QSam^a [4Q51]
V, 22 . . . . 100, 101

11QPsalms^a [11Q5]
XXVII, 2–11 186

11QT^a [11Q19]
XVIII–XXI 22
XXI, 3–4 77
XXI, 9b–10 80

Philo
Allegorical Interpretation
3.82 118

Contemplative Life
73–74 97
79–89 231

Creation
71 118

Dreams
2.183 79
2.246–47 85
2.248–49 85

Drunkenness
27 124
94 231
126–27, 129, 137–38 88
147–48 118
218 18

Flight
32, 166, 176 118

Good Person
13 118

Moses
2.153 68

Planting
50 181

126 231
154 38

Special Laws
1.98, 100, 247–50 88
1.134, 179 79
1.189 68
1.205 81
1.247–51 89
1.291 81
2.148 231
2.204 68
3.126 131

Virtues
95 77

Josephus
Against Apion
2.23 88

Antiquities
1.13.2 186
2.64 22
3.9.4 79
3.10.4 68
3.12.2 88
6.14.6 133
7.12.3 186
7.14.7 186
9.7.2 186
9.13.3 231
10.9.4 131
11.3.2–6 116
11.3.8 231
11.4.2 231
11.5.5 68
11.5.8 68
12.7.7 68
15.11.3 154
18.9.7 131
19.1.4 131

Jewish War
2.8.5 97
2.15.1 97
5.5.7 88
5.13.6 77

Mishnah, Talmud, and Related Literature

Mishnah

m. Avodah Zarah
2:3 105
2:3–4 45
4:8–12 . . . . 45, 105
5:1–12 . . . . 45, 105

m. Berakhot
7:5 34

m. Bikkurim
3:4 231

m. Middot
2:5 231

m. Mo'ed Qatan
2:2 81

m. Nazir
1:2 99
2:4 99
4:3, 5 99
6:1–2, 4, 9 99
8:2 99
9:1 99
9:5 100

m. Pesahim
3:1 27
5:7 231
10. . . . . 69, 213
10:7 213

m. Sheqalim
4:9 81

m. Sukkah
4:9–10 81
5:1–2 81
5:4 231

m. Tamid
7:4 231

m. Terumot
3:1 81
11:2–3 81

Tosefta
t. Menahot
9:9 81

t. Pesahim
10. 213

t. Sukkah
3:5 154

Talmud
b. Bava Batra
75. 196
97b. 81

b. Eruvin
61a. 69

b. Megillah
7b. 68
12b. 67

b. Pesahim
108b. 34

b. Sanhedrin
43a. 32

b. Sukkah
49a. 154

y. Pesahim
10:7–8 [23–24] 213

Targumic Texts
Fragmentary Targum Genesis
40:23 172

Targum Isaiah
5:2, 5 154
63:3–4 162

Targum Neofiti Deuteronomy
32:1 172

Targum Neofiti Genesis
40:23 172

Other Rabbinic Works
Genesis Rabbah
88:5 213

Song of Songs Rabbah
2:16 [§1] 154
7:13 [§1] 154

New Testament

Matthew
2:23 108
3:4 105
3:12 162
4:2 105
7:16 155
8:11 199
9:10 199
9:14 197
9:14–17 106
9:15 . . . . 139, 197
9:17 . . . . 19, 198, 203
11:16–17 107
11:18 107
11:18–19 251
11:19 . . . . 107, 114, 244
11:28–30 108
13:24–30, 36–43 162
13:33 . . . . 6, 159
14:9 199
16:6 . . . . 6, 159
16:11–12 6
20:1–16 . . . . 48, 154–155
20:20–21 173
20:21 173
20:22–23 173
21:12–17 190
21:28–32 155
21:31b–32 155
21:33 152
21:33–46 152
21:34–36 153
21:37 153
21:38–39 153
21:40–41 153
21:42 153
21:43 154
21:45–46 . . . . 153, 155
22:1–14 155
22:10 155
22:10–11 199
23:6 199
24. 136
24:38 . . . . 136, 137, 139
24:42 137
24:43 137

24:49–51 137	13:32–37 137	13–16 198–202
25:1–13 138	14:1 210	13:6 42
25:3–4 138	14:3 199	13:20–21 159
25:5 138	14:7 210	13:21 6
25:6 138	14:12, 14 210	13:22–30 199
26:7, 20 199	14:12–16 210	13:24–28 207
26:17 210	14:18 199	13:25 199
26:23 .... 23, 215	14:20 .... 23, 215	13:26–27 199
26:26 212	14:22 212	13:27–28 205
26:27–29 .... 69, 246	14:23 214	13:28 199
26:28 211	14:23–25 ...... 69, 246	13:28–29 201
26:28–29 14	14:24 211	13:29 .... 199, 205
26:29 ...... 19, 108, 202	14:24–25 14	14:1 199
26:30 .... 213, 231	14:25 ...... 19, 108, 202	14:7 199
26:36–46 172	14:26 .... 213, 231	14:7–11 199
26:39, 42 ...... 173, 214	14:32–43 172	14:8 199
27:34 .... 32, 214	14:36 173	14:9 199
27:48 .... 24, 191, 214	15:17 32	14:10 .... 199, 201, 204
	15:23 32	14:12–14, 21–23 204
Mark	15:36 ...... 24, 191, 214	14:12–24 199
1:6 105	16:14 199	14:13 199
1:12–13 105	16:18 244	14:13, 21, 23 205
2:15 199		14:14 200
2:18 197	***Luke***	14:15 .... 199, 200
2:18–22 106	1:7 106	14:16–17 200
2:19 .... 106, 197	1:15 .... 24, 106	14:18–20 200
2:19–20 .... 106, 197	3:17 162	14:21 200
2:20 .... 107, 197	4:2 105	14:22 200
2:21 .... 197, 198	5:27–32 198	14:23 200
2:22 .... 19, 46, 106, 197, 198, 203	5:29 199	14:24 .... 200, 205, 207
2:22b 198	5:33–39 106	15:1–2 202
6:14–29 131	5:37 198	15:11–32 202
6:22 199	5:37–38 .... 19, 203	15:22–24 202
6:26 199	5:39 ..... 19, 45, 198, 204, 249	16:19–31 ...... 201, 205, 206
8:15 .... 6, 159	6:44 155	16:21 201
10:37 173	7:31–32 107	16:22, 23 201
10:38–39 173	7:33 107	16:22–26 205
11:15–19 190	7:34 .... 107, 244	16:23 201
11:27 153	7:35 .... 107, 114	16:24 201
12:1 .... 43, 44	7:36 199	16:26 .... 201, 207
12:1–12 152	7:37 199	17:7 199
12:1b 152	7:49 199	17:26–27 136
12:2–5 153	10:34 111	17:27 137
12:6 153	11:37 199	17:28 137
12:7–8 153	12:1 .... 6, 159	19:45–48 190
12:9 .... 153, 154	12:13 153	20:9 152
12:10–11 153	12:19–21 123	20:9–18 152
12:12 153	12:35 137	20:10–12 153
12:39 199	12:36 137	20:14–15 153
13 136	12:37 .... 137, 199	20:16 .... 153, 154
13:1–37 173	12:45–48 137	20:17 153

20:19 153
20:46 199
21. 136
21:34 136
21:36 137
22:14 199
22:15 210
22:15–16 203
22:17 . . . . 212, 213
22:17–18 . . . . 14, 69, 246
22:18 . . . . 108, 202, 203
22:19 211
22:19–20 224
22:20 . . . . 14, 69, 211, 212, 213
22:21 215
22:24 203
22:24–27 204
22:27 199
22:27a 204
22:27b 204
22:28 204
22:29–30 204
22:30 204
22:39–46 172
22:42 173
23:36 . . . . 24, 214
24:30 . . . . 199, 228
24:30–31 221

John

1:14 . . . . 189, 244
1:29 . . . . 190, 191
1:35, 43 190
1:43–51 191
2. 33
2:1 190
2:1–10 187
2:1–11 . . . . 53, 197
2:4 . . . . 53, 191
2:6 189
2:9 15
2:10 . . . . 188, 242, 249, 250
2:11 189
2:13–22 190
2:14–17 190
2:18–22 244
2:19 190
2:21 190
4:21–24 190
6:4 217
6:11 217
6:14 217
6:23 217
6:25–59 225
6:29 . . . . 217, 218
6:32–33, 49–51, 58 217
6:35 . . . . 217, 218
6:40 219
6:41 217
6:48 217
6:51 217
6:51–58 218
6:52 217
6:53 217
6:53–56 217
6:53–58 14
6:54–56 217
6:55 217
6:56 218
7:6, 8, 30 191
7:37 68
7:37–39 . . . . 81, 190
8:20 191
8:33 104
9:7–15 82
11:25 219
12:2 199
12:23, 27–28 191
12:27 173
13–17 215
13:1 . . . . 191, 210
13:1–19 215
13:10 189
13:23 . . . . 199, 201
13:25 . . . . 199, 201
13:26 215
13:28 . . . . 199, 201
14:31c 215
15. . . . . 152, 216
15:1, 8 155
15:1–2 248
15:1–11 215
15:2 . . . . 42, 155, 156, 216
15:2, 6 42
15:3 . . . . 155, 216
15:4–5, 8, 16 155
15:4–7 216
15:5 216
15:6 . . . . 42, 155, 156
15:9–11 . . . . 216, 219
17:11 173
18:11 173
18:28 210
19:14 . . . . 191, 210, 215
19:28–30 23
19:29 . . . . 191, 214
19:31 . . . . 191, 210
19:31–37 191
19:34 191
19:42 191
21:9–13 228
21:20 . . . . 199, 201

Acts

2. 187
2:1–41 221
2:4 230
2:13 . . . . 22, 182, 203, 230
2:15 137
2:16–21 182
2:42, 46 221
2:42–47 221
4:11 187
7. 187
13:2–3 107
14:23 107
15:8 187
15:15–17 93
15:16–18 . . . . 184, 187
15:20 93
15:20b 164
15:29 . . . . 93, 164
16:34 221
20:7 221
21:25 . . . . 93, 164
27:33–36 221

Romans

1:29–31 95
2:8–9 95
12:2 244
13:11–13a 137
13:12 137
13:12b–13 137
14–15. 109–110, 114, 221, 222, 243
14:3, 17, 21 109
14:5–6a 109
14:13, 15, 19–21 110
14:14 109
14:17 227
14:17a 221
14:17b 221
14:22–23 110

14:23 243	11:26 224	*Colossians*
15:1–2 110	11:27 224	1:19 230
15:7–13 109	11:27–32 . . . . 224, 227	2:9 230
	11:28 225	2:12–15 109
1 Corinthians	11:28–32 173	2:16 109
3:16 230	11:29 . . . . 224, 225	2:20–23 109
5:1–13 225	11:30 225	2:23 107
5:6–8 . . . . 6, 159	11:33–34 225	3:5, 8–9 95
5:7 . . . . 210, 225	12 . . . . 225, 227	
5:11 . . . . 95, 96	12:12–13 246	*1 Thessalonians*
6:10 95	12:13 227	5:4–5 137
6:13 227	14:21 135	5:6 137
6:15–18 227	15:32 . . . . 123, 138	5:7 137
6:15a 227	15:34 138	5:8 137
6:17 227		5:22 244
6:19 230	*2 Corinthians*	
6:19–20 227	12:20–21 95	*1 Timothy*
8–10 . . . . 110, 223, 226		1:9–11 95
8:10 199	*Galatians*	3:3 93
9:4 77	2:11–14 222	3:8 . . . . 93, 111
9:7 77	2:16–17 222	4:1–5 . . . . 111, 113
9:13 77	2:19–20 222	4:2a 93
10–11 . . . . 220, 223–228	3:1–5 222	4:3b–5 93
10:1–4 225	5:9 . . . . 6, 159	5:17–25 110
10:1–5 218	5:19–21 95	5:22 110
10:2–4 227	5:21 . . . . 95, 96, 251	5:23 . . . . 93, 110, 111, 113
10:6, 11 225	5:22–23 . . . . 95, 251	
10:7 225	5:23 95	*2 Timothy*
10:8–10 226	5:24 251	3:1–5 95
10:14–22 . . . . 218, 223	6:15 252	4:6a 78
10:15 225		4:6b–7 78
10:16 . . . . 14, 224, 226	*Ephesians*	
10:16, 21 246	1:23 230	*Titus*
10:16–22 226	2:11–22 230	1:7 93
10:17 226	3:14–19 230	2:2 93
10:18 . . . . 226, 227	4:8–10 230	2:3 93
10:20–21 226	5:5 95	
10:21 226	5:15, 17 94	*Hebrews*
10:31 239	5:16 . . . . 94, 136	3–4 61
11 226	5:17 94	7:1–28 216
11:10 127	5:18 . . . 91, 93–94, 95, 96, 117, 124,	9:10 79
11:17–22 . . . . 94, 224, 232	136, 220, 223, 228–232, 251	9:12–14 216
11:17–34 223	5:18–21 . . . . 228, 231, 232	10:19 216
11:20 223	5:19–20 94	12:24 216
11:21 223	5:22–6:9 229	13:10 216
11:22 223	5:26 231	13:11–12, 20 216
11:23–26 224		
11:24–25 211	*Philippians*	*James*
11:25 . . . . 14, 69, 211, 212	2:17 78	3:12 155
11:25–26 246	3:18–19 109	5:5 53
11:25–27 226		

1 Peter
1:13 138
2:5, 9 232
2:5–8 232
3:18–22 127
4:3 137
4:7 . . . . 95, 137
5:8 138
5:9 138

2 Peter
2:4–5 127
2:13 222

1 John
2:15–17 244

Jude
6 127
12 222
12b–13 222

Revelation
1:9 174
3:20 168
6:6 206
13:16–18 206
14:4 162
14:8 . . . . 171, 172, 206
14:10 . . . 35, 37, 168, 171, 172, 206
14:14 162
14:14–16 161
14:15, 18 161
14:17 162
14:17–20 . . . . 14, 161, 162
14:19 206
14:19–20 . . . . 161, 168
14:20b 161
15–16 168
15:5–8 168
15:17 168
16:1 168
16:2, 3, 4, 8, 10, 12, 17 168
16:15 137
16:19 . . . . 168, 171, 172, 206
16:19b 6
17:1–2 206
17:2 . . . . 171, 206
17:4 . . . . 171, 172
17:4–6 164
17:6 . . . . 14, 164, 171, 174
17:9 164
17:18 164
18:3 . . . . 171, 172, 206
18:3, 9 206
18:6 . . . . 35, 37, 168, 172, 206
18:11–13, 15, 17, 19, 23 206
18:13 206
18:24 164
19:2 164
19:7–8 205
19:9 . . . . 205, 206
19:10 205
19:11–21 205
19:13 . . . . 162, 205
19:15 . . . . . 162, 168, 172, 205, 206
19:15b 162
19:17 206
19:17–21 163
19:18 206
19:21 206
20:1–10 206
21–22 206
21:1 207
21:4 206
21:22 207
21:23 207
21:25 207
21:27 207
22:1–2 228
22:3 207
22:5 207

Apostolic Fathers
1 Clement
30:1 95

Didache
9.1 157
9.1–2 216

Ignatius
To the Smyrnaeans
8.2 222

Martyrdom of Polycarp
14.2 172

Shepherd of Hermas
48:3 46
51.1–4 42
65.5–6 95

New Testament Apocrypha and Pseudepigrapha
Acts of Andrew
57[6] 95

Acts of John
35 95

Acts of Paul
25 97

Acts of Peter
2 97

Acts of Pilate
16.7–8 231

Acts of Thomas
36, 58, 124 95

Apocalypse of Paul
23–27 85
27.1–2a 202
29 186

Gospel of Thomas
47 198
65 152

Protevangelium of James
16 165

Classical and Ancient Christian Writings
Athenaeus
Deipnosophistae
2.40f–46f 112
2.45e 23
2.46d 113
10.426b–427c 34
10.427f 119
10.447b–c 55
II, 24 23

Cato
De agricultura
25 195
57 195
120 16

Columella

De arboribus
16. 42

De re rustica
3.2.1. 41
3.2.2. 41
3.3.1–15. 47
3.12.33, 38. 112–113
3.21.10. 45
4.19.3. 42
5.5.17. 42
5.6.5. 42
12.27, 37, 39 44
12.19. 16
12.19–21. 33
12.19.2. 38
12.20.3. 32
12.20.5. 32
12.21 17
12.21.4–5. 33
12.22–24 32
12.23.3. 33
12.25.1. 33

Euripides

Bacchae
1118–24. 133

Herodotus

Historiae
1.71 112
1.133 67
1.134 68
2.77 55

Hippocrates

Airs, Waters, Places
§7–11. 112

De natura hominis
§9 lines 24–25 112

Homer

Odyssey
9.193–215 34
9.371–74 132

Lucian

Saturnalia
§22. . . . . 188, 200

Plato

Laws
II 270e–272d 95

Respublica
8, 561c. 112

Pliny the Elder

Naturalis historia
13.24.46. 38
14.3.12. 42
14.3.15–19. 41
14.4.3. 42
14.4.22. 45
14.4.31–32. 17
14.6.54. 34
14.6.55. 33
14.8.63. 17
14.8.70. 40
14.9.73. 38
14.9.74. 38
14.9.85. 44
14.11.80. 14
14.11.80–85. 44
14.11.83. 16
14.12.86. 195
14.14.91. 188
14.14.121. 31
14.15.92–93. 32
14.17.107. 32
14.23.119. . . . . 37, 81
14.24.120. 32
14.25.122. 32
14.25.124. 32
14.25.127. 31
14.27.133–34. 31
23.34. 34
23.35–36, 38–39, 41, 44, 51 . . . 113
31. 112

Pliny the Younger

Epistulae ad Trajanum
10.96.7. . . . . 222, 232

Plutarch

Moralia
671D–E. 69

Strabo

Geographica
4.6.2. 38
17.1.14. 38

Varro

De re rustica
1.8.5–6. 73
1.8.6. 41

Xenophon

Cyropaedia
6.2.26–29. 112

SUBJECT INDEX

abiding, 216
Abigail, 132
Abimelech (king), 81, 83, 211
Abiram, 61
Abner, 132–33
Abraham, 57, 58, 199, 201, 216, 238, 240
Abrahamic covenant, 59, 65, 178
Abraham's side, 201
Absalom, 133
abstinence
   biblical justification and, 241
   blessing in, 239
   Daniel and, 104–5, 114
   from drunkenness, 251
   Esther and, 103–4, 113–14
   from food, 105
   Hannah and Samuel and, 100–101, 114
   Jeremiah and, 102, 113–14
   Jesus and, 105–8, 114
   Job and, 101–2, 114
   John the Baptist and, 105–8, 114
   for leadership positions, 93
   legislation regarding, 243
   in Nazirite vow, 26, 98–99, 101, 106, 239, 244
   overview of, 97–98, 113–14
   rationale behind, 114
   reasons for, 241, 242, 243, 244
   Rekabites and, 102–3, 114
   Samson and, 98–99, 114
   Timothy and, 110–13
   weak and strong and, 109–10, 114, 243
abundance
   in Abrahamic promises, 58
   bliss and, 193
   of blood, 161
   in the cup, 133
   future, 53–54, 69, 106
   idolatry and, 148
   mountains as dripping with sweet wine and, 181–87
   obedience and, 62, 63
   overview of, 176, 192–93
   prefiguring, 197
   rebellion and, 89–90
   restoration and, 9, 143, 176–79, 207
   revitalizing the temple and, 179–81
   of royal wine, 67
   sacred space and, 76
   stewardship and, 116
   in the temple, 84–85
   viticulture and, 58, 59, 65, 86, 141, 176–81
   wedding at Cana and, 187–92
abuse, 206
acetic acid, 23
Adam, 61, 126, 127
addiction, 52, 150, 241
Adonijah, 133
adultery, 165
Agag (king), 68
agitation, 167
agricultural devastation, 164–65
agricultural fertility, 58, 83–86. *See also* abundance
Ahab (king), 48, 64, 133
Ahasuerus (king), 18
alcohol. *See also* beer; wine; *specific aspects*
   background and experiences as shaping view of, 10–11
   categorizing of, in ancient world, 13–15
   complexity of issue of, 3–6
   diversity of terms for, 5, 6
   effects of excessive, 91
   glossary of Scriptural types of, 29
   hyperbolic statements regarding, 92
   introduction to biblical representation of, 3
   libations of, 78–83
   as life enhancement, 249
   as obstacle to faith, 243
   overview of references to, 10
   questions of characterization and representation regarding, 5
   questions of content regarding, 5
   questions of function regarding, 5
   risks regarding, 241
   ritual use of, 245–47
   statistics regarding, 240
   in symbolic varietals, 5–6
   tithes of, 76–78
   as truth-telling technology, 125
alcohol by volume (ABV), 13, 16, 26, 34–35, 54, 251
alertness, 136, 137, 138, 139
already/not yet kingdom of God, 244
Amalekites, 133
Amenhotep III (king), 47
Americano, 35
Ammon, 49
Amnon, 18, 133
amphorae, for wine storage, 46–47
ancient world, 13–15, 16
angels, 127, 162
anger, 99
animals, 79, 87, 98, 99, 118, 144, 151, 211
appearance of evil, 244
Arameans, 142
armor of God, 137
arrows, 163
art, 248–50
Ashkelon, 98
asis (grape must), 21–23, 160
Assemblies of God (AGUSA), 242
Assyria, 48, 142
Assyrian exile, 141

Baal, 82
Babylon, 48, 144, 149, 164, 170, 171–72, 237
Babylonian exile, 141, 148, 149, 161
banqueting. *See also* eschatological banquet; feasting; marriage supper of the Lamb
   of Belshazzar, 131
   customs of, 204

273

Greco-Roman, 34, 118, 212, 229
intimacy and, 125
marzeakh as, 53
in story of Esther, 67, 131–32
Wisdom's, 119
baptism, 173, 227
barrenness, 98, 100, 106
bath, 151
Bathsheba, 129–30
"The Battle Hymn of the Republic" (Howe), 162
bearing fruit, 155
beasts, in vineyards, 144, 148
Beaujolais, 5
beer. *See also* alcohol; *specific aspects*
    as brawler, 116
    economics of, 54–56
    as libation liquid, 79–80
    overview of, 24–28
    as party drink, 26
    process of, 28
    production of, 54–56
    shekar, 24–25, 26, 27, 28, 80
    sobe, 24
beer jugs, 55
Belhaven Best, 35
believers, as sober and alert, 136
belly button (navel), 72
Belshazzar (king), 131, 132
Benedictines, 249
Ben-Hadad (king), 133, 142
Benjamin, 125
Benjamites, 129
Bildad, 102
birthright, 58
Bittuni, 14
blessings
    of abundance, 250
    burden of, 65
    covenant, 75, 76, 89–90, 141, 143, 159, 238
    cup of, 168, 213, 224, 226
    of fertility, 182
    future, 176, 180
    to God, 101
    of the invitation, 205
    in the Last Supper, 213, 224
    obedience and, 75
    of the promised land, 58–59
    restorative, 237
    of sexuality, 70, 74
    temple and, 85
    theme of, 238
    in viticultural productivity, 141, 182, 196
    at wedding at Cana, 193
    wine and beer as, 18, 56, 57, 61–65, 102, 157, 174, 192, 239, 245
blood
    of animals, 87
    in cup of wrath concept, 164–68
    drunkenness and, 163
    of grapes, 19, 59, 160
    of Jesus, 70, 210–13, 217–19, 247 (see also Jesus)
    in the Last Supper, 217–19, 224, 226, 227
    libation of, 81
    prophecy regarding, 161
    at return of Jesus, 162, 205
    wine as compared to, 14
blood alcohol content (BAC), 124
blunting, 176–77
Boaz, 129, 130
bodies as temples concept, 244
boiling down, of wine, 16–17
Bordeuax, 5
bosom, 201
branch metaphor, 155
brandy, 25
brawling, 116–17
bread, 58. *See also* Eucharist; Last Supper
bride of Christ imagery, 71, 106–7, 197–98, 205–7. *See also* marriage supper of the Lamb
Burgundy, 5

Cabernet Sauvignon, 15
Canaan, 46, 57, 127
Canaanites, 44
capital punishment, 90
carbon dioxide, 19
Carthusians (Chartreuse), 249
casting bread upon water, 122
Catholicism, 248–49
Cato, 188
celebratory meals, purpose of, 194. *See also* banqueting; early Christian meals; eschatological banquet; feasting; marriage supper of the Lamb
celibacy, 239
cheerful heart, 118
Chemosh, 82
children, 141–42
choice vine (*soreq*), 14
Christianity, 240, 244, 245–47
church, 137–38, 228–32. *See also* temple
church leadership, alcohol restrictions for, 111
Cistercians, 249
clay vessels, 46–47
Clazomenae, 38
clothing, for mourning, 196
clothing parable, 198
coffee analogy, 15, 249–50
commercial wines, 45. *See also* wine
communion, 17. *See also* Eucharist; Last Supper
Consul Opimius, 33
consumptive habits, diversity of, 240–45
contemporary wines, 13–14. *See also* wine
convivium, wine and water mixture at, 34
Corinth, 223
Côtes-du-Rhône, 5
covenant
    Abrahamic, 59, 65, 178
    blessings, 75, 76, 89–90, 141, 143, 159, 238
    blood, 210–13
    curses of, 141
    disobedience and, 177
    disobedience to, 177
    with Israel, 211
    Mosaic, 141, 219
    new, 219
    promised land and, 61–65
    renewal of, 177, 219
    unfaithfulness to, 142
cows of Bashan, 53
creation, 247–48
creativity, 248–50
Cremisan, 15
crucifixion of Jesus, 172–74, 190, 191, 213–14. *See also* Jesus
cult, 76, 83, 185
cultic leadership, 153–54

cultic worship, 185
cup
    abundance in, 133
    of blessings, 168, 213, 224, 226
    Eucharistic, 224, 246 (see also Eucharist)
    gold, 171–72
cupbearers, 51–52
cup of wrath concept. See also wrath of God
    contents of the cup in, 164–68
    cup of Gethsemane and, 172–74
    overview of, 163–64, 174–75
    passing, 169–72
curses, 64, 141, 207
cursing God, 101–2
Cush, 42
Cyprus, 32
Cyrus the Great, 112

Dabouki, 14
Dagon, 82
Daniel, 104–5, 112, 114, 131, 240
Darius (king), 79, 131
date wine, 26, 27
Dathan, 61
Daughter Edom, 170
Daughter Zion, 170
David (king), 48, 50, 81, 129–30, 133, 183–87, 240
David's tent, 183–84, 185, 186–87
death, 121, 122, 194–97, 207
death penalty, 90
debauchery, 94, 124, 229
dedication, 100
Delilah, 98, 131, 133
dema (juice), 21
demons, 226
depression, 241–42
Destiny (god), 35
diets, 221
diluted wines, 33–38. See also wine
Dionysus (god of wine), 69, 133, 192
disciples, as branches, 155, 216
disobedience, 64, 141, 142–43, 177
distillation, 13, 25
divine judgment, 95–96, 136–39, 161–62, 171. See also judgment
divine punishment, 161
division, 223, 225

dizziness, 167
dopamine, 57
double portion concept, 171–72
dregs, 45, 167
drinking blood concept, 217–19
drink offerings, 78–83
drunkenness
    abstinence from, 251
    cultural dimensions of, 124
    debauchery and, 124
    defined, 10
    from diluted wine, 34–35
    disaster from, 139
    as distraction, 136
    to divine judgment, 136–39
    effects of, 91
    at Eucharistic gathering, 223
    foolishness of, 116, 117–18, 123
    harms from, 250–52
    hedging around, 242
    intemperance and, 94
    in judgment, 163, 166
    legal definitions of, 124
    metaphor of, 124
    negative side effects of, 124
    nobility and, 50
    overview of, 124–25
    prohibition of, 91, 92
    in Proverbs, 116
    in sacred space, 100
    sexual exploitation and, 125–30
    sexuality and, 124
    shame of, 127
    Spirit-filled community and, 228–32
    as vice, 95, 251
    to violence, 131–36
    worship and, 232, 250
dualism, 248

eagle imagery, 148–49
early Christian meals
    in 1 Corinthians 10-11, 223–28
    commonality at, 222
    identity and ethos at, 220–23
    overview of, 232–33
    segregation and, 222
    unity in, 220, 223, 225
eating, in the Last Supper, 217–18. See also Eucharist; Last Supper
ecological stewardship, 247–48

economics
    of beer, 54–56
    of vineyards, 47–49
    of wine consumption, 49–54
Edom, 160, 170
Egypt, 27, 28, 41, 55, 125, 149, 156
18th Amendment, 243
Elah, 133
elect, harvests of, 161, 162
Elihu, 22, 46, 100
Elijah, 24, 53–54, 64
Elisha, 48
elms, 42
embodiment, creation and, 247–48
Emmaus, 221
emotional benefits/risks of alcohol consumption, 241–42
Encratites, 97
enemies, 133–34, 138, 206
enjoyment, 120, 121, 123
Ephraim, 134
Ephraimites, 160, 161
Esau, 58–59, 162
eschatological banquet
    celebrating death of death, 194–97
    feasting in Jesus's Lukan parables and, 198–202
    hospitality in, 202
    inclusion in, 202
    Last Supper and, 202–4
    marriage supper of the Lamb and, 205–7
    overview of, 194
    teachings of Jesus and, 197–204
eschatology, 95–96, 136–39
Essenes, 97
Esther, 67–68, 103–4, 113–14, 131–32
eternity, 121
ethos, at early Christian meals, 220–23
Eucharist. See also Last Supper
    in 1 Corinthians 10-11, 223–28
    bread-of-life discourse and, 218–19
    commemoration in, 191, 205, 221
    judgment regarding, 227
    significance of, 238, 245–47
    suffering and, 173
    symbolism of, 216
    unity in, 225
Evans, Craig A., 32

Eve, 61, 126
excess, socioeconomic critique of, 150. *See also* abundance
exile, 48, 141, 148, 149, 161, 176–79

false teachers, 222
family, alcohol's destruction in, 252–53
famine, 145
fasting, 97–98, 103–4, 105–8, 112, 182, 197–98, 244
feasting. *See also* banqueting; early Christian meals; eschatological banquet; marriage supper of the Lamb
  abstaining from, 101
  to celebrate blessing, 63
  excessive, 68
  in Jesus's Lukan parables, 198–202
  life's futility and, 121
  liturgical cycle of, 244
  Purim and, 66–68
  sexual connotation and, 117–18
  violence in, 133
  vulnerability and, 132
  with wine, 58
Feast of Firstfruits, 78
Feast of Tabernacles, 68–69, 78, 81, 185–86
Feast of Trumpets, 66
Feast of Unleavened Bread, 210
feet, euphemism of, 129
Ferguson, Everett, 33
fermentation
  of beer, 54
  carbon dioxide in, 19
  description of, 46
  pasteurization and, 17
  process of, 15–16, 21, 88, 239
  stirring in, 45
  in vats, 45
Festival of Weeks, 78
fig tree, 82
firstfruits, 77, 162
flood, 126
foaming (*khemer*), 19
foaming wine, 167
folly, 91, 116, 117, 119, 123
food. *See also* banqueting; early Christian meals; feasting; marriage supper of the Lamb
  abstinence from, 105
  of folly, 119
  laws, 87
  as offered to idols, 223
  offerings, 79
  of wisdom, 119
fools, 116, 120
fortified wines, 246
foxes, 73, 99
France, 5
fruit of the Spirit, 95, 251
fruit of the vine, Jesus's reference to, 202–3. *See also* grapes; wine
fully fermented wine, 18–19, 26. *See also* wine
funerals, 145

Gaal, 83
Gabriel (angel), 106
gall, 32, 214
garden of Eden, 61, 65, 181
garments, blood-stained, 162
Gedaliah, 48
Gehazi, 48
gentiles, 88, 93, 109–10, 154, 187, 199, 205, 222
Gethsemane, 172–74
Gibeah, 48
Gibeon, 45
Gibeonites, 46
Gideon, 44, 81, 160–61
gifts from God, 239, 250–52
girding loins, 138
gleaning, 43, 160
gleukos (sugary wine), 22
glory, 189
glykasmos (sweetness), 22
Gnosticism, 248
God. *See also* wrath of God
  blessing, 101
  cursing, 101–2
  death and, 196
  as Father, 155
  as giver of all good gifts, 239
  glory of, 239
  as good shepherd, 133
  as gracious merchant, 179
  presence of, 85, 181–82, 189
  preservation by, 160
  protection from, 133–34, 178
  provision from, 62, 84–85, 122
  victory of, 195, 196
  as vintner, 146–47, 155, 157
Gog, 163
gold cup, 171–72
golden calf, 151
Gomorrah, 128, 152
good-for-nothing grape, 17
good fruit, importance of, 155
Good Samaritan, 111
grain. *See also* beer
  abundance of, 58, 61, 62, 63, 65
  beer production and, 54
  destruction to, 99, 144
  in famine, 49
  libations from, 80
  Nazirite vow and, 88
  as offering, 28, 53, 78
  as ration, 141–42
  shekar and, 27
  tirosh and, 20
  trade of, 122
grape juice (*mishrah*), 21, 245–46
grape must (*asis*), 21–23, 160
grapes. *See also* specific types
  broken skin on, 16
  destruction of, 144–45
  drying of, 44
  fermentation process of, 15–16, 88
  harvesting of, 43–45
  preservation process of, 41
  treading of, 43–45
grapevine, 5, 59, 126. *See also* vineyards
grappa, 25
great chasm, 201
greatness, inversion of, 204
Greco-Roman banqueting, 34, 118, 212, 229
Greek Retsinas, 32
Greeks, 33, 38
Greek symposium, 118
Greene King's IPA, 35
grog, 13
Guinness, 249, 253

Hades, 201
Hagar, 58
hair
  in Nazirite vow, 88, 98, 99, 100, 106, 108, 133

as offering, 89
uncut, 98, 100, 101
Ham, 127, 128, 130
Haman, 67, 68, 103–4, 131–32
Hannah, 79, 100–101, 114
harlot of Babylon, 37
harvesting, 43–45, 144–45, 160–63
Haupt, Paul, 32
Helbon, 14, 47
Hellenistic period, 14
herbs, as wine additive, 118–19
Herculaneum, 14
Herod (king), 131, 159
Herodias, 131
Hezekiah, 50, 142
holy days, wine consumption on, 65–70
Holy Spirit
    baptism of, 227
    as being filled with, 94
    in community, 221–22, 228–32
    filling of, 228–32
    John the Baptist and, 106
    as mediator, 227
    outpouring of, 177, 182, 221
    self-control and, 251
    unity and, 232
honey, 16, 59–60, 61, 81, 98, 118–19
hope, 152, 195
hospitality, 200, 202
house of David, 183–84, 185, 186–87
Howe, Julia Ward, 162
human body, associations with wine and, 72
hyssop, 191

identity, at early Christian meals, 220–23
idolatrous worship, 90
idolatry, 110, 143, 146, 147–48, 169, 223, 225
illness, 145
imbibing, 116–17
incest, 127, 128
infant dedication, 100
interpersonal benefits/risks of alcohol consumption, 241–42
intoxication, 10, 18, 19, 20, 35, 85, 166–67. *See also* drunkenness

Iron Age, 44
Isaac, 58, 65, 199, 211
Ishmael, 58
Israel
    bad fruit in, 150
    beer and, 28
    as blessing Judah, 59
    covenant with, 211
    disobedience of, 146–47
    exile of, 141
    as God's vineyard, 146–57, 196
    idolatry of, 143, 147–48, 225
    judgment to, 148, 151
    reliance on God by, 61
    remnant of, 160
    restoration of, 177–78
    sacramental rites of, 226
    socioeconomic critique of excess in, 150, 151
    soil type of, 40
    in song of the vineyard (Isaiah), 150–52
    topography of, 40
    as true vine, 156
    vineyards in, 42
    viticulture of, 7
    wineries in, 15

Jacob, 58, 59, 65, 128, 130, 199, 211
Jael, 131
James (disciple), 173
Jandali, 14
Jehoiachin, 149
Jehonadab, 102
Jehoram (king), 142
Jeremiah, 102, 113–14, 169
Jerusalem, 142, 146, 148, 149, 153–54, 169–72
Jerusalem Council, 93
Jesus. *See also* Last Supper
    abstinence by, 105–8, 114
    as banquet host, 204
    on banquets, 204
    blood of, 210–13
    as Branch, 108, 180
    as bridegroom, 107, 197–98, 205–7
    burden and yoke of, 108
    cleansing of the temple by, 153

    consuming of alcoholic drinks by, 240
    crucifixion of, 23–24, 32, 172–74, 190, 191, 213–14
    death of, 190–91
    on eschatological banquet, 197–204
    fasting by, 197–98
    at Gethsemane, 172–74, 214
    glory of, 189
    as harvester, 162
    Israel as God's vineyard in teachings of, 152–57
    as Lamb of God, 191
    at marriage supper of the Lamb, 205–7
    mutual abiding with, 216
    as Nazarene, 108
    on old wine, 45
    Olivet Discourse of, 136, 153
    as Passover lamb, 225
    on the present generation, 107
    as priest, 216
    as rabbi, 213
    recognition of, 221
    resurrection of, 190–91
    return of, 136–37, 162, 205, 224
    robe of, 205
    sour wine and, 23–24, 32, 191
    stone imagery regarding, 153–54
    as true vine, 155, 156
    as turning water into wine, 15
    union with, 227
    at Upper Room Discourse, 215–17
    vindication of, 204
    at wedding at Cana, 53, 54, 187–92, 197, 239
    wine as offered to, 23–24, 32
    as in winepress, 205
    on wisdom, 251
    wisdom of, 107–8
Jewish Christians, 109–10
Jews, 103–4, 131–32
Jezebel (queen), 48, 161
Joab, 133
Job, 22, 46, 48, 101–2, 114, 124
John (disciple), 173
John the Baptist, 105–8, 114, 131, 191, 197, 240
John the Seer, 240
Joseph, 51, 125

Joshua (high priest), 180
Jotham, 81–83
joy, 120, 121, 123, 178
Judah (man), 128–29, 130
Judah (nation)
   blessing on, 59
   exile of, 141, 148, 152, 156
   restoration of, 149
   treading of, 161
   vineyards of, 48–49
   woe against, 134
judgment. *See also* cup of wrath concept; wrath of God
   banquet following, 207
   blood in, 163
   drunkenness and, 128, 163, 166
   grape must (*asis*) imagery and, 160
   intoxication and, 166–67
   on Israel, 148, 151
   like-for-like, 135
   preparation for, 139
   privation as, 141–46
   pronouncement of, 194–95
   pruning as, 42
   restoration following, 196–97
   scenes of, 37
   in the temple, 190
   vulnerability to, 136–39
   winepresses and, 142, 144, 146, 161–62, 168, 169, 172, 174, 205, 206
   woes and, 150
juice (*dema*), 21

khamar (fully fermented wine), 18, 19, 35, 79, 167. *See also* wine
khemer (foaming), 19
kingdom of God, 159, 221
kings/rulers, abstinence by, 51
kissing, 72
kosher wines, 45
Koskenniemi, Erkki, 32
krater, 34, 118

Laban, 128, 130, 211
Lady Wisdom, 35
lament, 182
land, 143–44, 177–78
Last Supper. *See also* Eucharist
   covenantal blood and, 210–13
   Eucharist and, 191, 238

   fasting and, 108
   overview of, 202–4, 209
   as Passover meal, 209–10
   ritual practice in, 245
   third cup of, 213–15
   words of institution for, 224
Lazarus, 201
leadership
   alcohol restrictions for, 93, 111, 250
   feasting at proper time for, 119
   vulnerability of, 134
Leah, 128
leaven, 6, 159
Lebanon, 14, 148–49
lees, 45
Lemuel (king), 50, 90, 92, 119
Lesbos, 23
Levant, 14, 41, 59
Leviathan, 196
Levites, 77–78, 84
libationary offering, 212
libations, 37, 78–83, 226
locust plague, 21, 144
loins, girding, 138
Lot, 128, 130
love, 70–74
love feasts, 222
lovemaking, 71. *See also* sexuality
lying, 165

maceration, 14
Magog, 163
making glad, 85
mamtaqqim (sweet drinks), 22
manipulation, 125–30
manna, 218
Marawi/Hamdani, 14
Marcionites, 97
Maronean wine, 34
marriage supper of the Lamb, 205–7
martyrs, 164, 172
Mary (mother of Jesus), 165, 191
marzeakh (ritualized banquet), 53
"Master of Puppets" (Metallica), 150
meals, 220, 222, 223, 225, 232–33. *See also* banqueting; eschatological banquet; feasting; marriage supper of the Lamb
Medes, 131
medicine, wine as, 111, 112–13, 241–42
Meiomi Pinot Noir, 35
Melchizedek, 58, 65, 216
mental benefits/risks of alcohol consumption, 241–42
mental clarity, 138
Merlot, 5, 15
Mesopotamia, 27, 28, 41
metaphors, 70–71
Micah, 142–43
Midianites, 44, 160–61
military imagery, 137
milk, 31, 41, 59–60, 61, 85, 182
mishrah (grape juice), 21, 245–46
mishteh (feasting), 49–50. *See also* feasting
mixed drinks, 31–33. *See also specific drinks*
Moab, 45–46, 49, 146, 166
mocking, 116–17
Mordecai, 67, 68, 103, 131–32
Mosaic covenant, 141, 219
Moses, 42–43, 61, 64–65, 89, 151, 211
Mot (god of death), 196
mountains, 163, 181–87
Mount Ararat, 126
mourning, 145, 195, 196
mouth, associations with wine and, 72
Mt. Vesuvius, 220
myopia, 242
myrrh, 32, 214

Naaman, 48
Nabal, 18, 132
Naboth, 48, 161
nakedness, 127, 128
Naomi, 129
Nathanael, 191
nations, 146, 161, 196
Nazareth, 108
Nazirites, 88, 240
Nazirite vow, 21, 25–26, 88–89, 98–99, 101, 106, 108, 239, 244
Nebuchadnezzar (king), 48, 105, 149
Nehemiah, 52, 66
Neolithic period, 126
Nephilim, 127
new covenant, 219
new creation, 207

Newson, Carol, 105
new wine (*asis*), 21. *See also* wine
new wine (*tirosh*). *See also* wine
    abundance of, 62, 63, 116, 183
    in Assyria, 142
    destruction to, 64, 144, 178, 195
    as intoxicating, 20
    Jesus's reference to, 203
    lack of, 146
    Levites and, 77
    at messianic banquet, 200
    old wine as compared to, 45, 204
    overview of, 19–20
    parable of, 198
    at Pentecost, 22, 182, 230
    promise regarding, 182
    references to, 203
night, in new creation, 207
Noah, 125–28, 130

obedience, 62
offspring, blessing of, 58. *See also* Abrahamic covenant
Oholah, 169
Oholibah, 169
oinos (fully fermented wine), 19, 38. *See also* wine
old wine, new wine as compared to, 45, 204
Olivet Discourse, 136, 153
olive tree, 82
144,000, vision of, 162
Oreb, 160
oxygen, 23, 46

Palestine, wineries in, 15
parable of the Good Samaritan, 111
parable of the great banquet, 200, 204
parable of the narrow door, 199, 200, 201
parable of the prodigal son, 202
parable of the rich man and Lazarus, 201
parable of the ten virgins, 138–39
parable of the two sons, 155
parable of the wedding feast, 199–200, 204
parable of the wicked tenants, 152–55
parable of the wineskins, 19, 139, 197, 198, 203, 204
parody, 159, 238
Passover. *See also* Eucharist; Last Supper
    beer and, 27
    Esther and, 103–4
    Last Supper and, 209–11
    leaven and, 159
    libations in, 78
    third cup of, 213–15
    wine consumption at, 69–70
    wines, requirements of, 45
Pasteur, Louis, 17
pasteurization, 17
Pentecost, 22, 182, 230
Pentheus (king), 133
people of God, as bride, 205–7
permissibility, 3–4
Persian Empire, 49
Persians, 112
pestilence, 145
Pharisees, 97, 153, 159, 197
Philokalia, 15
Phoenicians, 44, 46–47
Pinot Noir, 5
pitch (tree resin), 31–32, 38
places of honor, 199–200
pleasure, 120, 237
pomegranates, 31
Pompeii, 220
poor/poverty, 51, 53, 199–200
present generation, 107
preservation of wine, in the ancient world, 16–17
priests, 88, 134, 231, 240, 250. *See also* Levites
princes, 119
privation, 141–46, 159
Prohibition, 243
prohibitions of alcohol
    in the New Testament, 93–96
    in the Old Testament, 87–93
promised land
    blessings and, 57, 58–59, 61–65
    covenantal stipulations regarding, 61–65
    description of, 142
    exile from, 142
    as gift, 62
    milk and honey in, 59–60
    overview of, 57–65
    viticultural potential of, 59–61
prophets, vulnerability of, 134
prophets of Baal, 64
protection, 133–34, 178
Proverbial wisdom on alcohol, 115–19
pruning, 42, 155, 178
Purim, 66–68

Qoheleth, 119, 120, 121–22
Queen of Sheba, 50
questions of characterization and representation, 5
questions of content, 5
questions of function, 5

Rachel, 128
rainfall, 40–41, 64
raisin wines, 44
rations, 141–42
readiness, 136, 139
rebellious sons, 89–90, 124
Recanati, 15
reclining, 199
red wine, 14. *See also* wine
regal figures, 149
Rehoboam (king), 50
Rekabites, 102–3, 114, 240, 244
repentance, 144, 182
resin (pitch), 31–32, 38
restoration
    abundance of wine at, 161, 207
    alcohol-related imagery and, 6
    economic leveling in, 53
    final covenantal word as, 64
    following judgment, 196–97
    God's eagerness for, 192–93, 252–53
    of Jerusalem, 171
    of the land, 65
    references to, 152
    of tent of David, 183–84, 185, 186–87
    viticulture and, 176–79
restrictions of alcohol
    in the New Testament, 93–96
    in the Old Testament, 87–93
resurrection, 138
rich, judgment on, 145–46
riddles, 98–99
ritualized banquet (*marzeakh*), 53
rituals, mourning, 145

ritual use of alcohol, 245–47
river imagery, 84, 85, 180–81
Roma (goddess), 37, 164
Romans, 33, 38
Roman soldiers, 23–24, 32
Rome, 164
Rothchild, Baron Edmond, 15
Ruth, 129, 130

Sabbath, 43, 64
Saccharomyces cerevisiae, 16
sacred space, drunkenness in, 100
Sadducees, 97, 159
salt water, as additive, 33, 38
salvation, 184
Samaria, 142, 143–44, 169
Samson, 98–99, 106, 114, 131, 133
Samuel, 79, 100–101, 106, 114
Sarah, 57
Saul (king), 48, 68, 132–33
Sauvignon Blanc, 5
Scorpion I (pharaoh), 47
Scripture, selectivity regarding, 4–5
sea, in new creation, 207
Seesemann, Heinrich, 32
segregation, at meals, 222
self-control, 251
self-harm, 169
Sennacherib, 142
serotonin, 241–42
sexual exploitation, 125–30
sexuality, 70–74, 117–18, 124, 227, 237
shame, 127
Shechemites, 82–83
sheepshearing, 101, 128, 130, 133
shemer (dregs or lees), 19
Shiloah, 84
Shiloh, 100
sickle, 161
signs and wonders, 192
sin, 206, 250
singing, 231
Sisera, 131
Slingerland, Edward, 33
sloth, 91
sobriety, 136, 137, 138, 139
social contagion, 226–27
socioeconomic inequality, 151
Sodom, 128, 152
Solomon, 47, 50, 63, 74, 84, 133

Song of Moses, 166
song of the vineyard (Isaiah), 150–52
sons of God (angels), 127
Sorek, 14
soreq (choice vine), 14
Sotah, 165
sour wine, 23–24, 46, 191, 214. *See also* wine
Southern Baptist Convention (SBC), 243
spears, 178
spices, as wine additive, 119
spirit of confusion, 36
spiritual armor, 137
spiritual unity, 220
stone imagery, 153–54
storage of beer, 55
storage of wine, 16, 45–47
Story of Aqhat, 127
straws, for beer consumption, 55
substance addiction, 150
suffering, 172–74
sugary wine (*gleukos*), 22
sukkah, 185–86
sun and moon, in new creation, 207
Susa, 52
sweet drinks (*mamtaqqim*), 22
sweet lesbian wine, 23. *See also* wine
sweetness (*glykasmos*), 22
sweet wine, 21–23, 181–87. *See also* wine
swords, 163, 169–70, 178
symbolic varietals, 5–6
symposia, 34

"Tale of Sinuhe," 60
Tamar, 128–29, 130, 133
tax collectors, 198
tears, as additive, 36
teeth, 176–77
temple cult, 145, 146
temple/temple system
 altar of, 227
 cleansing of, 190
 debauchery in, 229
 destruction of, 146, 161
 imagery of, 231–32
 judgment to, 190
 libations of alcohol in, 78–83
 neglecting, 145
 in new creation, 207

overview of, 76
presence of God in, 184
revitalizing of, 179–81
ritual use of alcohol in, 238
singing in, 231
as source of food and wine, 83–86
tithes of alcohol in, 76–78
wine storage at, 189, 244
wisdom and, 118
tenor, 71
tent of David, 183–84, 185, 186–87
Therapeutae, 97
thieves, 160
thornbush, 82
Timothy, 110–13
tithe, 25, 43, 76–78, 84
tower, in the vineyard, 44
trade of wine, 45–47
transubstantiation, 218
Trappists, 249
treading, 43–45, 160–63
tree of the knowledge of good and evil, 126
tree resin (pitch), 31–32, 38
true vine concept, 156
21st Amendment, 243
Two-Wine theory, 7, 15–18, 29
Tyre, 47

unclean, in new creation, 207
"under the sun," 119–23
unfermented wine, 17–18. *See also* wine
unity, 220, 223, 225, 228
Upper Room Discourse, 215–17
Uriah, 100, 129–30
Uzziah (king), 48

Valley of Jehoshaphat, 161
vats, 45, 237
vehicle, 71
vessels, for wine storage, 46–47
Vesuvius, Mount, 220
vices, 95, 251
vine, 82
vinegar, 23–24, 26, 28, 46, 88
vines of Sibmah, 146
vineyards
 destruction to, 146
 economics of, 47–49
 foxes in, 73

infrastructure for, 43–44
metaphorical, 73
origin of, 126
planting and cultivating of, 41–43
promise regarding, 142
in prophetic visions, 143–44
pruning in, 42
sabbath and, 43
symbolism of, 247
tower in, 44
value of, 48
vulnerability of, 49
vintners, 41–42, 43–44
violence, vulnerability to, 131–36
virtues, 251
viticulture
   biblical laws of, 45
   blessing, 59–61, 63, 65
   economic disparities and, 45
   of the Israelites, 7
   judgment and, 159
   land and, 65, 144
   new covenant and, 245
   rainfall and, 64
   restoration and, 176–79
   revitalizing the temple and, 179–81
   sexuality and, 71, 73, 74
   temple cult and, 145–46
vitis vinifera, 15
Volstead Act, 243
vomiting, 167
vows, 99, 103. *See also* Nazirite vow
vulnerability
   to divine judgment, 136–39
   Joseph and, 125
   of leadership, 134
   overview of, 139
   sexual exploitation and, 125–30
   to violence, 131–36

war imagery, 137–38
water, 28, 29, 33–34, 36, 164–65
water drinking, 111, 112–13
weak and strong, abstinence and, 109–10, 114, 243
wealth, 53, 122
wedding analogy, 106–7, 139, 197–98, 199–200

wedding at Cana, 53, 54, 187–92, 197, 239
Welch's grape juice, 17
wheat, 44
white wine, 14. *See also* wine
wicked, 117, 160
wickedness, 91
wine. *See also specific aspects; specific types*
   additives in, 31
   as additive to other wines, 33
   boiling down of, 16–17
   as celebration of place, 40
   as celebration of the land, 57
   classification of, 13–14
   dilution of, 25, 33–38
   diversity of terms for, 5
   as divine gift, 74–75
   as economic commodity, 206
   flavoring for, 32
   as food with two faces, 125
   as foreshadow of provisions, 58
   fully fermented, 18–19
   grapevine varietal of, 5
   Greek term for, 3
   health benefits of, 111, 241–42
   Hebrew term for, 3
   maceration and, 14
   medicinal usage of, 111, 112–13
   as mocker, 116
   preservation of, 16–17
   production of, 40–47
   as puppet master, 150
   as ration, 141–42
   regal connotations of, 51
   as regulated, 105
   as sparkling, 91
   statistics regarding, 15
   storage of, in ancient world, 16
   supremacy of, 116
   symbolic value of, 193
   symbols of, in Revelation, 206
   varietals of, 15
wine cellars, 45
wine consumption, economics of, 49–54
winemaking/wine production, 40–47, 159, 248–50. *See also specific aspects*

winepresses
   blood in, 160, 162
   construction of, 44, 150, 152
   crushing in, 160
   judgment and, 142, 144, 146, 161–62, 168, 169, 172, 174, 205, 206
   styles of, 44–45
wineskins
   judgment and, 164
   overview of, 46
   parable of, 19, 139, 197, 198, 203, 204
wisdom
   deeds and, 251
   Ecclesiastes and, 119–23
   feast of, 119
   futility of, 120
   home of, 118
   intoxication from, 118
   overview of, 115
   personification of, 118
   Proverbial, on alcohol, 115–19
   references to, 107–8
woes, 150, 151
women, 47–48, 53, 54–55, 92
Women's Christian Temperance Union, 243
wooden barrels, for wine storage, 47
worship, 52, 179, 232, 250
wrath of God, 6, 22, 37, 139, 159, 163–74, 206, 207. *See also* judgment

yayin (fully fermented wine), 18, 26. *See also* wine
year of Jubilee, 43
yeast, 14, 15–16, 17, 19, 26, 45, 54, 88, 246

Zadok, 133
Zealots, 97
Zechariah, 106
Zedekiah, 149, 156, 157
Zeeb, 160
Ziklag, 133
Zimri, 133
Zinfandel, 5
Zion, 152, 177, 197

AUTHOR INDEX

Abbott, T. K., 230
Abernathy, Andrew T., 179, 195
Adkins, Lesley, 37
Adkins, Roy A., 37
Adler, Yonatan, 189
Agourides, S., 186
Alexander, P., 199
Allaby, Robin G., 126
Allison, Dale C., 108, 154, 173, 174, 203, 211
Alroy, Odelia E., 88
Alter, Robert, 25, 28, 49, 52, 53, 64, 74, 117, 132, 135, 142, 144, 166
Ambrose, 111
Andersen, Francis I., 183
Anderson, Gary A., 83
Anderson, Paul N., 190
Aouizerat, Tzemach, 55
Arichea, Daniel C., 112
Arnold, Clinton E., 229, 230
Assis, Elie, 182
Athenaeus, 23, 34, 55, 112, 113, 119
Augustine, 111
Aune, David E., 162, 168
Averbeck, Richard E., 184

Bacchiocchi, Samuele, 7, 15, 16, 17, 20, 23, 49, 113
Barclay, John M. G., 62, 109
Barrett, C. K., 22, 224
Barton, John, 144, 160
Bauckham, Richard, 162, 187, 222
Beale, G. K., 154, 162, 171, 181, 230
Becker, Lothar, 7, 18, 19, 21, 36, 50, 66, 102, 112, 191, 195, 205
Bergsma, John S., 127
Berlin, Adele, 68, 142
Bewer, Julius A., 149
Black, Matthew, 154, 172
Blenkinsopp, Joseph, 24, 52, 196
Blij, Harm Jan de, 40
Block, Daniel I., 129, 149, 169
Blomberg, Craig, 107, 174, 201

Blount, Brian K., 162, 172
Bock, Darrell L., 107
Bokser, Baruch, 69, 214
Boring, M. Eugene, 153
Borneman, Anthony, 16
Borowski, Oded, 20, 42
Bovon, François, 106, 172, 201
Brenan, Megan, 243
Brooke, George J., 154
Broshi, Magen, 27, 44, 97
Brown, Raymond E., 157, 172, 210, 218
Bultmann, Rudolf, 218
Butler, Joel, 7, 15, 19, 46, 51, 58, 126, 251
Butler, Trent C., 98, 99

Caird, G. B., 161
Carpenter, Eugene, 21
Carroll, M. Daniel, 89
Carson, D. A., 190, 218
Casey, Maurice, 108, 203
Casper, Jayson, 243
Cato, 16, 195
Cavalieri, Duccio, 16
Charles, R. H., 163
Childs, Brevard S., 135, 150, 162
Cho, Kang-Kul, 196
Ciampa, Roy E., 211, 225, 227, 228
Clendenen, E. Ray, 191
Clifford, Richard J., 92, 181
Clines, David J. A., 101–102
Collins, Adela Yarbro, 154, 173
Collins, John J., 105, 116
Columella, 16, 17, 32, 33, 38, 41, 42, 44, 45, 47, 112–113
Cosgrove, Charles H., 226
Cowan, J. Andrew, 198
Cranfield, C. E. B., 174
Crenshaw, James L., 144

Dar, Shimon, 44, 45
Daube, David, 213
Davies, W. D., 108, 154, 173, 203, 211

Dayagi-Mendels, Michal, 14, 45
Dong, Yang, 126
Driver, S. R., 20
Drori, Elyashiv, 14
Dubach, Manuel, 7, 20, 21, 50, 92, 98, 117, 125, 128, 129, 135, 168
Duguid, Iain M., 72
Dunbabin, Katherine M. D., 37
Dunne, John Anthony, 32, 68, 173, 183, 214, 228, 230

Ebeling, Jennie, 27, 28, 54, 55
Eidevall, Göran, 52
Elliott, J. K., 179, 202
Euripides, 133
Evans, Craig A., 154, 203

Faas, Patrick, 23, 33, 46, 212
Falk, Daniel K., 185
Fee, Gordon D., 224, 225, 227
Feenstra, Ronald, 188
Fitzmyer, Joseph A., 22, 106, 211, 226
Fleischer, 19
Fleming, Stuart J., 34, 37
Forbes, Robert J., 113
Forsyth, Mark, 95, 238, 243
Foster, John L., 60
Foster, Robert L., 230
Fox, Michael V., 62, 91
Frankel, Rafael, 7, 21, 25, 33, 44, 81, 195
Freedman, David N., 183
Friesen, Courtney J. P., 192
Fu, Janling, 134, 196

Gaifman, Milette, 78, 168
Galen, 113
Garland, David E., 227
Garnsey, Peter, 55
Garrett, Duane, 71
Gaylord, H. E., 95
Geisler, Norman, 25, 33, 244
Gladwell, Malcolm, 242

Gorday, Peter, 111
Goswell, Gregory R., 185, 186
Gowers, Emily, 220
Grace, Virginia R., 46
Graybill, Rhiannon, 130
Green, Peter A., 42, 65, 185, 248
Greenberg, Moshe, 144
Grimm, Veronika, 97, 221
Grivetti, Louis, 125
Gstohl, Mark A., 17
Gundry, Robert H., 108

Habel, Norman C., 101
Haenchen, Ernst, 191
Hagner, Donald A., 203
Hahn, Scott W., 127
Hannah, Lee, 247
Harding, Julia, 41
Hatton, Howard A., 112
Haynes, Stephen R., 241
Hays, Richard B., 173
Heil, John Paul, 201, 230
Henschke, Paul A., 16
Herodotus, 112
Heskett, Randall, 7, 15, 19, 46, 51, 58, 126, 251
Hess, Richard S., 72, 74
Hippocrates, 112, 113
Holladay, William L., 102, 165, 169
Holmes, Michael W., 157, 216
Holt, Else K., 169
Homan, Michael M., 17, 25, 27, 28, 54, 55, 79, 122
Homer, 34, 132
Horrell, David G., 110
Hoskyns, Edwyn C., 218
House, Paul R., 71
Hoyt, JoAnna M., 183
Huey, F. B., Jr., 170

Ignatius, 222
Instone-Brewer, David, 214
Isaac, E., 183

James, Elaine T., 70, 74
Jenson, P. P., 50
Jeremias, Joachim, 108, 210, 213
Jerome, 111
John Chrysostom, 111
Johnson, Luke Timothy, 111
Jones, Jeffrey M., 243

Josephus, 22, 68, 77, 79, 88, 97, 116, 131, 133, 154, 186, 203, 231
Jouanna, Jacques, 113

Kahlo, Frida, 145
Kee, H. C., 94
Keel, Othmar, 84
Keener, Craig S., 191
Kelhoffer, James A., 105
Keown, Gerald L., 177
Kidner, Derek, 134
King, Philip J., 25, 27
Klein, Ralph W., 101
Klijn, A. F. J., 79, 167, 187
Klinghardt, Matthias, 212, 226
Klink, Edward W., III, 8
Knight, George W., III, 113
Koester, Craig R., 162, 168
Köstenberger, Andreas J., 230
Kreglinger, Gisela, 7, 111, 205, 214, 241, 248, 251
Kynes, Will, 115

Larkin, William J., 94
Levenson, Jon D., 181
Liu, Diana, 242
Lockett, Darian R., 8
Longenecker, Bruce W., 223
Longman, Tremper, III, 72, 119, 121, 122
Lovinger, David M., 241
Lucian, 22, 188, 200
Lukacs, Paul, 7, 17, 32, 113, 239
Lundbom, Jack R., 170
Lunde, Jonathan M., 191
Luz, Ulrich, 154

Macaskill, Grant, 156, 189, 190, 227, 230
MacDonald, Nathan, 8, 41, 45, 48, 55, 59–60, 61, 65, 67, 90, 98, 99, 105, 159, 168
Magness, Jodi, 97
Manning, Gary T., Jr., 156, 157
Mansfield, Stephen, 249
Marcus, Joel, 108, 203, 214
Marshall, I. Howard, 107, 201, 210, 241
Martini, Alessandro, 16
McCarter, P. Kyle, Jr., 101

McConville, J. Gordon, 78
McGovern, Patrick E., 7, 13, 14, 15, 16, 17, 26, 31, 32, 36, 44, 45, 46, 47, 54, 59, 60, 111, 126, 185
McGowan, Andrew, 97
McKane, William, 118, 165, 167, 170
McLaughlin, John L., 53, 145
Metallica, 150
Meyers, Carol L., 163
Meyers, Eric M., 163
Mitchell, Hinckley G., 20
Moffitt, David M., 216
Moore, George F., 82
Morales, Isaac Augustine, 231
Moritz, Thorsten, 94
Morris, Leon, 190
Mortimer, Robert, 16
Moule, C. F. D., 173
Mounce, William D., 110, 111
Murphy, Roland E., 71

Naeh, S., 20
Nekvasil, Nader, 242
Nelson, Max, 26, 55
Nelson, Richard D., 166
Neusner, Jacob, 27
Newsom, Carol, 105
Nielsen, Kirsten, 129
Nisula, Kirsi, 32
Nogalski, James D., 163, 182
Nolland, John, 106, 108, 210
Nutt, David, 241

Olson, S. Douglas, 23
Osborne, Grant R., 172
Oswalt, John N., 135, 151

Pace, Leann, 36, 53
Paul, Shalom M., 52
Philo of Alexandria, 18, 38, 68, 77, 79, 81, 85, 88, 89, 97, 118, 124, 131, 181, 203, 231
Pitre, Brant, 213–214
Plato, 95, 112
Pliny the Elder, 14, 16, 17, 31, 32, 33, 34, 37, 38, 40, 41, 42, 44, 45, 81, 112, 113, 188, 195
Pliny the Younger, 222, 232
Plutarch, 69, 88

Poirier, John C., 189
Polsinelli, Mario, 16
Prigent, Pierre, 206

Raabe, Paul R., 160, 170
Risch, Christina, 212, 213
Roberts, J. J. M., 20, 24, 27, 150, 151, 196
Robinson, John A. T., 190
Rogan, Wil, 189
Rogers, Cleon L., Jr., 229
Roi, Micha, 165
Rosenblum, Jordan D., 8, 68, 69, 118
Rosner, Brian S., 211, 225, 227, 228

Sasson, Jack M., 18, 88
Scalise, Pamela J., 177
Schart, Aaron, 185
Schipper, Bernd U., 118, 119
Schloen, J. David, 25
Schnabel, Eckhard, 22, 186, 231
Schweitzer, Albert, 202
Shelton, Jo-Ann, 23
Slingerland, Edward, 125, 242
Smart, Richard E., 41
Smith, Dennis E., 197, 212, 222
Smith, Gary V., 135
Smothers, Thomas G, 177

Snodgrass, Klyne, 154
Stager, Lawrence E., 25, 27, 55
Stein, Robert, 34, 37
Steinmetz, Devora, 127
Strabo, 38

Tait, Jennifer L. Woodruff, 246
Taussig, Hal, 220, 229
Teachout, Robert P., 7, 15, 16, 36
Thielman, Frank, 229, 230
Thiselton, Anthony C., 224, 225, 226
Thomas, Miles, 241
Toppari, Jorma, 32
Towner, Philip W., 110, 111
Travis, S. H., 168, 172
Trible, Phyllis, 130
Tsumura, David Toshio, 85, 132
Tupamahu, Ekaputra, 135

Ulfgard, Håkan, 68
Unwin, Tim, 7, 47

van Leeuwenhoek, Antonie, 17
Varro, 41, 73
Vogt, Peter, 65
von Rad, Gerhard, 125

Wallace, Daniel B., 203, 229, 230

Walsh, Carey Ellen, 7, 14, 20, 21, 24, 26, 28, 40, 41, 42, 44, 45, 47, 48, 58, 102, 125, 128, 185
Waltke, Bruce, 92, 116, 117, 118
Warde, Erin Jean, 240
Warren, Meredith J. C., 168, 218
Warren, Rick, 105
Watson, Francis, 109, 110
Webb, Barry G., 82, 99, 161
Weitzman, M. P., 20
Welch, Thomas Bramwell, 17
Wellhausen, Julius, 187
Welton, Rebekah, 7, 22, 36, 47, 49, 51, 53, 55, 60, 73, 79, 80, 90, 92, 107, 128, 143
Wenham, Gordon J., 127, 129
Williamson, H. G. M., 151
Wilson, Hanneke M., 126, 237
Wintermute, O. S., 70
Witherington, Ben, III, 227
Witkamp, L. Th., 24
Wolter, Michael, 220
Wright, N. T., 210, 245, 247, 253
Wright, Richard A., 229
Wyatt, Nicolas, 127

Xenophon, 112

Yonge, C. D., 231